Statement on the Research Study

The Commission was directed to "go as far as man's knowledge takes" it in searching for the causes of violence and the means of prevention. These studies are reports to the Commission by independent scholars and lawyers who have served on task forces and study teams; they are not reports by the Commission itself. Publication of any of the reports should not be taken to imply endorsement of their contents by the Commission, or by any member of the Commission staff, including the Executive Director and other staff officers, not directly responsible for the preparation of the particular report. Both the credit and the responsibility for the reports lie in each case with the directors of the task forces and study teams. The Commission is making the reports available at this time as works of scholarship to be judged on their merits, so that the Commission as well as the public may have the benefit of both the reports and informed criticism and comment on their contents.

MILTON S. EISENHOWER
Chairman

THE POLITICS OF PROTEST

A Report Submitted by

JEROME H. SKOLNICK, DIRECTOR

Task Force on Violent Aspects
of Protest and Confrontation
of the National Commission
on the Causes and Prevention of Violence

SIMON AND SCHUSTER
NEW YORK

FIRST PRINTING

SBN 671-20381-9 Trade edition
SBN 671-20416-5 Clarion paperback edition
Library of Congress Catalog Card Number: 75-91304
Manufactured in the United States of America

Staff

Director: Jerome H. Skolnick

General Counsel
Ira M. Heyman
School of Law
University of California
Berkeley

Asst. General Counsel
Edmund C. Ursin
Office of the General Counsel
Department of the Air Force

Accountant
Herbert Kalman, C.P.A.

Research Asst. to Director
Richard Speiglman

Research Assistants
Charles Carey
Howard Erlanger
Nancy Leonard
Sam McCormick
Alan Meyerson

Supporting Research Assts.
Susan Currier
Howard Schechter
Nelson Soltman
H. Frederick Willkie, III

Associate Director
Anthony Platt
School of Criminology
University of California
Berkeley

Assistant Director
Elliott Currie
Department of Sociology
University of California
Berkeley

Staff Administrator
Sharon Dunkle Marks

Asst. Staff Administrator
Lee Maniscalco

Office Staff
Kathleen Courts
Gabriella Duncan
Emily Knapp
Wendy Mednick
Sharon Overton
Charlotte Simmons

Supporting Office Staff

Mary Alden
Jayne Craddock
Judy Dewing
Sally Duensing
Sue Feinstein

Judy Foosaner
Vera Nielson
Elizabeth Okamura
Melba Sharp
Betty Wallace

v

Staff Consultants

David Chalmers
Kermit Coleman
Thomas Crawford
Frederick Crews
Amitai Etzioni
Richard Flacks
Joseph Gusfield

Irving Louis Horowitz
Marie-Helene leDivelec
Martin Liebowitz
Sheldon Messinger
Richard Rubenstein
Rodney Stark

Advisory Consultants

Richard Albares
Isaac Balbus
Herman Blake
Robert Blauner
Ed Cray
Harold Cruse
Caleb Foote
Allen Grimshaw
Max Heirich

David Matza
Henry Mayer
Phillipe Nonet
Thomas Pettigrew
Robert Riley
J. Michael Ross
Peter Scott
Charles Sellers
Philip Selznick

Contents

Staff   v

Staff Consultants   vi

Advisory Consultants   vi

Preface   xv

Summary   xix

Part One: Introduction   1

    Chapter I. Protest and Politics   3
        Problems of Definition   3
        Political Violence in American History   8
        Contemporary American Protest   21

Part Two: The Politics of Confrontation   25

    Chapter II. Anti-War Protest   27
        The Disorganization of the Anti-War
            Movement   30
        Why the Movement Grew   35
        The Social Bases of the Anti-War
            Movement   58
        Tactics and the Question of Violence   65

    Chapter III. Student Protest   79
        American Student Protest in International
            Perspective   81
        American Student Activism in the 1960's   87
        The Politics of Confrontation   105
        Black and Third World Student Protest   109
        Colleges and Universities in Crisis   111
        Response to Student Protest   120

    Chapter IV. Black Militancy   125
        The Roots of Contemporary Militancy   128
        The Impact of Riots   145
        The Direction of Contemporary
            Militancy   149
        Conclusion   171

Part Three: White Politics and Official Reactions   177

    Chapter V. The Racial Attitudes of White
        Americans   179
        Decline in Prejudice   181

The Validity of Racial Attitudes Surveys 183
The Widening Racial Gap: Social
    Perception in the "Two Societies" 201

Chapter VI. White Militancy 210
    Vigilantism and the Militant Society 211
    The South 218
    The Urban North 224
    White Paramilitarism 231
    Conclusion 239

Chapter VII. The Police in Protest 241
    The Police and Mass Protest: The
        Escalation of Conflict, Hostility,
        and Violence 241
    The Predicament of the Police 249
    Resources of the Police 252
    The Police View of Protests and
        Protesters 258
    Militancy as a Response to the Police
        Predicament: The Politicization
        of the Police 268
    Activism in Behalf of Material Benefits 272
    Activism in the Realm of Social Policy 274
    Conclusion 288

Chapter VIII. Judicial Response in Crisis 293
    The Lack of Preparation: An Overview 295
    The Role of Lawyers in Crisis 297
    High Bail as Preventive Detention 300
    Some Causes and Implications of Judicial
        Response 308
    The Lower Court as an Agency of Law
        Enforcement 313
    Recommendations 324

Part Four: Conclusion 327

Chapter IX. Social Response to Collective
  Behavior 329
    Theories of Collective Behavior 330
    Official Conceptions of Riots 339
    Social Control of Riots 342

Appendix: Witnesses Appearing at Hearings 347

Notes 349

Bibliography 397

Index 408

Foreword

by
Price M. Cobbs, M.D.
and
William H. Grier, M.D.

Authors of Black Rage

The National Commission on the Causes and Prevention of Violence has a grave task. If violence continues at its present pace, we may well witness the end of the grand experiment of democracy. The unheeded report of the Kerner Commission pinpointed the cause of our urban violence, and this Report presents the tragic consequences when those in power fail to act on behalf of the weak as well as the powerful. The Director and staff of this Task Force will have served the country well if this Report furnishes the Commissioners with that information needed for them to demand that the country institute solutions and not merely further studies.

This volume shows that an understanding of violence does not mean that it will be condoned, but that the better informed will be in a better position to remove its causes. This document further reminds us that if violence is to be eliminated in our society, then we must broaden its definition.

Our country seems only to respond to a visible domestic violence where people are killed or injured and property is destroyed. In the wake of this type of violence there are demands for law and order, and then promptly forgotten are the victims and causes of such violence.

As social psychiatrists we know that violence comes in many forms and that the psychological violence the nation inflicts is usually ignored. To debase a segment of the population on the basis of skin color is to do irreparable harm to them. To allow millions of Americans to remain hungry, to subsist in poverty and to live in unfit housing is as destructive to them as actual physical violence. If students burn draft cards and cite the war in Southeast Asia as an example of the hypocrisy of this country, are they being as violent as the military or the mayor of a city who says "shoot to kill?" To continue our brutality to the people of Vietnam and to our soldiers is to be violent. All of this must cease if our country is to reduce the level of violence and repair our national schisms.

Our hope is that Americans will read this book and initiate positive actions. A society solves a problem only when a majority of its people involves itself in the process of resolution. This country can no longer tolerate the divisions of black and white, haves and have-nots. The pace of events has quickened and dissatisfactions no longer wait for a remedy.

There are fewer great men among us to counsel patience. Their voices have been stilled by the very violence they sought to prevent. Martin Luther King, Jr., the noble advocate of nonviolence, may have been the last great voice warning the country to cancel its rendezvous with violence before it is too late.

The truth is plain to see. If the racial situation remains inflammatory and the conditions perpetuating poverty remain unchanged, and if vast numbers of our young see small hope for improvement in the quality of their lives, then this country will remain in danger. Violence will not go away because we will it and any superficial whitewash will sooner or later be recognized.

It has been said that this is a country with a tradition of violence, but we still wonder what is so special about the time in which we live that again we must struggle to maintain peace inside our nation. This analysis tells us that the kind of violence now involving us has occurred with regularity whenever a population committed to social change has confronted people committed to a defense of the status quo.

It seems that we never learn.

In colleges and universities, many educators have frequently acknowledged archaic admission standards and outdated curriculums, but they have done little to change them. Teachers, it has been said, should teach more and schools should relate to surrounding communities and involve themselves in the resolution of the problems of a modern world. Yet when black students ask for these same things, they are met with indifference and hostility. Who is to blame for the ensuing abrasions?

Over the past decade, black Americans have undergone profound changes in their conceptions of themselves and the world in which they live. It is ironic how many of these changes have remained unnoticed by many whites, even those white Americans purporting to make scientific inquiries into the thoughts, feelings and behavior of black people. Black Americans are undergoing a psychological revolution and, considering its implications, the wonder is that up to now it has been so peaceful.

In a short period we have seen a significant segment of Americans move from calling themselves colored, to Negro, to black, and now Black-American. A militant challenging posture has become a commonplace among blacks. They are determined to make America a better place for themselves and for all disenfranchised.

We take the position that the growth of this country has occurred around a series of violent upheavals and that each one has thrust the nation forward. The Boston Tea Party was an attempt by a few to alter an oppressive system of taxation without representation. The validation of these men rested on their attempts to effect needed social change. If the Boston Tea Party is viewed historically as a legitimate method of producing such change, then present-day militancy, whether by blacks or students, can claim a similar legitimacy.

Understood or not, this country is now in the midst of a major social revolution. Revolution suggests a drastic change and this is what black Americans are experiencing. A revolution turns from peaceful reform to violence when it encounters brutal, mindless resistance to change. If the black segment of our population is undergoing a maturing psychological and social change, and these maturing changes are not matched in white Americans, then the seeds of violence are sown. And if truth is the goal of any scholarly inquiry, we must conclude that too few white Americans are changing fundamental beliefs and behavior.

It is a contemporary tragedy that many leaders are in reality preaching the very violence they profess to deplore. They are inviting violence if they urge one part of the citizenry to stand pat while others are in transformation. Men who govern this country have a strange sense of leadership if they make appeals to law and order which are in effect thinly disguised messages to white Americans telling them they do not need to change their attitudes and actions. College administrators who respond to student demands as reactionary politicians rather than as progressive educators seem to ask to preside over institutions inviting more violence rather than less.

The way to avoid disorder is to appeal to the idealism of America; to facilitate change rather than resist it. If there is a streak of violence in the national character, then it is precisely that streak which sets itself in opposition to change. To resist necessary and healthy change in today's America is to invite social tumult and lay responsibility for it at the feet of black or student militancy.

Our history is filled with examples of the powerless determined to bring their grievances to a just hearing. We forget that many now powerful and entrenched social institutions were once engaged as a minority, and at times violently, in pressing claims to legitimacy.

Any American with union membership and a sense of fairness, who recalls the early stormy days of American unionism, should have immediate understanding of the struggles of contemporary black people.

While the communications media concentrate on the so-called excesses of students, this report shows clearly that most of the violence at universities is attributable to the policies of those in power—trustees, politicians, administrators, and finally, the unlawful actions of police called to campuses.

If the true instigators of violence are to be eliminated, how can we bypass the Police Establishment? In a few short years the ranks of law enforcement have become an ultraconservative social force which shrilly protests positive change. We submit that the violence done by this group will decrease only when every member of a minority group, whether racial or political, knows that the police will protect him as diligently as his white counterpart.

The Commission on Violence could serve no higher function than to commend this volume for reading by high government officials who seem determined to make violence much more a reality by appeals to rigidity and the "good old days." Men in high places must answer to history as well as conscience when they cite the black militant's style as an excuse for ignoring his just demands. They must live with their stupidity if they pander to a white bigotry which advocates resistance to any change that might threaten the status quo. Our country has achieved greatness by its ability to respond and grow, and history will deal harshly with those who block this growth by refusal to learn from the past.

Black Americans are now responding to their time in history and can no more be stopped than any idea whose time has come. They have been bred on the words of freedom, but immersed in bigotry and oppression, and their moment has arrived. Those who cannot see this are guilty of an inattention to the social ripenings that have enriched this land. There should be no mystery why students and antiwar protestors use the songs and style of black protest. Their own cause is strengthened when they share the momentum of a movement so eminently right and so certainly in the American tradition.

Violence is sure to increase if those who are responsible for the management of our country do not understand the driving force behind current protest. Our hope is that this Report will make more people see that there is a clear and present danger to our survival as a free society if fundamental changes are not made in American thought and institutions.

Justice has aligned itself with those who have been patient. The strivings of Blacks are on the side of democracy. Those who oppose these strivings, whether by appeals to law and order, states rights, or outright hatred, flirt with danger and with fascism.

Our clinical work has convinced us that all black Americans

are angry. All are asking for social change. There is a rage in black people which is a rage for justice. It demonstrates a passion for humanity at a time when few others are passionate.

And now there are stirrings among Spanish-speaking Americans, forgotten Indians, and poor and alienated whites, stirrings that tell us that a recalcitrant America has more than blacks to contend with.

We think that Americans can avert violence both in this country and the world by siding with rapid social evolution. If the relevant issues are race and poverty and peace, then we must move people to face these issues honestly and take action to reduce conflict. For those who doubt that many can change, we would say only that change is most rapid when the situation is most desperate.

We must abandon hypocrisy and aim for honesty. Can one find the answer to the question of poverty in a land of affluence by going to the poor alone, or must not inquiries be directed to the rich and powerful who are responsible for an unequal distribution of wealth and a system of taxation which subsidizes the affluent? Can we determine why the poor are sick by asking only them, or must we not go also to the major centers of medical care?

The leadership of this country has a solemn duty not to let this be another in a long series of such reports. The patriotism of our leaders must be called into question if the facts about a problem are clearly spelled out and people continue to suffer because no action is taken.

This Report clearly reveals that Americans must at last confront grievous wrongs and set swiftly to right them. The situation is critical and alternatives to violence must be found. Our leaders have a noble opportunity to demonstrate that change must not be feared but welcomed and embraced.

Price M. Cobbs, M. D.
William H. Grier, M. D.
San Francisco, California
May 15, 1969

Preface

This report is not an investigation, it is an analysis. It is based on facts collected from many sources over many years, plus some original field research begun and completed in a period of less than five months. The contract for the report was signed on August 28, 1968, and the final draft of the report was sent to the Commission on March 21, 1969. It is an attempt to understand the nature and causes of protest and confrontation in the United States, and their occasional eruption into violence. Our aim has been as much to describe what contemporary protest is *not* as to determine what contemporary protest *is*. The public response to protest is surrounded by misconceptions concerning the extent, nature, and goals of contemporary protest and the composition of protest groups. A major goal of our analysis, therefore, has been to challenge these misconceptions in order that responsible discussion may take place unencumbered by misunderstanding and distortion.

The assignment we were given was far-ranging, as the Table of Contents indicates. We have tried to be as objective as possible in our analysis, but objectivity is not synonymous with a lack of perspective. Our analysis makes no pretense at being "value-free." Our operating bias may be made explicit; we are partial to the values of equality, participation, and legality—in short, to those values we think of as the values of a constitutional democracy. We believe in due process of law and look toward a society in which order is achieved through consent, not coercion.

As social analysts we recognize, however, that violence has often been employed in human history, in America as elsewhere, to obtain social, political, and economic goals, and that it has been used both by officials and by ordinary citizens. For us, it is not enough to deplore violence—we seek to understand what it is and what it is not, as well as its nature and causes. Our title reflects our emphasis. This point of view was recently expressed in an article by Bruce L. R. Smith, coincidentally titled "The Politics of Protest." He writes:

> Violence has always been part of the political process. Politics does not merely encompass the actions of legislative assemblies, political parties, electoral contests and the other formal trappings of a modern government. Protest activities of one form or another, efforts to dramatize grievances in a fashion that will attract attention, and ultimately the destruction or threatened destruction of life and property appear as expressions of political grievances even in stable, consensual societies. In one sense, to speak of violence in the political process is to speak of the political process; the *ultima ratio* of political action is force. Political activity below the threshold of force is normally carried on with the knowledge that an issue may be escalated into overt violence if a party feels sufficiently aggrieved.

The intellectual freedom offered to us was absolute. Except for agonizing limitations of time, we were offered the best conceivable terms under which to do the job. In addition, the Commission staff was generous with its encouragement. No institution or affiliated organization, nor the Commission itself, nor the Task Force staff, is to be held responsible for the final report as it appears here. That responsibility rests solely with the Director of the Task Force.

The question of responsibility aside, however, whatever merit the report may have, and that it was completed on time, is to be attributed to a tireless and devoted staff and group of consultants. Five people should be singled out. Ira M. Heyman bore principal responsibility for organizing and conducting hearings before the Commission, and contributed wise counsel throughout the writing of the report. Elliott Currie, Anthony Platt, and Edmund C. Ursin were the workhorses of the staff. They not only drafted major portions of the report, they also were companions in the development of the tone and direction of the report as a whole. Sharon Dunkle Marks' title of staff administrator does not wholly indicate her contribution. In addition to administration, she made an intellectual contribution through discussion, writing, and interviewing. Besides, she brought some badly needed charm to the whole enterprise.

There were two classes of consultants: those who submitted papers (staff consultants), and those who submitted critiques (advisory consultants). The contributions of consultants to particular chapters were as follows: Chapter I drew heavily upon a paper by Richard Rubenstein and was informed by Amitai Etzioni's research; Chapter II drew heavily from a paper by Frederick Crews, and was further informed by a research contribution from Irving Louis Horowitz; both of them, moreover, contributed wise counsel at different times in the enterprise. Chapter III relied heavily upon the research of Richard Flacks and Joseph Gusfield and also drew upon a paper by Marie-Helene leDivelec; Chapter IV was informed by interviews conducted by, and in consultation with, Kermit Coleman; Chapter VI was informed by a paper submitted by David Chalmers. Thomas Crawford's paper served as the basis for Chapter V. Chapter VII drew upon a paper submitted by Rodney Stark and made use of materials collected by Ed Cray. Chapter VIII relies upon a variety of materials on courts during crisis, as well as some written materials prepared by Sheldon Messinger. Chapter IX was informed by a contribution from Martin Liebowitz.

Our base of operations was the Center for the Study of Law and Society, University of California, Berkeley. Its Chairman, Philip Selznick, and its Vice-Chairman, Sheldon Messinger, were gracious and generous with the facilities of the Center. As guests we were made to feel not merely welcome, but at home. Moreover, Drs. Selznick and Messinger were significant consultants throughout the development of the manuscript. Nine seminars on chapters and consultant papers were attended by Center Associates and guests. The seminars ranged in size from twenty to fifty persons, and especially valuable comments were made by Howard Becker, Herbert Blumer, Robert Cole, Sanford Kadish, William Kornhauser, David Matza, Neil Smelser, and Allen Grimshaw, among others. The seminars were an enormously valuable experience, and all the participants listed and unlisted deserve our gratitude.

Our advisory consultants are listed on a separate page.

Opinion research organizations generously provided helpful advice, numerous reports and tables summarizing opinion polls, and permission to publish data and tables: American Institute of Public Opinion; Louis Harris and Associates; Louis Harris Political Data Center; National Opinion Research Center; Roper Research Associates; and the University of Michigan Survey Research Center. Naturally, these organizations and their representatives are not responsible for the conclusions and interpretations we have drawn that may have differed from theirs.

Other members of the staff worked tirelessly to finish on time: Charles Carey, Howard Erlanger, Sam McCormick, and Richard Speiglman. Nancy Leonard was our Washington, D.C., research assistant, and was invaluable in getting necessary materials to the Berkeley staff. Our office staff was tireless, devoted, intelligent, and tolerant. Given our deadlines, we needed tolerance most of all.

Finally, my wife, Dr. Arlene Skolnick, served as a consultant on social psychology, helped with the editing, and, best of all, gave birth to Michael's brother, Alexander, on September 29, 1968.

Jerome H. Skolnick,
Center for the Study of Law and Society
University of California
Berkeley, California
March 21, 1969

Summary

Chapter I: Protest and Politics

There are three critical points about protest and violence in America:
—There has been relatively little violence accompanying contemporary demonstration and group protest.
It is often difficult to determine who was "responsible" for the violence when it does occur. The evidence in the Walker Report and other similar studies suggests that authorities often bear a major part of the responsibility.
—Mass protest, whether or not its outcome is violent, must be analyzed in relation to crises in American institutions.
For these reasons, serious analysis of the connections between protest and violence cannot focus solely on the character or culture of those who protest the current state of the American political and social order. Rather, our research finds that mass protest is an essentially political phenomenon engaged in by normal people; that demonstrations are increasingly being employed by a variety of groups, ranging from students and blacks to middle-class professionals, public employees, and policemen; that violence, when it occurs, is usually not planned, but arises out of an interaction between protesters and responding authorities; that violence has fre-

quently accompanied the efforts of deprived groups to achieve status in American society; and that recommendations concerning the prevention of violence which do not address the issue of fundamental social and political change are fated to be largely irrelevant and frequently self-defeating.

Chapter II: Anti-War Protest

Reasons for the existence of a broadly based and durable Vietnam peace movement must be sought in the reassessment of Cold War attitudes; in the absence of a "Pearl Harbor" to mobilize patriotic unity; and in the gradual accumulation of public knowledge about the history of America's involvement in Vietnam. Other sustaining factors have been the "credibility gap," the frustrating progress of the war, reports of extraordinary brutality toward civilians, and reliance on an unpopular system of conscription. In particular, critics of the war have been most successful in pointing up the relation between the war and the American domestic crisis; the need to "reorder priorities" has been a repeated theme. Anti-war feelings have been sustained by criticism of administration policy from highly placed sources in this country and abroad.

The movement's main base of support has been among white professionals, students, and clergy. A segment of the movement has been drifting towards "confrontationism"; physical injuries, however, have more often resulted from the actions of authorities and counter demonstrators. The most meaningful grouping of protesters separates those for whom tactics are chiefly a moral question from those who see tactics chiefly as the means to political ends. Most of the latter, though not ethically committed to nonviolence, have repeatedly turned away from possible bloody encounters. Having no single ideology or clearly formulated goals beyond an end to the war, the movement is dependent on government policy for its survival, growth, and tactical evolution. Still, the political consequences of the war may be profound since, in its wake, there has been a continuing reassessment of American politics and institutions, especially among students at leading colleges and universities.

Chapter III: Student Protest

The current student generation is more morally and politically serious and better educated than the generation of the 1950's. Its participation in the civil rights movement, in the Peace Corps, and in university protest reflects an idealism expressed in direct action. The increasing disaffection of student activists, their pessimism over the possibility of genuine reform in the university and larger society, and their frequent resort to tactics of confrontation cannot be explained away by referring to personality problems or to youthful intransigence or delinquency. On the contrary, research indicates that activists have usually been good students with liberal ideals not unlike those of their parents.

Stridency has increased with political frustration related to civil rights and the Vietnam War. Campuses have become the headquarters of anti-war protest. Not only have students challenged the war on its merits; they have also questioned whether a free society should force young men to fight a war they do not support, and whether school attendance and grades should be criteria for exemption from military service. They have been especially critical of the university's cooperation with the Selective Service System and of that system's policy of "channeling" students into careers and occupations deemed to be in the national interest by the director of Selective Service.

They have come to see the university as implicated in the industrial, military, and racial status quo. Disaffection has been intensified by the response of certain university administrations, which have been perceived as more susceptible to conservative pressures than to underlying issues. The introduction of police onto the campus, with its attendant violence, usually has reinforced these perceptions and aggravated campus conflict while decreasing support for the university outside the campus and diverting attention from substantive issues.

Chapter IV: Black Militancy

Black militants today—including black college students, a group that only a few years ago was individualistic, assimilationist, and politically indifferent—are repudiating conventional American culture and values. The theme of "independence" is stressed rather than "integration," and the concept of "non-violence" is being replaced by a concept of "self-defense."

Four factors have influenced this transition. First, the failure of the civil rights movement to improve significantly the social, economic, and political position of most Negro Americans has led to doubts about the possibility of meaningful progress through law. Second, urban riots in the 1960's, which symbolized this frustration, have been met with armed force, which in turn has mobilized militant sentiment within black communities. Third, the worldwide revolution against colonialism has induced a new sense of racial consciousness, pride, and affirmative identity. Fourth, the war in Vietnam has diverted resources away from pressing urban needs and reinforced the prevailing skepticism about white America's capacity or interest in addressing itself to the social, economic, and political requirements of black communities.

As a result, there has been increasing dissatisfaction with the United States and its institutions, and increasing identification with nonwhite peoples who have achieved independence from colonial powers. In response to the challenge of black militancy, Negroes of all occupations and ages are becoming increasingly unwilling to accept the assumptions of white culture, white values, and white power. The thrust toward militancy is especially pronounced among black youth, who tend to view the more militant leadership as heroic figures. As college students, these youth provide a fertile base for campus militancy.

Chapter V: The Racial Attitudes of White Americans

Recent studies indicate a long-term decrease in anti-Negro prejudice since the 1940's. While the social roots of prejudice are complex, it is especially characteristic of the less educated, older, rural segments of the population. Major trends in contemporary society, including urbanization and increasing educational opportunity, have undermined the roots of prejudice and may be expected to have a continuing effect in the future.

Although surveys show continuing rejection by many whites of the *means* by which blacks attempt to redress their grievances, most whites express support of the goal of increased opportunity for black Americans. Not surprisingly, blacks express less satisfaction with the quality of their lives, and are less optimistic about their opportunities, than are whites. Correspondingly, whites feel the need for change less urgently than do blacks. Nevertheless, recent studies show that a clear majority of whites would support federal programs to tear down the ghettos and to realize the goals of full employment, better education, and better housing for blacks, even if they would have to pay more taxes to support such programs.

Chapter VI: White Militancy

The most violent single force in American history outside of war has been a minority of militant whites, defending home, family, or country from forces considered alien or threatening.

Historically, a tradition of direct vigilante action has joined with racist and nativist cultural themes to create intermittent reigns of terror against racial and ethnic minorities and against those considered "un-American." It is difficult to exaggerate the extent to which violence, often aided by community support and encouragement from political leaders is embedded in our history.

Although most white Americans repudiate violence and support the goals of increased opportunity for blacks, there has been a resurgence of militant white protest, largely directed against the gains of the black communities.

The roots of such protest lie in the political and economic sources of white marginality and insecurity. In this sense, white militancy—like student, anti-war, and black protest—reflects a fundamental crisis of American political and social institutions. White protest is not simply the work of "extremists" whose behavior is peripheral to the main currents of American society. Similarly, capitulation to the rhetoric of white militancy, through simplistic demands for "law and order," cannot substitute adequately for concrete programs aimed at the roots of white discontent.

Chapter VII: The Police in Protest

The policeman in America is overworked, undertrained, underpaid, and undereducated. His job, moreover, is increasingly difficult, forcing him into the almost impossible position of repressing deeply felt demands for social and political change. In this role, he is unappreciated and at times despised.

His difficulties are compounded by a view of protest that gives little consideration to the effects of such social factors as poverty and discrimination and virtually ignores the possibility of legitimate social discontent. Typically, it attributes mass protest instead to a conspiracy promulgated by agitators, often Communists, who mislead otherwise contented people. This view leaves the police ill-equipped to understand or deal with dissident groups.

Given their social role, the police have become increasingly frustrated, alienated, and angry. These emotions are being expressed in a growing militancy and political activism.

The police are protesting. Police slowdowns and other forms of strike activity, usually of questionable legality, have been to gain greater material benefits or changes in governmental policy (such as the "unleashing of the police"). Direct police challenges to departmental and civic authority have followed recent urban disorders, and criticisms of the judiciary have escalated to "court-watching" by police.

These developments are a part of a larger phenomenon—the emergence of the police as a self-conscious, independent political power. In many cities and states the police lobby rivals even duly elected officials in influence. Yet courts and police are expected to be neutral and nonpolitical, for even the perception of a lack of impartiality impairs public confidence in and reliance upon the legal system.

Police response to mass protest has often resulted in an escalation of conflict, hostility, and violence. The police violence during the Democratic National Convention in Chicago was not a unique phenomenon. We have found numerous other instances where violence has been initiated or exacerbated by police actions and attitudes, although violence also has been avoided by judicious planning and supervision.

Police violence is the antithesis of both law and order. It leads only to increased hostility, polarization, and violence—both in the immediate situation and in the future. Certainly it is clear today that effective policing ultimately depends upon the cooperation and goodwill of the policed, and these resources are quickly being exhausted by present attitudes and practices.

Chapter VIII: Judicial Response in Crisis

The actions of the judicial system in times of civil crisis are an important test of a society's capacity to uphold democratic values and protect civil liberties. Our analysis, as the Kerner Commission found, finds that during recent urban riots defendants were deprived of adequate representation, subjected to indignities in overcrowded facilities, and held in custody by the imposition of high bail amounting to preventive detention and the suspension of due process. This was done under a "feedback to riot" theory that both lacks evidence and is implausible.

The inability of the courts to cope with civil emergencies encourages a further decline in respect for legal authority.

Black, student, and anti-war protesters have come to share a common view that legal institutions serve power and are incapable of remedying social and political grievances.

The crisis in the courts is explained by three considerations. First, the quality of justice in the lower criminal courts during routine operations is quite low; one would not expect more during emergencies. Second, in response to community and political pressures for immediate restoration of order, the counts tend to adopt a police perspective on "riot control," becoming in effect an instrument of social control, relatively unrestrained by considerations of legality. Finally, the courts are not suited to the task of resolving the political conflicts which occasion civil crisis and mass arrests.

Thus, reforms in the operations of the courts during crisis are only a temporary palliative, leaving untouched the political crisis. We nevertheless urge such reform to protect the constitutional rights of defendants and to increase the dignity and influence of the courts. We are especially concerned that the present trend toward devising "emergency measures" not become routinized as the main social response to crises that go deeper than the need to restore order.

Chapter IX: Social Response to Collective Behavior

Governmental responses to civil disorder have historically combined long-run recommendations for social change with short-run calls for better strategy and technology to contain disruption. We offer the following reasons for questioning such a two-pronged approach to the question of violence:

1. American society urgently requires fundamental social and political change, not more firepower in official hands. As the National Advisory Commission on Civil Disorders stated, "This nation will deserve neither safety nor progress unless it can demonstrate the wisdom and the will to undertake decisive action against the root causes of racial disorder."

2. We must set realistic priorities. Historical experience suggests that firepower measures—so seemingly simple, practicable, and programmatic—will receive favorable consideration over reform measures. We believe that the law must be

enforced fairly, and that the machinery of law enforcement needs upgrading; but we must carefully distinguish between increased firepower and enlightened law enforcement.

3. Police, soldiers, and other agents of social control have been implicated in triggering and intensifying violence in riots and other forms of protest. Sophisticated weaponry will not solve the social problems of America. To the young man in the ghetto, the "nonlethal" weapon is not seen as a humane response to his condition; to him it is still a weapon—aimed at him—and is viewed with hostility.

4. Evidence shows that it is incorrect to interpret riots merely as pathological behavior engaged in by riffraff. Neither are they "carnivals." More accurately, they are spontaneous political acts expressing enormous frustration and genuine grievance. Forceful control techniques may channel grievances into organized revolutionary and guerrilla patterns, promising a cycle of increased military force and covert surveillance.

5. In measuring the consequences of domestic military escalation, we must add the political and social dangers of depending on espionage as an instrument of social control, including its potential for eroding constitutional guarantees of political freedom.

If American society concentrates on the development of sophisticated control techniques, it will move itself into the destructive and self-defeating position of meeting a political problem with armed force, which will eventually threaten domestic freedom. The combination of long-range reform and short-range order sounds plausible, but we fear that the strategy of force will continue to prevail. In the long run this nation cannot have it both ways: either it will carry through a firm commitment to massive and widespread political and social reform, or it will become a society of garrison cities where order is enforced with less and less concern for due process of law and the consent of the governed.

Part One
Introduction

Chapter I
Protest and Politics

Problems of Definition

WE BEGAN the work of this Task Force by considering the relation between protest and group violence. Discussion and consultation with a variety of scholars made clear to us that the posing of the question biased the answer. As posed, the question seemed to imply that protest itself is the critical social problem demanding investigation and action.

Furthermore, as our factual material grew, we began to recognize three critical points about protest and violence in America, all of which will become more apparent in the chapters that follow:

1. One of our consultants examined every incident of protest reported in the *New York Times* and the *Washington Post* from September 16 to October 15, 1968. Of 216 incidents, 35 percent reportedly involved violence. Since protests resulting in violence are more likely to be reported, the actual proportion of violent incidents is doubtless much lower.[1]

2. It is often difficult to determine who was "responsible" for the violence. The reports of our study teams, however, clearly suggest that authorities bear a major responsibility.[2] The Kerner Commission findings reveal a similar pattern.[3] Of

the violent incidents reported above, in only half did the violence seem to have been initiated by the demonstrators, i.e., in only 17.5 percent of the total number of demonstrations.[4]

3. Mass protest, whether or not violence occurs, must be analyzed in relation to crises in American institutions. On all of these counts it may be suggested that a serious analysis of the connections between protest and violence cannot focus solely on the character or culture of those who protest the current state of the American political and social order. Nor does it appreciably advance our understanding to suggest, as has one commentator, that "the decisive seat of evil in this world is not in social and political institutions, and not even, as a rule, in the will or iniquities of statesmen, but simply in the weakness of the human soul itself." [5] Rather, the results of our research suggest that mass protest is an outgrowth of social, economic, and political conditions; that such violence as occurs is usually not planned, but arises out of an *interaction* between protesters and the reaction of authorities; and that recommendations concerning the prevention of violence which do not address the issue of fundamental social, economic, and political change are fated to be largely irrelevant and frequently self-defeating.

We have found the political character of these phenomena to be evident for at least five reasons. First, *"violence" is an ambiguous term whose meaning is established through political processes.* The kinds of acts that become classified as "violent," and, equally important, those which do not become so classified, vary according to who provides the definition and who has superior resources for disseminating and enforcing his definitions. The most obvious example of this is the way, in a war, each side typically labels the other side as the aggressor and calls many of the latter's violent acts atrocities. The definition of the winner usually prevails.

Within a given society, political regimes often exaggerate the violence of those challenging established institutions. The term "violence" is frequently employed to discredit forms of behavior considered improper, reprehensible, or threatening by specific groups which, in turn, may mask their own violent response with the rhetoric of order or progress. In the eyes of those accustomed to immediate deference, back talk, profanity, insult, or disobedience may appear violent. In the South, for example, at least until recently, the lynching of an "uppity" black man was often considered less shocking than the violation of caste etiquette which provoked it.

In line with the tendency to see violence as a quality of those individuals and groups who challenge existing arrangements, rather than of those who uphold them, some groups today see all instances of contemporary demonstration and protest as "violent." Such an equation obscures the very significant fact that protest takes various forms: verbal criticism; written criticism; petitions; picketing; marches; nonviolent confrontation, e.g., obstruction; nonviolent lawbreaking, e.g., "sitting-in"; obscene language; rock-throwing; milling; wild running; looting; burning; guerrilla warfare. Some of these forms are violent, others are not, others are hard to classify. Some protests begin peacefully and, depending on the response, may end violently. Most protest, we have found, is nonviolent.

Second, *the concept of violence always refers to a disruption of some condition of order; but order, like violence, is politically defined.* From the perspective of a given state of "order," violence appears as the worst of all possible social conditions and presumably the most costly in terms of human values. We have found this to be a questionable assumption. Less dramatic but equally destructive processes may occur well within the routine operation of "orderly" social life. Foreign military ventures come quickly to mind. Domestically, many more people are killed or injured annually through failure to build safe highways, automobiles, or appliances than through riots or demonstrations. And as the late Senator Robert Kennedy pointed out, the indifference, inaction, and slow decay that routinely afflict the poor are far more destructive than the bomb in the night.[6] High infant mortality rates or rates of preventable disease, perpetuated through discrimination, take a far greater toll than civil disorders.

It would not be implausible to call these outcomes "institutional violence," the overall effect of which far outweighs those of the more immediately observable kinds of social violence. For the sake of some precision, however, we have come to employ a less comprehensive definition of violence:

violence is the intentional use of force to injure, to kill, or to destroy property. Protest may be quite forceful without being violent, as the occupation of dozens of French factories in the summer of 1968 or the occupation of many campus facilities in America during the last few years testifies. This observation is not intended to applaud or condone the use of force; merely to recognize that it differs from violence—the point, after all, of an important legal distinction. Such a distinction should be helpful in separating violent and nonviolent forms of collective protest. There is a difference between a nonviolent "sit-in" and rock-throwing. But whatever the definition, there will always be marginal cases.

Third, *even as here defined, "violence" is not always forbidden or unequivocally condemned in American society.* Exuberant football crowds or fraternal conventions frequently produce considerable property damage, yet are rarely condemned. The violence of the poor against each other is substantially ignored until it spills out into the communities of the more comfortable, where it is called "crime in the streets." Generally, American society tends to applaud violence conducted in approved channels, while condemning as "violent" lesser actions which are not supportive of existing social and political arrangements. In contrast to the findings of the Chicago Study Team, a majority of the American people did not perceive the Chicago police as violent during the days of the recent Democratic National Convention.[7] A young black man setting fire to a Vietnamese hut is considered a dutiful citizen; the same man burning a grocery store is a dangerous criminal, condemned for "resorting to violence" and subject to the lawful exercise of deadly force. Violence, then, is proscribed or condoned through political processes and decisions. The violence of the warrior in the service of the state is applauded; that of the rebel or insurgent against the state condemned.

Fourth, *the decision to use or not to use such violent tactics as "deadly force" in the control of protest is a political one.* The interplay of protest and official violence, therefore, cannot be understood solely through an analysis of demonstrators and police. It must be seen in the light of the surrounding structure of authority and power and the conceptions that authorities hold of the nature of protest and the proper uses of official violence. Official violence is frequently overlooked. Through abstraction, the technical and instrumental elements of official violence are emphasized and its moral and political aspects obscured. Thus, "crowd control" may mean splitting open the heads of bystanders; a "looter" may in fact be an ordinary ghetto resident involved in a collective act of expropriating a pair of shoes or case of beer, or an ordinary ghetto resident trying to get off the street. By invoking the concept of "looter," however, public officials can conjure the picture of heinous crime, can sidestep the normal penalty structure of the criminal law, call for the use of deadly force, and be applauded for a firm stand on "law and order."

This consideration prompted us to adopt a general methodological position. Instead of accepting at face value the meaning of such terms as "police," "looters," "demonstrators," and "social control," we have found it wise to review the attitudes and behavior suggested by these abstractions. Too often, analyses of protest and disorder arbitrarily follow the analyst's preconception of motivation and purpose. We have tried to avoid this error. Therefore, we have tried to pay close attention to the viewpoints and the actual behavior of the participants in protest situations, whether demonstrators or police.

When the viewpoint of participants is taken seriously, a fifth aspect of the political character of protest becomes evident. *Almost uniformly, the participants in mass protest today see their grievances as rooted in the existing arrangements of power and authority in contemporary society, and they view their own activity as political action—on a direct or symbolic level—aimed at altering those arrangements.* A common theme, from the ghetto to the university, is the rejection of dependency and external control, a staking of new boundaries, and a demand for significant control over events within those boundaries. This theme is far from new in American history. There have been violent clashes over institutional control in this country from its beginnings. In the following section, we will examine some of these clashes in the hope that they will throw historical light on the political problems that now confront us.

Political Violence in American History [8]

Many commentators continue to write as if domestic political violence were a creation of the 1960's, as if the past had nothing to say to the present. It seems, as Clifford Geertz has said, that

> . . . we do not want to learn too much about ourselves too quickly. The fact is that the present state of domestic disorder in the United States is not the product of some destructive quality mysteriously ingrained in the substance of American life. It is a product of a long sequence of particular events whose interconnections our received categories of self-understanding are not only inadequate to reveal but are designed to conceal. We do not know very well what kind of society we live in, what kind of people we are. We are just now beginning to find out, the hard way. . . .[9]

Leading scholars of the 1950's believed that the United States was the one nation in which diverse groups had learned to compromise differences peaceably. American society had somehow succeeded in blurring divisions among a multiplicity of economic, social, political, and ethnic groups. For one reason or another (either because the land was fertile and the people hard-working, or because no true aristocracy or proletariat ever developed on American soil, or because the two-party system worked so well), any sizable domestic group could gain its share of power, prosperity, and respectability merely by playing the game according to the rules. In the process, the group itself would tend to lose coherence and to be incorporated into the great middle class. The result, these scholars argued, was something unique in world history: genuine progress without violent group conflict. In such an America there was no need—there never had been a need—for political violence. Rising domestic groups had not been compelled to be revolutionary, nor had the "ins" generally resorted to force to keep them out.[10] The conclusion drawn by many was that America, having mastered the art of peaceful change, could in good conscience presume to lead the Free World, if not the whole world.

This was the myth of peaceful progress, which, since the racial uprisings beginning in 1964, has spawned a corollary myth—that community violence is a uniquely Negro phenomenon—for clearly the only way to explain what happened in Watts, Newark, or Detroit, without challenging anyone's belief in the essential workability of established machinery for peaceful group advancement, was to assume that black people were the great exception to the law of peaceful progress. A "conservative" could emphasize black laziness, loose morality, and disrespect for law. A "liberal" could discuss the weakness of Negro family structure inherited from slavery, the prevalence of racial discrimination or the culture of poverty. Either way, it was assumed that the existing political and economic system could make good on its promise to blacks without radical institutional change.[11] The situation could be salvaged, white faith in America confirmed, and violence ended without any great national political upheaval, provided the government was willing to spend enough money on both reform programs and law enforcement.

"This then is the mood of America's absolutism," wrote Louis Hartz, "the sober faith that its norms are self-evident." [12] What if the black community were not unique, however, but rather the latest of a long line of domestic groups motivated to resort to political violence? What if the institutions designed to make economic and political advancement possible had broken down frequently in the past, and other groups had embraced the politics of violence? What if political violence on a large scale was, as H. Rap Brown stated, "as American as cherry pie"? Then, clearly, the myth of peaceful progress—and the immunity of hallowed political institutions from fundamental criticism—would be in danger.

Especially if prior outbreaks of violent revolt in the United States fell into a pattern, the suspicion would arise that not just "violence-prone" or "exceptional" groups were responsible, but rather American institutions themselves—or, at least, the relationship between certain groups and certain institutions. In such an event, modern Americans might be compelled to wonder whether something fundamental was wrong —something not merely capricious and temporary, but socially structured and predictable. That this has not yet happened testifies to the remarkable tenacity of the myth of peaceful progress. We are therefore compelled to analyze in more detail the ways in which this myth has shaped American attitudes toward political violence, in order to clear away some of the ideological underbrush which has so hampered exploration in the past.

Whether in Congress or in the streets, reactions to modern outbreaks of political violence have demonstrated a widely held belief that such outbreaks were "un-American": that they had occurred infrequently in the past, and that they bore little relationship to the way past domestic groups had succeeded in gaining political power, property, and prestige. (Those most vociferous in denouncing the violent were often those who believed, rightly or wrongly, that *their* ethnic, economic, or occupational groups had "made it" in American society without resorting to violent conduct.) Historical study, on the other hand, reveals that under certain circumstances the United States has regularly experienced episodes of mass violence directly related to the achievement of social, political, and economic objectives. The following is a partial list of major groups which have been involved in violent political movements: [13]

1. Beginning early in the seventeenth century, *American Indians* engaged in a series of revolts aimed at securing their land and liberty against invasion by white settlers supported by colonial, state, and federal governments. In the eighteenth century, following Britain's victory over France, Eastern tribes participated in such uprisings as Pontiac's Conspiracy, Little Turtle's War, the Blackhawk War, the Revolt of the Creeks and Cherokees, and the Seminole War—a series of unsuccessful resistances to white settlement and "removal" to Indian territories west of the Mississippi. For the Indians of the West who fought in the post-Civil War rebellions of the Sioux, Sac and Fox, Navajo, Apache, and others, the price of defeat was imprisonment on reservations and the loss not only of land but also of liberty and livelihood. Calling these conflicts "wars" against Indian "nations" does not, of course,

alter their character; they were armed insurrections by domestic groups to which the United States had determined to deny the privileges of citizenship as well as the perquisites of nationhood. The suppression of Indian revolts was the chief occupation of the U.S. Army for more than a century after its creation.

2. *Appalachian farmers* living in the western regions of the Eastern Seaboard states participated in civil disorder from the 1740's, when Massachusetts farmers marched on Boston in support of a land bank law, until the 1790's, when farmers and mountain men fomented the Whiskey and Fries Rebellions in Pennsylvania. The series of revolts now known as the Wars of the Regulators (North and South Carolina), the War of the New Hampshire Grants (New York–Vermont), Shays's Rebellion (Massachusetts), and the Whiskey Rebellion (Pennsylvania) were the principal actions engaged in by debtor farmers protesting half a century of economic exploitation, political exclusion, and social discrimination by the East Coast merchants, shippers, and planters who were in substantial control of the machinery of government. In state after state, civil disobedience of hated laws was followed by intimidation of, or physical attacks on, tax collectors and other law enforcers, by the closing down of courts to prevent indictments and mortgage foreclosures from being issued, by the rejection of halfway compromises proffered by Eastern legislatures, and finally by military organization to resist the state militia. Although most insurgent groups were finally defeated and dispersed by superior military force, the rebellions did not end until Jefferson's election provided access for Westerners to the political system, and new land created fresh economic opportunity. Where political and economic systems were especially rigid, as in New York's Hudson Valley, agitation and sporadic violence continued well into the nineteenth century.

3. *American colonists,* as we know, gained their independence from Britain after a decade of civil strife and eight years of revolutionary war. What is now becoming clearer is the extent to which the struggle pitted Americans against Americans, with the insurgents resorting to political violence and the authorities to repression. This pattern was repeated again

and again in American history. The decade beginning in 1765 with the Stamp Tax controversy saw a steady rise in civil disorder in the forms of massive civil disobedience, urban rioting, economic boycotts, sabotage of government property, terrorism of government officials, and finally military organization—paralleled, of course, by simultaneous escalation of attempts at suppression by the colonial authorities and their local supporters. Such groups as the Sons of Liberty, operating chiefly out of East Coast cities, organized campaigns against British colonial legislation, directing both economic and physical coercion against Tories, merchants who refused to participate in boycotts of British goods, and other "collaborators." With the outbreak of hostilities against the British, civil strife increased in both intensity and scope, spreading into rural areas such as New Jersey and South Carolina, where roving guerrilla bands played nightmare games of armed hide-and-seek with the Tories. The violence of the rebellious guerrillas resulted in a massive Tory emigration. Indeed, it seems likely that this emigration, which began in the last years of the war, probably saved the United States from the sort of prolonged revolutionary violence and emigré retaliation which characterized the French Revolution.

4, 5. In the years between 1820 and 1860, *white Southerners* became a conscious minority. This was the period in which Southerners committed themselves economically to an agricultural system based on slave-breeding and plantation farming; in which the dream of emancipation fled the South and became the exclusive property of Northern abolitionists; and in which thinkers such as John C. Calhoun constructed vain theoretical defenses against increasing Northern economic and political power, while Southerners, with a pride born of increasing desperation, dreamed the "purple dream" of a Southern Empire stretching from the Mason-Dixon Line to Tierra del Fuego. How Southerners moved from abortive civil disobedience (the Nullification Controversy of 1828 to 1830) to war by proxy (in "bleeding Kansas" during the 1850's) and finally to outright secession is well known, as is the parallel movement of *Northern abolitionists* from disobedience of the Fugitive Slave laws to the fielding of a settler army in Kansas, support of John Brown's raid on Harpers

Ferry, and (in coalition with Northern Whigs) the election of a President committed to the preservation of the Union by force.

Less well known, however, is the guerrilla war waged after the surrender at Appomattox by terrorist groups (principally the Ku Klux Klan) supported by the mass of white Southerners. The purposes of this struggle—to prevent freed Negroes from voting or participating in politics; to restore the substance of the prewar Southern social and economic systems; and to drive "carpetbagger" officials and their "scalawag" collaborators out of office and out of the South—were largely realized by 1876, when President Hayes withdrew the last of the Northern troops. This was not the end of Southern violence, however; continued racial domination was maintained in postwar years by the lynching of great numbers of blacks, the driving of dissenting whites out of the South, and the meting out to "outside agitators" of painful and sometimes deadly punishment.

6, 7. *White, Anglo-Saxon, Protestant Americans* (WASPs) engaged in a long series of riots, lynchings, mob actions, and abuses of power in their effort to protect their political preeminence, property values, and life-styles against the immigrant onslaught. WASPs, organized politically as "Native Americans," tore apart the Irish section of Philadelphia in 1844; similar riots occurred in Baltimore, Boston, and other port cities. On the West Coast, Chinese and Japanese immigrants were victims of both riots and discrimination. Italians were lynched in New Orleans and Jews attacked in New York, and WASPs resorted to fierce violence in collaboration with other American groups against German-Americans during World War I (riots, intimidation, boycotts, etc.) and against Japanese during World War II (internment in concentration camps, regardless of citizenship or alienage).

For their part, later *immigrant groups* sometimes responded in kind, although their hostility was more often directed socially downward, toward the blacks and newer-arrived immigrants who were often the "scabs" in labor disputes.

During the terrible New York Draft Riots in 1863, for example, the Irish of New York not only burned draft offices and Yankee homes but went on a rampage against the blacks, numbers of whom were left swinging from New York lampposts. Following the Civil War, attacks on ghetto blacks in border state cities became frequent, and when, in the present century, race riots struck Northern cities like Chicago, more recent immigrant groups fearful of the black "invasion" were in the forefront of the white attackers.

8. Beginning in the 1870's, *workingmen* attempting to organize for collective action engaged in more than half a century of violent warfare with industrialists, their private armies, and workers employed to break strikes, as well as with police and troops. The anthracite fields of western Pennsylvania were Molly Maguire territory during the 1870's; after losing a coal strike early in the period, the Mollys sought to regain control of the area by systematic use of violence, including sabotage and assassination, and were successful until penetrated and exposed by a Pinkerton spy. In 1877, when a railroad strike spread throughout the nation, unorganized workers engaged in a series of immensely destructive riots to protest wage cuts, the use of scabs, and probably loss of jobs during a depression. Baltimore and Pittsburgh were hardest hit; although the total cost in life and property has never been estimated accurately, one commentator has reported that the destruction in Pittsburgh alone was greater than that experienced during all the labor and racial riots of 1919. The Haymarket Square bombing and retaliation against anarchists in 1886 followed the railroad strike of 1877; the Homestead Strike at the Carnegie Steel plant was followed by an anarchist attempt to kill Henry Clay Frick in 1892; the Pullman Strike became particularly violent after President Grover Cleveland called in troops over the protest of the Governor of Illinois in 1894; the *Los Angeles Times* was bombed by persons associated with the AFL in 1910; the IWW led a textile strike at Lowell, Massachusetts, in 1912; and there were national strikes against railroads and steel, with troops called out in several cities, in 1919. These are just a few of the major battles.

Meanwhile, in the mining and timber industries of the West, an initial blowup in the Coeur d'Alene region of Idaho (1892) was followed by twenty years of the most intense and sanguinary struggle, ranging from Goldfields, Nevada, and Ludlow, Colorado, to the West Virginia–Kentucky border. On the eve of passage of the New Deal's pro-union Wagner Act, CIO auto workers were engaging in sit-down strikes in Michigan auto plants and fighting pitched battles with strike-breakers and police. Legislative transformation of labor-management relations, especially provisions for grievance and arbitration machinery, ended this principal period of labor war in the United States, although continued skirmishes accompanying hard-fought strikes seem now a part of our way of life.

9. *Black Americans* participated during the years of slavery in at least 250 abortive insurrections and were, after the end of the Civil War, the victims of white attacks in dozens of cities ranging from Cincinnati (1866) to East St. Louis (1917). Blacks retaliated violently against white attacks in the Chicago and Washington, D.C., race riots of 1919 and in the Detroit riot of 1943.

10. Prior to the passage, in 1920, of the Nineteenth Amendment granting female suffrage, *women* engaged in militant action to protest their exclusion from American politics. The idea of women gaining a voice in politics was widely considered to amount to a radical assault not only on the political order but on the very fabric of society. "Were our state a pure democracy," wrote Thomas Jefferson, "there would still be excluded from our deliberations . . . women, who, to prevent deprivation of morals and ambiguity of issues, should not mix promiscuously in gatherings of men." [14] Although the struggle for woman suffrage did not include mass political violence of the kind that marked the struggles of many other groups for a share of political power, it frequently involved aggressively militant tactics. In 1917, for example, militant women engaged in hunger strikes, picketed the White House, and burned copies of Presidential speeches.[15]

This list, although incomplete,[16] does provide a historical background against which to test the most important implication of the myth of peaceful progress—the idea that political violence in the United States is, and always has been, relatively rare, needless, without purpose, and irrational. The proposition that domestic political violence has been unneces-

sary to achieve political goals is ambiguous, but it is historically fallacious no matter how one interprets it. If it means
that the established machinery has permitted major "out-
groups" to move nonviolently up the politicoeconomic ladder,
it is demonstrably false. On the contrary, American institutions seem designed to facilitate the advancement of talented
individuals rather than of oppressed groups. Groups engaging
in mass violence have done so only after a long period of
fruitless, relatively nonviolent struggle.

Similarly, the proposition is false if it means that the established order is self-transforming, in that groups in power will
always or generally share that power with newcomers without
the pressure of actual or potential violence. The Appalachian
farmer revolts, as well as tumultous urban demonstrations in
sympathy with the French Revolution, were used by Jefferso-
nians to create a new two-party system over the horrified protests of the Federalists. Northern violence ended Southern
slavery, and Southern terrorism ended radical Reconstruction.
The transformation of labor-management relations was
achieved during a wave of bloody strikes, in the midst of a
depression and widespread fear of revolution. And black people made their greatest political gains, both in Congress and
in the cities, during the racial strife of the 1960's.

All this does not mean, however, that violence is *always*
effective or *always* necessary. Such a belief would merely create a new myth—a myth of violent progress—which could
easily be refuted by citing examples of violence without progress (such as the American Indian revolts) and progress
without violence (such as the accession of Jews to positions
of influence).

The point, really, is to understand the inertia of political
and economic power, which is not as easily shared or turned
over to powerless outsiders as the myth of peaceful progress
suggests. The demands of some domestic groups for equality
and power have been impossible to meet within the existing
political and economic systems. The admission of Indian
tribes, members of labor unions, or the mass of oppressed
black people to full membership in American society would
have meant that existing systems would have had to be transformed, at least in part, to make room for the previously ex-

cluded and that, in the transformation, land-hungry settlers, large corporations, or urban political machines and real estate interests would have had to give ground. Transformation and concomitant power realignments were refused to the Indians; were granted, at least partially and after great social disorder, to workers; and are currently in question for black people in American society. The moral is not that America is a "sick society" but that, like all other societies, it has to confront the oldest problem of politics—the problem of the nonviolent transfer of power.

Disposing of the myth of peaceful progress may also shed some light on another current illusion: the notion that domestic ethnic groups that escaped from their ghettos nonviolently are somehow superior to those that did not. In the first place, "nonviolence" is a misleading term. European immigrants participated, at various times and in differing proportions, in political movements often productive of disorder —socialist, anarchist, populist, and fascist. Whether German, English, Irish, Italian, East European, or Russian, their struggle to unionize implicated them deeply in labor-management warfare. Immigrants in urban areas fought each other for control of the streets, participated in race riots, and engaged in a kind of politics not meant for those with weak stomachs or weak fists. They sometimes used criminal activity both as a way of exercising community control and as a method of economic advancement when other routes were closed.[17] And they did not hesitate, once some power had been obtained, to employ official violence through control of local governments and police forces against emerging groups as militant as they had once been.

Second, it is clear that those groups which rose rapidly up the politicoeconomic ladder (and not all immigrant groups did) were the beneficiaries of a happy correspondence between their group characteristics (including economic skills) and the needs of a changing economic and political system. To put it baldly, they were lucky, since collective virtues which are an advantage at one stage of national development may be irrelevant or disadvantageous at another. Were immigrants of rural peasant stock, such as the Irish or the southern Italians, to come to the United States today, they would find themselves in a position very similar to that of rural Southern blacks and whites now entering Northern cities, their skills almost valueless and their traditional social institutions irrelevant. Even immigrants with crafts or commercial skills and an urban outlook, such as the Jewish arrivals of 1890–1920, would find themselves less mobile today, small entrepreneurs in an age of corporate concentration and post-industrial automation, like the Puerto Ricans of present-day New York. Politically, earlier immigrants reaped the benefits of decentralization—the possibility of taking over an urban machine or a state legislature—and were the chief beneficiaries of the political realignment created by the Great Depression. In short, the steady pace of national centralization and unification on all levels, political as well as economic, has made it progressively more difficult for powerless groups to break into the power structure.

The myth of peaceful progress offers intellectual support for existing political arrangements and validates the suppression of protest. It also serves to conceal the role of official violence in the maintenance of these arrangements.

Official violence has been a major element in the pattern of domestic mass violence discussed thus far. Ever since the eighteenth century, those wishing to justify individual instances of revolt on grounds of self-defense have pointed to prior acts of violence by those in authority. In the midst of the Green Mountain Boys' uprising, for example, Ethan Allen wrote the Governor of New York, "Though they style us rioters for opposing them and seek to catch and punish us as such, yet in reality themselves are the rioters, the tumultuous, disorderly, stimulating factors . . ." [18]

Once mass revolt has begun, the most common question is whether "official violence," reform, or some combination of force and reform will end it. Military suppression has ended some rebellions, such as those of the Indian peoples; capitulation to the insurgents, as in the case of the Klan during Reconstruction, terminated others. At most times during their history, however, Americans confronted by violent uprisings have responded ambiguously, alternating the carrot of moderate reform with the stick of mild suppression. During the ghetto uprisings of the past few years, police and troops called in to suppress disorders have often used excessive violence, as in Newark and Detroit, but have not committed massacres—for example, by machine-gunning looters. With a few exceptions (such as the U.S. Army's treatment of the Indians) this has been the recurrent pattern of attempted suppression of domestic revolts: frequent excesses of official violence without mass murder. And along with suppression has gone moderate reform, from the offers of state and colonial legislatures to remedy some of the grievances of the Appalachian farmers to the civil rights legislation of the 1960's, enacted almost directly in response to Southern sit-ins and Northern rioting. The problem, however, is that these methods are seldom effective. The historical data suggest that once law-abiding Americans reach the point of mass disobedience to law, their revolts will be ended neither by moderate force nor by moderate reform.

Both techniques were attempted during the eighteenth-century farmer uprisings; revolts in New Jersey, the Carolinas, Pennsylvania, New York, and Massachusetts were squelched in relatively bloodless battles, while legislatures held out the olive branch of compromise on such issues as legislative apportionment, taxation, and court procedure. Still, until the Jeffersonian accession, the revolts continued. Similarly, the North-West axis which came to control Congress in the decades before the Civil War attempted to end Southern insurgency by combining law enforcement (e.g., Jackson's Force Act, passed in response to South Carolinian "nullification" of the Tariff of 1828) with a series of famous compromises on the issue of slavery. Despite the offer of the Crittenden Compromise of 1860, the South seceded. Even during the labor-management warfare of the later nineteenth and early twentieth centuries, the pattern persisted. The force used to suppress strikes and riots was not massive enough to destroy the entire labor movement; reforms achieved in the form of recognition of some unions, victory in some strikes, and a pro-labor attitude on the part of the Wilson administration were not sufficient to meet the movement's demands and needs. At present, it appears that gentle enforcement of civil rights laws and court decisions in the South will not integrate Southern schools or alter fundamental patterns of racial discrimination, while a similar combination of police action and legislative reform is proving ineffective to end the revolt of ghetto blacks in the North.

Whether on the frontier on in the factory, in rural Southern communities or in urban ghettos, what rebels have demanded is the satisfaction of their group interests, including interests in exercising political and economic power and in controlling their own social systems. Metaphorically, these desires translate into "independence"—the integration into American society not just of scattered members of the group but of the entire group considered as a cultural, economic, political, and occasionally territorial unit. Prior to and during their struggle for greater autonomy, insurgent groups experience a sharp increase in collective pride and in political awareness. They reject old-style leaders and choose new ones reflecting this new awareness. Old links with outside society are discarded as obsolete; new ones are forged in the heat of revolt. The achievement of a greater degree of local autonomy makes possible the creation of group economic institutions, more rapid internal modernization, and an increase in national political power based on group solidarity (e.g., the "bloc vote"). Therefore, paradoxically, revolts or insurrections seen by those in power as divisive, separatist, or even anarchic have often had the effects of restoring social order to the group and reuniting the insurgents on a new basis with the larger body politic. "Independence," then, implies a new interdependence, based no longer on favors asked and received but on the respect which power owes to power. It may be argued, of course, that this is not a final state but a phase of group development. Even so, it would seem to be an essential phase; all successful American groups, including WASPs, have passed or are passing through it on their way to maturity and power. At the same time, the official approach to the problem of violent mass revolt has been to offer the rebels the benefits of individualism—reforms which promise members of the insurgent group fairer treatment, more votes, more jobs, and so on—provided only that they give up "unrealistic" demands for control of territory, recognition of collective political and economic interests, and the like. Naturally, such offers are rejected by the insurgents.

This compromise has been repeatedly acted out. American colonists, Western farmers, Southern secessionists, labor union men, urban blacks, and others have all been offered the benefit of integration *as individuals* into a preexisting social system, provided that they renounce the goal of exercising independent, collective power. In each case, rejection of such compromises paved the way for escalated conflict. In each case, what finally terminated the conflict was either massive military suppression or some collection of events which so transformed the preexisting social system as to permit integration of the insurgent *group*, not just some of its members individually, into American society.

It is worth noting that, as a rule, the means of such integration have been either accidental or improvised, since our individualistic political and economic systems have lacked the machinery for advancing the interests of groups qua groups. Methods of group advancement which now seem "traditional"—e.g., political parties, political machines, business corporations, labor unions, and community organizations—were all considered at their inception as dangerous and un-American. Moreover, the integration of large out-groups into American society generally took place not as a result of in-group generosity or reform but in the wake of system-transforming "explosions," such as westward expansion, civil or world war, and depression. That the great immigration waves of 1880–1920 coincided with the transformation of the United States from an agricultural-rural to an industrial-urban society goes far to explain why some groups were able to achieve integration fairly quickly and with a minimum of organized violence, although even among these immigrants both the pace of integration and the frequency of recourse to violence varied significantly from group to group.

Contemporary American Protest

The number of participants in demonstrative protest seems to be increasing and includes an ever larger proportion of the members of society. Anti-war demonstrations in the United States, for example, are estimated to have grown almost continuously from the spring of 1965 to the spring of 1968.[19] The student population, castigated in the 1950's as the "silent generation," produced at least 221 demonstrations in 101 colleges between January 1 and June 15, 1968, involving 38,911 participants, according to a study conducted by the National Student Association.

Demonstrations are often viewed as the political tool of only a few dissident factions, such as students and Negroes. Actually, the number and variety of social groups resorting to this mechanism seem to be increasing. Various middle-class groups as well as "respectable" professionals have been involved in demonstrations. Teachers have picketed schools in New York City.[20] Doctors, nurses, researchers, and others from the medical profession have demonstrated against the war in Vietnam.[21] Clergymen have similarly protested. On several Sundays in September and October, 1968, parishioners demonstrated near Catholic churches in Washington, D.C., to protest sanctions against priests who did not support the Pope's edict against artificial birth control. Even the staffs of law enforcement agencies have not refrained from demonstrating. For instance, on October 1, 1968, one hundred "welfare patrolmen" picketed New York City's Social Services Department.

Nor are the demonstrators all of one particular political persuasion. Among those who have resorted to this mode of expression are students who demonstrated *for* Humphrey (urging Senator Eugene J. McCarthy to support him) outside the San Francisco Civic Center Auditorium on October 15, 1968, *against* the sit-in at Columbia University, *for* the war in Vietnam, and *for* stricter enforcement of the law.

Wide segments of the public condemn protest indiscriminately. James Reston observed that "the prevailing mood of the country is against the demonstrators in the black ghettos and the universities," even though most of the demonstrations are peaceful.[22] *Life* magazine states, "Certainly it is a matter of concern when Americans find the ordinary channels of discussion and decision so unresponsive that they feel forced to take their grievances to the street." [23] The majority of the citizenry tends to focus its attention on the communicative

acts themselves, condemning both them and their participants. For instance, 74 percent of the adult public in a California poll expressed disapproval of the student demonstrations at Berkeley in 1964,[24] although those demonstrations
were actually nonviolent. Perhaps media reports of the
"Berkeley riots" shaped public opinion.

Asked explicitly about the right to engage in "peaceful"
demonstrations ("against the war in Vietnam") 40 percent of
the people sampled in both December, 1966, and July, 1967,
felt that the citizenry had no such right. Fifty-eight percent
were prepared to "accept" such demonstrations "as long as
they are peaceful." So a major segment of the public seems
unaware that such demonstrations have the same legal status
as writing to a congressman or speaking up at a town
meeting.[25]

The situation is somewhat similar to the first appearances
of organized labor strikes. Not only the owners and managers
of industrial plants but also broad segments of the public at
the beginning of the century did not recognize the rights of
workers to strike and to picket factories if their grievances
were unheeded. Strikes are more widely accepted now, even
though they have frequently been associated with violence by
workers, management, and the police. According to a Harris
poll, "The majority (77 percent of those sampled) feel that
the refusal to work is the ultimate and legitimate recourse for
union members engaged in the process of collective bargaining. . . ."[26]

It is important to note that as more of the public learned
to accept strikes, they erupted less frequently into violent
confrontations; the most important factor seems to have been
an increased readiness to respond to the issues raised by the
strikers rather than merely responding to the act of striking.
Perhaps contemporary social protest will provoke similar
transformations both in the public mind and in social institutions.

In the chapters that follow, we present a social history of
anti-war, student, and black protest. Our analysis is intended
to illuminate the reasons for the development of these protest
movements, with the hope that such an exposition will both

contribute to increasing understanding of how and why these movements came about, and serve as background for consideration of what society's response to these movements ought to be.

Part Two
The Politics of Confrontation

Chapter II
Anti-War Protest

In the past three years, protest against American involvement and conduct in Vietnam has become so familiar to our national life that it has almost acquired the status of an institution. Few people today would think of asking why this social force came into existence or how it has sustained itself and grown; even the movement's opponents seem resigned to its inevitability. In many respects, however, the very existence of a broadly based, militant opposition to foreign policy marks a sharp departure from long-standing and deeply embedded traditions, and future historians will probably marvel at the outpouring of protest and seek to explain it by reference to unprecedented conditions.

In some advanced countries, such as Japan, protest has been virtually ritualized over the years. Attendant street violence is predictable and the issues are likewise stable—military pacts, foreign bases on native soil, delay in the return of confiscated territory, hospitality to nuclear submarines, and so forth. American war protest, by contrast, has until recently been a marginal, easily ignored phenomenon. The 1863 anti-draft riots had more to do with ethnic rivalries than with principled objections to the Civil War, and in other wars a magnified patriotism has obscured the voices of dissent.[1] Once a war has gotten under way, those who formerly counseled against participation in it have sometimes emerged as its staunchest champions; World War II is perhaps the best example of this. Furthermore, although American wars have varied in the enthusiasm of their reception at home, nothing like the Vietnam protest movement has previously appeared.

It is especially interesting that the wars most closely resembling the current one did not generate a comparable reaction. In the 1840's the United States annexed a large portion of Mexico and suppressed a "native uprising" under the cover of dubious legal arguments. Few listened to Henry Thoreau's protests against this action, and when Abraham Lincoln rose in the House of Representatives to detail the President's sophistries, he doomed his chances for reelection. In the 1890's the United States aligned itself temporarily with Philippine nationalism in order to destroy Spain's colonial power, and then turned to suppression of the nationalists themselves. Despite the fact that there were more than 100,000 Filipino casualties, mostly civilians, no concerted protest was heard; indeed, American historians are still reluctant to see the Philippine episode as the cynical and brutal adventure described by Mark Twain.[2] A similar mental blackout has accompanied the numerous American incursions into Latin America, first by private filibustering expeditions and later by the Marines. There were no significant protests when Secretary of State Knox remarked, upon the sending of Marines into Cuba in 1908, that "The United States does not undertake first to consult the Cuban Government if a crisis arises requiring a temporary landing somewhere." [3]

Turning to recent history, we must note that the chief public objection to the invasion-by-proxy of Cuba in 1961 was that the invasion failed. And President Johnson was able to mobilize congressional and public support for the invasion of the Dominican Republic in 1965, first on grounds of protecting American civilians and then with the retrospective justification that the "Sino-Soviet military bloc" had been behind the Dominican revolution.[4] This support was mobilized despite organized opposition that may have been a precursor to the anti-Vietnam war movement.

There have actually been significant exercises of American power that the American public has hardly noticed at all: few Americans are aware of the United States' invasion of Russia after World War I, coups in Iran and Guatemala, the intervention of U.S. troops in Lebanon, the attempted overthrow of the neutralist government of Laos, and the quiet deployment of 55,000 troops in Thailand. Finally, in seeking to explain recent protest it is especially useful, for purposes of contrast, to recall the Korean War, which resembled the Vietnam War in several respects and occurred within the memory of many current protesters. Though the similarities between South Korea under Syngman Rhee and South Vietnam under Ngo Dinh Diem were extensive and profound, no mass protest against intervention occurred. Even today, fifteen years after the Panmunjom Truce, few Americans know about, and fewer question, the presence of more than 50,000 American troops in South Korea. It is thus evident that a tradition of anti-interventionism is not in itself a significant factor in the shaping of American public opinion. Obviously, something more is required to account for the growth of a broad protest movement in this country.

The case of Vietnam would thus appear to be a unique exception to the support which the American public habitually grants its leaders in matters of national security. There is, of course, a correlation between the degree of our military involvement and the size of protest; the first significant dissent against the war was heard in the spring of 1965, when the first "nonretaliatory" air attacks against North Vietnam began and the first acknowledged combat troops were landed in South Vietnam. Since then, the scope of protest has grown with the scope of hostilities. But the Korean example reminds us that the degree of American involvement and sacrifice cannot account for the level of protest; it was not until the spring of 1967 that American casualties in Vietnam surpassed those in Korea, and the total number of American combat deaths is still (November, 1968) lower for this war than for its predecessor.[5] Whereas the high casualties in Korea chiefly served the arguments of those who wanted to extend the war into China, the high casualties in Vietnam have chiefly been emphasized by proponents of negotiation or withdrawal.

It is plain, therefore, that an unprecedented constellation of factors must have gone into the making of the anti-war sentiment that prevails today. In analyzing these factors, we begin with an examination of the organization of the anti-war movement. This examination indicates that organizational structure per se is of little value in accounting for its growth. Indeed, the movement is best understood as a result of events, not as a generator of future actions. These events, which were widely communicated, led to a deep skepticism about the war among wide segments of the American public and also led an amorphous set of organizations to oppose the war. Thus our analysis turns to an examination of these events and why they had the effect they did.

The Disorganization of the Anti-War Movement

There is little general agreement about the makeup and nature of the Vietnam protest movement. From within, the movement seems disorganized to the point of chaos, with literally hundreds of ad hoc groups springing up in response to specific issues, with endless formation and disbanding of coalitions, and with perpetual doubts as to where things are headed and whether the effort is worthwhile at all. From without, as in the view taken by some investigating committees and grand juries, the movement often looks quite different—a conspiracy, admittedly complex but single-minded in its obstruction of American policy. In the latter interpretation, leaders and ideology are of paramount importance; in the former, the movement is simply people "doing their own thing."

The interpretation offered here will be that the peace movement does have some broad continuities and tendencies, well understood by the most prominent leaders, but that its loosely participatory, unstructured aspect can scarcely be overestimated. Would-be spokesmen can be found to corroborate any generalization about the movement's ultimate purposes, but the spokesmen have few constituents and they are powerless to shape events. Tom Hayden's influence on the developments outside the Democratic Convention in Chicago, for example, was probably minuscule compared to that of the Chicago authorities; and Hayden's subsequent call for "two, three, many Chicagos" has no status as a strategical commitment. If there are to be more "Chicagos" it will require similar occasions, similar attitudes on the part of civic and police authorities, similar causes for political desperation, and similar masses of people who have decided on their own to risk their safety. No one, not even Tom Hayden, is likely to show up for ideological reasons alone or because someone told him to.

The more one learns about the organizational structure and development of the peace movement, the more reluctant one must be to speak of its concerted direction. As the following pages will show, the movement has been and remains in a posture of responding to events outside its control; the chief milestones in its growth have been its days of widespread outrage at escalations, bombing resumptions, draft policies, and prosecutions. As Chart II-1 shows, the size of demonstrations varies directly with the popular opposition to the war during the period 1965 to 1968. Thus, the strength of the movement would seem to be causally related to widespread American attitudes and sentiments toward the war.

When we reflect on the variety of the critics of the war, we can well understand why the movement has never yet had the luxury, or perhaps the embarrassment, of defining either its parameters or its long-term aims. There is a widespread feeling among those who participate in active criticism of the war that the movement would collapse without the presence of a worsening military situation and a domestic social crisis, and this feeling gains credence from the slackening of protest after President Johnson's speech of March 31, 1968, and the preoccupation with "straight" politics during the McCarthy and Kennedy campaigns. Although it may seem tautological to say so, one must bear in mind that the chief sustaining element in the Vietnam protest movement has been the war in

Chart II-1: Size of Anti-War Demonstrations and Percentage of Anti-War Sentiment

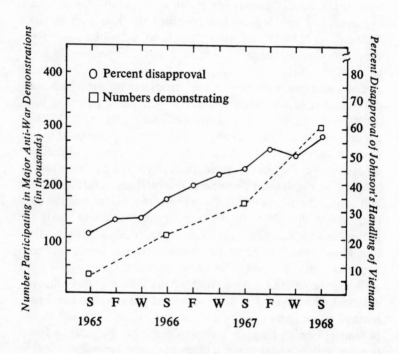

Source of data: Percent disapprovals, Gallup Polls; numbers of participants in anti-war demonstrations involving 1,000 or more persons, *New York Times Index* and *Facts on File*.

S = Spring
F = Fall
W = Winter

Vietnam. Not even the most avid partisans of the movement
can guarantee its continued growth when the issues become
less immediate and dramatic.

This fact needs to be emphasized repeatedly in view of the
widely divergent political opinions of people who must be
counted as having served the movement. The Chinese-ori-
ented Progressive Labor Party has been part of the movement, but so have United States senators. The Communist
journalist Wilfred Burchett has had less impact than Harrison
Salisbury, and the Republican Blue Book on Vietnam probably contributed more than Bertrand Russell's International
War Crimes Tribunal. For that matter, it is unlikely that any
demonstration mobilized American opinion as effectively as
Premier Ky did when he declared his only hero was Adolf
Hitler.[6] Innumerable small events such as that casual remark
drew great numbers of normally apolitical American citizens
into signing petitions, participating in vigils and marches, and
supporting peace candidates. One must resist the tendency,
fostered both by would-be leaders of the movement and by
those who want to blame them as the source of all trouble, to
identify the movement with its most radical and estranged
segment, or to take too seriously the political impact of demonstrations. The anti-war movement is not a fixed group of
people; it is something that has been happening to America.
And demonstrations are typically an *outcome* of events un-
controlled by the movement, rather than a generator of future actions. Moreover, it is usually the *response* to the demonstration that catapults it, as in the Chicago demonstration,
into the status of an "event."

Several other considerations reinforce an attitude of caution about describing the peace movement in terms of its organizational structure. The most effective groups in marshal-
ing mass protest, such as the National Mobilization Committee to End the War in Vietnam and the Students for a Democratic Society, have extremely fluid membership and virtually
no national control over their membership's behavior. In fact,
the former committee has no real membership at all; it is
merely a coalition of "leaders" from various smaller groups
who would disagree with one another on a number of fundamental points but are willing to appear in the same march or

demonstration. The very name of the most prominent group in New York City, the "Fifth Avenue Peace Parade Committee," expresses the prevailing subordination of ideology to coalition tactics. It is only a small exaggeration to say that the role of organizational leadership in the movement is restricted to applying for permits, holding press conferences, announcing the time and place of demonstrations, and mailing appeals for funds.

Again, it should be understood that anti-war groups tend to spring up to give focus to activities that already exist. A few pacifists picket the Naval Weapons Depot at Port Chicago, California, they decide to stay there indefinitely, as the Port Chicago Vigil, and the vigil rallies support from the anti-war community. Draft cards are destroyed by individuals, prosecutions begin, the press takes notice, and, in response, an organization called The Resistance is formed. The Resistance in turn poses a challenge to draft-ineligible sympathizers who see their young friends being treated as criminals, and so additional organizations like RESIST and the Committee for Draft Resistance are formed. Businessmen, VISTA volunteers, writers and artists, clergymen, doctors, student body presidents, and so forth typically get together in ad hoc groupings whose sole aim may be to place an advertisement in a newspaper; the political work of forming common attitudes has been done in advance by the mass media and a general awareness of facts about the war.

There are, of course, very many groups that do have long-range purposes and articulated leftist ideologies, but none of them is especially influential, and they have learned over the past few years that their only hope of broad support is to participate in such paper mergers as the National Mobilization Committee and the Student Mobilization Committee and to get their names associated with large and dramatic rallies. One must also realize that the participatory style of decision-making epitomized in the Students for a Democratic Society has gained much currency, thus further limiting the meaningfulness of an analysis in terms of leadership structure. "Party discipline" has vitually disappeared as a code of behavior. Indeed, a dilemma facing the movement is its lack of discipline; in exchange for spontaneity and political autonomy, it forfeits control over the smallish elements whose demeanor is provocative of violence. It is significant in this light that the American Communist Party has been among the most peripheral and least noticed components of the peace movement, and also among the least spirited in tactics.

A partial exception to the rule that organizations can be either ideological or effective, but not both, can be found in groups like the American Friends Service Committee, the Committee for Nonviolent Action, and the Committee for a Sane Nuclear Policy. The ideology in question is, to be sure, merely peace and nonviolence, but one could defend calling this an ideology on the grounds that it is a fully thought-out commitment that is not negotiable and not dependent on the existence of any particular crisis. These three groups have achieved significant results in shaping opinion among people who are resistant to traditional political rhetoric, and they have also formed an important bridge between the peace movement and such critical institutions as the U.S. Congress and the United Nations. Their very commitment to nonviolence has given them a political weight that the more "political" groups have found difficult to acquire. Furthermore, the nonviolent activists developed innovative tactics of protest in the 1950's and focused interests on the issues of militarism and the nuclear arms race that have subsequently entered the national political dialogue.

Why the Movement Grew

So the reasons for the growth of the anti-war movement must be found outside the organization of that movement, and the movement is best understood as a result of events. Accordingly, we now turn to an examination of these events and the multitude of factors which conditioned their impact and which lent the movement its occasional capacity for desperation and fury.

A War with Time to Think

One of the most telling of those factors was the prolonged public attention given to Vietnam before the battle was fully joined. In this respect Vietnam stands in marked contrast to Korea.

The Korean War broke into public consciousness all at once with an invasion from the Communist North; the public had no more time to reflect than did President Truman. Few Americans had given any thought to the complexities of Korean politics—particularly, to the nature of the Syngman Rhee regime, its degree of popular support in South Korea, or the manner in which it had been placed in power under American direction. The intellectual climate in 1950 was not conducive to detached thought concerning the war; there were hardly any Americans who questioned the Cold War policy of containment, except, of course, for those who favored "rollback" and "liberation" of Communist-occupied territories. The rise of Communist China abroad and of McCarthyism at home did not allow for the development of a respectable anti-war segment of opinion.

Vietnam was different. The American public had become increasingly aware of the country and its issues over a period of years. Americans had been vaguely aware of the fall of Dienbienphu in 1954, the Geneva Accords and the establishment of the Diem regime in the same year, and the alleged success of Premier Diem in establishing a "democratic one-man rule." Until his deposition and assassination in November, 1963, Diem was portrayed favorably in American press releases. The State Department White Paper of 1961 supported his claim that South Vietnam was a victim of unprovoked aggression from without. Numerous statements from high government officials promised an early end to the Communist threat in Vietnam. At the same time, Diem's treatment of dissenting political factions, the failure of the strategic hamlet program, the Buddhist protests beginning in May, 1963, and the self-immolations beginning in the following month, together with the colorful and newsworthy deportment of the Premier's sister-in-law, Mme. Nhu ("I would clap hands at seeing another monk barbecue show"), all served to focus American interest on Vietnam. This interest could hardly be characterized as protest, but when the Diem regime was replaced by a succession of strongmen, juntas, and shadow governments and the war continued to grow, the

American public was aware and becoming increasingly disturbed.

The Promises of the 1964 Campaign

The American Presidential election campaign of 1964 can hardly be overrated as a precondition of the protest movement. In that campaign President Johnson recommended himself as the candidate of peace, as opposed to a man who would defoliate forests, bomb the North, and "supply American boys to do the job that Asian boys should do." [7] It seems fair to say that the anti-Vietnam War movement has been energized in part by a deep personal bitterness against the speaker of those words, and without the promises of 1964 the movement might have assumed a milder character. President Johnson's 1964 victory was overwhelming and was widely described as a "landslide." Certainly, he was perceived as a man of enormous executive ability. Perhaps because of the confidence given him in 1964, large numbers of normally apolitical citizens have felt misled or even betrayed, and this feeling was exacerbated by the insistence of the Johnson administration that its policies merely honored commitments made by Presidents Eisenhower and Kennedy.

President Roosevelt, too, campaigned as a peace candidate and then made war, but the public felt no contradiction; America had been "stabbed in the back" by other powers. World War II and the Korean War as well conformed to the national expectation that conflicts are always begun by others. Only a vague and dubious analogue to this claim could be made in the case of the Vietnam War, and doubts about it could incubate for months and years as the government reiterated its position. The Tonkin Gulf incidents of August 2–4, 1964, and the Pleiku airbase attack of February 7, 1965, were no substitute either for a "Pearl Harbor" or a northern invasion. The very effort to minimize American involvement lowered morale, not only because the assertions were regularly disputed but also because the absence of official jingoism discouraged formation of the patriotic myopia that often prevails in a fully mobilized country. Public ambivalence and dismay only increased as escalations were denied and assessments of the strength of the South Vietnamese regime were shown to have been fanciful. In short, the American people had to cope with some of the risks and anxieties of war without benefit of a "wartime emergency" mentality.

The Failure of Administration Arguments—
Factual and Legal

At any given phase the majority of protesters claimed readiness to be reconciled to the government if certain questions could be satisfactorily answered. The mood of injury and estrangement that has increasingly characterized the anti-war movement has had much to do with the failure to provide answers which satisfied them. Protesters who read the Geneva Accords of 1954 expressed puzzlement at President Johnson's description of the aim of U.S. policy as "observance of the 1954 agreements which guaranteed the independence of South Vietnam," [8] since the Geneva Accords make no mention of South Vietnam and indeed provide a timetable for the reunification of the northern and southern parts of the country.[9] Similarly, the government claim that we are in Vietnam to guarantee self-determination has not proved credible to many students of the post-Geneva period, in which Premier Diem explicitly refused to follow the election procedures laid down in the Accords.[10] Students of the Vietnam situation who observed that the 1965 State Department White Paper omitted any mention of the elections pointed out that the Department's Blue Book of 1961 had praised the South Vietnamese government for avoiding the "well-laid trap" of the proposed elections.[11] The 1965 version did not even look consistent with itself, since the claim of massive North Vietnamese military involvement over a five-year period was backed with only twenty-three biographical sketches of "North Vietnamese" prisoners, seventeen of whom were, in fact, born in South Vietnam. As books about the war proliferated, growing numbers of Americans began to learn how the current Vietnamese situation had evolved from the unstable conclusion of the Indochinese War, in which the United States had openly supported French colonialism against the Vietnamese. As more and more facts fell into place, increasing numbers of American citizens began to question whether their government was being truthful about its real purposes in Vietnam.

The most important part of the government's case for intervention—that it was opposing a clear case of aggression from Hanoi—looked less impressive when the fact emerged that in 1963 the 16,000 American "advisors" were opposing a revolutionary movement that was at least 98 percent indigenously South Vietnamese.[12] As regime after regime in Saigon fell, it seemed more and more likely that it was the ARVN, rather than the Viet Cong, which survived only as a result of outside support. As a Saigon official reportedly told *New York Times* correspondent Charles Mohr:

> Frankly, we are not strong enough now to compete with the Communists on a purely political basis. They are organized and disciplined; the noncommunists are not—we do not have any large, well organized political parties and we do not yet have unity.[13]

As for the political nature of the NLF, and its relation to Communism, the Buddhist Thich Nhat Hanh wrote:

> The majority of the people in the Front are not Communists. They are patriots, and to the extent that they are under the direction of the Communists, it is an unconscious acceptance of control, not allegiance to Communist ideology. I know it is a hard fact for Americans to face, but it is a fact that the more Vietnamese their troops succeed in killing, and the larger the force they introduce into Vietnam, the more surely they destroy the very thing they are trying to build. Not only does the Front itself gain in power and allegiance, but Communism is increasingly identified by the peasants with patriotism and takes an increasingly influential role in the direction of the Front.[14]

While most peace advocates were willing to concede the NLF's dependency on the North Vietnamese government, few, if any, could accept the theory, reiterated by Secretary Rusk and others, that the insurgents in South Vietnam were carrying out a master plan drawn up in Peking.[15] Too much was known about indigenous grievances behind the fighting: the refusal to implement the Geneva Accords, the American replacement of French power in protection of the old Vietnamese ruling class, the excesses of the Diem´regime in the internment and torture of dissenters, the persecution of non-Catholics, and the restoration of a feudal landholding structure. There were, to be sure, comparable factors in the South Korea of Syngman Rhee, but they had seemed insignificant when set against North Korea's aggression. Moreover, in Korea the United States fought as part of a United Nations force which lent moral and political support that was notably absent in Vietnam.

Moreover, in the years since 1950 Communism had lost the image of a monolithic force of conquest. The Sino-Soviet dispute, the fragmentation of the East European bloc, the U.S. government's own efforts at détente with Russia, all served to undermine the official picture of Diem's opponents as an invading army equipped and dispatched by "world communism." Indeed, the statistics offered in the 1965 White Paper, "Aggression from the North," left an implication that nearly all the enemy's military equipment must have been introduced into Vietnam (in disregard of the Geneva terms) by the United States.[16]

The issue of the legality of American intervention in Vietnam [17] has been a continual irritant to American war protesters, and the government's claims in this area have been repeatedly challenged. President Johnson's repeated assertion that "three Presidents . . . have committed themselves and have promised to help defend this small and valiant nation" [18] seemed to many students and protesters to be a serious misrepresentation of the attitude of President Eisenhower toward the Diem government and at best an allusion to informal plans rather than to binding commitments.[19] Instead of satisfying critics of the war, government appeals to the Geneva settlement focused attention on our refusal to sign the Accords and our installation of the Diem regime in the hope of preventing the implementation of their provisions. Nor have critics been placated by retroactive citations of the SEATO pact, which does not seem to them to justify the unilateral measures taken in defense of the South Vietnamese regime.[20] The administration's references to the U.N.

Charter have similarly failed to placate critics who saw inconsistencies between the document and American actions.

Opponents of the Vietnam War have long argued that it violates the U.S. Constitution, which grants Congress the sole authority to make war. One possible retort is that made by Under-Secretary of State Nicholas Katzenbach, who told the Senate Foreign Relations Committee on August 17, 1967, that the constitutional clause at issue "has become outmoded in that international arena." [21]

The more usual line of reasoning, however, is that Congress granted the President full power to make war in the Tonkin Gulf Resolution of August 7, 1964, when he was authorized "to take all necessary measures to repel any armed attack against the forces of the United States and to prevent further aggression." [22] This broad interpretation of the resolution's meaning has been explicitly repudiated by some of the senators who voted for it (e.g., Senator Gaylord Nelson) [23] and the floor sponsor of the resolution, Senator Fulbright, who subsequently described his sponsoring role as something "I regret more than anything I have ever done in my life." [24] War critics have been fortified by the researches of Senator Fulbright and others into obscurities surrounding the background and nature of the Tonkin Gulf incidents.[25] These critics concluded that the attacks on the *Maddox* and the *Turner Joy* were not wholly unprovoked, and that the administration suppressed a good deal of compromising knowledge in pressing for immediate passage of the resolution. Furthermore, it has been widely reported that the substance of the Tonkin Resolution had been drafted long before the Tonkin incidents occurred, thus giving rise to speculation that the subsequent acts of escalation had been decided upon earlier—in fact, during the period when President Johnson was denouncing Senator Goldwater's "reckless" recommendation of the same measures.[26] Whatever the merits of this obscure case, the anti-war segment of American opinion has had ample incentive to depreciate the Tonkin Resolution.

Thus anyone seeking to understand the anti-war movement and the occasional willingness of peace activists to defy the law should bear clearly in mind the widely held opinion in the anti-war movement that the war itself is illegal: a violation of the Constitution, the U.N. Charter, and numerous treaties.

Implicit in all above is the fact that the embittered atmosphere of the peace movement must also be seen in the context of the so-called credibility gap. On every aspect of the war—the explanation of its origins, characterization of our role, praise of the South Vietnamese regime and its progress toward democracy, description of the unfailing success of all American military operations, minimization of civilian casualties, astronomical "body counts," [27] and denials of enemy and neutral gestures toward negotiation—the American government has been charged with duplicity by many of those who disagree with its policies. And this effect was heightened by the coupling of American assurances of willingness to negotiate with renewed escalations. James Reston expressed the confusion of many Americans when he asked, "Do these policies complement one another or cancel each other out? Does half a war offensive and half a peace offensive . . . add up to a whole policy or no policy?" [28] When all shades of misgiving about the war were scorned as cowardly and unpatriotic—the timidity of "nervous nellies" and "cussers and doubters" [29]— the effect was to turn disagreement into rage.

Opinion Leaders, the Media, and the Spread of Anti-War Sentiment

It may well be asked how the peace movement was able to sustain confidence in its own view of the war when the administration consistently challenged that view. One important part of the answer is that television thrust the citizenry into vicarious attendance on the battlefield every day. The documentary material gathered by reporters and cameramen has been consistently more eloquent than the military dispatches (known in the Saigon press corps as "The Five O'Clock Follies" and recently referred to by an "American official" as "vaudeville performances . . . so often produc[ing] antagonism and incredulity" [30]). This is the most fully reported war in history; one could go further and say that this is the only war in which millions of citizens in their homes have been granted access to immediate experience and background knowledge that would enable them to doubt their own government's version of what was happening.

Another factor favoring the movement's growth has been the refusal of many highly placed persons to go along with the administration policies and assertions. Senate "doves" such as Fulbright, Morse, Hatfield, McGovern, Gruening, Gore, Kennedy, Mansfield, Hartke, and McCarthy provided continual incentive to further dissent, and they were sometimes joined in criticism by "hawks" like Symington, Stennis, and Russell. While some members of the Kennedy administration stayed in office under President Johnson and helped to make war policy, many others did not; men like Galbraith, Reischauer, Kennan, Schlesinger, Sorenson, and Hilsman strengthened the widespread feeling that President Kennedy would have handled things differently. Influential war correspondents like Neil Sheehan, Malcolm Browne, David Schoenbrun, Richard Halberstam, Peter Arnett, and the late Bernard Fall also had an important hand in shaping public opinion, as did the columns of Walter Lippmann. Disillusioned veterans like Don Duncan, rebels within the armed services like Ronald Lockman and Howard Levy, young draft resisters facing jail, firsthand observers of the Vietnamese countryside like former International Voluntary Services director Don Luce, clergymen and scholars at home, and distinguished foreigners like U Thant, Pope Paul, Gunnar Myrdal, and Arnold Toynbee, all gave encouragement to critics of the war. By 1968 the opinion polls declared that the dissenting minority had become a majority (see Chart II-2).

This is not to say, however, that advocates of negotiated or unilateral withdrawal had become a majority. Charts II-2 and II-3 show that while "doves" came very close to outnumbering "hawks," they could not by themselves have produced the overwhelmingly negative popular judgment that American involvement in Vietnam was mistaken. This is a point of some consequence, since it shows that the movement was temporarily aided by segments of opinion that could not have been counted on for continued support if the war had been waged more successfully. The "anti-war majority" is thus not what it seems, for many citizens who disapprove of the government's policies might welcome an intensification of the same policies if they believed that more efficient results would be forthcoming. More people believe the war to have been "mistaken" than regard themselves as "doves."

Chart II-2: Gallup Poll Answers to the Question, "In view of the developments since we entered the fighting in Vietnam, do you think the U.S. made a mistake sending troops to fight in Vietnam?"

	Yes	No	No Opinion
August '65	24%	61%	15%
March '66	25	59	16
May '66	36	49	15
September '66	35	48	17
November '66	31	51	18
February '67	32	52	16
May '67	37	50	13
July '67	41	48	11
October '67	46	44	10
December '67	45	46	9
February '68 (early)	46	42	12
March '68	49	41	10
April '68	48	40	12
August '68	53	35	12
October '68 (early)	54	37	9

Chart II-3: Gallup Poll Answers to the Question, "How would you describe yourself, as a 'hawk' or a 'dove'?"

	Hawk	Dove	No Opinion
December '67	52%	35%	13%
January '68	56	28	16
February '68 (early)	61	23	16
February '68 (late)	58	26	16
March '68	41	42	17
April '68	41	41	18
October '68 (early)	44	42	14

It was not altogether coincidental that dissent reached its peak in the election year of 1968. The Senate Republican Policy Committee decided in early 1967 that peace sentiment would be a decisive factor in the next Presidential election; accordingly, a ninety-one-page Republican Blue Book, *The War in Vietnam,* was issued in May, 1967, embracing nearly all the contentions of the peace movement. Instead of repeating the customary calls for early victory, the Blue Book frankly located the source of the Vietnam War in Premier Diem's refusal to hold free elections, his religious and political persecutions, and his abolition of village elections. "Many of the revolutionists in the South," it stated, "were not necessarily Communist to begin with, but rather anti-Saigon and anti-Diem." It challenged the administration's account of the Tonkin Gulf incidents, tracing them, as earlier anti-war critics had, to an American-sponsored naval raid by South Vietnamese ships against North Vietnamese radar and naval installations. And it spelled out the costs of the war—the actual money costs, such as $300,000 for each dead Vietnamese alleged to be an enemy soldier, and the costs in American casualties, the devastation of Vietnam, and the weakening of domestic unity and morale. Many activists were startled to find the Republican Party on their side, but this was within the logic of the American political calendar.

On the same day that the Blue Book appeared, the *Wall Street Journal* declared the war unwinnable and likened it to an "incurable disease." And indeed, the New York stock market responded with great enthusiasm when President Johnson announced his revision of bombing policy on March 31, 1968. In record trading, the market rose sharply. Financial analysts estimated that the President's decision not to run for reelection was probably less important than the prospect of lower interest rates and a redress of the balance-of-payments difficulties which the war had exacerbated.[31] " 'Peace is bullish,' summed up the general response of the executives interviewed." [32]

The Course of the War

Of all ingredients of anti-war sentiment, there can be little doubt then that one has been paramount: the course of the war itself. Presumably a brief and successful assault against the enemy in Vietnam could not have aroused sustained criticism in this country; there is nothing in the previous history of American interventions to suggest otherwise. Never before had the American public been offered so many official predictions not borne out by events or been given so much documentary evidence of military and political frustration. Eventually, government optimism produced a deep skepticism in the public. Critics like Robert F. Kennedy commented that in view of statistics released by this country, "it would seem that no matter how many Viet Cong and North Vietnamese we claim to kill, through some miraculous effort of will, enemy strength remains the same. . . . Who, then, is doing the fighting?" [33] Others asked why, if the war was so one-sided, was it lasting so long? Why were South Vietnamese desertions in the order of 100,000 a year? [34] Why were the provinces and even cities becoming less instead of more secure? Clare Hollingworth, writing in the conservative *London Daily Telegraph* on November 2, 1968, estimated that the enemy had by then gained administrative control of 1,800 of South Vietnam's 2,500 villages and over 8,000 of its 11,650 hamlets. "Indeed, Saigon administers less than eight million of the total population of 17 million and of this eight million some four-and-a-half million are soldiers and civil servants paid by the state." Senator Kennedy pointed out that it was an illusion to unswervingly pursue military victory in the interest of the people of Vietnam:

> Their tiny land has been devastated by a weight of bombs and shells greater than Nazi Germany knew. . . . More than two million South Vietnamese are now homeless refugees. . . . it is the people we seek to defend who are the greatest losers.[35]

Understandably, the greater part of American public interest was centered on the vicissitudes of our own troops. Great heroism was displayed in the successful defense of Con Thien in the fall of 1967 and again of Khe Sanh in the eight months preceding July, 1968; but the strategic significance of these costly outposts was challenged by critics. Two hundred eighty-seven Americans were reported to have died in the November, 1967, "Battle of Dak To," including the celebrated capture of Hill 875; the hill was abandoned ten days later. Newspapers were full of bitter comments from GI's who had lived through the ordeal and wondered why it had been necessary.

As the war dragged on, media commentators began to strike a gloomy note. Lou Cioffi's ABC Forecast for 1967 stated that "The American people must get used to the idea of American troops there for the next five, ten or eighteen years. The South Vietnamese army is badly trained and badly equipped, and its officers are more interested in politics and graft." *U.S. News and World Report,* on March 6, 1967, described the failure of such massive sweeps as Operation Junction City, and asked rhetorically, "Is victory possible?" In August of 1967, R. W. Apple of the *New York Times* wrote an extraordinarily pessimistic series of evaluative essays under such headings as "Growing Signs of a Stalemate."

Most analysts agreed that the Tet Offensive of early 1968 called for a serious reassessment of the American position in Vietnam. Beverly Deepe remarked in the *Christian Science Monitor* (February 3, 1968), "The Communists' three-day blitz war . . . has opened up the possibility of the United States losing its first major war in history." The Tet Offensive seems to have marked the nadir of official credibility in the public mind, after which the government's statements about the war gradually became more modest. The American public was profoundly upset, as Chart II-4 makes plain. Public skepticism was epitomized in the Herblock cartoon showing an American officer turning out communiques ("We now have the initiative. . . . The enemy offensive has been foiled. . . . Besides, we knew about it in advance") in the wrecked headquarters of the American mission. "Everything's okay," he says on the phone, "—they never reached the mimeograph machine." Conceivably the skepticism was wrong, but its existence helps to show why the domestic peace movement continued to gather strength.

The Plight of Draft-Age Men

Everything that has been said thus far is pertinent to an understanding of the way many draft-eligible young men felt and feel about the war. For them, however, the overriding question was not merely whether to lend approval to the American effort, but whether to lend it their bodies and perhaps their lives. There have always been conscientious pacifists, but the Vietnam War has been the first to produce a sizable number of draft *resisters,* men willing to spend several years in federal prison rather than fight in a *particular* war that they considered immoral. The attitude of Congress, the

Chart II-4: Gallup Poll's Correlation Between Hawk/Dove Sentiment and Key Military Events (December, 1967, to April, 1968)

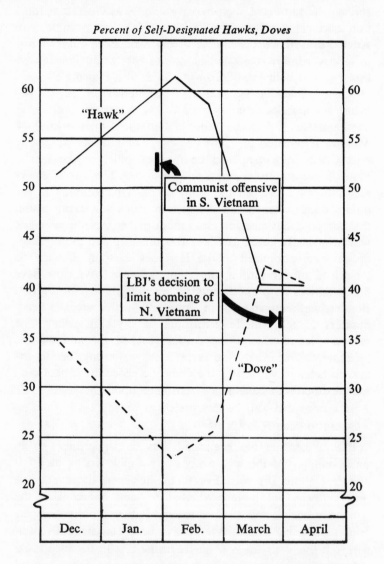

Percent of Self-Designated Hawks, Doves

"Hawk"

Communist offensive
in S. Vietnam

LBJ's decision to
limit bombing of
N. Vietnam

"Dove"

| Dec. | Jan. | Feb. | March | April |

The proportion of self-designated hawks increased immediately after the Tet Offensive in late January, but decreased somewhat in late February. A tremendous drop in the number of hawks was recorded in early March.

Selective Service System, and the courts has been that such persons are indeed criminals; as the prosecutor of George Dounis, who received four years in prison for draft refusal, stated, "Crimes of conscience are more dangerous than crimes of greed and passion." Conscientious objection was respected only if the objector could swear that he opposed war in any form, as a result of convictions arising from religious training and belief.[36] On October 26, 1967, the national director of Selective Service recommended that local draft boards issue punitive reclassifications to unruly peace demonstrators.[37] The effect of such measures, when combined with the impression made by the war itself, was to drive some young men into open resistance, others out of the country, and still others into seeking occupational and educational deferments.

The announcement in early 1968 that most such deferments would be cancelled made the issue of cooperation or noncooperation inescapable for large numbers of youths who opposed the war. Even before that announcement, 22 percent of the respondents to a survey of Harvard senior men said they would go into exile or jail rather than serve in the army; 94 percent disapproved of the conduct of the war.[38] And the posture of such young men forced many of their elders to choose whether to lend them moral support or allow them to be generally regarded as disgraced felons. It is often alleged that men like Dr. Spock, the Reverend Mr. Coffin, and the brothers Berrigan have urged resistance upon the young, but their actions can also be interpreted as having been taken in response to such resistance and in sympathy with it. The conviction and sentencing of these men has served to multiply support for their position. Here again the Vietnam War has introduced a new and surprising element into American public life.

Military Tactics and the War Crimes Issue

In attempting to understand how such a reversal of traditional attitudes could have been effected, historians of this period will surely put stress on the peculiarly vivid impression that the *tactics* of the Vietnam War have made on the public, chiefly through television films. Napalm in particular has touched the imagination of the public, as in the following description by Martha Gellhorn in the *Ladies Home Journal,* January, 1967:

> In the children's ward of the Qui Nhon provincial hospital I saw for the first time what napalm does. A child of 7, the size of our 4-year olds, lay in the cot by the door. Napalm had burned his face and back and one hand. The burned skin looked like swollen, raw meat; the fingers of his hand were stretched out, burned rigid. A scrap of cheesecloth covered him, for weight is intolerable, but so is air. His grandfather, an emaciated old man half blind with cataract, was tending the child. A week ago napalm bombs were dropped on their hamlet. The old man carried his grandson to the nearest town. . . . Destitute, homeless, sick with weariness and despair, he watched every move of the small racked body of his grandson.[39]

Or again, the account by Richard E. Perry, M.D., in *Redbook,* January, 1967:

> The Vietcong do not use napalm; we do. . . . I have been an orthopedic surgeon for a good number of years. . . . But nothing could have prepared me for my encounters with Vietnamese women and children burned by napalm. It was sickening, even for a physician, to see and smell the blackened flesh. One continues for days afterward getting sick when he looks at a piece of meat on his plate because the odor of burned flesh lingers so long in memory. And one never forgets the bewildered eyes of the silent, suffering napalm-burned child.[40]

Widely available reports like these may help to explain why the manufacture and use of napalm became almost as great an issue for anti-war activists as the total war policy to which it contributed. Moreover, dissenters were particularly infuriated by their perception that government responses to their allegations of civilian bombing, use of gas and fragmentation bombs, and the depopulating of whole districts usually consisted in denial of the facts—followed later by partial or full concession when, as in the case of Harrison Salisbury's *New York Times* dispatches from Hanoi in December, 1966, further denial would no longer be believable. The seriousness and importance of these allegations to the anti-war movement cannot be underestimated. Dissenters pointed to treaties banning warfare, and to numerous international conventions regarding mistreatment of prisoners, use of chemical warfare, "ill treatment or deportation ́. . . of civilian population from occupied territory . . . wanton destruction of cities, towns or villages," etc.[41] Indeed, the "war crimes" issue has been of central importance in the drift of many protesters toward a stance of personal resistance—appealing to the principle of the Charter of the Nuremberg Tribunal that "The fact that [a] defendant acted pursuant to the order of his Government or of a superior shall not free him from responsibility." [42]

Harrison Salisbury's reports of the effect of American bombing on the population of North Vietnam constituted one of the major episodes in the growth of the anti-war movement. But the much greater devastation of South Vietnam was a subject of public concern as soon as major American operations began in 1965. As Charles Mohr remarked from Saigon in the *New York Times* of September 5, 1965, "This is strategic bombing in a friendly, allied country. Since the Viet Cong doctrine is to insulate themselves among the population and the population is largely powerless to prevent their presence, no one here seriously doubts that significant numbers of innocent civilians are dying every day in South Vietnam." The same article continued:

> In [a] delta province there is a woman who has both arms burned off by napalm and her eyelids so badly burned that she cannot close them. When it is time for her to sleep her family puts a blanket over her head. The woman had two of her children killed in the air strike which maimed her last April and she saw five other children die. She was quite dispassionate when she told an American, "More children were killed because the children do not have so much experience and do not know how to lie down behind the paddy dikes." [43]

It was no secret that peasant villages were more often destroyed by explicit command than by mistake; as Secretary of the Navy Paul Nitze explained in defense of village-burning, "Where neither United States nor Vietnamese forces can maintain continuous occupancy, it is necessary to destroy those facilities." [44] The same tactical considerations in part dictated the policy of occasional "sweeps" such as Operation Cedar Falls and Operation Junction City. The Iron Triangle campaign of January, 1967, was explicitly designed to make an inhabited section of the countryside uninhabitable. The effect was described vividly in Jonathan Schell's book, *The Village of Ben Suc,* and more succinctly by prizewinning correspondent Peter Arnett: "Burning homes, crying children, frightened women, devastated fields, long lines of slowly moving refugees." [45] A later A.P. report from Saigon described the general strategy of which such episodes partook:

> The United States high command, preoccupied for two years with hunting down North Vietnamese regulars, now is looking more toward the populated valleys and lowlands where the enemy wields potent political influence and gets his sustenance. Quick gains are hoped for by forced resettlement of chronically Communist areas, followed up with scorched-earth operations that deny enemy troops all food, shelter, and material support. Central highland valleys are being denuded of all living things; people ringing the Communist war zones in the South have been moved. Some American observers recently in the Mekong Delta say that the Vietnamese Army, long hated and feared, now is regarded as less of a threat to the countryside than the Americans. [46]

There was, of course, terrorism on both sides of the Vietnam War, but the domestic peace movement did not regard the enemy's practices as justifying our own. Indeed, there appeared to be a qualitative difference. That the enemy could blend into the population necessarily resulted in more indiscriminate assaults from the American side. Whereas the NLF might assassinate a village chief, the Americans would be more likely to destroy the village itself with 500-pound bombs, helicopter gunships, riot gas to smoke the inhabitants out of hiding, and cluster bomb units to finish them off.

A dispassionate and expert account of air weaponry and tactics can be found in Frank Harvey, *Air War—Vietnam,* a book written with the cooperation of U.S. Navy and Air Force officers. [47] One learns from Harvey not only the range of the American arsenal and the manner in which targets are chosen by forward air controllers, but also the sort of attitudes that pilots and helicopter gunners need to cultivate. Thus:

> . . . it was fortunate that young pilots could get their first taste of combat under the direction of a forward air controller over a flat country in bright sunshine where nobody was shooting back with high-powered ack-ack. He learns how it feels to drop bombs on human beings and watch huts go up in a boil of orange flame when his aluminum napalm tanks tumble into them. He gets hardened to pressing the fire button and cutting people down like little cloth dummies, as they sprint frantically under him. He gets his sword bloodied for the rougher things to come.[48]

Such information as this, widely disseminated in a paperback book, understandably contributed to the peace movement.

Similarly, the revelation of the use of chemical and gas warfare strengthened the movement. "Dr. Jean Mayer, a Harvard nutrition expert reported that crop-poisoning chemicals had little effect on mobile enemy soldiers, but the tactics of starvation worked effectively against small children, pregnant women, the aged, and the sick." [49] The AAAS and other scientific groups expressed concern over the impact of large-scale use of herbicides, especially in Vietnam. The Department of Defense commissioned and published a report on the Vietnam defoliation and crop destruction program which was designed to silence its critics.[50] This report provoked the following response from Thomas O. Perry of the Harvard University Forest:

> Through the simple process of starvation, a land without green foliage will quickly become a land without insects, without birds, without animal life of any form. News photographs and on-the-spot descriptions indicate that some areas have been sprayed repeatedly to assure a complete kill of the vegetation. There can be no doubt that the DOD is, in the short run, going beyond mere genocide to biocide. It commandeered . . . a sufficient amount [of chemicals] to kill 97 per cent of the aboveground vegetation on over 10 million acres of land (about 4 million hectares)—an area so big that it would require over 60 years for a man to walk on each acre.[51]

The use of poisonous chemicals to destroy *civilian* crops is in the class of prohibited belligerent actions recognized by the U.S. Army's own Field Manual, FM 27-10, Sect. 37. And the *New York Times* pointed out in an editorial of March 24, 1965, that the "nonlethal" gas which Secretary McNamara belatedly announced we were using in Vietnam "can be fatal to the very young, the very old, and those ill with heart and lung ailments." [52] (The use in war of "asphyxiating, poisonous, or other gases" is prohibited by a number of international agreements, notably the Geneva Protocol of 1925, which the United States signed but did not ratify.[53]) Even placid Americans were affected when, during the early weeks of 1968, American forces attempted to dislodge guerrillas from Hue, Ben Tre, and Saigon itself by saturation bombardments of heavily populated areas. "We had to destroy the city in order to save it," said one American officer in a much-quoted remark about Ben Tre.

The South Vietnamese Regime

The fact that the South Vietnamese government (or governments—there have been ten since 1963) lent encouragement to such assaults against the South Vietnamese population directed interest to the question of which social forces were being favored by the American presence. Despite the rapid turnover at the top, critics saw the faction best protected by U.S. power to be that which was opposed to full Vietnamese independence in the days of the Indochinese War. The *New York Times,* in an editorial of October 11, 1966, raised the possibility that "if the United States 'wins' this war, it will be for the old ruling classes," [54] and Asian scholar George McT. Kahin has discussed "the understandable tendency for many South Vietnamese to regard an American-supported Saigon regime as having a good deal in common with its French-supported predecessor—particularly when almost every senior army officer and the overwhelming majority of top civilian officials collaborated with the French." [55] Most Americans who were disturbed about the war stressed certain features of the Saigon regime: religious persecution, corruption and inefficiency, reluctance to undertake full mobilization or to participate in dangerous operations, eagerness to have the war extended by the Americans, rigged elections, press censorship, laws forbidding advocacy of neutralism, arbitrary imprisonment of dissenters, summary executions, etc. Most important than any of these tendencies, however, was the relationship of the regime to the peasant farmers who make up an overwhelming majority of the population. To some peasants, "pacification" meant death. To most peasants, it meant the American-sponsored return of absentee landlords who would collect rents as high as 60 percent of a rice crop and "extort back rents for the time they fled the Viet Cong." [56] Indeed, American backing of the hated landlords may, in the final analysis of this war, turn out to have been more decisive for its outcome than all the military engagements taken together.

The reason this aspect of the war deserves mention in a study of the American peace movement is that a negative assessment of the Saigon government has formed part of the political education of many demonstrators. If, as Representative Gerald Ford charged, Americans were being asked to "pay more to make Saigon interests richer and the Vietnamese people more completely dependent on us," [57] and if Premier Ky was correct in saying that the Communists "are closer to the people's yearnings for social justice and an independent national life than our Government," [58] then it was natural for large numbers of Americans to ask themselves why we were willing to deliver and receive so much suffering to keep that government from being overthrown. Even Secretary Clifford has recently criticized the Saigon government. His impatience was felt much earlier by critics of the war, and for reasons previously discussed, the official explanations in terms of fostering self-determination, honoring commitments, and preventing world conquest left many citizens unsatisfied. In the absence of government arguments acknowledging our support of Vietnamese feudalism or our long-range interests in Southeast Asia, dissenters were left to draw their own inferences. Some concluded that we were preparing for war with China. Some, taking note of our $1,600,000,000 base construction program in Vietnam, decided that we had no intention of abandoning such an investment in the event of a truce.

Young Americans began paying attention to those "Old Leftists" who had been saying for years that the United States, with its vast foreign investments and its deployment of troops around the globe, was, in fact, the expansionist power to be most feared. Even a respected leader like Senator Fulbright suggested that "America is showing some signs of that fatal presumption, that over-extension of power and mission which brought ruin to ancient Athens, to Napoleonic France and to Nazi Germany." [59] And the late Martin Luther King, Jr., felt compelled to call his government "the great purveyor of violence in the world today." [60] For many, disapproval of the American role in Vietnam spilled over into scrutiny of our attitude toward numerous oligarchies in Latin America, Asia, and southern Europe. The concept of a "Free World" devoted to "democracy" began to look faulty, and the history of the Cold War was reassessed as a power struggle rather than as a morality play.

Even the term "imperialism," once the exclusive property of sloganeers of the left and right, gained currency as a respectable characterization of American behavior. It was argued that we had become the world's major counterrevolutionary power, prepared, as Secretary Rusk announced, to intervene anywhere with or without treaty commitments. The Secretary's exact words, spoken before the Senate Preparedness Committee on August 25, 1966, were as follows: "No would-be aggressor should suppose that the absence of a defense treaty, Congressional declaration or U.S. military presence grants immunity to aggression." [61] Many observers interpreted the Secretary's statement as implying that no legal restraints would prevent the United States from forcefully imposing its will on other nations to prevent internal change. The same observers argued that this influence was being constantly exercised already in the form of economic and military subsidies to fascist regimes, counterinsurgency training programs, and actual infiltration of other governments—as, for example, in the successful placing of admitted CIA agent Antonio Arguedas in the Bolivian cabinet as Minister of the Interior.

The Domestic Scene

During the period of the Vietnam War there were other developments within the structure of American society that gave impetus to radical dissent. The racial polarization described in the report of the Kerner Commission assumed frightening proportions, and was worsened by the diversion of "Great Society" funds into war spending. The major political parties did not prove very responsive to sentiment for peace, and when a strong third party arose it drew strength from race hatred and sword-rattling. The Vietnam expenditures, which had possibly averted a recession in 1965, later contributed to a serious inflation. Moreover, critics felt that because of war expenditures, problems of conservation, traffic, and pollution were neglected. Assassination haunted our public life and contributed to the feeling of despair and frustration which affected many in the anti-war movement. Universities, the unofficial headquarters of the peace movement, were hampered by federal research cutbacks and shaken by student protest which often focused on such war-related activities as the development of biological warfare weapons.

The anguish of many protesters was summed up in Senator Fulbright's remark that we have become a "sick society." "Abroad we are engaged in a savage and unsuccessful war against poor people in a small and backward nation," he told the American Bar Association. "At home—largely because of the neglect resulting from twenty-five years of preoccupation with foreign involvements—our cities are exploding in violent protest against generations of social injustice." [62]

These facts and these feelings, then, provide the basis for understanding how the anti-war movement emerged and grew —why there was great skepticism about the war and why this skepticism might yield to frustration, anguish, and even desperation. The significance of such an alienation from the prevailing national policy is made even more apparent when one considers that the anti-war movement is largely composed of persons who, prior to Vietnam, would not have been thought to hold such feelings. Thus we turn now to an examination of the social bases of the anti-war movement.

The Social Bases of the Anti-War Movement

Insofar as the anti-war movement has an ongoing membership, it can best be characterized along social as opposed to organizational lines. The most striking fact about the movement, and its most obvious handicap, is that it has had to rely largely on middle-class professionals and preprofessional students. The worker-student collaboration that surfaced in France in the spring of 1968 seems remote from the American scene. Labor officials such as George Meany and Jay Lovestone have taken more "hawkish" positions than the Johnson administration, and the AFL-CIO is known to be working closely with government agencies in such projects as the surreptitious combating of leftism in affiliated Latin American unions. With notable exceptions, rank-and-file American workingmen have not supported the peace movement, either because they felt that the war was necessary and justified or because they disliked the style of the most colorful protesters, or because they were outside the institutions where an anti-war consensus was allowed and encouraged, or because they had friends or relations in the service whom they felt they had to "support" by supporting the war, or simply because they have in a fundamental way become the most conservative of political actors—they tend to follow the lead of government, especially if the government is supported by the unions. Workingmen, like businessmen, were made uneasy by such side effects of the war as inflation and high taxes, but they were largely indifferent to arguments couched in terms of disillusionment with the Cold War or violations in international law. To the degree that the peace movement emphasized disarmament, sympathy with foreign guerrillas, and self-consciously anti-bourgeois styles of protest, it actually drove the labor movement away. The confusion of many workers was revealed by the finding that some of them who had supported Robert Kennedy in the 1968 primary elections intended to vote for George Wallace in November.[63]

Within its middle-class and relatively well-educated base of strength, the peace movement seems to have drawn most heavily from teachers, students, and clergy. It would be facile to call these categories the movement's mind, body, and conscience, respectively, but there is some truth to such a description. The teachers were instrumental in learning and making known the history of American involvement in Vietnam and in engaging government spokesmen in debate. Students performed this function, too, and in addition they provided the confrontational tactics and the sheer numbers of demonstrators that could keep up continual pressure on public opinion. And the clergy raised moral issues and often dramatized them with bold acts of individual protest. Each of these three groups deserves extra comment because of their distinctive contributions.

The role of teachers and of intellectuals generally has been prominent from the beginning of the movement. Although there was a good deal of scattered protest in 1964, many observers feel that the movement properly started with the spring, 1965, undertaking of college teach-ins—a tactic still in use, but which seems to have been especially appropriate to that period when less was known about the war and when more militant forms of protest were unpalatable to many dissenters. The teach-in was by nature a form of hesitation between respectful inquiry and protest, and its campus setting emphasized that objections to the war were still mostly on the intellectual plane. The failure of government "Truth Teams" to satisfy their college audiences, and sometimes their failure to appear at all, gave a strong impetus to the further evolution of campus protest. The enlistment of professors in rational dialogue about the war was an ideal way of introducing them into the movement's work.

Although intellectuals in America are not reputed to enjoy the popular influence possessed by counterparts in Europe, several factors favored their prominence in the Vietnam protest movement. The movement itself consisted largely of people who *do* pay attention to intellectuals, and the movement conceived its first task to be a scholarly one: to expose the contradictions and half-truths in the standard government account of the war. The absence of widely respected left-of-center political spokesmen made for a vacuum into which the intellectuals were drawn. Professors like Noam Chomsky,

Staughton Lynd, Franz Schurmann, and Howard Zinn not only disseminated information but also helped define the movement's consciousness—as, for example, in Professor Chomsky's influential essay, "The Responsibility of Intellectuals." [64] Other academics who had held high posts within the Kennedy administration made less sweeping critiques of the war but had a large impact on public opinion by virtue of their defection from the official view; the same was true of former policy advisers such as Marcus Raskin and Hans Morgenthau. And literary figures like Norman Mailer, Mary McCarthy, and Robert Lowell became increasingly conspicuous as they participated in significant acts of protest and shared their reflections with readers who had followed their earlier work.

The centrality of college students to the growth of anti-war sentiment is generally recognized, and much effort has been put into the task of explaining why this should be so. Revealing investigations have been made into the rearing, family attitudes, and social background of the student generation which first entered American political life in the civil rights movement of the early sixties and then turned to agitation against the war and the universities.[65] But such an emphasis should not be used to undervalue the determinative influence of the war itself. While justice for blacks has been a deeply held theme of conscience for a vanguard of middle-class white students, it has been outside the normal scope of their lives; they have had to seek out battlefields in the Deep South or in unfamiliar ghettos. The Vietnam War, by contrast, has directly affected them in several respects. Most obviously, students have been subject to the draft; their academic studies have been haunted by the prospect of conscription and possible death for a cause in which few of them believe. When the manpower needs of the war eventuated in the cancellation of many graduate deferments in early 1968, the anti-war movement was naturally strengthened. From the beginning, however, the war had been an on-campus reality by virtue of the presence of military and war-industry recruiters, the extensive cooperation of university institutes and departments with Pentagon-sponsored research, the tendency of universities to award honorary degrees to public officials who are also official spokesmen for the war, and, of course, the normal campus atmosphere of controversy and debate. By 1968, as for example in the Columbia rebellion, it was becoming difficult to distinguish the anti-war effort from the effort to remake the internal structure of the universities.

Clergymen have been especially prominent in the peace movement in contrast to their relative silence during former wars. Partly as a result of the decline of abstract theology and the humanizing influence of figures like Pope John, partly because of their experience with nonviolent protest in the civil rights movement, but above all because they found difficulty in reconciling the claims of religious doctrine with the demands of the Vietnam War, religious leaders have increasingly placed themselves in the opposition. As the most active group, Clergy and Laymen Concerned About Vietnam, declared in a position paper of early 1967:

> Each day we find allegiance to our nation's policy more difficult to reconcile with allegiance to our God. . . . We add our voice to those who protest a war in which civilian casualties are greater than military; in which whole populations are deported against their will; in which the widespread use of napalm and other explosives is killing and maiming women, children, and the aged. . . .

Such well-known clerics as William Sloane Coffin, Robert McAfee Brown, Philip and Daniel Berrigan, and even Martin Luther King, Jr., associated themselves with the cause of draft resistance,[66] while Cardinal Spellman was picketed by fellow Catholics for his enthusiastic support of United States policy in Viet Nam.[67] Even President Johnson could not attend church without risking exposure to an anti-Vietnam sermon—a new vicissitude among the many burdens of the Presidency.

Another component of the peace movement deserves special consideration, not so much for its decisive role as for its future potential. The effort of white radicals to enlist black Americans in their ideological ranks is a long-standing feature of American leftism, and has become a subject of general concern in the wake of the serious urban uprisings of the past few years. People both within and outside the anti-war movement would like to assess the degree to which black political consciousness has been altered by participation in the movement and by exposure to the war. This interest often has to do with the long-range prospect of black insurrection rather than with any immediate hope of bringing the Vietnam War to an end. The question is not whether blacks will turn out in large numbers to demonstrate and march, but whether the issues of war protest will feed naturally into the so-called black liberation movement, as the issue of racial integration (insofar as it concerned white activists) to some degree laid the groundwork for the anti-war movement itself.

There are two opposite and perhaps equally plausible interpretations. If attention is restricted to the overt involvement of blacks in the anti-war issues as defined by white radical and pacifists, little evidence can be found to indicate real coalition. Insofar as they are militant, black Americans are unsympathetic to the nonviolent ethic of the pacifists; insofar as they are economically deprived, they desire the material goods which the radicals despise as tokens of an unjust economic system; and insofar as movement tactics court exposure to police billy clubs, blacks cannot work up the requisite enthusiasm. Unlike the alienated middle-class whites, they already know what it means to be dealing with antagonistic police on a daily basis, and they find it difficult to appreciate the value of getting publicly clubbed so as to expose the system's latent violence. Nor, by and large, have blacks rushed willingly into open and principled draft resistance. Many of them have been willing to risk death in Vietnam in exchange for the squalor and indignity of American ghetto life, and others who have preferred not to serve have not cared to pass two to five years in federal prison for this reason. Those who are oppressed from birth onward do not seek out occasions to prove their oppression.

Many instances could be shown of the white movement's failure to enlist blacks on a mass basis. In Oakland, California, to take one example, Stop the Draft Week (October 16–20, 1967) was planned to involve the ghetto community in "white" confrontation tactics, but the blacks ended by having their own separate rally and by largely avoiding the planned showdown with the Oakland police, with whom they were already well acquainted. One should not be misled by the fact that CORE and SNCC were among the earliest organizations to oppose the war; positions taken in those days were usually representative of a consensus reached among black and white activists.[68] As blacks developed their own themes of protest and began disaffiliating themselves from the white movement, it became clear that Vietnam was a relatively minor issue, distant from the emergency of the American cities although, of course, related to it in numerous intangible ways.

There is, however, another side to this question. The abstention of black masses from white-sponsored rallies seems less noteworthy when one considers that the white working class has also been poorly represented; it could well be that the movement, with its dominant strain of moral outrage and intellectuality, has neglected issues that would touch deprived Americans generally. Certainly there have been numerous signs from prominent blacks that Vietnam could become a major focus for ghetto discontent. Consider the fact that the most beloved black man of modern times, Martin Luther King, Jr., found that in order to sustain his self-respect and the momentum of his organization (SCLC) he had to denounce the war and its racist aspects.[69] Consider also that one of the most prominent black athletes of the 1960's, Muhammad Ali, having been denied the status of a conscientious objector, has chosen draft resistance and faces a long prison term. And Malcolm X, whose influence was not stilled by assassination any more than Dr. King's was, spoke out forthrightly against the Vietnam War in 1965 and drew lessons from it about the guerrilla's strategic advantages over the colonizer.

There have been several highly significant instances of black anti-Vietnam protest, but their significance seems largely to have been appreciated by "movement" whites rather than by great numbers of blacks. A typical example was the appearance of Private Ronald Lockman at the New Politics convention in 1967, where he electrified the white activists with the following statement:

> I am to report to Oakland, California, September 13 to leave for Vietnam. My position on my orders is simply no. I won't go. I can't go. I will not be used any longer. My fighting is back home in Philadelphia's ghettos where I was born and raised. I will not be sent 10,000 miles away from home to be used as a tool of the aggressors of the Vietnamese people. I feel that it is time to follow my own mind and do what I know is right. I think most of the fellows in my company, white and black, fear the war but they also fear the military structure. I think most of the guys in my company support what I am doing. But they are afraid to take a stand, so I am asking for the support of people all over the nation and especially black people, the black brothers and sisters, to join me and support me in my struggle.[70]

Private Lockman was greeted with a tumultuous ovation, and he was indeed given extensive support during and following his court-martial. However, despite similar individual instances, black resistance to the war has not materialized on a large scale.

Nevertheless, there are certain moments in the history of the anti-war movement that bear mention as possibly indicating an emergent trend for blacks. One might add to the foregoing instances the expressions of resentment at Secretary of Defense McNamara's August, 1966, "salvage" plan for ghetto residents through military discipline, the refusal of Howard University students to allow General Hershey of the Selective Service System to address them in March, 1967, Eartha Kitt's challenge to Mrs. Johnson at a White House luncheon, and perhaps most importantly, the refusal of forty-three black soldiers to be transported to Chicago in anticipation of possible rioting at the time of the Democratic National Convention.[71] It remains to be seen whether resistance of this sort will spread, but there seems to be reason to doubt that blacks will be only too happy to choose Vietnam over unemployment and discrimination at home. Black radicals from Malcolm X and Robert Williams through Stokely Carmichael and Eldridge Cleaver have told their brothers that they are in effect the colonized Viet Cong of America. If that perspective is adopted by great numbers of blacks, it could well prove to be the most serious of the Vietnam War's domestic effects.

Tactics and the Question of Violence

From Dialogue to Resistance: A Qualifying Analysis

Violence within the current anti-war movement has been a focus of considerable attention on the part of reporters and analysts, and pro-movement theorists have sharpened this attention with a good deal of talk about the necessary passage "from dialogue to protest to resistance." In a rough and ready way this outline of the movement's changes in attitude is serviceable, but only if certain reservations are kept in mind.

First, much of what is called resistance has taken the form of nonviolent civil disobedience by individuals or groups whose purpose has been moral witness. Individual draft resisters have engaged in a form of noncooperation which has dramatized their outrage at the war but has not impeded its implementation. And nearly all the violence that has occurred in mass demonstrations has resulted, not from the demonstrators' conscious choice of tactics, but from the measures chosen by public authorities to disperse and punish them. Even after the bloody "battle of Chicago" it can be said that the American anti-war movement has not yet deliberately embraced violence. Peace demonstrators are still going through a mental adjustment to the physical precariousness of protest.

It is less than the whole truth to say that the movement has been drifting toward confrontationism. This does apply to some long-standing activists, but many have recently given their energies to conventional electoral politics. The McCarthy and Kennedy campaigns, the "abdication" of President Johnson on March 31, 1968, and the subsequent Paris negotiations renewed, at least for a while, the traditional tendency of dissent to express itself through established channels. The enthusiasm and energy with which many college protesters joined the "Children's Crusade" of the McCarthy campaign should serve as a reminder that there is nothing final about a posture of resistance. America remains, as it has always been, a country in which genuinely revolutionary or even obstructionist activity is rejected by the great majority of dissenters. Significantly, the first serious incident of anti-war violence following the President's March 31 speech occurred outside the Democratic Convention in August, and the Chicago Study Team's report clearly points to the contribution of the city administration and the police in the development of the violence.

One must also note numerous exceptions to the apparent rule that "resistance" tactics have come later than the tactics of mere protest. Significant instances of draft resistance occurred as early as 1964,[72] and recently some young men who were formerly intending to refuse induction have decided to accept it and "bore from within." [73] Examples of obstructionist action on the part of pacifists were plentiful as early as 1965 and seem to have fallen off somewhat in 1968. And even the pattern of developing confrontation between street demonstrators and police is far from simple. The march on the Pentagon on October 21, 1967, and the Chicago clashes seem to mark peaks of militancy, before and after which the movement has adopted different stances, and even in those instances the issue of violence is not simple. There was no planned violence in the Pentagon march: off-limits territory was symbolically invaded, but property and persons were not attacked, and in any case the great majority of demonstrators abstained from even this token defiance. Before the Chicago convention, public authorities rejected permit applications for peaceful assembly, even though they might have known from a clash four months previously that this would lead to violence.[74] Between April and August the demonstrators had become *more* willing to reach an accommodation with city officials; it was the latter who ensured that on both occasions heads would be cracked.[75]

Violence Directed at Protesters

In this connection it is essential to note that, while there have been scattered acts of real violence committed by anti-war activists, by far the greater portion of physical harm has been done *to* demonstrators and movement workers, in the form of bombings of homes and offices, crowd-control measures used by police, physical attacks on demonstrators by American Nazi Party members, Hell's Angels, and others, and random harassment such as the Port Chicago Vigil has endured. Counterdemonstrators have repeatedly attacked and beaten peace marchers, sometimes with tacit police approval.[76] Sometimes, as in the San Francisco Police Tactical Squad assault on demonstrators and bystanders picketing Secretary Rusk on January 11, 1968, and in Chicago, a minority of demonstrators have provoked police violence with violent or provocative acts.[77] In such cases the unstructured and undisciplined nature of the demonstration unfortunately permits the confrontationists on both sides to have their way, and both demonstrators and police have been injured. It must be said, however, that while militant demonstrators do have the power to ensure that brutal police tactics will be used, they do not have the power to prevent them. Persons aware of the events of the past year in Chicago should also be aware by now that when police are encouraged by public officials to regard free assembly as subversive, they do not need much provocation in order to attack even innocent bystanders. When, as at Chicago, it appears that police provocateurs mingle among the demonstrators and "incite" their fellow officers to violence by such acts as helping to lower the American flag, it is even less likely that the spirit of nonviolence will prevail.[78]

Rights in Conflict, the report of the Commission's Chicago Study Team, not only provides ample documentation for what the study group called the "police riot" at Chicago; it also offers a paradigm of the way in which violence can emerge, not from the schemes of individuals, but from the volatile mixture of elements that are drawn together in such an event. The report makes clear that there were indeed provocative tactics on the part of some demonstrators—tactics that were intended to "expose the inhumanity, injustice, prejudice, hypocrisy or militaristic repression" of the society.[79] Few, if any, demonstrators anticipated or welcomed the extent to which the forces of law were in fact provoked to violence, and it is clear in retrospect that such violence was inherent in the attitudes of police and civic authorities toward the demonstrators. The Chicago Study Team's report also documents the largely futile efforts of National Mobilization Committee leaders to arrive at tactical ground rules that would be honored by all demonstrators.[80] The inability of leaders to give guarantees of peaceable behavior was a factor in the denial of parade permits, which in turn was a factor in the brutal excesses committed by the police. In retrospect, it would appear that the most critical decision leading to violence was the denial of Lincoln Park to the demonstrators. Once the police and city officials decided to clear the park of some 1,500 to 2,000 people, violence was a certainty.

Thus, much of what passes for the violence of the anti-war movement is done *to* rather than *by* protesters, and much of the tactical debate within the movement itself has not been about whether to commit violence but whether to expose oneself to it. The issue is not whether to be violent; it is whether nonviolence shall be cooperative or provocative. The stated purpose of those advocating this exposure is educational—to reveal the brutality and hypocrisy of a system that has maintained democratic forms.

Varieties of Protesters and Protest

In order to make sense of the great variety of tactics employed within the peace movement, one must bear in mind a primary distinction between two broad groupings of protesters: those for whom tactics are chiefly a *moral* question and those who see tactics chiefly as *means to political ends*. Nearly all pacifists fall into the first of these categories. For them, the ethical posture of nonviolence is no less important than the cause for which they may be agitating. Believing in a government of law, they insist on making themselves liable to the law's penalties; they hope to persuade others by the example of their sacrifice. Most nonpacifists, in contrast, are more interested in impeding the war than in achieving a "correct" moral posture, and they are not bothered—or not so deeply bothered—by the idea of tactics which "hurt the enemy" while enabling the protester to avoid arrest. This is not to say that this group's tactics actually are more politically effective than the pacifists'; that is a matter of continual debate within the movement. The point is that in studying the movement's tactical evolution we must recognize the influence of a serious philosophical disagreement which prevents that evolution from being simple or wholly explainable in pragmatic terms.

The difference was epitomized in Stop the Draft Week of October 16 to 20, 1967. The organizers of this series of demonstrations found that they could not agree among themselves on the best means of "shutting down the Oakland Induction Center." As a result, October 16 and 18 were given over to those of pacifist orientation, who sat in the doorway of the induction center in small, orderly groups, and allowed themselves to be peaceably arrested, while October 17 and 20 were given over to the mass-mobile tactics of the "militants." These demonstrators, along with newsmen and spectators, were severely beaten and sprayed with MACE as they blocked the arrival of busloads of inductees, and they retaliated with harassing tactics. They attempted, on the whole successfully, to avoid arrest, although their leaders were later prosecuted for "conspiracy to commit misdemeanors." The pacifists were more successful in literally preventing the induction center from functioning, but the militants argued that their operation made a greater impact on the public. Assuming, however, for the purposes of argument that both sides could agree on the superior effectiveness of one approach or the other, it is still unlikely that the two groups would then have coalesced. Radical militants are as averse to the posture of meekly courting arrest as the pacifists are to hit-and-run vandalism. Both parties, therefore, are inhibited by their life-styles from adopting a certain range of tactics, and their means of protest are bound to diverge.

There are, of course, many tactics that both groups can agree on, such as peaceful marches, mass rallies, ballot initiatives, picketing, agitation against the draft, and community-organizing projects like Vietnam Summer. Recognizing this, movement coordinators have increasingly turned to unstructured demonstrations in which ideological lines are not insisted upon and protesters are free to take the sort of action that suits them individually. The movement as a whole has been singularly relaxed in this respect, drifting with events instead of following a fixed timetable, placing more reliance on a developing consensus of anti-war feeling than on the adoption of a "correct" political line. There have been quarrels and tensions, but they have been minor in consideration of the vast differences that would appear within the movement if it ever had to set forth its positive vision of the good life.

There can be no simple equation of militancy and violence or of pacifism and nonviolence. The truth is that neither wing of the peace movement has been violent in comparison with comparable movements in other times and countries. Surprisingly, the tactics of obstruction have been most richly explored by the pacifists, whose record of personal and small-group confrontation with the military extends back into the days of Pacific nuclear testing, before Vietnam was an issue. Sit-downs before the White House and the Senate and war factories, the tying of canoes to troopships and munitions ships, the boarding of destroyers, the chaining of demonstrators to AWOL soldiers, the destruction of draft files, the sailing of medical supplies into Haiphong harbor under American aerial bombardment—these gestures have all been conducted by pacifists. No "militant," furthermore, has done anything so extreme as the Quaker Norman Morrison's self-immolation before the Pentagon on November 2, 1965.[81]

The attention of public authorities is nevertheless concentrated on the non-pacifist militants, and understandably so, for they are the ones who are not prevented by ethical scruples from passing into a more "revolutionary" phase. Like the blacks, they arouse interest more for what they might later decide to do than for anything that has happened yet. Within this grouping there has certainly been a development—haphazard and halting and always subject to reconsideration—toward confrontationism. This trend, moreover should not be obscured by the fact that confrontation tactics could be found quite early, as in the blocking of troop trains in Oakland and Berkeley in August, 1965. That action grew out of the peculiarly radical traditions of the Berkeley campus and the San Francisco Bay Area, whereas later militancy has sprung up in every section of the country, with new recruits each year. This is especially evident in campus protest, which began at Berkeley but rapidly spread across the country, affecting small private schools and large public universities alike. Today the anti-war movement is still not wedded to confrontation as a favorite style of action, but the number of protesters who find it philosophically acceptable and politically meaningful has been increasing.

The reason for this trend is plain. The movement at its best has only succeeded in producing negative effects, such as President Johnson's announcement, two days before the Wisconsin primary, that he would not stand for reelection. The snubbing by government spokesmen, the accusations of cowardice and betrayal, the relative unresponsiveness of Congress to anti-war sentiment, and especially the clubbings by constituted law enforcement officials have bred desperation. It is safe to say that by now the only effective countermeasure against the bitterness that leads to violence would be a termination of the war in Vietnam. Until that occurs, the more moderate element within the movement will find itself increasingly out of touch with the small minority who actually seek violence and can claim that milder tactics have proved unsuccessful. Curiously enough, the very achievement of the movement in finally obtaining majority support for peace has played into the hands of the supermilitants, who point out that the warmakers have not capitulated merely because of public opinion. In the eyes of many of those opposing the Vietnam War, recent events—such as the nomination of two champions of President Johnson's war policy—point to a serious defect in the democratic process. As in the "black liberation" movement, time may be running out for those who counsel prolonged patience and trust.

It must be stressed, however, that even when movement spokesmen have counseled "resistance," they have not meant such things as the bombings of draft boards and ROTC buildings, but rather acts of obstruction such as mill-ins, the blocking of traffic, the temporary and symbolic "seizure" of university buildings, the "imprisonment" of CIA or Dow recruiters, the granting of "sanctuary" to discontented soldiers, and the harassment of pro-government speakers. One can disapprove of such acts and still recognize that they do not constitute the instrumental use of force to conquer political opposition. They have a symbolic and expressive character that is less violent than the use of nightsticks and MACE and rifle butts. This has been true even of the most colorful acts of defiance, such as pouring blood on draft files or even napalming them, as was done by the "Milwaukee Fourteen" and the "Catonsville Nine." [82] These religious activists were willing to mutilate some pieces of property and incur long prison terms to raise moral issues about the violence of the Vietnam War. They were not literally attacking an enemy, but dramatizing what they felt to be the intolerable savagery of the military system.

By far the greater part of movement obstructionism has been conducted by college students, usually on their own campuses and in response to university cooperation with the war effort. Significantly, most of the agitation has had to do with the draft, first over the question of releasing class ranking to the Selective Service System, then over the punitive reclassification of protesters, and then over the cancellation of whole categories of deferment. Other draft-related activities —such as protests at induction centers and the organizing of "Vietnam Commencements" to dramatize the plight of graduating seniors who were to be conscripted into a war they found abhorrent—were fed by discontent with the entire draft structure and its announced purpose of "channeling" deferred men into defense-related work.[83] Similarly, a general malaise over the gradual militarization of national life contributed to the obstructionist mood that prevailed on dozens of campuses in the 1967–68 harassment of Dow and CIA recruiters. Students justified their tactics by referring to the violence of the war and their inability to stop that violence through ordinary means.[84] Many people within the movement, including nonpacifists, thought that the students were jeopardizing their own academic freedom in resorting to abridgements of free assembly and speech, but the students replied that university and national administrators had shown themselves indifferent to more decorous forms of dissent.[85]

For many protesters the phrase "from protest to resistance" has nothing to do with physical obstruction of any sort; it means instead that individuals, having exhausted normal channels of dialogue and petition, feel they must take a personal stance of noncompliance with the war. Tax refusal, the declaration of medical students that they would refuse to serve, the turning down of government grants and prizes and invitations to the White House are all examples of such resistance. The overridingly important categories, however, have been draft resistance and the association of draft-ineligible persons with draft resisters. It is reasonable to suppose that this has been the point of maximum common focus between the peace movement and its antagonists. Nothing has aroused greater anxiety and outrage among people outside the movement than the burning of draft cards and the willingness of eminent citizens to stand beside resisters and applaud their patriotism. The Justice Department and local grand juries and prosecutors have been similarly absorbed in this aspect of the peace movement; perhaps the most widely noticed and debated event in the movement's history has been the Boston trial of Dr. Benjamin Spock. Reverend William Sloane Coffin, Jr., Marcus Raskin, Mitchell Goodman, and Michael Ferber for "conspiracy" to aid draft resistance.

In a technical sense the "Spock trial" has so far been a success; four of the five defendants were convicted. If, however, the main purpose of the trial was to prevent draft resistance and its adult support, the effect produced was exactly the opposite. The Spock case became a rallying point for the entire movement, an inducement for thousands of wavering dissenters to throw in their lot with the defendants by declaring their "complicity," and a subject of national misgiving over the use of a figurative notion of conspiracy to inhibit acts thought by many to be real and symbolic speech. The second thoughts inspired by this trial were best summarized by one of the jurors, Frank Tarbi, who later wrote:

> How and why did I find four men guilty? All men of courage and individuals whom I grew to admire as the trial developed. As I searched my conscience, I had to admit I profoundly agreed with these defendants. . . . Just as a gang of dissenters dumped a cargo of tea into the drink and were declared patriots for their action, so were these men protesting against a war they termed unjust and brutal. . . . These four men were trying to save my sons whom I loved dearly. Yet I found them guilty. To hell with my ulcer. After four or five

stiff hookers (I lost count) I began to cry bitterly, locked up in my room. Maybe it was temporary insanity? Or was it remorse for a world gone mad? [86]

Another lengthy quotation, from one of the defendants, spoken before the indictments were handed down, will perhaps help to explain why the "Boston Five" acted as they did and why neither they nor their supporters have abandoned a posture of resistance:

> If there is such a thing as a just war, then there is such a thing as an unjust war; and whether just or unjust is finally a matter of individual conscience, for no man can properly surrender his conscience to the State. Our Puritan fathers came to these shores because they were committed to this principle. At the Nuremberg trials we faulted an entire nation for not accepting it.
>
> Now let us suppose that a man has conscientiously done his homework on the war in Vietnam, and that his homework has led him to the following conclusions: that while it is true that we are fighting communists, it is more profound to say that we have been intervening in another country's civil war; that despite the billions of dollars of aid, the heroic labor and blood of many Americans, the Saigon government from Diem to Ky has been unable to talk convincingly to his people of national independence, land reform, and other forms of social justice; that the war is being waged in a fashion so out of character with American instincts of decency that it is seriously undermining them (which is not to say the V.C.'s are Boy Scouts, which they clearly are not); that the strains of the war have cut the funds that might otherwise be applied to anti-poverty efforts at home and abroad (which is the intelligent way to fight communism); and finally, that the war would have a good chance of being negotiated to an end were we to stop the bombing in North Vietnam.
>
> If a man's homework leads him to these conclusions, then surely it is not his patriotic duty to cheer or stand silent as good Americans die bravely in a bad cause.
>
> Surely, too, he does not engage in civil disobedience—not as a first resort. Rather he speaks out, writes letters, signs petitions, attends rallies, stands in silent vigils—all in the best American tradition. But now let us suppose he has done all this, many times and for years. Does he then tuck his conscience into bed with the comforting thought, "Well, I have done my best, the President continues to escalate the war, and the law of the land is clear"? Or does he decide that

having chosen the road of protest he has to choose to pursue it to the end, even if this means going to jail?

Which decision he makes clearly depends on how wrong he thinks the war is and how deeply he cares.

My own feeling is that the war is so wrong, and that we are so wrong in not seeking to end it by the serious bombing pause suggested by Senator Kennedy, that it is time for those of us who feel this way to come out from behind exemptions and deferments, take our medicine like men, or as the more recent expression goes, "put our bodies on the line."

I feel this is particularly true of religious people, who have a particular obligation to a higher power than that of the State. I therefore proposed in Washington on February 21 that seminarians and younger clergy opposed to the war surrender their 4-D exemption and declare themselves Conscientious Objectors to this war, which is against the present law of the land. I further proposed that older clergy publicly advocate their doing so that all might be subject to the same penalties. Finally, I suggested that students opposed to the war consider organizing themselves to do likewise.

Now let us be very clear: this is not to advocate violence. I am against violence, as I am against draft card burning, which I consider an unnecessarily hostile act. This is also not to advocate anarchy, for when a man accepts the legal punishment he upholds the legal order. This is not even to advocate withdrawal. I am against withdrawal, for negotiation.

But this is to advocate—as a last resort—a form of civil disobedience which I view as a kind of radical obedience to conscience, to God, and I would add to the best traditions of this country which won for us the respect of allies we no longer have in this venture. So if in the eyes of many this be subversion, then may it at least be understood as an effort to subvert one's beloved country into its former ways of justice and peace.

Finally, let me say that I would hope that such an action would stir the uninformed citizens of today to become better informed citizens tomorrow. For this war is not being waged by evil men. In our time all it takes for evil to flourish is for a few good men to be a little bit wrong and have a great deal of power, and for the vast majority to remain indifferent.[87]

Resistance within the military services has also been of growing importance to the anti-war movement. Considerable support has been mustered for noncooperators like "the Fort Hood Three," Private Lockman, and Captain Howard Levy. Court-martialed and sentenced to military prison, these men

are nevertheless heroes to the movement—all the more so because they stood up to the system after they had foregone the
protection of civilian law. Repugnance for the war has become so strong that retired officers like Admiral Arnold True
and former Marine Corps Commandant General David M.
Shoup have spoken freely against it; and veterans have been
prominent in anti-Vietnam activities.[88] Deserters in Sweden
and elsewhere have been greeted with sympathy, reservists
have made legal challenges to their activation, AWOL soldiers have been given sanctuary in churches and universities,
and others have participated in pray-ins and peace marches
as well as flocking to "GI coffee houses" and reading anti-war
newspapers sponsored by the movement. These acts hardly
constitute an insurrection against American policy. They do,
however, indicate that it is becoming increasingly difficult to
instill a "proper" attitude of unthinking obedience into American conscripts.

The Future of the Anti-War Movement

This raises the large question of where the peace movement is heading next. Everything that has been said here
should inspire caution on this matter, for we have seen that
the movement's options have been continually defined by unanticipated events, and this will surely remain the case. The
most one can do is extrapolate from recent tendencies and
add that American society at large—and especially the mak-
ers of national policy—will finally determine whether the
movement's desperation will be accentuated or overcome. As
in the past, the movement can be counted on to respond
more according to its temporary mood than according to ideology or a strategic plan.

Having made that caveat, we can perhaps suggest that two
lines of development within the peace movement are especially likely to flourish. One is the increasing preference for
structural analysis as opposed to moral protest. After a certain number of months and years of begging their elected
leaders to take mercy on the people of Vietnam and to meet
the crisis at home, protesters inevitably begin asking themselves whether they have been conceiving the problem truly.

Why, protesters ask, has the United States become, in Robert Hutchins' words, "the most powerful, the most prosperous, and the most dangerous country in the world"? [89] Is it possible that our Vietnam involvement is "not a product of eminent personalities or historical accidents, [but] of our development as a people"? [90] Many protesters are questioning whether the war might not be a natural result of the bureaucratic welfare state, with its liberal rhetoric, its tendency to self-expansion, its growing military establishment, and its paternalism toward the downtrodden. Doubts like these have been gradually eroding party loyalties and creating a broad public for radical thought and dialogue. The result will not necessarily be a swelling of the ranks of Marxists, but almost certainly a thorough questioning of current institutions and political style. As John McDermott has remarked, the movement's own tactics have produced "a growing appreciation of the creative role of social conflict, and accordingly a growing rejection of the pluralist consensus views which have dominated American political and social theory for so long." [91]

The second development has to do with the question of violence versus nonviolence. A minority of alienated activists may flirt with terrorism, but they are unlikely to cause serious damage to the "war machine" or even to gain the support of other dissenters. There seem at present to be built-in limitations on the possibilities for effective movement-initiated violence; American society is simply unready for revolutionary bloodshed. Nonviolence, on the other hand, has been making some unexpected converts within the peace movement, not because of a rising tide of pacifism, but because activists have begun to understand that their first target must be the psychology that acquiesces and delights in war. The use of "guerrilla theater"—radical sentiments expressed in songs and skits—and the bringing of anti-military culture to American soldiers in the form of coffee houses and newspapers and "GI teach-ins" thus have an importance beyond their current degree of effectiveness; they suggest that major figures in the peace movement are turning from despairing gestures to attempts to convert those who must be converted if the movement is to grow. In David Dellinger's words:

We will come closer to achieving our goals of subverting an inhuman system and undermining its ability to rely on fascist methods when we conduct teach-ins for the police and soldiers and fraternize with them rather than insulting them by calling them "pigs" or raising their wrath by stoning them. We must make a distinction, both philosophical and tactical, between institutions and the people who have been misled into serving them. . . . The traditional pacifist has been misled by the gentility and gentleness of the men who order out armies, napalm, bombs and Mace. The unthinking revolutionist is misled by the crudity of the actions that police and soldiers can be conditioned into performing.[92]

There is nothing to guarantee that the peace movement will evolve further in the directions pointed here, and there is a residue of bitterness which nothing will easily erase. Yet if the Vietnam War is sustained by policy-makers in the face of worldwide indignation and the apparent apathy of the soldiers who must fight it, it seems reasonable to suppose that the movement's current mood of disenchantment with existing institutions will both generate new forms of militancy and spread into new segments of the American public, creating possibilities for social changes which neither the movement's supporters nor its opponents have yet imagined. The anti-war movement is tied inextricably to the student and black protest movements, even as its historical roots lie with the symbolic confrontations of the pacifists. And as we will discuss in the next two chapters, the war has been a significant spur to each of these movements—it has become a primary rallying point of campus protest, and it has compounded the difficulties of fulfilling promises of progress made to the black communities of America earlier in the decade.

Chapter III
Student Protest

THE BERKELEY student rebellion of 1964 sent shock waves through the academic community and puzzled the nation. Today, campuses throughout the country have been rocked by student protest, and the major campus that has not experienced a certain amount of turmoil and disruption is the exception. According to the National Student Association, during the first half of the 1967–68 academic year there were 71 separate demonstrations on 62 campuses—counting only those demonstrations involving 35 or more students. By the second half of the year, the number had risen to 221 demonstrations at 101 schools.[1] On several campuses, massive student demonstrations have become a familiar and almost banal occurrence. Moreover, there has been a discernible escalation of the intensity of campus conflict, in terms of both student tactics and the response of authorities. Indeed, the early months of 1969 were characterized by a hardening of official response to student protest on many campuses, as evidenced by the presence of bayonet-wielding National Guard troops at the University of Wisconsin and the declaration of a "state of extreme emergency" at Berkeley.[2]

Further, student protest now involves a wider *range* of campuses and a wider range of students. The past few months have seen the rise of intense protest by black and other Third World students, on both "elite" and "commuter" campuses.

The scope and range of contemporary student protest make certain kinds of explanation grossly inadequate. To explain away student protest as the activity of an insignificant and unrepresentative minority of maladjusted students is inaccurate on two counts. First, as a recent *Fortune* magazine survey suggests, roughly two fifths of the current college-student population express support for some "activist" values.[3] Second, fact-finding commissions from Berkeley to Columbia tend to present a rather favorable group portrait of student activists. In the words of the Cox Commission report on the Columbia disturbances:

> The present generation of young people in our universities is the best informed, the most intelligent, and the most idealistic this country has ever known. This is the experience of teachers everywhere.
>
> It is also the most sensitive to public issues and the most sophisticated in political tactics. Perhaps because they enjoy the affluence to support their ideals, today's undergraduate and graduate students exhibit, as a group, a higher level of social conscience than preceding generations.
>
> The ability, social consciousness and conscience, political sensitivity, and honest realism of today's students are a prime cause of student disturbances. As one student observed during our investigation, today's students take seriously the ideals taught in schools and churches, and often at home, and then they see a system that denies its ideals in its actual life. Racial injustice and the war in Vietnam stand out as prime illustrations of our society's deviation from its professed ideals and of the slowness with which the system reforms itself. That they seemingly can do so little to correct the wrongs through conventional political discourse tends to produce in the most idealistic and energetic students a strong sense of frustration.[4]

Empirical research into the personalities and social backgrounds of student activists tends to confirm this portrait. These studies recurrently find student activists to have high or at least average grades, to come from politically liberal families whose values can be described as "humanist," and to be better informed about political and social events than nonactivists.[5]

The dimensions of student protest must be understood as part of a worldwide phenomenon. At the same time, the American student movement developed in the context of American institutions in general and of the American university in particular. Accordingly, in the first section of this chapter, we examine American student activism in international perspective. Next, we trace the development of student activism in America in the 1960's, giving special attention to the rise of the Students for a Democratic Society; and briefly, to black and Third World student protest. We then consider the organization of colleges and universities in the United States in relation to campus conflict. Finally, we consider some implications of our analysis for administrative response.

American Student Protest in International Perspective [6]

Our understanding of the current American student movement can perhaps be advanced by analyzing some of the ways in which it resembles or differs from student movements in other nations.

To the casual observer it is clear that student protest is now a worldwide phenomenon. In 1968 alone, student demonstrations and strikes paralyzed universities in nations as far apart, geographically and culturally, as Japan, France, Mexico, West Germany, Czechoslovakia, Italy, and Brazil. Indeed, a recent study commissioned by the United Nations estimated that those in the 12–25 age group now number 750 million and will total a billion by 1980. At that time, the study predicted, "Youth of the world will begin to predominate in world affairs.

"World opinion is going to become increasingly the opinion of the world's youth and the generational conflict will assume proportions not previously imagined.

"Young people in all walks of life," they add, "are prepared to march, to demonstrate and to riot if necessary in support of views which may not be those of the electorate, nor of the majority; nor yet of the government." [7]

Conventional wisdom is much given to the view that youth is "naturally" rebellious. We are not surprised when young persons experiment with adult ways and criticize those who enforce constraints, because we know that youth is "impatient." Nor are we unduly shocked when young persons protest the failure of adults to live up to their professed values, since we know that youth is "idealistic." Such views, whatever their ultimate truth, have the virtue of providing comfort for adults and, no doubt, for many young people. Such views assume that young people will outgrow their impatience and will experience the difficulties of actualizing ideals. Moreover, adults who hold these views need feel no special responsibility or guilt over the rebelliousness of youth, since it is "inevitable." And, equally inevitably, it will pass away. As S. M. Lipset has pointed out, nearly every country has a version of the saying: "He who is not a radical at twenty does not have a heart; he who still is one at forty does not have a head." [8]

Unfortunately, conventional wisdom neglects the salient fact that widespread student movements, such as we are witnessing in the United States today, do not occur at all times and places, nor do they exhibit the same characteristics and orientations everywhere.

First, student idealism has not always been revolutionary. Students were very active in the right-wing movements that led the rise of fascism in Western Europe in the 1930's. Far from demanding basic social change, they were concerned with the defense of tradition and order against the threats and insecurities of change.

Second, even where they are oriented toward progress and change, student movements do not always express an autonomous rebellion against the larger society. A good example is the contemporary Czechoslovakian student movement, which is more directly linked to liberalizing movements in Czechoslovakian society as a whole than to any distinct student radicalism.

Third, historically the phenomenon of revolutionary student movements has been primarily a feature of transitional societies—that is, societies in which traditional, agrarian-based cultures breaking down and modern values congenial to industrialization were becoming influential. Thus, student revolutionary activity was a constant feature of Russian life during the nineteenth century; it played a major role in the revolutions of 1848 in Central Europe; the Communist movements in China and Vietnam grew out of militant student movements in those countries; and, in Latin America, student movements have been politically crucial since the early part of this century.

Such societies tend to promote the formation of autonomous student movements for several reasons. First, traditional values, transmitted by the family, are increasingly irrelevant to participation in the emergent industrial occupational structure. Students are acutely aware of this irrelevance in the relatively cosmopolitan atmosphere of the university and in their training for occupations which represent the emerging social order. Second, although students are ostensibly being trained to constitute the future, more modern elite, it is usually true that established elites continue to represent traditional culture, resist modernizing reform, and refuse to redistribute power. Paradoxically, established elites typically sponsor the formation of the university system to promote technical progress while simultaneously resisting the political, social, and cultural transformations such progress requires. In this situation, students almost inevitably come into conflict with established institutions.

If any generalization can be made, it would be that student movements arise in periods of transition, when, for example, the values inculcated in children are sharply incompatible with the values they later need for effective participation in the larger society, or when values which are prevalent in universities are not supported by established political elites in the larger society. As S. M. Lipset writes:

Historically . . . one would learn to expect a sharp increase in student activism in a society where, for a variety of reasons, accepted political and social values are being questioned, in times particularly where events are testing the viability of a regime and where policy failures seem to question the legitimacy of social and economic arrangements and institutions. And more observation shows that in societies where rapid change, instability, or weak legitimacy of political institutions is endemic, there is what looks like almost constant turmoil among students.[9]

In other words, the formation of student movements *in general* may be a reflection of technological, cultural, and economic changes that require new forms and mechanisms for distribution of political power. Political expressions of discontent arise if political authorities are identified as the agents of the status quo. Intellectuals and students are most likely to criticize established authorities because they, more than any other stratum of society, are concerned with the problem of creating and articulating new values. When an existing political order loses its legitimacy, the young intellectuals search for alternative forms of authority, new grounds for legitimacy, and ideological rationales for their attack on the established order. Characteristically (and both the "classical" and "new" student movements are similar in this respect), the emergent ideology of the student movement is populist, egalitarian, and romantic. That is, it justifies its attack on established authority by asserting that the true repository of value in the society is the people rather than the elites; it seeks to undermine deferential attitudes toward authority by asserting anti-hierarchical and democratic principles; it defends the rejection of conventional values by celebrating the idea of free expression and individualism; and it provides inspiration to its participants by emphasizing that the conflict of generations must be won by the young, since the old must die.

This analysis might lead one to expect that advanced industrial societies of the West would be the least likely places for radical student movements to emerge. In these societies, it is said, the move to modernity has been made, and sharp value conflicts are absent; Western nations are not ordinarily seen as "developing" or "in transition." Yet such movements have appeared with increasing frequency in Western societies during the past decade. How can we understand this? The American situation differs from classical ones in that it does not arise from the standard problems of modernization. But the existence of a student movement in America and other advanced industrial societies forces on us the conjecture that these societies, too, are "transitional"—not in the same terms as developing countries, and perhaps more subtly, but just as meaningfully. While educated youth in developing countries experience the irrelevance of traditional, religious, prescientific, authoritarian values for modernization, industrialization, and national identity, educated youth in the advanced countries perceive the irrelevance of commerical, acquisitive, materialistic, and nationalistic values in a world that stresses human rights and social equality and requires collective planning. Politicized young people in the developing countries were usually absorbed by socialist, communist, or other working-class movements, since these appeared to be offering opposition to the old society and culture and to be addressing the problems of modern society. But in advanced industrial societies, the organized left has moved toward integration into the established political system and abandoned its radical vision. In the United States the labor movement became similarly integrated, purged itself of radical influence, and organized radicalism slid into obscurity. Thus it has devolved upon students in the West to reconstitute radical political action and ideology. In so doing, they adopt the populist, egalitarian, romantic, and generational rhetoric and style which characterized the classical student movements in the early stages of their development. But they also reject the ideological orientations and modes of action that were characteristic of the revolutionary left in earlier phases of industrialization and modernization.

Of all the new student movements, that among white American students shows the least resemblance in its origins to the classical model. The French student movement, although it probably has some of the same roots as the American, resembles the classical case in some respects: it is in part a call for modernization, and a rebellion against traditional culture and the archaic forms of authoritarianism that still pervade French society and the organization of its universities.

West Germany's student movement has similar characteristics. On the one hand, West Germany, like the United States, is dominated by giant corporate bureaucracies, by increasing centralization of political life, by an absence of organized and effective political opposition to corporate capitalism, and by militarization; on the other hand, it is also marked by a greater persistence of traditional cultural and political values. Like its American counterpart, the German student movement appeals to an idealized conception of democracy in modern society; it differs in its emphasis on the rejection of the archaic forms of authority and status distinctions Europe has inherited from its feudal past. It is aware that many of the cultural and political factors that contributed to Hitlerism have not been eradicated, while it is itself imbued with a profound hatred of the legacy of Nazism.

Thus the current wave of student protest throughout the world is, in part, the result of coincidence: on the one hand, the student movements in Latin America and Asia continue to function as part of a relatively long tradition of student activism; on the other hand, new student movements in the West have emerged in response to rather different problems and issues. Despite the differences among student movements in developed and underdeveloped countries, however, it is clear that a process of mutual influence is at work among them. For example, the white student movement in America received inspiration in its early stages from dramatic student uprisings in Japan, Turkey, and South Korea. More recently, American activists have been influenced by street tactics learned from Japanese students and by ideological expressions emanating from France and West Germany. The French students were certainly inspired by the West Germans, and the Italians by the French. The symbols of "alienated" youth culture, originating in Britain and the United States, have been adopted throughout Eastern and Western Europe. The spread of ideology, symbols, and tactics of protest is, of course, powerfully aided by television and other mass media and also by the increased opportunities for international travel and study abroad available to European and American students. The increasing cross-fertilization and mutual inspiration which are certainly occurring among student movements are, then, the outcome of mass communication and informal contact. Whatever similarity exists among stu-

dent movements around the world is thus neither completely
spontaneous nor centrally coordinated.

American Student Activism in the 1960's

Those who believe that disorder and conflict are unique to
the campuses of the 1960's are unacquainted with the history
of American colleges. Dormitory life in nineteenth-century
America was marked by violence, rough and undisciplined
actions, and outbreaks of protest against the rules and regulations through which faculties and administrations attempted
to govern students.[10] Although collegiate life became more
peaceful after the turn of the century, protest, activism, and
collective action continued to be part of college life. The
depression of the 1930's and the pre-World War II period of
the 1940's were marked by protest, often of a political character. An examination of college and university disruption
even during the 1950's provides a notable record of activity.

Student activism during the 1960's appears, however, to
have unprecedented qualities. Compared to earlier activism,
that of the 1960's involves more students and engages them
more continuously, is more widely distributed on campuses
throughout the country, is more militant, is more hostile to
established authority and institutions (including radical political organizations), and has been more sustained. Such activism seems better considered as part of a student *movement,*
something largely unknown before in the United States,
rather than as a collection of similar but unconnected events.
And although it involves issues of special interest to students,
the movement has usually integrated student concerns with
political issues of wider currency.

The emergence of such a movement in the 1960's is particularly striking. The ten previous years—despite outbreaks of
campus disruption—were notable mainly as a period of political indifference or privatized alienation among students.[11]
Campus observers at that time remarked on student conformity to conventional values and private goals. Social scientists
hardly anticipated that large numbers of students would become engaged in substantial social action.

Still, the student movement in the sixties does have some roots in the previous decade. During the late 1950's, liberal and radical dissenters became increasingly active at several universities. At Berkeley a campus political party, SLATE, challenged the domination of student government by more conservative, fraternity-oriented students. In particular, SLATE expressed opposition to restrictions of freedom of speech and argued for student participation in off-campus political activity.[12]

Although SLATE's activity seems prophetic of what was to happen nationally, it had little impact beyond the Berkeley campus. In February of 1960, however, Negro students began to attack segregation in public facilities by "sitting-in" at segregated Southern dime-store lunch counters. Northern students supported these demands by picketing and boycotting Northern branches of Woolworth's and Kresge's. The success of the Southern sit-ins led to the formation of the Student Nonviolent Coordinating Committee (SNCC). Northern white student groups formalized their organizations to support the Southern movement.

At the same, time, other issues emerged. At Berkeley, students demonstrated to protest the execution of Caryl Chessman. In a particularly dramatic instance, Bay Area students protested hearings of the House Un-American Activities Committee in San Francisco. The anti-HUAC demonstrations received national publicity. HUAC itself publicized a film of the protest, intended to expose "Communist influence" among the youth. Instead, the film turned out to be self-caricature and dramatized to many students that demonstrations and direct action could have positive effects in challenging hostile authority.

By late 1961, students consciously began to use civil rights techniques of nonviolent direct action—marches, vigils, and pickets—to protest aspects of American foreign policy. Student concern over the nuclear arms race, nuclear testing, and civil defense prompted the first national student demonstration in several decades—the Washington Peace March of February, 1962.[13]

Students who participated in these activities saw them primarily as moral responses to *specific* issues, yet some began to perceive *general* political implications. Most activists read widely, and they were influenced by radical social criticism in the United States and Western Europe. The work of C. Wright Mills on the power elite and the Cold War was especially influential. By 1962, "little" student magazines critically examined the classic doctrines of radicalism.[14] They called for a new radical ideology, stressing links between civil rights, disarmament, and poverty. Meanwhile, in England, university-based intellectuals formed what they called a "new left," which broke with communist and social democratic orthodoxies and sought to regenerate socialist thought.

According to data collected by Richard Peterson of the Educational Testing Service, there were, in 1965, "student left" organizations on 25 percent of American campuses; by 1968, the number had grown to 46 percent.[15] Students for a Democratic Society has become the most widely publicized and perhaps the most influential of student political groups formed in the early 1960's. SDS now claims about 7,000 "national" (i.e., dues-paying) members and at least 35,000 members in its several hundred local chapters.[16] SDS began in competition with other new and old left groupings; by now, however, SDS vastly overshadows in size and reputation the other left-wing groups (such as the DuBois Clubs, the Young Socialist Alliance, and Progressive Labor).

From its inception, SDS's primary purpose was to develop a new radical movement to significantly affect American politics. Although its founders and members were students, their ultimate concern was not with student issues as such, but rather with the organization of students for social change in the larger society. To this end, SDS envisioned an invigoration of the democratic process in America. This could result, they believed, if universities could become centers of controversy and arenas for active discussion of alternatives to present policies; if the civil rights and anti-war movements could succeed in activating large numbers of people at the grassroots level; and if established reform groups, such as the labor movement, liberal organizations, and religious bodies, would join forces with the civil rights, peace, and student movements to offer new alternatives to the electorate at the local and national levels.

A major hope of many members of SDS was for a political "realignment" in which the Democratic Party would become the voice of the rising social movements. Under these conditions, they hoped, a majority coalition could be constructed to move the country away from its commitment to the Cold War and toward a policy of disarmament, relaxation of international tensions, and a domestic program aimed at ending poverty and racial inequality.

In addition to these short-range political goals, SDS, at its convention at Port Huron, Michigan, in June, 1962, announced a further vision—a society based on "participatory democracy." In a society that was becoming increasingly centralized, SDS leaders argued, men were less and less capable of controlling decisions affecting their lives. Technological development and mass education could, however, create new forms of decentralization and local democracy in neighborhoods, factories, schools, and other social organizations. SDS urged disenfranchised and powerless people to organize themselves and press their interests in opposition to the already powerful. Such local insurgency should have two effects: immediately, to generate a climate for reform of national policy; in the longer run, to teach the possibility and meaning of participation.[17]

As this brief history suggests, the emerging thrust of the student movement in the early sixties was toward the reform of society rather than the university as such. Even prominent "on-campus" issues show this impulse: there were rallies and protests concerned with removing university restraints on political expression and activity, such as bans on controversial speakers. (In 1956, for example, Adlai Stevenson was not permitted to speak on the Berkeley campus under the then prevailing interpretation of political "neutrality.") So-called campus concerns also had broader meaning. Students saw that protest against racial and ethnic discrimination in fraternity systems and against compulsory ROTC had a wider political significance. By and large, the university itself remained a neutral, or even positively valued, base of operations. For many student activists, the university represented a qualitatively different kind of social institution, one in which radical social criticism could be generated and constructive social change promoted.

It should also be noted that between 1960 and 1964, student campaigns either employed such "normal channels" as student government or invoked such conventional protest techniques as petitions, picketing, and public meetings. Although many students sympathized with the use of civil disobedience and other forms of direct action in behalf of racial equality and peace, the use of these techniques on campus during the period was decidedly uncommon, and student radicals regarded them as means of bringing issues to the attention of persons who would then pursue them through conventional political processes. It seems evident that, on balance, the student movement began with a firm commitment to nonviolence and with considerable optimism regarding the responsiveness of authorities.

The summer of 1963 marked a high point of optimism. The signing of a nuclear test-ban treaty and a pending civil rights march on Washington augured well for passage of significant legislation. Student activists projected new civil rights work, particularly in the area of voter registration. In addition, such books as Michael Harrington's *The Other America* had developed in young activists an awareness of economic as well as racial inequality. During that summer, SDS began to mobilize students for community organization among poor whites and other minorities, in much the same way as the Southern civil rights movement had been working among poor Negroes. This new commitment to off-campus work in poverty areas was undertaken in a relatively optimistic spirit: if the poor could be organized in their own interest, then the national climate of reform could be moved beyond the issue of segregation and voting rights to an effective attack on poverty and unemployment.[18]

The period of optimism began to wane with the assassination of President Kennedy in November, 1963. Still, in 1963–1964, the student movement engaged in an effort to draw students into volunteer and full-time work in the Southern black belt, Appalachia, and Northern urban slum areas. By the summer of 1964, thousands of students were involved in such activities, their legitimacy bolstered by President Johnson's announcement of a "war on poverty." In Mississippi, nearly one thousand volunteers aided in the effort to build the Mississippi Freedom Democratic Party.

The Mississippi experience was an extraordinary one for many of its participants. Three young men were murdered, and many others saw at first hand the character of Southern repression.[19] The experience intensified feelings of urgency about justice, social and legal, for Negroes; it demonstrated the complicity of the legal order in perpetuating repression of Negroes; and it produced profound discontent with the indifference and superficiality of white middle-class life, including collegiate life. Many returned to campus with strong convictions about the necessity of direct action and confrontation for bringing change.

The Mississippi summer culminated with the Freedom Democratic Party's effort to unseat the segregationist Mississippi delegation at the Democratic Party National Convention in Atlantic City. Their failure, particularly the refusal of white liberal Democrats to support wholeheartedly the Mississippi challenge, proved deeply disillusioning to the leaders of SNCC and their black and white supporters. The Atlantic City compromise seemed of a piece with the reluctance of the federal government to enforce existing laws protecting civil rights workers in the South. The events of that summer in the South led SNCC to a profound reevaluation of its commitment to building a nonviolent grass-roots protest movement, since that commitment depended on the belief that the national authorities would be responsive to and supportive of the movement. Just as SNCC's initial program had helped spark the white student movement in the North, so its disillusionment deeply affected Northern students.[20] Despite these events, SDS in the fall of 1964 announced that it supported Lyndon Johnson in preference to Barry Goldwater and issued a button, "Part of the Way with LBJ," which signified its continued though partially disillusioned connection to conventional political processes.[21]

Shortly after classes began at Berkeley in the fall of 1964, the campus was rocked by a series of massive protest demonstrations, culminating in December in a large-scale sit-in at

the administration building, mass arrests, and a strike. The
Free Speech Movement began, conventionally enough, over
suddenly imposed restrictions on students who used the campus "to support or advocate off-campus political or social
action." [22] Although removal of these restrictions remained a
prominent issue, as the struggle on campus developed, a
larger issue, with strong ideological overtones, took prominence: the Berkeley demonstrations became not simply a protest against particular violations of students rights, but rather
an expression of an underlying conflict between students as a
class and the "multiversity" and its administration—a struggle
between two fundamentally opposed interests in and orientations toward higher education.

The Free Speech Movement had a special importance in
the history of the student movement. Although there were
precedents—for example, University of Chicago students
held a sit-in at the administration building to protest alleged
discrimination against Negroes in the rental of university-
owned housing, and New York City College students staged a
strike to protest a ban against communist speakers on campus, both before 1964—the Berkeley protest, which was
widely publicized, demonstrated the feasibility of involving
large numbers of students in direct action techniques on campus. It also suggested that such techniques might be necessary
to effect campus reforms—and that they might be successful
for this end.[23]

Moreover, Berkeley events focused attention on the policies, programs, and organization of the university—both internally and in its connections with the larger society. Student
activists, before the Free Speech Movement, had viewed campus issues as trivial compared to the civil rights struggle. The
only way for white students to display their commitment to
social change, to put themselves "on the line," was to move
off the campus. The Free Speech Movement showed how the
campus itself might become a front line. Students now saw
that what happens on campus could really matter politically,
and that a local campus uprising could have national and international importance.

It seems fair to say that the Free Speech Movement at
Berkeley in 1964 marked a turning point in the American

student movement. Other events, of course, contributed to the change. By 1965, the era of white student participation in the Southern civil rights movement was drawing to a close. The period of concern with nuclear war had culminated in an apparently firm agreement between the United States and the Soviet Union to stop atmospheric nuclear tests, relax tensions, and control the pace of the arms race. President Johnson had been elected with a massive mandate to avoid expanding the war in Vietnam and to preserve and enlarge the welfare state program. The Berkeley uprising gave the student movement a new prominence and evoked a new interest among students and others in university reform and educational innovation.

In this atmosphere, SDS and other activist groups searched for new programmatic directions. These groups preferred to work in local urban situations in grass-roots community organization among the poor; the involvement of students in this kind of action rose steadily, but the war in Vietnam became increasingly important. In December, 1964, SDS abandoned its practice of concentrating only on domestic issues by deciding to call for a national student march in Washington against the war, to be held in April, 1965. Six weeks later, the bombing of North Vietnam began; the Administration reiterated its refusal to negotiate an end to the war; and support for the April march began to build rapidly. Some 20,000 students and others participated in the first nationally visible protest against U.S. policy in Vietnam. SDS was catapulted to national prominence, receiving wide coverage in the media; its membership grew rapidly, and by the end of the school year it had achieved wide recognition as *the* nationally organized expression of the student movement.[24]

After the April, 1965, march, hundreds of campuses witnessed "teach-ins" and other organized activities concerning Vietnam; during this period no sector of the American public received as much information about and analysis of the war as the student body. Vietnam soon became the central, overriding preoccupation of activist students. New waves of demonstrations were held in the fall, largely at the initiative of the Berkeley Vietnam Day Committee; they were organized locally by SDS chapters and by the scores of ad hoc "committees to end the war in Vietnam" which had sprung up around the country in the preceding months.

Early anti-Vietnam War activity was characterized by the use of conventional forms of protest and by the encouragement of debate and discussion through such forms as the teach-in. Some draft cards were burned, and some Berkeley students tried to block troop trains in September, 1965, but, generally, "legal" techniques of opposition were used, or civil disobedience was employed in order to dramatize the movement's cause. The majority of SDS members even refused to endorse a national program of opposition to the draft, the aim of which was merely to increase the number of young men seeking conscientious objector status.

But there was increasing disillusionment during the year with the efficacy of such protests; each major march had more participants but was shortly followed by some new escalation of the war. Many disillusioned students argued that the main function served by peace marches was to maintain America's image as a democratic society permitting dissent, so that the war effort could continue without significant internal or external opposition. Meanwhile, depictions in the media of the effect of the war on civilians in Vietnam, of the corrupt and unrepresentative character of the South Vietnamese regime, of Administration failure to seize opportunities for negotiation, and of the ways in which the rising costs of the war hampered domestic reform programs in the United States were widely discussed on the campus and heightened the urgency of the student protests.[25]

In the spring of 1966, General Lewis Hershey announced that some students would have to be drafted, and that student deferments would be terminated for those whose class standings were poor or who failed to reach a certain level of performance on a soon-to-be administered Selective Service Qualification Test. The reaction on the campus was sharp and immediate. Professors protested against the use of grades for Selective Service purposes. There was rising tension at many schools; some students became anxious about the possibility of being drafted, others upset about competing with their peers to avoid the draft; students and faculty resented the cooperation of universities with the draft in supplying class standings and facilities for the administration of the test.

At several schools, SDS chapters demanded that universities withold such cooperation. At the University of Chicago, five hundred students, led by SDS, staged a sit-in at the administration building, seizing control of the building for three and one-half days. Similar seizures and sit-ins occurred at Wisconsin, City College of New York, Oberlin College, and other institutions. The Chicago action was the first successful closing of a university administration building and the first time that SDS had undertaken a direct confrontation with a university administration. The "anti-ranking" protests thus signified the spread of the "Berkeley situation" to other campuses. As at Berkeley, the confrontation developed when student activists perceived university administrators as cooperating actively with outside agencies in opposition to student interests and democratic values, and undertaking such cooperation without prior consultation of students. As at Berkeley, the Chicago students had attempted to use regular channels to change policy before resorting to a sit-in. As at Berkeley, widespread support for the demands of the protest was evident among nonparticipating students. And, as at Berkeley, the Chicago and other anti-ranking protests won immediate, widespread attention from the mass media.

The Chicago sit-in did not elicit punitive action by the university administration, and the students eventually abandoned the building. Nor did it have an immediate effect on university policy concerning the draft (although the faculty senate voted to support punitive action in the event of further disruptive protest, and a year later the faculty council voted to end the transmission of "male class ranks" to draft boards). But the anti-ranking actions at Chicago and other universities did spark a nationwide debate on the draft, did lead some schools to refuse to send class rank information to draft boards, and did help popularize the concept of refusing to cooperate with the draft as a means of resisting the war.[26]

For SDS, these sit-ins provided a new strategic orientation and a new phase in its development. This new phase was inaugurated at an SDS convention in June, 1966. At that meet-

ing, a new generation of leadership came into office. For the
first time since its formation, SDS was to be run largely by
people without ties to the original founders of the organization. The "new guard" were students who had joined SDS
after the inception of its anti-Vietnam program, and who
came from schools without much tradition of student activism. They tended to conceive of SDS as a *student* organization, and they believed its greatest promise lay in reaching
uncommitted students on issues that concerned *them,* rather
than in simply working against the war or working on general political programs without specific relevance to the campus. The new thrust was at first called "student syndicalism,"
a term borrowed from the European student movement and
its tradition of organizing students along trade unionist lines.
The new orientation demonstrated a desire to build on the experience of Berkeley, the anti-rank protests, and similar confrontations, by working for what eventually came to be called
"student power"—that is, organized student unions or parties
working for such reforms as the abolition of grades, smaller
classes, and greater student participation in shaping curricula.

It was not a program to disrupt the universities, but rather
an effort to increase the "class-consciousness" of students and
break down what SDS saw as the bureaucratic quality of university life, the paternalistic treatment of students, and the
authoritarian pattern of education, which, they alleged, was a
source of student discontent and also produced widespread
political apathy and passivity. To implement this program,
SDS created a team of traveling campus organizers who were
to assist in the formation of chapters, and, as the year wore
on, various forms of "student syndicalist" activity emerged.
On a number of campuses, SDS leaders, running on plat-
forms advocating "student power," were elected as student
body presidents. Across the country, there were more and
more demands for liberalization of dormitory rules and of
the grading system, for free speech, and the like. These demands had been building up before SDS's new programmatic
thrust; probably the main effect of SDS was to enhance the
skill with which these demands could be made.[27]

But "student syndicalism" was not a stand which SDS
could maintain for very long. Although demands for student

power were consonant with SDS's orientation to participatory democracy, they were not well suited to deal with the general political situation, particularly the continued escalation of the war and the intensification of black rebellion in the cities. Besides, many SDS members were convinced that university reform was futile, that the universities could not be substantially changed until there was basic change in the society as a whole.

Then, in December, 1966, Berkeley activists tried to set up an anti-draft literature table next to a Navy recruiting table in the Student Union. A massive sit-in and student strike ensued as a result of efforts by the administration to eject the protesters from the Student Union and to defend the ejection on the grounds that, as a state university campus, Berkeley had to offer government agencies the special privilege of setting up recruiting tables in areas of the Student Union where students were forbidden to set up their tables. A month later, SDS members at Brown University organized the first protest against Dow Chemical Company recruiters. During the following spring, scores of demonstrations and sit-ins occurred protesting the presence of military, CIA, and Dow recruiters on the campus. At Columbia, SDS and its followers engaged in physical battle with other students as a result of their protests against Marine recruiters.

The anti-rank sit-ins and the anti-recruiter demonstrations provided a way for SDS to combine its opposition to the war and to militarism with its interest in approaching students on their own ground. On the one hand, these demonstrations and some disruptive effect on the military machine by impairing the ease of its relations with the university. On the other hand, unlike general protests against the war, these demonstrations could more easily affect uncommitted students, since they protested a war that was increasingly relevant to the student body as a whole. Moreover, such demonstrations could be linked to student power concerns, since the university-military connections were undertaken without consulting students.

Similar strategic considerations underlay the even more militant anti-Dow demonstrations in the fall of 1967 [28] and the SDS-led protests against university involvement in the Institute for Defense Analyses which culminated in convulsive rebellion at Columbia in the spring of 1968. By 1967–68, the organization of on-campus confrontations, especially those concerning university involvement with military agencies, became a central purpose of SDS. After several years of oscillating between university reform and student power versus general political issues, SDS had at last found an issue—the military connections of the university—that could mobilize both students primarily concerned with campus reform and students primarily interested in general politics.

But the reason for SDS's turn toward confrontation with university authority lay deeper than its discovery of new strategic and tactical possibilities.[29] The history of the student movement in general and SDS in particular reveals that underlying the changes in strategies and tactics and the shifts in the issues which motivated protest were more fundamental changes in the way student activists perceived authority in the nation and in the university and in the way they defined their relation to it. What happened in the eight years we have just briefly reviewed was a precipitous decline in the degree to which active participants in the student movement attributed legitimacy to national authority and to the university.

The two general phases of the movement—before and after 1965—may be viewed as follows: In phase one, the student movement embodied concern, dissent, and protest about various social issues, but it generally accepted the legitimacy of the American political community in general and especially of the university. In those years, many students believed that the legitimacy of the existing political structure was compromised by the undue influence of corporate interests and the military. They made far-reaching criticisms of the university and of other social institutions, but their criticisms were usually directed at the failure of the American political system and of American institutions to live up to officially proclaimed values. Thus, despite their commitment to reform and to support for civil disobedience and direct action, the student activists in the first half of this decade generally accepted the basic values and norms of the American political community. And despite their discontent with the university, they usually operated within the confines of academic tradition and felt considerable allegiance to the values of the academic community.

In phase two of the student movement, a considerable number of young people, particularly the activist core, experienced a progressive deterioration in their acceptance of national and university authority. The ideology of this phase of the movement was recently stated by Mark Rudd, leader of the local SDS during the Columbia crisis:

> Many have called us a "student power" movement, implying that our goal is student control over the "educational process," taking decision-making power away from the administrators and putting it in the hands of "democratic" student groups. . . . Student power used to be the goal of S.D.S., but as our understanding of the society has developed, our understanding of the university's role in it has also changed.
>
> We see the university as a factory whose goal is to produce: (1) trained personnel for corporations, government and more universities, and (2) knowledge of the uses of business and government to perpetuate the present system. Government studies at Columbia, for example, attempt to explain our society through concepts of pluralism and conflicting group interest, while the reality of the situation is quite different.
>
> In our strike, we united with many of the people who have been affected by the university's policies—the tenants in Columbia-owned buildings, the Harlem community, the university employees. Many other people throughout the world saw us confront a symbol of those who control the decisions that are made in this country.
>
> In France, the workers and students united to fight a common enemy. The same potential exists here in the United States. We are attempting to connect our fight with the fight of the black people for their freedom, with the fight of the Mexican-Americans for their land in New Mexico, with the fight of the Vietnamese people, and with all people who believe that men and women should be free to live as they choose, in a society where the government is responsive to the needs of all the people, and not the needs of the few whose enormous wealth gives them the political power. We intend to make a revolution.[30]

The process of "delegitimation" and "radicalization" was gradual, and it may be useful to suggest key events and experiences contributing to it.

1. *The Nonviolent Southern Civil Rights Movement.* The treatment of civil rights workers and Negroes seeking to exercise constitutional rights by Southern police officials and racist groups was seen as brutal by civil rights organizers and their student allies, and as never adequately responded to by federal authorities. Instead, the latter were thought to be primarily interested in "cooling off" the movement rather than in achieving full implementation of political rights. These events marked the beginning of the sharp split between the student left and established liberal leadership and organization, and disillusionment with the idea that the federal government could be a major agency for protection of rights and promotion of equality and welfare. This disillusionment increased with the failure of the Democratic Convention to grant recognition to the Mississippi Freedom Democrats, and the associated unwillingness by prominent liberal Democrats to wage a floor fight in their behalf.

2. *The "War on Poverty."* Young people saw the rhetoric of public officials as overstated and unfulfilled. Young poverty workers alleged that political machines and other established agencies used federal funds to preserve existing power relationships, saw the erosion of the promise of "maximum feasible participation by the poor" as a basic element of the new programs, regarded public bureaucracies as callous toward the poor, and saw local police being used to attack legitimate protest activity by indigenous organizations of the poor. SDS and other student groups that had embarked on anti-poverty activities had hoped that the new federal programs signified the beginning of significant reform efforts, and that the new programs would facilitate the political organization of deprived groups. The failure of these expectations was a severe disillusionment.

3. *The Events at Berkeley.* These marked a change in the perception of university administrators by campus activists. Administrators came to be seen as actively interested in preventing students from effectively organizing for off-campus protest, as more responsive to political pressure from conservative interests than to student concerns or traditional principles of civil liberties, and as devious and untrustworthy

in negotiating situations. Moreover, President Clark Kerr, in his book *The Uses of the University,* supplied ideologically oriented activists with an image of the university as fundamentally hostile to humane values, to undergraduate education as such, to internal democratic functioning—and as necessarily involved in servicing the needs of powerful interest groups. The combination of actual experience with university authority at Berkeley with exposure to administrators' self-proclaimed values helped to change students' perception of the university from an essentially congenial institution—needing reform—to an institution whose primary functions were directly opposed to the needs, interests, and values of activist and intellectual students.

4. *The Escalation of the War in Vietnam.* Escalation occurred despite campaign promises of President Johnson. Peaceful protest activity had no discernible impact on policy, which continued to harden while students became increasingly aware of the diverse moral, legal, and practical arguments for disengagement from Vietnam. Administration officials often refused to participate in campus debates on the war; when spokesmen for the President's policy were present, their arguments were often based on historical and political grounds which many students and professors regarded as questionable. Particularly damaging were the frequent instances of deceitfulness on the part of Administration spokesmen—the mass media providing much documentation for the view that the Administration was misrepresenting the facts about the war and the diplomatic situation. Many students were as deeply affected by the "credibility gap" as they were by the war itself.

5. *Cooperation by Academic Institutions with the War Effort and with Military Agencies Generally.* An early revelation was the fact that faculty members at Michigan State University had worked with U.S. intelligence agencies in South Vietnam to bolster the regime of Ngo Dinh Diem. Shortly thereafter, an extensive research operation concerning biological warfare was publicized at the University of Pennsylvania. Finally, there were widely publicized revelations of the covert sponsorship of research by the Central Intelligence

Agency, operating through a variety of bona fide and "paper" foundations, and the concomitant subsidy by the CIA of various student, labor, religious, and educational organizations in their overseas operations. These revelations, plus the obvious fact that major universities depended on Defense Department funds for large portions of their budgets, raised deep questions in the academic community about the intellectual independence of universities and of the scholarly enterprise in general. For student activists, they provided further evidence of the untrustworthiness and bias of the universities, and provided easy targets for politically effective protest against university authority. The involvement of the universities and the scientific and scholarly disciplines in the war effort and with the defense establishment, while continuing to proclaim their "nonpartisanship," "neutrality," and insistence on academic values, has been a severe and continuing reason for the erosion of university authority for many students and academics.

6. *The Draft.* Student immunity from the draft began to weaken in 1966, with General Hershey's announcement of restrictions on student deferments. This announcement focused students' attention on the possibility that they themselves would have to participate in the war; it also made them aware of the fact that young men were in competition to avoid the draft, and that their student status had provided them with a special privilege—one that was not available to lower-income, noncollege youth. Many students entertained doubts about a system of compulsory service in a society that celebrated individualistic and voluntaristic values: many had doubts about the use of conscription for a war that had not been declared and for which no general mobilization had been undertaken. Of course, many had strong moral objections to participation in or support for the war in Vietnam in particular, or to war in general; the Selective Service law's narrow definitions of conscientious objection, however, prevented most pacifists and other moral objectors from achieving exemption for their claims of conscience. Moreover, the legitimacy of the draft was weakened by the frank admission by Selective Service, in a widely circulated document, that the threat of the draft was useful in "channeling" young men into

"socially useful" careers, that avoiding the draft by legitimate means involved a considerable amount of self-deception as well as deception of others, that in fact the very course of one's youth and young adulthood was shaped and distorted by either the fear of the draft or officially encouraged calculation to avoid it. At the same time, many middle-class students deeply resented the interruption of career and the frustration of plans and aspirations which the draft represented, especially if they felt that no adequate justification for this interruption had been provided. Considerable cynicism about the operations of the system prevailed as a result of widely disseminated folklore about techniques for evading the draft through the faking of disabilities. Finally, many young people resented the imposition of the draft by a political system in which they had no voice or representation and which seemed entirely unresponsive to their opinions regarding the war. Further resentment was encouraged by the use of the draft to punish anti-war dissenters.

7. *Race, Poverty, and Urban Decline.* The failure of the political system to deal effectively with these problems has been a continuing source of student disaffection. Students in large numbers saw the war as a major barrier to effective action on domestic problems; in addition, they saw considerable hypocrisy in the efforts of the government to "preserve freedom" in and "pacify" a remote country when these goals could not be achieved in America's cities. For white activists, whose original interest in social action had been sparked by the civil rights movement, the increasing militance of black youth created new problems, especially when ghetto rebellions were met with massive police repression. For many white activists, the moral and political choices had narrowed to that of siding with black revolutionaries or remaining identified with white authority, which was increasingly defined as "colonial" in nature. Black militants constantly, and understandably, challenged the commitment and seriousness of whites who claimed to be their allies; in this context, tactics of aggressive resistance seemed the only morally commensurate response for white radical students. Thus, for example, at Columbia, the SDS-led protest turned into a serious effort to seize control of university buildings only after black stu-

dents openly expressed doubt that the white students were prepared to take serious action. Similar events occurred on many campuses.

8. *Police on Campus.* Unquestionably, a major source of disaffection—perhaps especially for moderate or previously uncommitted students—has been the nature of campus encounters with the police. Even commentators who are unsympathetic to the goals of the Columbia SDS have agreed that police violence contributed greatly to the radicalization of the Columbia student body during the 1968 crisis. Daniel Bell, for example, describes this process as follows:

> In all, about a hundred students were hurt. But it was not the violence itself that was so horrible—despite the many pictures in the papers of bleeding students, not one required hospitalization. It was the capriciousness of that final action. The police simply ran wild. Those who tried to say they were innocent bystanders or faculty were given the same flailing treatment as the students. For most of the students, it was their first encounter with brutality and blood, and they responded in fear and anger. The next day, almost the entire campus responded to a call for a student strike. In a few hours, thanks to the New York City Police Department, a large part of the Columbia campus had become radicalized.[31]

Thus, however one may criticize the strategic and tactical responses of the student radicals, their ranks are characteristically enlarged by a sense of moral outrage at what students take to be the ineffectiveness, insincerity, and finally tactics of harsh repression on the part of the authorities. Therefore, a "politics of confrontation" has become the most effective strategic weapon of student radicals, thrusting such groups as SDS into positions of campus leadership when they can develop a sense of outrage in students and faculty, and isolating them, in numerous instances, when they cannot.

The Politics of Confrontation

During the past three years, "resistance" and "confrontation" have come to occupy an increasingly prominent position in the strategy and tactics of the student movement. "Resistance" and "confrontation" refer to such forms of direct action as deliberate disruption of or interference with normal, routine operations of persons or institutions by large masses of persons; deliberate violation of authoritative orders to disperse; forceful retaliation against police use of clubs, chemicals, or other force; the use of barricades or "mobile tactics" to prevent or delay police efforts to disperse a crowd; the use of ridicule, rudeness, obscenity, and other uncivil forms of speech and behavior to shock, embarrass, or defy authorities; refusal to comply with orders or to accept authoritative commands or requests as legitimate.

Even so, confrontations arranged by students have been usually more "symbolic" than "disruptive" or "destructive." Much rhetoric flows in university circles, and elsewhere, about "interference with institutional functioning." Whatever the intent of radicals, however, they have usually not been successful in disrupting the routines of most university members—until massive police formations were called to campus.

Doubtless some student radicals hope for physical confrontations with the police. But there is little evidence that such a hope is widespread. Further, there is little evidence that many students are willing (much less able) to disrupt functioning, attack persons, or destroy property in the university. But they are willing to engage in symbolic protest—to symbolically "throw their bodies on the machine." This leads to showdowns with the police, and then to violence from the police —and retaliation by some students.

Many observers who have tried to understand the student movement and who express sympathy for many of its objectives find the turn toward confrontation, disruption, and incivility highly irrational and self-destructive. Increasingly, SDS and the "new left" are criticized for the style of their actions and rhetoric. Although many such critics can understand the frustration which contributes to extreme militancy, they argue that the strategy of confrontation serves only to defeat the aims of the movement, and that student radicals ought to exercise self-restraint if they sincerely wish to achieve their political and social ends. For example, it is frequently argued that confrontation tactics accomplish little more than the arousal of popular hostility, thus fueling the fires of right-wing demogoguery and increasing the likelihood of government repression. Confrontation tactics in the university, the critics argue, do not promote reform; they mainly achieve the weakening of the university's ability to withstand political pressure from outside, and consequently they threaten to undermine the one institution in society that offers dissenters full freedom of expression. Some critics conclude their arguments by assuming that since in their view the main effect of new left activity is to create disorder, intensify polarization, increase the strength of the far right, and weaken civil liberties, then these must be the results actually desired by the student radicals.

We have interviewed new left activists in an effort to understand the basis for their actions from their point of view. The following is an attempt to present the case for confrontation tactics as the militants themselves might make it.[32]

1. *Confrontation and militancy are methods of arousing moderates to action.* The creation of turmoil and disorder can stimulate otherwise quiescent groups to take more forceful action in their own ways. Liberals may come to support radical demands while opposing their tactics; extreme tactics may shock moderates into self-reexamination. Student radicals can claim credit for prompting Senator McCarthy's Presidential campaign, for increased senatorial opposition to the Vietnam War, and for the greater urgency for reform expressed by such moderate bodies as the Kerner Commission.

2. *Confrontation and militancy can educate the public.* Direct action is not intended to win particular reforms or to influence decision-makers, but rather to bring out a repressive response from authorities—a response rarely seen by most white Americans. When confrontation brings violent official response, uncommitted elements of the public can see for themselves the true nature of the "system." Confrontation, therefore, is a means of political education.

3. *Confrontation, militancy and resistance are ways to prepare young radicals for the possibility of greater repression.* If the movement really seriously threatens the power of political authorities, efforts to repress the movement through police state measures are inevitable. The development of resistant attitudes and action toward the police at the present time is a

necessary preparation for more serious resistance in the future. Fascism is a real possibility in America; and we don't intend to be either "Jews" or "good Germans."

4. *Combative behavior with respect to the police and other authorities, although possibly alienating "respectable" adults, has the opposite effect on the movement's relationships with nonstudent youth.* Educated, middle-class, nonviolent styles of protest are poorly understood by working-class youth, black youth, and other "dropouts." Contact with these other sectors of the youth population is essential and depends upon the adoption of a tough and aggressive stance to win respect from such youth. Militant street actions attract a heterogeneous group of nonstudent youth participants who have their own sources of alienation from middle-class society and its institutions.

5. *The experience of resistance and combat may have a liberating effect on young middle-class radicals.* Most middle-class students are shocked by aggressive or violent behavior. This cultural fear of violence is psychologically damaging and may be politically inhibiting. To be a serious revolutionary, one must reject middle-class values, particularly deference toward authority. Militant confrontation gives resisters the experience of physically opposing institutional power, and it may force students to choose between "respectable" intellectual radicalism and serious commitment to revolution, violent or otherwise.

6. *The political potency of "backlash" is usually exaggerated.* Those who point to the possibility of repression as a reaction to confrontation tactics wish to compromise demands and principles and dilute radicalism. Repression will come in any case, and to diminish one's efforts in anticipation is to give up the game before it starts.

Some movement spokesmen would add that the possibilities of polarization, repression, and reaction do require more careful attention by the movement if it wishes to win support and sympathy among middle-class adults. They would argue that such support can be obtained, even as militant action is pursued, by concerted efforts at interpretation to and education of such adult groups. The Chicago convention demonstrations are cited as an instance in which adult moderate and liberal sympathy was *enhanced* by militant action, because some care was taken to maintain good relations with these groups, and because the actual events in the street were directly observable by the general public.

We have no way of knowing how many participants in such actions share these perspectives; many rank and file participants may engage in militant or violent action for more simple and direct reasons: they have been provoked to anger, or they feel moral outrage. The rationale we have tried to depict is at least partly the result of student outbursts rather than the cause—after an event (e.g., Columbia), movement stategists try to assimilate and rationalize what occurred. Nevertheless, when movement participants maintain that confrontation and resistance are politically necessary, the arguments described above are those most frequently used.

To a large extent, acceptance of the moral or practical validity of these arguments depends on one's view of the nature of American society and of the university as an institution. Radical activists base their commitment to a politics of confrontation on a kind of negative faith in the repressive and illiberal character of American institutions, including the university. These perceptions have been augmented by an increasing sense that the American university is deeply implicated in the perpetuation of racial injustice. The increasing protest of nonwhite students has brought the issue to the foreground of campus conflict in recent months.

Black and Third World Student Protest

Without doubt, the most far-reaching challenge to the moral authority of the university has begun to emerge from nonwhite students. We have had little to say about this phenomenon.[33] It is of recent origin and is not ordinarily understood as coextensive with the student movement, although the latter, as we have suggested, emerged in part as an effort to extend the gains of Southern black student civil rights activists. Black Student Unions and Afro-American Associations exist on most campuses that have significant numbers of black students. Until a few years ago, black students tended to be individualistic, assimilationist, and politically indifferent; the drive for black power, however, has offered a clear ,opportunity for educated blacks to give collective expression to their grievances and to identify with the black community.

Black student protest cannot be understood outside the framework of the historical status of the black man in American society or without reference to contemporary protests against that status burgeoning within the black communities of America. In the following chapter we examine these issues. Yet any speculation on the origins of black student protest must look to two sources that have increasingly been converging. One important source has been the Negro colleges in the South. In a recent book tracing the history of the black liberation movement, James Forman [34] has shown how the original Student Nonviolent Coordinating Committee began as a response by middle-class, young, Southern black men and women against what they perceived to be their social distance from the black lower classes and the complacency evidenced by their own parents. (In this respect, the black student movement seems akin to features of generational criticism characteristic of white radicals.) Moreover, as the civil rights movement became an increasingly "black" movement, rejecting first the leadership and then the companionship of whites, black students in the movement also became increasingly conscious of parallel movements of protest within the urban black communities of the North. Thus there seem to be two streams feeding into contemporary black student protest. One is from the middle classes of the Southern black community; the second, and increasingly more dominant stream, is from the urban ghettos of the North. In recent years, both sources of black protest have converged and found a congenial response among high school youth. It is these youth, with roots in the urban black communities, steeped in the ideas and ideals of black militancy, who are now beginning to attend the universities and colleges of America in greater numbers.

Black student spokesmen are at least as militant as white radicals, especially in the tactics they advocate and use. But black student organizations have been more oriented toward negotiating specific reforms and concessions than have white radicals. At the same time, the militant stance of black students has been a factor in increasing the militancy of white students, whose expressions of commitment to justice and equality are often greeted with skepticism and derision by blacks.

At San Francisco State College, black militants and students of Asian- and Mexican-American background have joined together to form a "Third World Liberation Front," reflecting the identification with Africans and Asians that is increasingly coming to characterize nonwhite university students.[35] A Third World Liberation Front is also pressing a list of demands at the University of California at Berkeley.

Nonwhite student protest—with its demands for an autonomous nonwhite faculty, curriculum, student body, and self-governed standards of admission—constitutes at least symbolic protest from nonwhite communities as a whole, and thus involves wider interests and concerns than the campus. Presumably, a university embodies and transmits the fundamental traditions and values of the society. At its heart, militant black and Third World student protest challenges those values and ideas as they are currently embodied in curricula, admissions, and hiring practices, and accordingly demands a separate line of authority over resources to develop its own distinctive values and traditions. In effect, it questions the fundamental and unstated assumption underlying much of higher education: the cultural *superiority* of Western civilization.

Ultimately, black and Third World student protest demands that the university reassess its currently institutionalized aims and purposes, and maintains that its present goals are not relevant to the needs of modern urban society. With this in mind, we turn to a brief examination of the structure of the contemporary American university.

Colleges and Universities in Crisis

Student protest has turned many American campuses into arenas of political conflict. To many people both in and out of the universities, the very idea of the politicization of the campus is abhorrent, for it conflicts sharply with a cherished image of the university as a forum for free inquiry, academic values, and "civility": in short, an institution whose fundamental concerns transcend politics. The conception of the university as a *community,* sharing common values and culture and standing apart from both internal political conflict and external political influence, is embedded in academic tradition and, not infrequently, in law. Tradition has conferred a kind of sanctity on the special character of the university as an institution. To many people concerned with the university, the character of student protest in the 1960's marks an unwarranted and inappropriate assault on this sanctity; an injection of profane concerns into what is felt to be a sacred institution.

Indeed, an insistence on the profane character of the university characterizes contemporary student activism and, as we have suggested, is basic to the radical tactics of the late 1960's. The radical image of the university is that of an institution which functions as an integral part of the "system," providing that system with the skilled personnel and technical assistance required for the furthering of its political objectives.

In fact, most universities and colleges can best be seen as falling somewhere between these two conceptions. The university has long since ceased to be—if indeed it ever was—purely a community of shared values; on the other hand, it has become deeply involved in the larger political community without conscious direction and occasionally without intent, and without careful consideration of the problematic character of its enlarged commitments. This is the context of its current crisis.

The Changing Role of Higher Education

In 1900, approximately 1 percent of the college-age population attended academic institutions; by 1939 this had grown to 15 percent. It nevertheless remained true that both private and public institutions of higher learning largely served upper-income groups in the United States. The plenitude of denominational colleges in the United States is evidence of the ways in which colleges served specific ethnic or religious populations. Public universities were hardly different: state schools largely served the agricultural and business needs of local and state groups.

In recent years the American university has become a national institution; its students are likely to be drawn into occupational groups and communities outside the local confines of its formally designated clientele. Denominational colleges have lost a great deal of their special cultural character. Research has become diverse as the populations served have extended through many institutional areas of society and as federal needs have become a major competitor with state and local demands. The University of California at Berkeley currently lists 101 departments in 15 colleges and schools and has 89 separate research institutes, centers, and laboratories. Private universities draw significant proportions of their funds from federal and private foundation research monies, and large state universities depend heavily on the same sources.

Behind these nationalizing and homogenizing trends lies the central role which education and research have come to play in the American economy. The development of new products, new procedures, and new programs is a major dynamic in an economic structure geared to scientific advancement. In addition, welfare and human relations programs have created an intense demand for training and research in social sciences. These technological trends are reinforced by the capacity of an affluent economy for distributing more and more education as a consumer good. By 1970, it is expected that approximately 50 percent of college-age persons will be attending institutions of higher learning. The present college and university population of 6,500,000 includes representatives of most social levels in the population, although it is still true that children of laborers and nonwhites are underrepresented. Whether they wish it or not, American universities, both public and private, are deeply embedded in the social institutions of American life and have become greatly affected by public policy and public interests.

Most universities, indeed, have developed an ethos of service to community and nation. The provision of technical services and trained personnel by centers of higher learning is indispensable in an advanced society at a high level of technological development. So too is the extension of higher education to wider and wider segments of the community. These services, however, necessarily and substantially increase the university's involvement in matters of political significance. The model of the university as a "neutral" institution probably described its pretensions more closely than its uses, even in the past. In our time, at any rate, it is clear that the university is not and cannot be "neutral" if this means, as some seem to think, not at the service of any social interests. Nor, clearly, is the university, as presently constituted, "neutral" in the sense of being equally at the service of all legitimate social interests. In our time, the university is an important cultural and economic resource; it is also much more fully in the service of some social interests than others. The provision of defense research, for example, necessarily aligns the university with the course of national foreign policy and military strategy. In thus entering the service of the political order, the scientific and technological functions of the university become politicized. Given these circumstances, it is understandable that the university has become the scene of conflict and protest focused on control over the nature and direction of the services it provides, or fails to provide, to actual and potential publics.

Moreover, the extension of higher education to lower-income and minority groups usually means the attempt to extend norms and values of privileged classes and cultures. Lower-income and minority groups may find it difficult to assimilate the cultural artifacts of the privileged, at least on a competitive basis. Moreover, the established culture may conflict with the claims of minority groups for cultural autonomy. Under these conditions, the accepted values of the university—including its norms defining the nature of competence and academic qualification—become contested political issues.

In thus extending their sphere of interest, influence, and involvement, American universities have gained neither clarity of purpose nor direction. They are not necessarily willing or able to assess the relative importance and value of their greatly extended interests, or the problematic character of certain of their own value premises and standards. Few would deny that the basic "service" the university offers to society is understanding and criticism. Yet the university's independence from outside agencies, political powers, and interest groups may be seriously compromised by the high cost of both education and research, which requires the university to seek financial support from the very groups which its scholars are obliged to study and criticize. As a recent study of university governance suggests:

> We have imperceptibly slumped into a posture in which the demands of external interests—strongly reinforced by economic lures, rewards of prestige and status, and other powerful resources which only those with power can marshall and wield—have increasingly dominated the ethos of the university and shaped the direction of its educational activities.[36]

The Fragmentation of University Interests

These basic problems in the relation of the university to the society at large are compounded by the development of different bases of interest and influence among the various segments of the university community. Put simply, the university barely resembles a community at all, if by community is meant a group sharing common interests and values. Given this fragmentation of interests, the university is unable to deal effectively with conflict, whether internal or external; it has been unable to develop new modes of governance in line with its increased and disparate commitments. Whether it *can* develop effective modes of governance while retaining its present commitments is a matter of considerable doubt. It is certain that it cannot do so without substantial alteration of its structure of power. This is evident from an analysis of the nature of the internal divisions within the university.

Trustees

The governing boards of colleges and universities vary greatly in composition, attitudes, and interests, depending on the type and quality of the institution. Nevertheless, a recent survey by the Educational Testing Service of over 5,000 college and university trustees sheds some light on the characteristics of trustees as a group. From these data, a troubling picture emerges; the trustees tend to be strikingly indifferent to academic values and uninformed about issues and problems in contemporary higher education, and very much convinced of the inappropriateness of student and faculty decision-making power on crucial academic issues.[37]

The average trustee is in his fifties; over 98 percent are white; over half have yearly incomes exceeding $30,000; over 35 percent are business executives. The majority regard themselves as politically "moderate." Their attitudes toward certain issues involving academic freedom reflect their frequent distance from campus concerns.

Over two thirds of the trustees surveyed, for example, advocate a screening process for campus speakers. Thirty-eight percent agreed that it is reasonable to require loyalty oaths from faculty. Twenty-seven percent *disagreed* with the statement that "faculty members have a right to free expression of opinions." Many trustees—especially those with business connections—agreed that running a university is "basically like running a business."

The attitudes of trustees concerning the location of university decision-making tend to be strongly at variance with those of many students and faculty. Trustees tend to feel that student decision-making, to the extent that it should exist at all, should concern only "traditional" student concerns such as fraternities and sororities, student housing regulations, and student cheating. Seventy percent of the trustees surveyed believed that students and faculty should not have major authority in choosing a university president; 64 percent felt that students and faculty should not have major authority on tenure decisions; 63 percent felt students and faculty should not have major authority in appointing an academic dean.

It should be stressed again that these attitudes vary considerably depending on the type of university represented. Still, the overall picture is inconsistent with a conception of the university as an integrated academic community. Distant in values and interests from most faculty and students, the average trustee has little conception of the problematic nature of campus issues. For that matter, as the ETS data make clear, most trustees rarely bother to remain well-informed about trends and problems in higher education; the vast majority have not read many major books on higher education, and are unfamiliar with most of the relevant periodicals.

Faculty and Administration

In using the term "multiversity," Clark Kerr indicates the fragmented character of the contemporary American institution of higher learning, its separation into specialized units united in nothing save connection to a central administration.[38] One important cause of this fragmentation is the development of professors and graduate students from generalists into specialists.[39] This process, made necessary by a veritable explosion of information in all fields of study, has resulted in a trend toward professionalism—that is, identifying oneself more with one's colleagues everywhere and less with one's local community. Increasingly, it is according to the demands of his field of study, not those of the local campus community, that a scholar's values, success, and acceptance are determined. Only a few universities, such as Harvard and Chicago, have traditions of sufficient prestige to assure the loyalty of their faculties. Then, too, the members of these faculties come from all over the world. In general, the prestige of any institution comes from the eminence of its individual scholars rather than from the mystique of the institution itself.[40]

This derivation of prestige from the faculty makes for an academic seller's market, with sellers whose interests are professional and national, if not international, and buyers whose interests are largely organizational and local. Such disparity of interests is a major source of conflict, in which the faculty opposition is more effective today than it has been in the past.[41] Whatever their sources, mistrust and animosity between faculties and administrations are very much in evidence at many American universities, and this hostility is very little assuaged by a sense of common commitment to the university as a repository of unique values and traditions.

Studies of student activists indicate that they have close ties to faculty; activists are not unknown and anonymous faces in the classroom.[42] But outside the classroom, faculty have little effect on rules governing student conduct. At Columbia there was no senate or single body in which the undergraduate faculty met regularly to consider policy of any kind. The distance of the faculty from decisions related to student life—especially the final say in disciplinary proceedings—has led to mistrust and resentment of administration by both students and segments of the faculty.

In most student confrontations and protest actions on campus, the administration is singled out as the target. Students tend to accept the premise that these officials can, at will, develop and carry out policies in major areas of political concern. For example, "new left" critiques of universities imply that research policy and use of government funds is largely a matter of administrative decision rather than of faculty desire. Yet the administration's capacity for controlling the content of faculty research is greatly limited by the universities' need for capable research personnel. At major institutions, significant portions of the faculty adopt a research-oriented perspective that stresses the requirements of their particular discipline. Appointments and promotions typically stress ability within the discipline, rather than teaching or university service. The result is that faculty tend to follow the reward structure, which they themselves have created.

University policy is usually arrived at by a series of compromises, committees, and balancings of interests. University officials are severely limited in both power and authority by faculty values and interests.

Faculty interests fail to generate bonds with the university as an institution. There is no definition of what the university "stands for" around which to rally the university "community" when crises occur. There are few shared criteria of university operation to which appeals can be made.

The lack of power or authority of administrators within their faculties makes the faculties in turn seem capricious and irresponsible while the administration seems intransigent and unresponsive. When officials do speak, it is difficult to know whether they represent faculty or students, trustees, or other interested parties. The "double-talk" and evasion about which students so often complain is a standard defense against clear commitments in situations where great constraints exist.

Students

The existence of powerful student movements has meant a significant increase in the power and influence of students on American campuses. Such power is not entirely new. Throughout the history of higher education in the United States, students have wielded some influence. At times they have developed activities which, while extracurricular, served as important sources of new educational content. Student culture, whether congruent or not with faculty or administrative goals, has influenced curriculum, university regulations, and policy through informal pressures.[43] But this influence has rarely amounted to genuine and formal participation in university governance. That students are beginning to be heard and considered in university policies is largely a result of the political activity and organization of students in recent years. Out of the agitation and activism of nonacademic issues, student power within academic and campus affairs has grown.

The activism of students may be seen as one response to situations in which student opinion and influence have been ignored in the administration of colleges and universities. Lacking effective representation for the expression and alleviation of grievances, students have resorted to more militant measures. In this sense, the character of contemporary student protest can be seen as one consequence of the lack of genuine political mechanisms within the university. As is the case with any social institution, where "normal channels" for participation and influence are underdeveloped, political action tends to take place outside those channels. In the process, hostility and conflict over the *style* of protest and response tends to displace substantive issues as the focus of concern.

It is particularly at this critical point that the fragmentation of interests within the university becomes most significant. A distant governing board, uncommitted to academic values, may invoke simplistic calls for order on the campus, perhaps backed by threats of punitive action. A managerial administration, under pressure and fearful of conservative community reaction, may respond to protest with force and bureaucratic intransigence. A faculty concerned with professionalism may retreat from serious involvement in the issues. Under these conditions, the university drifts further and further away from the possibility of constructive change.

Response to Student Protest

It should be clear that there are no programmatic solutions to the problems raised by contemporary campus conflict. As Morris B. Abram, President of Brandeis University, has recently observed, the mere application of conventional means of social control is a hopelessly inadequate response:

> Handling campus disruptions is a herculean task. University security forces are generally limited, and, historically, the use of outside police is abhorrent to the campus community and leads to a divisiveness that may be irreparable. Nor is it easy to apply conventional university disciplinary measures, especially harsh ones. Like the use of outside police, these tend to evoke sympathy for the offenders and escalate the problem. (This is especially true in the case of expulsion, which is tied up with draft deferment and which, because of student feeling toward the Vietnam war, is emotionally equated—morally and literally—with a death sentence.)
> Yet a community of several thousand people including a majority of young adults cannot survive without discipline and order . . . to attempt to maintain order, what courses are open to it? I see three:
> 1. The university can surrender to every whim to avoid confrontation—but if it does, it will not long be a place of excellence or, indeed, an institution of learning.
> 2. The university can resist by using outside force—which probably would result in it becoming both bitter and divided.
> 3. The university can attempt to set agreed limits as a community, and try internally to enforce this code. Such rules must originate primarily with the students and faculties. They must be a statement of necessities as seen by the persons to be governed, and they will, it is hoped, have an internal validity which makes them almost self-enforcing.[44]

In short, if order is to be restored to the university community, the university must first take major steps toward developing forms of governance appropriate to its increased implication in the wider social and political order. This involves attention to the delicate balance between the need for autonomy and the need for responsiveness to the surrounding community.

We have argued that the fundamental problems of the university lie in two directions: one external, in the university's erratic and unexamined excursions into the political order; the other internal, in a disputed and largely anachronistic structure of power and authority. It follows that an adequate response to campus conflict requires substantial alterations in both of these areas.

A thorough discussion of these matters is beyond the scope of this report, but a few general comments are appropriate.[45]

First, as we previously suggested, it seems doubtful that the university can expect a substantial reduction of conflict as long as it continues its present commitments to supplying research in certain politically contested areas. This is particularly true in the case of war-related government research. We have already indicated the complexity of the university's commitment to this kind of enterprise; it is not simply a question of administrative intransigence, but also of faculty interests and, therefore, involves issues of professional autonomy and academic freedom. Thus a demand for the removal of this kind of research from the campus is overly simplistic; but universities must develop means for assessing the relevance of such research to the values and purposes of an academic institution.

Second, if the university is to function academically, serious questions must be raised concerning its structure of power. Foremost is the problem of the attenuation of the university's autonomy from distant interests, as manifested in the location of decision-making power in the hands of trustees whose values and interests so frequently conflict with those of an academic community. Any serious attempt to come to grips with the issues raised by contemporary student protest must consider the problematic character of this form of governance. It may be that trustee government has lost its usefulness; as Riesman and Jencks have argued, boards of trustees "seem in many ways to cause more trouble than they are worth."[46] On the other hand, the answer may lie in the direction of structuring boards into closer accordance with the social and political makeup of the community as a whole. The overriding issue is whether an educational system can endure without the consent and support of faculty and students, and whether such higher authorities as trustees, boards of regents, and legislatures can expect tranquillity on a campus that is governed on controversial issues by remote authorities whose understanding of academic values is minimal and who are empowered to undercut academic and administrative decisions with which they disagree. Reform of the present condition of university governing boards is a prerequisite to campus order in the future.

Another prerequisite is the increased participation of students in university decision-making and policy-making. The inclusion of students in campus policy-making is a recognition that formal political means are necessary to provide adequate representation. It is neither realistic nor justifiable to expect contemporary students to remain content as second-class citizens within the university. When the university was less important, both in terms of its social and political significance and in terms of its decisive influence on the student's life-chances, such representation was correspondingly less critical. Today, the university—like other large social institutions—commands such critical importance in those areas that it has in effect made of students a new kind of group with new kinds of legitimate interests, and it must revise its structure of representation accordingly.

Similar considerations apply to the need for reformation of current disciplinary standards and procedures. Most of the disciplinary procedures in American universities were developed when students were themselves committed primarily to traditional roles; such procedures were designed to deal with the excesses of student highjinks. Issues of drinking, curfew hours for girls, cheating on examinations, and other aspects of housekeeping and student privacy were then major concerns before disciplinary boards.[47] When universities sought to promote "character education," and students were tied to the university by extracurricular bonds fashioned out of athletics and "student activities," a quasi-informal disciplinary body with vague standards and even vaguer procedures could nevertheless command the allegiance of students.

This concept of authority is fast becoming anachronistic in American higher education. In line with the changing character of the university, the basis of the internal legal order of the campus must undergo a difficult and complex transition from the concept of "discipline" to that of "due process." [48]

The development of workable internal mechanisms of order and justice is critical, since the alternative is recurrent outside intervention. The reduction of campus disorder seems unlikely unless universities possess the means to commit themselves decisively and consistently to the autonomous resolution of political disputes. Resort to force and the unleashing of official violence against student protesters is the clearest way for an administration to effectively destroy an academic community. In this regard, Daniel Bell has commented:

> It was SDS which initiated the violence at Columbia by insisting that the university was the microcosm of the society, and challenging its authority. After some confusion, the administration, in its actions, accepted this definition and sought to impose its authority on the campus by resorting to force. But in a community one cannot regain authority simply by asserting it, or by using force to suppress dissidents. Authority in this case is like respect. One can only *earn* the authority—the loyalty of one's students—by going in and arguing with them, by engaging in full debate and, when the merits of proposed change are recognized, taking the necessary steps quickly enough to be convincing.[49]

The remarks of a University of Chicago official after the recent student occupation of the University's administration building are instructive:

> We were prepared to lose that building or any other building by occupation or by arson right down to the last stone rather than surrender the university's ability to govern itself without the police, the courts, or the Guard.[50]

Particularly in the case of public universities, this kind of administrative response requires a similar commitment on the part of outside authorities to the value of campus self-governance. Nothing is more destructive of a university's efforts to resolve conflicts than simplistic demands for "law and order on the campus" and indiscriminate use of police and troops by public officials.[51]

A final issue is raised by the themes of Third World student protest. Again, we have no simple answers to the academic problems attendant on the thrust toward cultural autonomy and educational self-determination. It is clear that a simple call for campus autonomy does not adequately encompass these problems. As we suggested previously, Third World protest is at bottom a *community* protest, aimed toward the extension of the resources and services of the university to new communities and on new terms. In a perceptive comment on the meaning of the Columbia gymnasium dispute, Roger Starr writes:

> The question asked of the Columbia gymnasium by the most potent of its adversaries is whether a gymnasium incorporating the standards of Ivy League sport and physical training is *relevant* to the needs of the people who live nearest it. And if the gymnasium is not, as they put it, "relevant," can the institution itself be relevant? When Columbia faculty and administrators are asked why there are so few (reportedly, six) Negro faculty members, the answer comes back that it is hard to find qualified faculty. The militants then pose the question as to whether the qualifications should not be adjusted to the human candidates, not merely by lowering the standards for acceptance, but by changing the taught subject matter, changing the curriculum, changing the student body, changing—perhaps entirely—the value system of the university. Perhaps, in the atmosphere of the new cities, a university must become an educational institution with wholly different aims: to teach race pride, applied sociology, pedagogic reform, small business techniques, revolutionary strategy.[52]

These issues transcend the university; they involve the larger questions of race, culture, and power in America. Accordingly, in the following chapter we examine the meaning of black protest in the 1960's.

Chapter IV
Black Militancy

WE BEGIN this chapter with a number of misgivings. This is by no means the first official commission to investigate violent aspects of black protest in America. On the contrary, official treatments of the "racial problem" may be found far back in American history, and official investigations of racial violence have been with us since 1919.[1] Occasionally, these investigations have unequivocally condemned the participants in racial disorder, both black and white, while neglecting the importance of their grievances. More often, their reports have stressed that the resort to violence is understandable, given a history of oppression and racial discrimination. All of these reports, nevertheless, have insisted that violence cannot be tolerated in a democratic society. Some have called for far-reaching programs aimed at ending discrimination and racism; all have called for more effective riot control. None of them appear to have appreciably affected the course of the American racial situation.

The cycle of protest and response continues. Violence occurs; it is again investigated, again understood, and again deplored.

There are grounds for skepticism, therefore, concerning yet another report on black militancy. And we are faced with a number of more specific problems. Our subject is too vast and complex to the dealt with adequately in a single chapter. Black protest cannot be properly studied apart from the larger political and social structure and trends of American society. We have not been able to do a measurable amount of field research (although we have done some interviewing) due to time limitations and also to the suspicion with which this Commission is viewed by many militant black leaders. Finally, it is difficult to add much to the recent and exhaustive Kerner Report.

Consequently, our analysis is limited to certain specific issues. We have avoided generalizations about the "racial problem" and its solutions. Those wishing to understand the broad social and economic conditions of black Americans, and the kinds of massive programs needed to remedy those conditions, should look to the Kerner Report and to the vast body of literature on the subject. Much of this has been said before, and we see little point in saying it again. Our general aim, rather, is to examine the events of the past several years to understand why many black Americans believe it increasingly necessary to employ, or envision, violent means of effecting social change.

This chapter is divided into three main sections. In the first, we examine the interaction between black protest and governmental response which caused many participants in the civil rights movement to reject traditional political processes. Our analysis considers the importance of anti-colonialism in providing new meaning and ideological substance for contemporary black protest. We have found it particularly important to stress that, for many black militants, racial problems are international in scope, transcending the domestic issue of civil rights. The urban riots have been a second major influence on contemporary militancy, and this section concludes with an analysis of the meaning of riots for the black community and for black organizations.

The second section considers some major themes in contemporary black protest, and examines their origins in the history of black protest in America, the anti-colonial movement, and the present social situation of black Americans. Many of these themes are most clearly expressed in the actions of militant youths in the schools. The final part of this section analyzes the nature and extent of this increasingly significant youth protest.

We conclude with an analysis of the extent and direction of ghetto violence since the publication of the Kerner Report, and the future implications of the political response to that violence.

Two related points should be understood. First, this chapter does not attempt to encompass the entire spectrum of black protest in America. Rather, it is concerned with new forms of political militancy that have recently assumed increasing importance in black communities. Its general outlines are fairly clear, even though, as we write, new militant perspectives are being generated. We regard what follows as an *introduction* to a phenomenon whose importance has been inadequately appreciated.

Second, it is important to keep the violent aspects of black protest in perspective. The connection between black militancy and collective violence is complex and ambiguous. There has so far been relatively little violence by militant blacks in this country—as compared to nonviolent black protest—despite the popular impression conveyed by the emphasis of the news media on episodes of spectacular violence (or threats of violence). This is true historically, and it is largely true for the contemporary situation. It must also be remembered that much of the violence involving blacks has originated with militant whites (in the case of the early race riots and the civil rights movement) or from police and troops (in the case of the recent ghetto riots). On the other hand, we cannot be optimistic about the future. Recent developments clearly indicate that black Americans are no longer willing to wait for governmental action to determine their fate. At the same time, we find little that is reassuring in the character of the present governmental response to black protest. We can only agree with the Kerner Commission that "this nation will deserve neither safety nor progress unless it can demonstrate the wisdom and the will to undertake decisive action against the root causes of racial disorder." [2]

The Roots of Contemporary Militancy

Those who profess to favor freedom, and yet deprecate agitation, are men who want crops without plowing up the ground.[3]

FREDERICK DOUGLASS

You show me a black man who isn't an extremist and I'll show you one who needs psychiatric attention.[4]

MALCOLM X

Black men in America have always engaged in militant action. The first permanent black settlers in the American mainland, brought by the Spanish explorer Lucas Vasquez de Ayllon in 1526, rose up during the same year, killed a number of whites, and fled to the Indians.[5] Since that time, black protest has never been altogether dormant, and militant blacks have experimented with a wide variety of tactics, ideologies, and goals. No simple linear or evolutionary model covers the complexity of those developments.[6]

It is inaccurate, for example, to suggest that black protest has moved from peaceful use of orderly political and legal processes to disorderly protest and, finally, to rejection of nonviolent means. Leaving aside the history of Southern slave insurrections,[7] a number of black writers before the Civil War called for violent action. David Walker, in his *An Appeal to the Coloured Citizens of the World* (1829), called white Americans "our natural enemies" and exhorted blacks to "kill or be killed." [8] The abolitionist Frederick Douglass, discussing the kidnapping of escaped slaves and their return to the South under the Fugitive Slave Act, argued that "the only way to make the fugitive slave law a dead letter, is to make half a dozen or more dead kidnappers." In supporting John Brown's armed raid at Harpers Ferry, Douglass advocated the use of any and all means to secure freedom: "Let every man work for the abolition of slavery in his own way. I would help all, and hinder none." [9] There is a remarkable similarity between Douglass' statement and the more recent dictum of Malcolm X: "Our objective is complete freedom, complete justice, complete equality, by any means necessary." [10]

At the same time, the use of legal argument and of the ballot is far from dead in the contemporary black protest movement. The history of black protest is the history of the temporary decline, fall, and resurgence of almost every conceivable means of achieving black well-being and dignity within the context of a generally hostile polity, and in the face of unremitting white violence, both official and private. Where black protest has moved toward the acceptance of violence, it has done so after exhausting nonviolent alternatives and a profound reservoir of patience and good faith.

This is the case today. In this section, we examine the events leading up to the most recent shift in the general direction of militant black protest—the shift from a "civil rights" to a "liberation" perspective.

Civil Rights and the Decline of Faith

From the decline of Garveyism [11] in the 1920's until quite recently, the dominant thrust of black protest was toward political, social, economic, and cultural inclusion into American institutions on a basis of full equality. Always a powerful theme in American black militancy, these aims found their maximum expression in the civil rights movement of the 1950's and early 1960's. Today, these aims, while actively pursued by a segment of militant blacks, are no longer at the forefront of contemporary militancy. Several features of this transition stand out:

1. The civil rights movement was largely directed at the South, especially against state and local laws and practices, and, in general, it saw the federal government and courts as allies in the struggle for equality. The new movement for black liberation, while nationwide in scope, is primarily centered in the black communities of the North and West, and is generally antagonistic to both local and federal governments.

2. The civil rights movement was directed against explicit and customary forms of racisim, as manifested in Jim Crow restrictions on the equal use of facilities of transportation, public accommodations, and the political process. The libera-

tion movement focuses on deeper and more intractable sources of racism in the structure of American institutions, and stresses independence rather than integration.

3. The civil rights movement was largely middle-class and interracial. The liberation movement attempts to integrate middle- and lower-class elements in rejection of white leadership.

4. The civil rights movement was guided by the concepts of nonviolence and passive resistance. The liberation movement stresses self-defense and freedom by any means necessary.

For the civil rights movement, the years before 1955 were filled largely with efforts at legal reform, with the NAACP, especially, carrying case after case to successful litigation in the federal courts. Among the results were the landmark decisions in *Shelly v. Kraemer*,[12] striking down restrictive covenants in housing, and the series of cases leading up to *Brown v. Board of Education*,[13] declaring that the doctrine of "separate but equal" was inherently discriminatory in the public schools. The Supreme Court directed Southern school jurisdictions to desegregate "with all deliberate speed," but in the following years little changed in the South. The great majority of black children remained in segregated and markedly inferior schools; blacks sat in the back of the bus, ate in segregated facilities, and were politically disenfranchised through the white primary and the poll tax. Southern courts and police continued to act as an extension of white caste interests. Established civil rights organizations, lulled by judicial success in the federal courts, lapsed into a state of relative inactivity.[14] There was a considerable gap, however, between the belief of the NAACP and other groups that major political changes were in sight and the reality of the slow pace of change even in the more "advanced" areas of the South. The gap was even greater between the conservative tactics and middle-class orientation of the established civil rights organizations and the situation of the black ghetto masses in the North.

Since the NAACP, the Urban League, and other established groups continued to operate as before, new tactics and new leaders arose to fill these gaps. In 1955, Mrs. Rosa Parks of Montgomery, Alabama, refused to give up her bus seat to a white man, and a successful boycott of the bus system materialized, led by the Reverend Martin Luther King, Jr. Around the same time, with less publicity, another kind of organization with another kind of leadership was coming into its own in the Northern ghettos. Elijah Muhammad and the Nation of Islam gained wide support among those segments of the black community that no one else, at the moment, was representing: the Northern, urban, lower classes.

Neither the direct-action, assimilationist approach of the Reverend Dr. King nor the separatist and nationalist theme of the Nation of Islam was new. Both were traditional themes which had been adopted in response to specific situations. Direct action was used by the abolitionists prior to the Civil War,[15] by left-wing ghetto organizers in the 1930's, and by CORE in the early 1940's; it had been threatened by A. Philip Randolph in his March on Washington in 1941, but called off when President Roosevelt agreed to establish a Federal Fair Employment Practices Commission.[16] The roots of separatism are equally deep, beyond Marcus Garvey to Martin Delaney and the American Colonization Society in the eighteenth century.[17]

The move to direct action in the South brought civil rights protest out of the courts and into the streets, bus terminals, restaurants, and voting booths, substituting "creative disorder"[18] for litigation. Nevertheless, it remained deeply linked to the American political process and represented an innate faith in the protective power of the federal government and in the moral capacity of white Americans, both Northern and Southern. It operated, for the most part, on the implicit premise that racism was a localized malignancy within a relatively healthy political and social order; it was a move to force American morality and American institutions to root out the last vestiges of the "disease."

Nowhere were these premises more explicit than in the thought and practice of Martin Luther King, Jr. Nonviolence was for him a philosophical issue rather than the tactical or strategic question it posed for many younger activists in SNCC and CORE.[19] The aim was "to awaken a sense of moral shame in the opponent."[20] Such a philosophy presumed that the opponent had moral shame to awaken, and that moral shame, if awakened, would suffice. During the 1960's many civil rights activists came to doubt the first and deny the second. The reasons for this did not lie primarily in white Southern terrorism as manifested in the killing of NAACP leader Medgar Evers, of three civil rights workers in Neshoba County, Mississippi, of four little girls in a dynamited church in Birmingham, and many others. To a large extent, white Southern violence was anticipated and expected.[21] What was not expected was the absence of strong protective action by the federal government.

Activists in SNCC and CORE met with greater and more violent Southern resistance as direct action continued during the sixties. Freedom Riders were beaten by mobs in Montgomery; demonstrators were hosed, clubbed and cattle-prodded in Birmingham and Selma. Throughout the South, civil rights workers, black and white, were victimized by local officials as well as by night-riders and angry crowds. It was not surprising, then, that student activists in the South became increasingly disillusioned with nonviolent tactics of resistance. Following the shotgun murder in 1966 of Sammy Younge, Jr., a black civil rights activist at Tuskegee Institute, his fellow students organized a protest march:

> We had no form, which was beautiful. We had no pattern, which was beautiful. People were just filling the streets, and they weren't singing no freedom songs. They were mad. People would try and strike up a freedom song, but it wouldn't work. All of a sudden you heard this, "Black Power, Black Power." People felt what was going on. They were tired of this whole nonviolent bit. They were tired of this organized demonstration-type thing. They were going to do something.[22]

Despite the passage of civil rights legislation and legal support for integration, Southern courts continued to apply caste standards of justice. Official violence of the past—beating, shooting, and lynching—was supplemented and sometimes replaced by official violations of the law. Judges, prosecutors, and local bar officials explicitly attempted to suppress the civil rights movement, without any pretense of harmonizing

competing interests within the ambit of the law.[23] Many celebrated aspects of democracy, the jury system, for instance,
worked to maintain terrorist racism instead of prosecuting
and punishing it. In the same manner the constitutional inhi-
bitions on federal intrusion into state sovereignty became
from the black viewpoint a mockery of democracy instead of
a keystone.

The problems of white violence and Southern judicial intransigence were compounded by political constraints on the
federal government, such that it failed to move decisively toward radically altering the Southern situation.

White liberals and government officials did not deny the legitimacy of the activist's claims; on the contrary, they affirmed them. Nevertheless, in practice, field operatives of the
government, especially agents of the FBI, were accused of
vacillation, particularly in protecting civil rights workers.
"Maintaining law and order," said a Justice Department
official, "is a State responsibility." [24] Later, in the aftermath
of ghetto riots and riot commissions, militants were to ask
why law and order was a state responsibility when white
Southerners rioted, but a problem needing massive federal intervention when black Northerners did. At the time, many
activists—and even some "established" members of older organizations—began questioning the integrity of a government
which praised its own sponsorship of civil rights legislation
while failing to challenge Southern violence.

The deepest or most entrenched meaning of racism began
to emerge, and it made considerable sociological as well as
historic sense: a society that has been built around racism
will lack the capacity, the flexibility, the institutions to combat it when the will to change belatedly appears. The major
American institutions had developed standards, procedures,
and rigidities which served to inhibit the Negro's drive for
equality. It was as if a cruel joke had been played; the most
liberally enshrined features of democracy served to block the
aspirations to equality—local rule, trade unionism, referen-
dums, the jury system, the neighborhood school. And to complete the irony, perhaps, the most elitist aspect of the constitutional system—the Supreme Court—was for a time the cut-

ting edge of the established quest for equality, for which it came under considerable populist fire.

At the March on Washington in 1963, John Lewis of SNCC voiced the growing lack of enthusiasm for more civil rights bills. "This bill will not protect young children and old women from police dogs and fire hoses for engaging in peaceful demonsrations . . ." [25] Federal policy also began to show less enthusiasm for the civil rights movement. Federal government officials were often unable to obtain a strong popular or congressional consensus, even for their moderate efforts at enforcement, and responded accordingly. In Albany, Georgia, the federal government prosecuted civil rights demonstrators who picketed a local grocery, while local police officials who attacked and severely beat the demonstrators were not prosecuted under available federal law.[26] Events like these led many militants to ask, with Lewis, "Whose side is the government on?" [27] Howard Zinn wrote:

> The simple and harsh fact, made clear in Albany, and reinforced by events in Americus, Georgia, in Selma, and Gadsden, Alabama, in Danville, Virginia, and in every town in Mississippi, is that the federal government abdicated its responsibility in the Black Belt. The Negro citizens of that area were left to the local police. The U.S. Constitution was left in the hands of Neanderthal creatures who cannot read it, and whose only response to it has been to grunt and swing their clubs.[28]

Even many moderates agreed with the Urban League's Whitney Young that the government was "reacting and not acting" [29] in the drive for Negro rights. Activists who had been in the South were inclined to agree with a white observer that the American government seemed "uncommitted emotionally and ideologically to racial equality as a first-level value." [30] In 1963, some civil rights workers were beginning to lose faith in that government and in the major political parties. "We cannot depend on any political party, for both the Democrats and the Republicans have betrayed the basic principles of the Declaration of Independence." [31]

Faith in the political process, and especially in the traditional alliance between blacks and the liberal elements in the

Democratic Party, suffered another blow in the failure to seat the Mississippi Freedom Democratic Party delegation at the 1964 Democratic convention.[32] The MFDP represented both a rejection of Southern white-only Democratic politics and a fundamental belief in the good offices of liberal Democrats, whose compromise offer of two seats among the regular Mississippi delegation was seen as an insult.

The MFDP episode climaxed a growing disillusionment with the white liberal. As a black commentator wrote in 1962, "Negroes are dismayed as they observe that liberals, even when they are in apparent control, not only do not rally their organizations for an effective role in the fight against discrimination, but even tolerate a measure of racial discrimination in their own jurisdictions." [33] The recognition that civil rights laws would not suffice to bring blacks into full equality in American society furthered the search for more intractable causes of disadvantage in American institutions. Militants begin to examine the reasons why discriminatory practices remained in such traditionally "liberal" institutions as labor organizations, schools, and civil service. The liberal's motives became suspect. Suspicion extended to another traditionally "friendly" institution—academic social science, and its representatives in the federal welfare "establishment." The Moynihan Report, which many blacks took as an affront, was interpreted as an attempt to place the blame for continued discrimination in the Negro community and not on the structure of racism.[34]

The increased criticism of liberals, academics, and federal bureaucracies was part of a broader turn to a renewed critique of the situation of blacks in the North. To a large extent, and despite such evidence as the Harlem uprisings of 1935 and 1943, most white Northerners had congratulated themselves on the quality of their "treatment" of the Negro vis-à-vis that of the South. But with the explosion of Harlem again—along with several other Northern cities—in 1964, attention began shifting to the problem of institutional racism in the North, and this shift was accelerated by the Watts riot the following year. In a real sense, the riots surprised not only liberal and academic whites, but civil rights leaders as well. While undermining the moral credibility of liberal

Northerners, the riots deprived most civil rights leaders of a vocabulary for expressing the deeper problems of the Northern ghettos. There was a widespread sense that civil rights leaders either could not or would not speak to the kinds of issues raised by the riots, and that a wide gulf separated those leaders—mostly of middle-class background—from the black urban masses. During the 1964 Harlem riot, for example, Bayard Rustin and other established civil rights leaders were booed and shouted down at rallies and in the streets, while crowds shouted for Malcolm X.[35]

By the mid-1960's, then, civil rights activists had petitioned the federal government and the white liberals and found them wanting. They also found themselves increasingly out of touch with the vocal ghetto masses. At the same time, another issue began to emerge. Militants began to ask whether there was not a contradiction between the lack of action at home and American commitments overseas: "How is it that the government can protect the Vietnamese from the Viet Cong and the same government will not accept the moral responsibility of protecting people in Mississippi?" [36]

For some blacks, this contradictory performance further indicated the government's lack of concern for the Negro. In 1965, the McComb branch of the Mississippi Freedom Democratic Party issued a leaflet which caught the mood of disillusionment and suspicion:

> 1. No Mississippi Negroes should be fighting in Vietnam for the White Man's freedom, until all the Negro people are free in Mississippi. . . .
> 2. No one has a right to ask us to risk our lives and kill other colored people in Santo Domingo and Vietnam, so that the white American can get richer. . . . We don't know anything about Communism, Socialism, and all that, but we do know that Negroes have caught hell right here under this American Democracy.[37]

Concern with the war and its implications for black people intensified along with the war itself. In January, 1966, SNCC issued a statement on Vietnam:

> We believe the United States government has been deceptive in claims of concern for the freedom of the Vietnamese

people, just as the government has been deceptive in claiming concern for the freedom of colored people in such other countries as the Dominican Republic, the Congo, South Africa, Rhodesia, and in the United States itself.

We of the Student Nonviolent Coordinating Committee have been involved in the black people's struggle for liberation and self-determination in this country for the past five years. Our work, particularly in the South, taught us that the United States government has never guaranteed the freedom of oppressed citizens and is not yet truly determined to end the rule of terror and oppression within its own borders.[38]

A few months later, when Stokely Carmichael of SNCC brought the new direction of civil rights activists into the public eye with the slogan of "Black Power," it became clear that a shift of major importance had occurred.

This change of direction away from the established political process toward a critique of larger American policy at home and abroad did not occur in a vacuum. The civil rights movement had been organized on an assumption of the responsiveness of American institutions and especially of the federal government. As these assumptions were viewed more critically, as the movement began looking at the North as well as at the South, and as it became clear that racism was not simply a localized phenomenon confined to the Southern bigot, activists began to look harder in two directions: inward toward the social structure of the urban ghetto and the increasing protests of those caught within it, and outward toward American foreign policy and to the emerging anti-colonial movement. In looking inward to the urban ghetto, many civil rights activists met and merged with the voices of black, Northern, urban, lower-class protest. In looking toward the anti-colonial struggle, black militants acquired a new conception of their role in the world and new models of collective action.

The Impact of Anti-Colonialism [39]

Throughout most of the past century the world was dominated by whites. The domination was political, economic, social, and cultural; it involved nothing less than the reclassification of the majority of the world's population as somewhat less than human. "Not very long ago, the earth numbered two thousand million inhabitants; five hundred million men, and one thousand five hundred million natives." [40]

Today this is no longer true. The great majority of lands formerly under colonial domination have gained at least formal autonomy. The impact of this development has yet to be completely assessed, but it is clear that no discussion of the character of racial conflict in America can ignore it.

Black militants in America have frequently looked to Africa for recognition of common origins and culture, and the influence has been reciprocal. W. E. B. DuBois saw that the "problem of the color line" was international in scope and was a guiding force behind the movement for Pan-African unity. The ideas of Marcus Garvey and other American and West Indian black nationalists stimulated the development of African nationalism and informed the intellectual development of such African leaders as Kwame Nkrumah.[41] The successful revolt against colonialism in Africa and other non-white regions has created, in many American black militants, a heightened sense of the international character of racial conflict. Beyond this, it has stimulated a reexamination of the nature of the American racial situation and of the links between black subordination in Africa and in the United States. As LeRoi Jones has put it: "The kind of unity I would like to see among black Americans is a unity that would permit most of them to understand that the murder of Patrice Lumumba in the Congo and the murder of Medgar Evers were conducted by the same people." [42] Jones' analysis reflects an undeniable fact—that the situation of black men everywhere has been conditioned by the expansion of white European politics, commerce, and culture over several hundred years. By defining nonwhites and their beliefs as inferior, wherever they were found, white domination laid the groundwork for the current international consciousness of common interest among blacks. "The Negroes of Chicago," wrote Frantz Fanon, "only resemble the Nigerians or the Tanganyikans in so far as they were all defined in relation to the whites." [43]

The revolt against colonialism has affected American black protest in three ways. It has substantially overthrown the image of blacks as people without culture or history; it has created a host of new states run by nonwhites, whose influence in the world increases daily; and it has provided attractive models of ideology and action.

Culture

Colonialism operates on several different levels: as a political order, an economic system, and a set of cultural arrangements. In conjunction with its political and economic aims, colonialism attempted to deny, depreciate, or destroy indigenous cultures. The revolt against colonialism, therefore, is in part a revolt against cultural dispossession.

The white man's intervention in Africa and Asia was rationalized as a "civilizing mission." Thought to be lacking in history and culture, and certainly lacking in Christianity, "natives" were held to be in desperate need of cultural and spiritual tending. Colonialism was not entirely a system of raw exploitation; it is better conceived as "an association of the philanthropic, the pious, and the profitable." [44] Like all philanthropy, the colonial concern for the native was predicated on the idea of the social and sometimes innate inferiority of the recipient vis-à-vis the donor. "The nonexistence of Negro achievements was fundamental to colonial ideology." [45] The conception of Africa as a land peopled by cultureless savages was fostered by colonialism and elevated to scientific status in the doctrines of "scientific racism." It was assimilated by many American Negroes, who were inclined to look down on their African origins and to minimize their connection with the "Dark Continent." [46]

These conceptions of black culture and of Africa had been attacked by scholars like Basil Davidson and Melville Herskovits prior to the Second World War. Herskovits, arguing that their acceptance functioned only to justify racial prejudice, exhaustively demonstrated the sophistication of early African religious, political, and economic systems, showing them to have been comparable in complexity to European society at the same period in history. He placed special emphasis on the link between black culture in America and in Africa. Nevertheless, the conception of the Negro as "a man without a past" [47] dominated racial contacts here and abroad, and the denial that blacks possessed anything of cultural value shaped many aspects of colonial policy.

The assimilationist policy of the French, Portuguese, and Belgian colonial administrations allowed black men to attain legal rights by becoming as nearly white, in culture and manner, as possible, Thus the advancement of blacks to full legal rights in Portuguese colonies, for example, meant taking a test to prove that the candidate had transcended his cultural origins.[48] These arrangements, and the white cultural hegemony which they reflected, have obvious parallels in the American situation, and their effects cut deeply into the self-image of blacks. The rejection of color, hair and facial features could be found wherever these policies against black people developed, in Brazil and in West Africa as well as Chicago.[49] "The first attempt of the colonized is to change his condition by changing his skin." [50]

A limited rebellion against this cultural and historical dispossession has long been an undercurrent of black protest in America and Africa. The concept of black self-affirmation which was present in Garveyism and Pan-Africanism came alive in the post-World War II drive for African independence. This resulted in part from the limitations of assimilationist policy itself. "The candidate for assimilation almost always comes to tire of the exorbitant price which he must pay and which he never finishes owing." [51] The thrust toward black self-affirmation was also encouraged by questioning the monolithic character of European culture and values: ". . . as time went on, African intellectuals began to ask . . . why it should automatically be assumed that it is an unadulterated virtue to accept Western values." [52]

The assault on the dominance of Western culture was deeply implicated in the quest for political independence from white rule. After the Second World War, African nationalist movements began a process of reconstruction of African history and reevaluation of African culture which continues today. Much scholarship is devoted to charting and analyzing the growth of early African civilizations, and affirming their high level of cultural and technological development. The strength of these efforts at cultural reconstruction reflects the pervasiveness of white stereotypes of black inferiority. Cultural autonomy is important because it has only been recently and precariously attained.

Nevertheless, the cultural impetus of anti-colonialism has substantially reversed for many blacks, especially for the new militants, the negative stereotypes which suffused Western thought for centuries and which still linger in white conceptions of black culture and black achievements. The significance of black independence is inestimable. If nothing else, it has involved a reappraisal by American black militants of the potential of nonwhites, and hence of themselves. Malcolm X, a central figure in promoting the new international outlook of American black militancy, found himself deeply moved by the very existence of a technological society in Egypt: "I believe what most surprised me was that in Cairo, automobiles were being manufactured, and also buses. . . ." [53] "I can't tell you the feeling it gave me. I had never seen a black man flying a jet." [54]

Power

The successful revolt against colonialism has changed the structure of power in the world, and this fact has not been lost on black militants in America. It demonstrated that peoples supposed to be culturally and technologically "backward" can triumph over ostensibly superior powers; and it has developed in many militants a consciousness that, in global terms, nonwhites represent the majority.

Successful anti-colonial movements are evidence that the military and technological supremacy of the major Western powers is incapable of containing movements for national liberation. The eventual victories of such movements in Algeria and Kenya, and the inability of a massive and costly American effort to deflect the course of the national liberation movement in Vietnam, are not lost on American blacks. If nothing else, these facts demonstrate that should urban insurgency come to this country, it would require a massive and frustrating effort to control, at enormous costs to all involved. Perhaps above all, the aura of invulnerability which may have surrounded the technologically powerful white nations has substantially crumbled: "Two-thirds of the human population today," wrote Malcolm X, "is telling the one-third minority white man, 'Get out.' And the white man is leaving." [55]

Perhaps most significantly, the recognition that whites are an international minority necessarily changes the meaning for many black militants of their national minority position. Malcolm X emphasized this point repeatedly: "There are whites in this country who are still complacent when they see the possibilities of racial strife getting out of hand. You are complacent simply because you think you outnumber the racial minority in this country; what you have to bear in mind is wherein you might outnumber us in this country, you don't outnumber us all over the earth." [56]

Beyond the question of mere numbers, the political and technological achievements of nonwhite countries produce a sense of pride and optimism: "For the Negro in particular, it has been a stirring experience to see whole societies and political systems come into existence in which from top to bottom . . . all posts are occupied by black men, not because of the sufferance of white superiors but because it is their sovereign right." [57]

American Negroes across the political spectrum, according to one observer, uniformly showed a certain amount of pride in response to the successful explosion of a nuclear device by China.[58] Again, the partial identification with Oriental nations is not completely new; there were elements of ambivalence among some Negroes about fighting the "colored" Japanese in World War II.[59] What is new is the sense of pride in the growing power of the nonwhite nations.

There were four African and three Asian nations in the UN in 1945; twenty years later there were thirty-six African and fifteen Asian countries represented.[60] The rise of these new states, especially when coupled with the exigencies of Cold War diplomacy, has meant that since World War II American leaders have been well aware that the way blacks are treated at home has important ramifications for world affairs. A number of American black militants have looked to the UN specifically as an arena for bringing black grievances before the world. Malcolm X urged African leaders to bring up the plight of Afro-Americans in UN meetings [61] and urged American Negro leaders to visit nonwhite countries, where they "would find that many nonwhite officials of the highest standing, especially Africa, would tell them—privately—that they would be glad to throw their weight behind the Negro cause, in the UN and in other ways." [62] As colonialism disappears, the previously unquestioned authority of the white world likewise disintegrates, and with it the capacity of a predominantly white society to maintain its privileges. Black militants are aware of this, and recognize the impact it may have: ". . . the first thing the American power structure doesn't want any Negroes to start," wrote Malcolm X, "is thinking internationally." [63]

Politics, Ideology, and Violence

Anti-colonialism provided, directly or indirectly, a cultural resurgence and a sense of international influence among American blacks. It also provided new models of ideology and action which, with greater or lesser relevance, could be applied to the American situation. Two themes especially stand out: the politicization of conflict and the redefinition of the meaning and uses of violence.

White domination of nonwhites shared with other forms of political domination an attempt to define the situation in non-political terms. In Africa, as previously suggested, political domination was cloaked in philanthropic or religious sanctions. As a result, early expressions of anti-colonial conflict tended to take forms which were not explicitly political:

> Every colonial administration has aimed at establishing a depoliticized regime or has emphasized maximum depoliticization of all the expressions of native life. . . . Consequently, political reactions against the colonial situation were expressed indirectly at first, for example, through new syncretist religious movements loaded with revolutionary implications.[64]

Again, the American parallels are not hard to find. Black religious movements of this kind—best typified by the Nation of Islam—have generally drawn recruits from the most oppressed sectors of the American black population.[65]

The success of the movements for political independence in the colonial countries required a recognition that the plight of the "native" was a political problem, and that political action was the most effective vehicle of major social change. Early nationalist movements in Africa, therefore, sought to turn nearly every aspect of life into a political issue.[66] This was especially true of the area of culture. The quests for political and for cultural autonomy had a reciprocal influence; the rebuilding of culture served as a basis of political organization. The political importance of culture lay in the fact that "natives," as people without history or culture, were also seen as people without political claims of their own, and therefore as people to be dealt with from above—benevolently or otherwise. Black culture was—and still remains—a "contested culture"[67] whose very existence is a political issue of the greatest importance, in the United States as in Africa.[68]

Through the same process of politicization, instances of black resistance in history were redefined as precursors of contemporary political struggles. "Native" crime was redefined as early revolutionary activity; instances of rebellion were sought in the past and their significance amplified.[69]

In viewing history as an arena of white violence and native resistance, the anti-colonial perspective stressed the intrinsically violent character of colonial domination. Colonialism was seen as dependent on the routinization of violence, both physical and psychological, against the native. Consequently, revolutionary violence against the colonial regime was deemed not only necessary, but justifiable, on both political and psychological grounds. Colonialism, wrote Frantz Fanon, "is violence in its natural state, and it will only yield when confronted with greater violence."[70] Further, "at the level of individuals, violence is a cleansing force. It frees the native from his inferiority complex, and from his despair and inaction; it makes him fearless and restores self-respect."[71]

Anti-colonial writers defined the situation of nonwhites as one of subordination under a political, social, economic, and cultural order intrinsically hostile to the interests of nonwhites, and therefore not susceptible to change through orderly political processes; "revolt is the only way out of the colonial situation, and the colonized realizes it sooner or later. His condition is absolute and calls for an absolute solution; a break and not a compromise."[72] The rejection of compromise meant a corresponding rejection of the native middle class, which was seen as parasitical, timid, and generally antagonistic to the struggle of the native masses for liberation.[73] The motive force of the anti-colonial revolution, for these writers, lay in the *lumpenproletariat* of the cities. Through revolutionary violence, Fanon wrote, "these workless less-than-men are rehabilitated in their own eyes and in the eyes of history." [74]

The Impact of Riots

Although it is difficult to assess accurately the various influences on contemporary black militancy, the Northern urban riots are surely important. Whereas anti-colonialism provided, directly or indirectly, a model of cultural identity and a sense of international influence, riots both dramatized the failure of the American polity to fulfill the expectations of the civil rights movement, and demonstrated the gap between black leaders and the prevailing sentiments of their constituencies.[75] The urban riots, then, have had important consequences for black leaders as well as for governmental action. Newer and younger faces and organizations have emerged in recent years to represent the interests of the urban lower classes, and the older representatives of the civil rights movement have been required to redefine their political programs to accommodate these new forms of militancy. A recent statement by Sterling Tucker, Director of Field Services of the National Urban League, indicates that established black leaders are well aware of the new militancy:

> I was standing with some young, angry men not far from some blazing buildings. They were talking to me about their feelings. They talked out of anger, but they talked with respect.
> "Mr. Tucker," one of them said, "you're a big and important man in this town. You're always in the newspaper and we know that you're fighting hard to bring about some changes in the conditions the brother faces. But who listens, Mr. Tucker, who listens? Why, with one match I can bring about more change tonight than with all the talking you can ever do."

Now I know that isn't true and you know that isn't true. It
just isn't that simple. But the fact that we know that doesn't
really count for much. The brother on the street believes
what he says, and there are some who are not afraid to die,
believing what they say.[76]

The "Riffraff" Theory

Until recently, riots were regarded as the work of either
outsiders or criminals. The "riffraff" theory, as it is known,
has three assumptions—that a small minority of the black
population engages in riot activity, that this minority is composed of the unattached, uprooted, and unskilled, and that
the overwhelming majority of the black population deplores
riots.[77] This theory helps to dramatize the criminal character
of riots, to undermine their political implications, and to uphold the argument that social change is possible only through
lawful and peaceful means. If riots can be partly explained as
the work of a few agitators or hoodlums, it is then much easier to engage wide support in repudiating violent methods of
social protest.

Official investigations generally publicize the fact that normal, ordinary, and law-abiding persons do not instigate riots.
According to the FBI, riots are typically instigated by a
"demagogue or professional agitator" or by "impulsive and
uninhibited individuals who are the first in the mob to take
violent action or to keep it going when it wanes." [78] Thus,
"hoodlums" were responsible for the 1943 riot in Detroit,
"marauding bands" of criminals in Watts, "a small fraction
of the city's black population" in Chicago in 1968, and "self-
appointed leaders, opportunists, and other types of activists"
in Pittsburgh.[79] The recent Chicago Commission noted that
the riot was an "excuse for lawlessness, destruction and violence" on the part of some "leaders and followers." They also
suggested that "irresponsible advocates are encouraging the
black youth of this city to join in a wholesale rejection of our
national traditions, our public institutions, our common goals
and way of life. Advocates of black racism encourage political rebellion in the place of political participation, violence in
the stead of non-violence, and conflict rather than cooperation." [80] Implicit in the "riffraff" theory is the idea that riots

are unilaterally violent, that public officials and agencies merely respond in defense against the violence of "irresponsible advocates," and that the riots have little wider meaning in the black community.

The "riffraff" theory has been challenged by various studies. As long ago as 1935, the Harlem Commission reported that "among all classes, there was a feeling that the outburst of the populace was justified and that it represented a protest against discrimination and aggravations resulting from unemployment." [81] More recently, a study of participants in the Watts riot suggests that 46 percent of the adult population in the curfew zone were either actively or passively supporting the riot. The riot had a "broad base" of support and was characterized by "widespread community involvement." [82] Although participants in the Watts riot were predominantly male and youthful, support for rioting was as great from the better-educated, economically advantaged, and long-time residents as it was from the uneducated, poor, and recent migrants. [83]

The Kerner Report provided further evidence to contradict the "riffraff" theory, but its significance was lost in the mass of facts and figures. The most convincing attack on this theory came from Fogelson and Hill's study of participation in the 1967 riots which was published at the end of the Kerner Commissions supplemental studies. The authors found that (1) a substantial minority, ranging from 10 to 20 percent, participated in the riots, (2) one half to three quarters of the arrestees were employed in semiskilled or skilled occupations, three fourths were employed, and three tenths to six tenths were born outside the South, and (3) individuals between the ages of fifteen and thirty-four and especially those between the ages of fifteen and twenty-four are most likely to participate in riots. [84]

Riots are generally viewed by blacks as a useful and legitimate form of protest. Survey data from Watts, Newark, and Detroit suggest that there is an increasing support, or at least sympathy, for riots in black communities. Over half the people interviewed in Los Angeles responded that the riot was a purposeful event which had a positive effect on their lives. [85] Thirty-eight percent of the population in the curfew area said that the riot would help the Negro cause. "While the majority expressed disapproval of the violence and destruction," writes Nathan Cohen in the Los Angeles Riot Study, "it was often coupled with an expression of empathy with those who participated, or sense of pride that the Negro has brought worldwide attention to his problem." [86]

That riots are seen by many as a legitimate and instrumental method of protest has drastic implications for the "riffraff" theory. Fogelson and Hill ask:

> Is it conceivable that . . . several hundred riots could have erupted in nearly every Negro ghetto in the United States over the past five years against the opposition of 98 or 99 percent of the black community? And is it conceivable that militant young Negroes would have ignored the customary restraints on rioting in the United States, including the commitment to orderly social change, unless they enjoyed the tacit support of at least a sizeable minority of the black community? [87]

Studies of riot participation suggest that "rioters" represent a cross section of the lower-class community. The young people who participate are not known to be psychologically impaired or especially suffering from problems of masculine identity. Juveniles arrested in the 1967 Detroit riot were found by a psychological team to be less emotionally disturbed and less delinquent than typical juvenile arrestees.[88] Furthermore, the recent riots have served to mobilize the younger segments of the black community and to educate them to the realities of their caste position in American society:

> Today it is the young men who are fighting the battles, and, for now, their elders, though they have given their approval, have not joined in. The time seems near, however, for the full range of the black masses to put down the broom and buckle on the sword. And it grows nearer day by day. Now we see skirmishes, sputtering erratically, evidence if you will that the young men are in a warlike mood. But evidence as well that the elders are watching closely and may soon join the battle.[89]

The Direction of Contemporary Militancy

By the mid-1960's, many militant black leaders had become convinced that the aims and methods of the civil rights movement were no longer viable. The failures of the federal government and of white liberals to meet black expectations, the fact of the urban revolts, and the increasing American involvement overseas all served to catalyze a fundamental transformation in black perceptions of American society. The anti-colonial perspective, rather unique when expressed by Malcolm X in 1964, now provided many blacks with a structured world-view. For the Black Panther Party, for example, it provided the "basic definition":

> We start with the basic definition: that black people in America are a colonized people in every sense of the term and that white America is an organized Imperialist force holding black people in colonial bondage.[90]

Many articulate black spokesmen saw the final hope of black Americans in identification with the revolutionary struggles of the Third World. Even political moderates began pointing to the discrepancy between the massive commitment of American resources abroad and the lack of a decisive commitment to end racism at home. Martin Luther King wondered why "we were taking the black young men who had been crippled by our society and sending them 8,000 miles away to guarantee liberties in Southeast Asia which they had not found in Georgia or East Harlem." [91] He also questioned the official condemnation of the ghetto poor for their "resort to violence":

> As I have walked among the desperate, rejected, and angry young men I have told them that Molotov cocktails and rifles would not solve their problems. . . . But they asked—and rightly so—what about Vietnam? . . . Their questions hit home, and I knew that I could never again raise my voice against the violence of the oppressed in the ghettos without having first spoken clearly to the greatest purveyor of violence in the world today—my own government.[92]

By the mid-1960's, then, criticism of fundamental American policies at home and abroad was widespread among intellectuals in the black community. The dominant themes in contemporary black protest reflect this basic mood. Three major themes stand out: self-defense and the rejection of nonviolence; cultural autonomy and the rejection of white values; and political autonomy and community control. These trends do not exhaust the content of contemporary militancy, and they are held in varying combinations and in varying degree by different groups and individuals. All of them, however, share a common characteristic: they are attempts to gain for blacks a measure of safety, power, and dignity in a society that has denied them all three.

Self-defense

Traditionally, Americans have viewed self-defense as a basic right. The picture of the armed American defending his home, his family, his possessions, and his person has its origins in frontier life but is no less a reality in modern suburbia. In that picture, however, the armed American is always white. The idea of black men defending themselves with force has always inspired horror in whites. In some of the early slave codes, black slaves were not permitted to strike a white master even in self-defense.[93] In the caste system of the Southern states, Negroes were expected to accept nearly any kind of punishment from whites without retaliation; openly showing aggression meant almost certain violent retaliation from whites.[94] Still, individual blacks occasionally fought back in the face of white violence in the South; and blacks collectively resisted attacking whites in the race riots of 1917, 1919, and 1943.[95]

The civil rights movement, under the leadership of Martin Luther King, and the sit-ins and freedom rides of the 1960's stressed nonviolence and what some called "passive resistance." As a result of the failure of local and federal officials to protect civil rights workers in the South, however, a number of activists and their local allies began to arm themselves against attacks by the Ku Klux Klan and other white terrorist groups. It was only too obvious that local police and sheriffs

in the South were at best only halfheartedly concerned with
the welfare of rights workers, and at worst were active participants in local terrorist groups. The latter was the case in
Neshoba County, Mississippi, for example, where the local
sheriff's department was deeply implicated in the killing of
three civil rights workers. More often, civil rights groups
found they could not depend on Southern officials for protection. In 1959, the head of the NAACP chapter in Monroe,
North Carolina, had organized local blacks into a rifle club as
an armed defense against repeated assaults by the Ku Klux
Klan.[96] A notable result was that "the lawful authorities of
Monroe and North Carolina acted to enforce order *only
after, and as a direct result of*, our being armed." [97]

Following the bloody Southern summer of 1964, local defense groups sprang up in several black communities in the
South. Their primary purpose was to protect nonviolent civil
rights workers in the absence of police protection and to end
white terrorism against black communities. As a rule, they favored nonviolence as a civil rights tactic, but felt that it could
only operate where nonviolent demonstrators were protected
from assault.[98] A study of one such group in Houston, Texas,
concluded that the overall effect of an organized showing of
armed force by blacks was to decrease the level of violence in
the community. White vigilantes were deterred from action,
and police were forced to perform an effective law enforcement role.[99]

During this period, the focus of attention began to shift
to the ghettos of the North. The dramatic episodes of police
harassment of demonstrators in the South had overshadowed,
for a time, the nature of the routine encounters between police and blacks in the ghetto. The ghetto resident and those
who spoke for him, however, had not forgotten the character
of the policeman's daily role in the black community, or the
extent of private white violence against Northern blacks in
history. The writings of Malcolm X spoke from Northern,
rather than Southern, experience in demanding for blacks the
right to defend themselves against attack:

> I feel that if white people were attacked by Negroes—if
> the forces of law prove unable, or inadequate or reluctant to

protect those whites from those Negroes—then those white people should be able to protect themselves against Negroes using arms if necessary. And I feel that when the law fails to protect Negroes from white attack, then those Negroes should use arms, if necessary, to defend themselves.

"Malcolm X Advocates Armed Negroes!" What was wrong with that? I'll tell you what was wrong. I was a black man talking about physical defense against the white man. The white man can lynch and burn and bomb and beat Negroes —that's all right. "Have patience" . . . "The customs are entrenched" . . . "Things are getting better." [100]

After the Watts riot of 1965, local blacks formed a Community Action Patrol to monitor police conduct during arrests. In 1966, some Oakland blacks carried the process a little farther by instituting armed patrols. From a small group organized on an ad hoc basis and oriented to the single issue of police control, the Black Panther Party for Self-Defense has grown into a national organization with a ten-point program for achieving political, social, and economic goals.[101] In the process, the name has been condensed to the Black Panther Party, but the idea of self-defense remains basic: "The Panther never attacks first, but when he is backed into a corner, he will strike back viciously." [102]

The Black Panther Party has been repeatedly harassed by police. After the conviction of the party's leader, Huey P. Newton, for manslaughter in the death of a white policeman, Oakland police fired into the Black Panther office with rifles and shotguns presumably because they felt that a conviction for first-degree murder would have been more appropriate.[103] On September 4, a group of 150 whites, allegedly including a number of off-duty policemen, attacked a group of Panthers and their white supporters in the Brooklyn Criminal Court building.[104] The confrontation between the Panthers and some elements of the police has become a feud verging on open warfare. This warfare highlights the fact that for the black citizen, the policeman has long since ceased to be—if indeed he ever was—a neutral symbol of law and order. Studies of the police emphasize that their attitudes and behavior toward blacks differ vastly from those taken toward whites.[105] Similar studies show that blacks perceive the police

as hostile, prejudiced, and corrupt.[106] In the ghetto disorders
of the past few years, blacks have often been exposed to indiscriminate police assaults and, not infrequently, to gratui-
tous brutality. Many ghetto blacks see the police as an occupying army; one of the Panthers' major demands is for stationing UN observers in the ghettos to monitor police
conduct.[107]

In view of these facts, the adoption of the idea of self-defense is not surprising. Again, in America self-defense has always been considered an honorable principle, and the refusal
to bow before police harassment strikes a responsive chord in
ghetto communities, especially among the young. In Oakland,
ghetto youths emulate the Panthers; the Panthers, in turn, attempt to direct youth into constructive channels:

> We have the Panther Youth Corps, kids from the age of
> about ten to thirteen. And after school I would teach them
> history and tutor them in mathematics, and it all started be-
> cause the kids have always been very enthusiastic, and they
> always identify with the Panther. We have this office . . . and
> the kids would gather up outside because I wouldn't let them
> inside the office because we had weapons inside, and because
> I didn't want them hurt or fooling around with the weapons.
> . . . So finally I organized them . . . as a Panther group, but
> to get in, they would have to show that they were working
> very industrious in school, because Panthers always get the
> highest grades in school. . . . I would have them every report
> card period give me their report cards to see how they were
> progressing.[108]

The Black Panther Party has remained defensive and has
been given credit for keeping Oakland cool after the assassination of Martin Luther King, but this has not stemmed from
any desire on their part to suppress black protest in the community. Rather, it has stemmed from a sense that the police
are waiting for a chance to shoot down blacks in the streets.
Continued harassment by the police makes self-defense a necessary element of militant action for the Panthers and for
similar groups, such as the Black Liberators in St. Louis.

Beyond this, society's failure to commit itself to ending
racism leads many militants to feel that there is no end in
sight to the long history of white violence and repression. Ad-

vocates of self-defense can easily point to instances of official violence employed at one time or another against a variety of groups in the United States. With the approval of the government in Washington, Southern whites militarized their entire society between 1830 and 1860, terminated the education of Negro slaves and deprived them of all human rights, restricted their movements, and punished real or alleged revolts by summary execution of suspects. Mob violence tacitly sanctioned by the government was employed with terrible effect against West Coast Chinese as well as against Southern blacks in the decades following the Civil War. Systematic political persecution by the government, using techniques of discriminatory legislation, nighttime raids, mass deportation, officially condoned mob violence, and jailing of political prisoners, was employed against rebellious political minorities like the IWW and socialists of 1917 to 1922. During the First World War, most resident Germans were suspected of disloyalty and many were physically attacked or had property destroyed by mobs; during the Second World War, virtually the entire West Coast Japanese community was removed by the United States government to concentration camps in the West. Most prominent in these allusions to violence is the 250-year campaign of suppression waged against the American Indians, the one example in United States history of official violence raised to a genocidal scale. For some militants, the history of this struggle deserves particular attention in the light of contemporary events, for it provides a scenario for massive suppression of a large racial minority.[109]

As a militant black leader argues, "We have been assaulted by our environment." [110] For some American militants, this neutralizes all restraints against the use of counterviolence, seen not as aggression but as defensive retaliation. And as a Seattle Panther recently stated, "You see, we've been backed into a corner for the last 400 years, so anything we do now is defensive." [111]

Cultural Autonomy

The strain toward black liberation mixes indigenous and international influences. The resurgence of interest in cultural autonomy reflects both of these influences, as well as the unique problems confronting black Americans during the mid-1960's. Three elements of that situation are especially significant.

First, with the rise of an international outlook and a concomitant recognition of America's role in supporting oppressive regimes overseas, black Americans found themselves in a society that appeared to be bent on suppressing nonwhite ambitions on a worldwide, as well as a domestic, scale. "A rising tide of consciousness that we are Africans," writes James Forman, "an African people living in the United States and faced with the problem of sheer survival, dominates the thoughts of many black college students today." [112] Looking backward at the long history of white domination in this country, and outward at American neocolonialism, militants questioned the cultural basis of American values: "I do not want to be a part of the American pride. The American pride means raping South Africa, beating Vietnam, beating South America, raping the Philippines, raping every country you've been in." [113]

The exclusion of blacks from the mainstream of American culture has made rejection of that culture less difficult, for as James Baldwin suggests:

> The American Negro has the great advantage of having never believed that collection of myths to which white Americans cling; that their ancestors were all freedom-loving heroes, that they were born in the greatest country the world has ever seen, or that Americans are invincible in battle and wise in peace, that Americans have always dealt honorably with Mexicans and Indians and all other neighbors or inferiors, that American men are the world's most direct and virile, that American women are pure.[114]

The thrust toward cultural assimilation became considerably weakened or reversed by these understandings. As Baldwin put it, "Do I really want to be integrated into a burning house?" [115] Unimpressed by the performance of this country under the dominance of white, Western culture, blacks looked to their own cultural heritage as a source of affirmation of a different set of values. "We reject the American

Dream as defined by white people and must work to construct an American reality defined by Afro-Americans." [116]

A second element of the situation was intrinsic. Supported by the revival of awareness of African history and culture accompanying the anti-colonial movement, blacks grew more and more impatient with the attempt of the American cultural apparatus—especially the schools and mass media—to enforce cultural standards which either ignored or depreciated the independent cultural heritage of Afro-Americans.

> The systematic destruction of our links to Africa, the cultural cut-off of blacks in this country from blacks in Africa are not situations that conscious black people in this country are willing to accept. Nor are conscious black people in this country willing to accept an educational system that teaches all aspects of Western Civilization and dismisses our Afro-American contribution . . . and deals with Africa not at all. Black people are not willing to align themselves with a Western culture that daily emasculates our beauty, our pride and our manhood. [117]

In addition to demanding recognition of a rich cultural heritage, militant blacks resented the policy implications of the rejection of that heritage by whites. American social science has traditionally—with the exception of men like Herskovits—argued that the Negro is only "an exaggerated American" [118] without values of his own; "the Negro is only an American and nothing else. He has no values and culture to guard and protect." [119] Two corollary notions, both of which have important implications for social policy, flow from this conception. On the one hand, the current cultural arrangements become relatively immune from independent criticism by blacks; on the other hand, the distinctness of black behavior comes to be seen as pathological.

> Yesterday's rural Negro may have had something like a folk culture, so the myth goes, but today's urban Negro can be found only in a set of sociological statistics on crime, unemployment, illegitimacy, desertion, and welfare payments. The social scientists would have us believe that the Negro is psychologically maladjusted, socially disorganized and culturally deprived. [120]

This elitist perspective implies that something must be done to bring blacks up to the cultural standards of the "community" or, at the extreme, that blacks themselves have to clean their own houses—literally and figuratively—before "earning" admittance into the American mainstream.[121] A long-term result of the denial of black culture was the entire set of conceptions centering around the notion of "cultural deprivation": black children failed in schools because they came from a "cultureless" community, not because the schools did not teach.[122] Central to this perspective was the ideology of American public welfare, with its commitment to raising the moral standards of the poor and its public intrusions into the family arrangements of ghetto blacks.[123]

The drive toward cultural autonomy, therefore, was in part a rejection of the cultural vacuum of "welfare colonialism" into which the black community has been thrown. It was also an organizational response to the failure of white liberals to fulfill the promise of the civil rights movement of the 1950's. For the most part, white supporters of the movement for civil rights thought in assimilationist terms. Their object was to open opportunities for the Negro to enter the mainstream of American life. Many blacks, however, questioned the cost involved in aiming for inclusion on terms that were irrevocably the terms of white culture. Many whites, too, tended to assume that their function in the movement for civil rights was to guide, instruct, and otherwise lead the movement from the top. These facts, coupled with the rise of identification with nonwhites on an international basis and increased contact with the black masses in the North, led black activists to move toward limiting the role of whites in their organizations. The Student Nonviolent Coordinating Committee excluded whites from leadership positions in 1966, citing these reasons:

> The inability of whites to relate to the cultural aspects of Black society; attitudes that whites, consciously or unconsciously, bring to Black communities about themselves (western superiority) and about Black people (paternalism); inability to shatter white-sponsored community myths of Black inferiority and self-negation; inability to combat the views of the Black community that white organizers, being "white,"

control Black organizers as puppets; . . . the unwillingness of whites to deal with the *roots* of racism which lie within the white community; whites though individually "liberal" are symbols of oppression to the Black community—due to the collective power that whites have over Black lives.[124]

The rejection of white leadership was mistakenly viewed as a form of "racism in reverse" by many white and some black commentators.[125] But this rejection was not necessarily or consistently a withdrawal from whites *qua* whites. Rather, it was an assertion of the ability of blacks to control their own organizations, and a rejection of white claims, symbolic or explicit, of political leadership. As such, it represented one aspect of a general thrust toward black political independence.

Political Autonomy and Community Control

The movement of black militants toward a concern for political autonomy, with a corresponding rejection of traditional political avenues and party organizations, is a result of several influences. One we have already noted—the failure of traditional politics to play a meaningful part in the drive for black dignity and security. Passing civil rights legislation is not the same as enforcing it. Pleading for goodwill and racial justice from the relative sanctuary of Congress, the courts, or the White House is a good deal easier than committing a massive federal effort to eradicate institutional racism. On a local level, it occasions no great difficulty to appoint a few Negroes to positions of some influence; the crucial test is whether local government acts decisively to correct the problems of the ghetto and to provide a genuine avenue of black participation in community decision-making. On all of these counts, most local governments have failed or, more accurately, have hardly tried. The result is that local government has become, to those beneath it, oppressive rather than representative. Certainly, there are "differences within the system," the structure of political power in a given community is usually less monolithic than it appears from below, and there may be several loci of influence rather than an organized and cohesive "power structure." But these points are only meaningful to those who enter the system with some preestablished influence. A critical fact about the black ghettos of the cities, and of the black belt communities of the South, is their traditional lack of such a base of influence. Without this, blacks have participated in the political process as subjects rather than citizens.[126] Traditionally, black political leaders have been less a force for black interest than middlemen in a system of "indirect rule": "In other words, the white power structure rules the black community through local blacks who are responsive to the white leaders, the downtown, white machine, not to the black populace." [127]

A recent study of decision-making positions in Chicago illustrates the extent of black exclusion from the centers of influence. Of a total of 1,088 policy-making positions in federal, state, and local government in Cook County, only 58, or 5 percent, were held by Negroes in 1965. Yet, blacks made up at least 20 percent of the county's population. Blacks were especially underrepresented in local administrative positions, including city and county governments, the Board of Education, and the Sanitary District, as well as in Federal Civil Service and Presidential appointive positions.[128] There was no black representation at all in the decision-making positions in the Metropolitan Sanitary District, for example, and only 1 percent of local administrative positions were held by blacks.[129] Further, "Not only were Negroes grossly underrepresented in Chicago's policy-making posts, but even where represented they had less power than white policy-makers. The fact is that *the number of posts held by Negroes tended to be inversely related to the power vested in these positions —the more powerful the post, the fewer the black policy-makers.*" [130] And the study concludes:

> . . . even where represented their actual power is restricted, or their representatives fail to work for the long-term interests of their constituency. It is therefore safe to estimate that Negroes really hold less than 1% of the effective power in the Chicago metropolitan area. Realistically, the power structure of Chicago is hardly less white than that of Mississippi.[131]

The critical character of the lack of black participation in decision-making is obvious; control over the centers of decision-making means control over the things about which decisions are made. This includes, of course, such traditional civil rights issues as housing, employment, and education, as well as newer focal points of black protest like the police and the welfare apparatus. As the civil rights movement showed, blacks cannot expect major changes in their political interests when control over the speed, direction, and priorities of change is held by whites who are at best less urgently committed, and at worst openly hostile, to black aims.

A major factor influencing the thrust for black political autonomy is the fact that racism itself has created the conditions for effective black political organization. Residential segregation has meant that, in the black belt South as well as the urban North and West, blacks occupy whole districts en bloc. With the growing influx of blacks to the central cities, and the corresponding exodus of whites to the suburbs, larger and larger areas of the inner cities are developing black majorities. This fact is critical since, as the Chicago study shows, ". . . Negroes simply do not hold legislative posts in city, state, or federal government *unless* they represent a district that is mostly black. No district with Negroes in the minority had a Negro representative, even when Negroes constituted the single largest ethnic group." [132]

In light of these facts, black political organization is both feasible and imperative. Historically, blacks have responded to their political exclusion in America in a variety of ways. There has been a traditional strain of separatism, manifested in schemes for removal to Africa or for setting aside certain areas in the United States for all-black control; several militant groups express similar aims today.[133] For the most part, however, contemporary black protest is oriented to the idea of black community control and/or the development of independent black political bases and a black political party. The response to the idea of "Black Power" has ranged from accusations by black intellectuals of liberal pragmatism and anti-intellectualism,[134] to white criticism of its inherent racism and retreat from the goals of integration. The Kerner Report argued that advocates of Black Power had "retreated into an unreal world," that they had "retreated from a direct confrontation with American society on the issue of integration and, by preaching separatism, unconsciously function as an accommodation to white racism." [135] This argument constitutes a misinterpretation of American political history, of the decline of the civil rights movement, and of the goals of contemporary black protest.

As we suggest in several places in this report, the interpretation of American political history as one of peaceful and orderly inclusion of diverse groups into the polity is inaccurate. We need not recapitulate here. Many groups have used violence as an instrument of social change; some minorities have been forcibly repressed. It is highly unrealistic to depend on the mere goodwill of the larger society to meet black grievances. As James Forman has observed, "Those in power do not concede or relinquish their position without a fight, a skirmish, a struggle, a war in which violence and force will be used to keep the powerless oppressed." [136] The idea of black political organization is based on the hard fact that no political order transfers its power lightly and that if blacks are to have a significant measure of political control they must organize into a position of bargaining strength:

> Before a group can enter the open society, it must first close ranks. By this we mean that group solidarity is necessary before a group can operate effectively from a bargaining position of strength in a pluralistic society. Traditionally, each new ethnic group in this society has found the route to social and political viability through the organization of its own institutions with which to represent its needs within the larger society. [137]

The notion that advocates of black autonomy have "retreated from a direct confrontation" with white society "on the issue of integration" is misleading. It ignores both the fact that the decline of the goals of the early civil rights movement came about as the direct result of societal, and especially governmental, inaction, and that blacks may be expected to modify their tactics after decades of such inaction. It also fails to appreciate the fact that black protest now aims, at least in theory, at a transformation of American institutions rather than inclusion into them.

> Thus we reject the goal of assimilation into middle-class America because the values of that class are in themselves

anti-humanist and because that class as a social force perpetuates racism. . . . Existing structures . . . must be challenged forcefully and clearly. If this means the creation of parallel community institutions, then that must be the solution. If this means that black parents must gain control over the operation of the schools in the black community, then that must be the solution. The search for new forms means the search for institutions that will, for once, make decisions in the interests of black people.[138]

This is not separatism, nor is it racism. Militant leaders from Malcolm X to Huey P. Newton have stressed the possibility of coalitions with white groups whose aim is radical social change.[139] The Black Panther Party has links with the Peace and Freedom Party, and its candidate, Eldridge Cleaver, ran for President on the Peace and Freedom ticket. For the most part, the new black stance is better described as a kind of militant pluralism, in which not whites, but traditional politics and politicians of both races, are rejected.

Militant Youth

It is for young blacks that the "new spirit of revolutionary militancy"[140] has had special relevance. The Kerner Report observed that there was enough evidence by 1966 to indicate that a large proportion of riot participants were youths. It also suggested that "increasing race pride, skepticism about their job prospects, and dissatisfaction with the inadequacy of their education, caused unrest among students in Negro colleges and high schools."[141] The events of 1968 support and go beyond this finding. The schools are more and more becoming the locus of a whole spectrum of youthful protest, from negotiation to violence. This section attempts to describe the nature of this phenomenon and to account for its significance and apparent increase in the last few years.

The transition from a "civil rights" perspective to a "liberation" perspective has had a profound impact on the ideology and activities of black youth. The following changes are the most significant:

1. The civil rights movement was for the most part nonviolent, directed at Southern racism, and recruited its most active members from the colleges. The new movement has

shifted its focus to cities in the North and West, regards non-violence as only one of many tactics for achieving power and autonomy, and recruits its most active members from high schools as well as colleges.

2. The civil rights movement was concerned with integrating schools, eliminating de facto segregation, and providing equal educational opportunities for blacks. The new movement stresses cultural autonomy, community control of schools, and the development of educational programs which are relevant to black history and black needs.

3. During the civil rights movement, high school youth often participated in demonstrations, sit-ins, and marches. But this participation was limited in terms of activity and responsibility. In recent years, however, youth have become integrated into the liberation movement, often in leadership roles. One of the most significant features of the new militancy is the increasing political consciousness of black youth; this trend is reflected in the formation of Afro-American organizations in high schools and in the proliferation of youth chapters of militant political organizations.

Since 1960, there have been dramatic changes in the character and quantity of high school protests. Even allowing for varying fashions in news reporting and the tendency of the press to underreport nonviolent protest, it is nevertheless evident that there has been a significant increase in militant action among black (and white) high school youth.[142] There are two significant aspects to this new militancy: first, young blacks are now engaging in collective political action and are less involved in internal gang warfare; and second, the educational system is intrinsically important to the movement for liberation because, as it is argued, cultural autonomy and black dignity are only possible if children are taught by persons responsible and sympathetic to the black community.

It is only recently that students have begun to regard themselves as potential power holders in the institutions which they attend. Youthful militants have focused on the school, for it is here that for the first time expectations are cruelly raised and even more cruelly crushed.[143] Whereas the last year has seen increasing protests by middle-class black students in colleges and universities, the high school has been the main target of militant action for lower-class urban youth and for a significant segment of middle-class youth as well. The protests raise many issues: black student unions, curriculum reforms, black teachers, democratic disciplinary procedures, "soul" food, bussing, boycotts, amnesty for "political" offenders, community control, police brutality, and many others.

In the last two years, most urban school systems have been disrupted by militant protest. In 1967, 17 percent of civil disorders involved schools to some degree. In January through April, 1968, 44 percent involved school. Of the April disorders following Dr. King's death, nearly half took place entirely in schools or adjacent grounds, while nearly another third began in schools and spread to surrounding areas.[144] Most of these school disorders were connected in one way or another with the assassination of Dr. King. But, according to the Lemberg Center for the Study of Violence, "a continuation of the rate of civil disorders involving schools was uncovered *irrespective* of the King tragedy, which served to intensify the trend." [145]

This finding is supported by a cursory examination of school disorders unrelated to riots. At the beginning of the 1967 school year, police and students fought outside Manual Arts High School, in Los Angeles, in October of 1967; the school was boycotted by over half the student body on October 23, while the president of the faculty association petitioned the Board of Education for "adequate personnel to maintain supervision and security in order that the teachers may teach." [146] New Jersey schools were disrupted when interracial fighting, vandalism, and strikes occurred at Barringer High School in Newark and at Trenton High School.[147]

Chicago was the scene of two major school disturbances in 1967. A rally to protest police brutality, held outside Forrestville High School on the South Side, ended in fifty-four arrests and twelve injuries.[148] A local gang leader was credited with clearing the street when the police were ready to use force.[149] Nevertheless, the police were required to fire warning shots in order to disperse the rally. The next day, a spokesman for Students for Freedom, a militant group within the high school, promised to "initiate a boycott . . . unless the police and others who patrol the school as if it were a prison are removed." [150]

The second Chicago disturbance occurred in the middle-class suburb of Maywood after it became known that no black girl was on the list of five homecoming queen finalists. Blacks make up about 20 percent of Proviso East High School's enrollment of 3,700 students. Black and white students boycotted the school for over a week; at one point, attendance was down to less than 30 percent; city officials imposed a 9:00 P.M. curfew after incidents of sniper fire and looting; sixty adults were arrested over the weekend; the school's security force was tripled and plainclothes policemen patrolled the corridors; at the end of the week, police were required to use tear gas to disperse crowds.[151]

Maywood's black students were represented by local officials of the NAACP who presented a list of grievances to the superintendent of schools. "There was pressure from many sources, some of the school board, to have uniformed police with riot sticks and helmets in the building," the superintendent said, "but I absolutely refused. A public school that has to be turned into an armed camp has reached the lowest point in desperation. It presents an image of pupils that we can't afford to have." During the middle of the boycott, school officials agreed to a number of demands, including (1) an in-service program in human relations for teachers, (2) adequate teaching of black history, (3) abolition of corporal punishment except in self-defense, and (4) investigation of complaints about cafeteria service. The school board and Proviso East's superintendent worked out an agreement despite the hostility of local whites who, like the Mayor's wife, felt that the "rioters" should have been "put down. They haven't anything to cry about. What hurts me is that the few spoil it for the good ones." [152] To school officials, however, the grievances seemed to be widely supported in the local black community. "We have responded," said the superintendent, "to some legitimate needs that were presented with impact."

The significance of the Maywood disturbance lies in the participation of middle-class youth and NAACP officials. Maywood is a middle-class suburb with a substantial percentage (almost 30 percent) of Negro residents. Its median family income is $9,450 and the median home value is almost $18,000. One quarter of the forty-man police force is black and two of the town's six trustees are Negroes.[153] The successful protest at Proviso East seriously contests the idea that school disorders are limited to a minority of poor, lower-class, delinquency-prone youth.

School protests by black students escalated in 1968. In Cincinnati, sit-ins and demonstrations in six of the city's eight high schools resulted in the suspension of 1,300 and arrests of 100 students, most of whom were black. Racial antagonism in East St. Louis forced the closing of a number of schools in late April. In South Bend, Indiana, seventy-two adults and fifty-nine juveniles were arrested after a sit-in at the school system's administration building. The sit-in was a protest against the use of armed guards in two high schools and an elementary school in a predominantly black community. In Pittsburg, California, all of the city's eleven schools were closed on April 18 after a day of racial violence. Police were called into Central High School in Flint, Michigan, to break up a sit-in protesting the selection of only one Negro among six cheerleaders.[154]

Militant protest was resumed with greater intensity in the fall. Interracial fights broke out at Bladensburg High School, in Washington, D.C., following complaints of discrimination against black students. "We're going to participate in everything and nobody is going to stop us," said one spokesman for the dissident students. After a boycott and sporadic violence, officials of the school met with student representatives and agreed to an amnesty.[155] Interracial violence recurred at Trenton High School for the fourth time in nine months, resulting in a boycott by two thirds of the school's 3,000 students. Blacks were challenged by white students chanting "Wallace for President." Further confrontations were prevented by riot police who intervened between the two groups.[156] Other disturbances occurred in New Jersey: black demonstrators and white counterdemonstrators protested at Linden High School after a black student was suspended for allegedly striking two white teachers; and about five hundred black students boycotted classes at Montclair High School in order to protest a change in faculty leadership of the Black Student Union.[157] The teaching of black history was another central issue in many protests, such as the boycott of three high schools in Waterbury, Connecticut.[158]

Massive student boycotts occurred this year in Chicago and New York. On October 21, about twenty thousand black students boycotted classes and presented the Chicago Board of Education with an extensive list of demands, including locally controlled schools, student participation in decision-making, more black teachers and history courses, more technical and vocational training, greater use of black business services to schools, and holidays to commemorate the birthdays of Dr. King, Malcolm X, Marcus Garvey, and W. E. B. DuBois.[159]

In summary, high school protests by black students have significantly increased in the last few years. Both middle- and lower-class youth participate in such protests, often with the active support of their parents and local community organizations. The success of boycotts and other instrumental protests suggests the increasing political consciousness of youth. Although interracial violence continues in varying intensity, black and white students occasionally demonstrate more solidarity than they have in the past. "It's the youngsters versus the system," commented the Mayor of Trenton, New Jersey, after a school disorder, "rather than the students versus the students." [160] High school activists have generally impressed school officials with the sophistication and legitimacy of their demands. Despite the general hostility of the white community and press, some ameliorative concessions have been made to black students while more fundamental disputes over school control and decentralization are still being contested.

The pervasiveness and strength of youthful militancy must be appreciated in the context of the black liberation and student movements. Traditional discussions of high school youth have invariably focused on "troublesome" and "abnormal" forms of "acting-out" behavior—disturbances at dances, athletic events, and parties, vandalism, gang fights and disputes over gang territory, etc. Much of this activity was seen as a function of youthful exuberance, or of adolescent restlessness, or of lower-class culture. Theorists and experts have shown a special interest in explaining the negative and pathological attributes of gangs, but they have rarely been concerned with examining collective youth action from a political perspective. There is a strong tendency to regard the political activities of youth in terms of "conspiracy" and "anarchy" [161]—an attitude which underestimates the popular appeal and purposeful character of the student movement.

Similarly, much attention has been directed to the problem of why young people cause so much trouble for the schools, whereas the equally legitimate question of why schools cause so much trouble for youth has been seriously neglected.[162] The problematic aspects of the educational process are widely attributed to students' cultural and family backgrounds, or to their inability to adjust to the demands of school life, or to their failure to cooperate with teachers and school administrators. Fighting, vandalism, truancy, disobedience, and other "disrespectful" behavior are handled as a form of psychological immaturity and cultural primitivism, commonly associated with adolescent "acting-out."

The militant activities of black youth have served to revise popular conceptions about the immaturity and independence of youth, as well as to focus considerable attention on the deficiencies and irrelevance of most ghetto high schools. Government and school officials have in some instances recognized the power of youth by agreeing to negotiate student demands, by creating special programs of job training, and by "consulting" with youth and gang leaders in the development of community projects. Often this recognition is motivated by an awareness that youth organizations, like the Blackstone Rangers in Chicago, are becoming more and more capable of mobilizing vast numbers of young people with a view to political or even guerrilla action. After the death of Dr. King, the Blackstone Rangers helped to "cool" Chicago's South Side. According to one commentator, "This was their way of saying, 'You have to reckon with us because, if we cannot stop one [a riot], well, you know the alternative.' This was a naked display of power." [163]

The politicization of black youth reflects the growing political interest of youth in general. During 1968, for example, students in New York high schools formed a union to protest racism and the war in Vietnam as well as to enable participation in local school issues.[164] On April 26, thousands of high school students attended a rally to protest the war.[165]

More specifically, however, student militancy has its roots in the black liberation movement for political and cultural autonomy. Several years ago, school protests focused almost uniquely on the problem of de facto segregation. Black adults and their children boycotted local schools to protest their failure to comply with federal standards on integration. White crowds, particularly in the South, gathered outside newly integrated schools to jeer, harass, and even attack Negro students.[166] Civil rights organizations engaged student support to protest segregated facilities, but always insisted on the use of nonviolent tactics. In late 1960, for example, a representative of the Southern Christian Leadership Conference predicted a widespread resumption of demonstrations against segregation: "I certainly judge from the students' activity," he said, "that they are mobilizing for a big push in the fall. They are going to find unique ways to apply the technique of nonviolence." [167] Traditional civil rights organizations, especially the NAACP, were quick to condemn violence, even from black youths seeking revenge against white attacks.[168]

The new directions of the black movement have influenced and in turn been influenced by urban, lower-class youth. Separatism has replaced integration as a primary objective, and nonviolence has become for many another tactic of resistance rather than a moral creed. It is the spirit and determination of black youth that moved James Forman to describe the 1960's as the "accelerating generation, a generation of black people determined that they will survive, a generation aware that resistance is the agenda for today and that *action* by people is necessary to quicken the steps of history." [169] The militancy of youth has received considerable support from adults and community organizations.[170] "If we had done this twenty years ago, our children wouldn't have to be doing this today. These children will make us free." [171]

Perhaps the most significant reason for the militancy of youth is the fact that education is central to the liberation perspective. The Nation of Islam has long recognized the importance of recruiting and socializing a whole new generation of proud and masculine youths:

> The education and training of our children must . . . in-
> clude the history of the black nation, the knowledge of civili-
> zations of man and the Universe, and all sciences. . . . Learn-
> ing is a great virtue and I would like to see all the children
> of my followers become the possessors of it. It will make us
> an even greater people tomorrow.[172]

New militant leaders and students themselves have come to
appreciate the value of this perspective, realizing that only
through control of the educational system can they build a
political movement and instill pride, dignity, self-appreciation, and confidence in black Americans.

The struggle for educational autonomy is both a cultural
and political struggle. It is a cultural struggle in the sense that
the school can provide youth with an education which gives
proper attention to black history and black values, thus providing a positive sense of self-appreciation and identity. But it
is also a political struggle, for it is widely felt that the educational system is a predominant means used by those in power
to teach people to "unconsciously accept their condition of
servitude." [173] According to Edgar Friedenberg, a white sociologist who has written extensively on education, "the
school is the instrument through which society acculturates
people into consensus before they become old enough to resist
it as effectively as they could later." [174] Thus, local control of
the educational system will provide an opportunity to build a
resistance movement as well as to achieve some cultural independence from the values of white America. "We don't want
to be trained in ROTC to fight in a Vietnam war," says one
black youth. "We want ROTC to train us how to protect our
own communities." [175]

The available evidence suggests that we are presently witnessing the rise of a generation of black activists, enjoying
wide support from their communities and relatives, committed to the principles of local community control and cultural
autonomy, and disenchanted with techniques of peaceful protest associated with the civil rights movement of the 1950's.
Given this militant participation by black youth, it is difficult
to accept the Kerner Report's conclusion that "the central
thrust of Negro protest in the current period has aimed at the
inclusion of Negroes in American society on a basis of full

equality rather than at a fundamental transformation of American institutions." The available evidence suggests that "inclusion" and "integration" have become largely irrelevant to black youth. "Considering the opportunities for being a Negro man in 1967 that society has held out to them," writes an adviser to the Blackstone Rangers, "they feel very fortunate to have rejected them. . . . They want a mainstream all their own." [176] Demands of the groups like the Black Panthers for cultural autonomy and decentralized power are gaining ascendancy. As Herman Blake testified before this Commission:

> You can't go through any community without seeing black youth with Huey P. Newton buttons and "Free Huey." Many of them who have no connection with the Panthers officially, wear the Panther uniform. We all groove on Huey. No two ways about it. We dig him. And I use that rhetoric because that's the way it is. Not for any exotic reasons.[177]

And, as the Reverend John Fry has suggested, in Chicago's South Side ghetto, "What it means to be a man is to be a Blackstone Ranger." [178] Whatever differences may exist between militant black groups, their programs generally speak to self-defense, political independence, community control, and cultural autonomy. These themes challenge American social arrangements at a deeper level than did the movement for "civil rights," and, in doing so, they reveal problematic aspects of our national life which have been taken for granted, at least by whites. Thus, since the publication of the Kerner Report, the thrust of black protest, especially among the young, has shifted from equality to liberation, from integration to separatism, from dependency to power.

Conclusion

As we have pointed out throughout this report, group political violence is not a peripheral or necessarily pathological feature of American political history. For many black Americans today, violent action increasingly seems to offer the only practical and feasible opportunity to overcome the effects of a long history of systematic discrimination. The events of 1968 suggest that violent racial incidents have, at least temporarily, become part of the routine course of events rather than sporadic calamities.

Martin Luther King, Jr., was killed on April 4, 1968. In the aftermath, civil disorders occurred throughout the country, following an already rising incidence of disorder in the first three months of the year.[179] The following facts are significant: (1) The month of April *alone* saw nearly as many disorders as the entire year of 1967, and more cities and states were involved than in all the previous year. (2) There were more arrests and more injuries in April, 1968, *alone* than in all of 1967, and nearly as much property damage; and there were more National Guard and federal troops called more times in April, 1968, than in all of 1967.[180]

Major riots—none of which, individually, matched in dead or injured the largest riots of the past three years—took place in several cities during the month of April. In Chicago, 9 were killed and 500 injured; in Washington, D.C., 11 died, with 1,113 injuries. There were 6 deaths and 900 injuries in Baltimore, and 6 more deaths in Kansas City, Missouri. Racial violence of some degree of seriousness occurred in 36 states and at least 138 cities.[181]

Considered in isolation, the summer itself was less "hot" than that of the previous year, but it was hardly quiet. Racial violence occurred in July, for example, in Seattle; in Paterson, New Jersey; in Jackson and Benton Harbor, Michigan; in San Francisco and Richmond, California. In Cleveland, a shoot-out between black militants and police ultimately left eleven dead, including three policemen.[182] And any aura of relative quiet over the summer should be dispelled by the fact that racial violence in 1968 did not end with the end of the summer. The opening of schools in the fall was accompanied by an increase in school disorders; sporadic assaults on police, and by police, continue as of this writing in many cities and on college and high school campuses.

Two general points emerge in considering the extent of racial disorder in 1968. First, generally speaking, the violence began earlier and continued longer. The year 1967 also witnessed spring violence, but not to the same degree; and not all of the increase in the spring of 1968 can be attributed to the assassination of Dr. King.[183] It has become more and more difficult to keep track of violent racial incidents.

Second, 1968 represented a new level in the massiveness of the official response to racial disorder. In April alone, as noted, more National Guard troops were called than in all of 1967 (34,900 to 27,700) and more federal troops as well (23,700 to 4,800).[184] *Never* before in this country has such a massive military response been mounted against racial disorder. Troops in the streets of the cities are well on the way to becoming a familiar sight. In one city—Wilmington, Delaware—armed National Guard troops, enforcing a series of harsh anti-riot and curfew provisions, occupied the city from April, 1968, until January, 1969.[185]

Although it is far too early for certainty, limited evidence suggests that the massive ghetto riot—typified by the uprisings in Watts, Newark, and Detroit—may be a thing of the past. None of the disorders of 1968 matches these in scope. The specific explanation for this is far from clear. It lies somewhere in the interaction between more massive and immediate "riot control" efforts by authorities and the apparent perception by many blacks that the "spontaneous riot," as a form of political protest, is too costly in terms of black lives. It is clear that some militant ghetto organizations, such as the Blackstone Rangers in Chicago and the Black Panther Party in Oakland, have made direct and markedly successful efforts to "cool" their communities, especially in the wake of the King assassination. These efforts have been spurred in part by the belief that a riot would provide the opportunity for police attacks on ghetto militants: "We don't want anything to break out that will give them [the police] the chance to shoot us down. They are hoping that we do something like that but we are passing the word to our people to be cool." [186] Blacks did not participate, except peripherally, in the Chicago events during the Democratic National Convention. There were no riots in the black neighborhoods of Chicago.[187] If this is a genuine trend, the decline of the large-scale riot has important analytical implications. It provides a kind of test for competing perspectives on the sources and meaning of riots. If the decline of riots means the decline of disorders in general, then the view of riots as controllable explosions rooted in black "tension" makes a good deal of sense. If, on the other hand, the decline of the riot means only a change in the character of violent black protest, then the roots of black violence may go deeper and reach more profoundly into the structure of American institutions.

There is some evidence—highly tentative—to suggest that the decline in the scale of riots coincides with an increase in more strategic acts of violence and a shift from mass riots to sporadic warfare.[188] In July, as previously noted, Cleveland police battled with armed black militants, and the resulting disorder saw three police killed. There were several attacks on police in Brooklyn in the late summer; in August, two policemen were wounded by shotgun fire; in early September, two policemen were hit by sniper fire as they waited for a traffic light.[189] In mid-September, a police communications truck was fire-bombed, slightly injuring two policemen.[190] In Harlem, two policemen were shot and wounded, reportedly by two black men, as they sat in a parked patrol car.[191] Two September attacks on police took place in Illinois; in Kankakee, a policeman was wounded in what police termed an "ambush" in the black community;[192] in Summit, black youths reportedly fired shotguns at two police cars, injuring two policemen.[193] In the same month, eighteen black militants were arrested in St. Louis following a series of attacks on police, including shots fired at a police station and at the home of a police lieutenant.[194] During October, the San Francisco Bay Area was the scene of the bombing of a sheriff's substation and sniper fire against firemen in the black community. Finally, in recent months, black students have made increasing use of strategic acts of violence including the occasional fire-bombing of homes as well as campus buildings.[195]

Correspondingly, as we indicate in Chapter VII and more generally in the last chapter, the police and social control agencies increasingly view themselves as the political and military adversaries of blacks. This official militancy has even taken the form of direct attacks on black militant organizations. Black youth has become a special target for governmental and police action. Despite frequent successes in high schools, youthful militancy has often met with tough-minded programs of social control on the part of police and school officials. Most "helping" programs—job training, summer outings, athletic events, tutoring and civic pride projects, etc. —are seasonal and employ short-term recreational strategies to "keep a cool summer" and distract youths from more militant kinds of activities. Some authorities feel, for example, that "riots are unleashed against the community" from high schools and that the granting of concessions to students will only encourage further rioting.[196]

Consistent with this policy, intelligence units are supplementing youth offices within police departments and are developing sophisticated counterinsurgency techniques of gang control.[197] The size of the gang intelligence unit in Chicago has been increased from 38 to 200.[198] Governmental programs on behalf of urban youth rarely involve young people in the decision-making process. A modest program of job training in Chicago which appointed local youth leaders to positions of administrative responsibility was harassed by police and discredited by a Senate investigation.[199] Rather than increasing opportunities for the exercise of legitimate power by adolescents, public agencies have opted for closer supervision as a means of decreasing opportunities for the exercise of illegitimate power.[200]

At the same time, it is clear that the massive national effort, recommended by the Kerner Commission, to combat racism through political and peaceful programs has not materialized and shows few signs of doing so in the near future. Despite widespread agreement with the Commission's insistence that "there can be no higher priority for national action and no higher claim on the nation's conscience," [201] other priorities and other claims still seem to dominate the nation's budget.

Part Three
White Politics and Official Reactions

Chapter V
The Racial Attitudes of White Americans

THE MOST significant conclusion of the National Advisory Commission on Civil Disorders (The Kerner Commission) was that "White racism is essentially responsible for the explosive mixture which has been accumulating in our cities since the end of World War II." [1] Yet most Americans reply "not guilty" to the charge of racism. In an opinion survey conducted in April of 1968, white Americans disagreed by a 53 to 35 percent margin with the contention that the 1967 riots were brought on by white racism. [2]

Perhaps part of the disagreement between public opinion and the Kerner Commission stems from different definitions of "white racism." The average person is likely to reserve the emotionally loaded term "racism" for only the most extreme assertions of white supremacy and innate Negro inferiority. Finding that few of his associates express such views, he rejects the central conclusion of the riot commission. Perhaps he would be somewhat more likely to agree that *historically* white racism is responsible for the position of the black man in American society. The Kerner Commission Report, however, not only asserts that "race prejudice has shaped our history decisively" but claims further that "it now threatens to affect our future." The Commission validated its charge of racism by pointing to the existing pattern of racial discrimination, segregation, and inequality in occupation, education, and housing. But a distinction must be made between *institutional* racism and *individual* prejudice. Because of the influence of historical circumstances, it is theoretically possible to have a racist society in which most of the individual members of that society do not express racist attitudes. A society in which most of the good jobs are held by one race, and the dirty jobs by people of another color, is a society in which racism is institutionalized, no matter what the beliefs of its members are. For example, the universities of America are probably the least bigoted of American institutions. One would rarely, if ever, hear an openly bigoted expression at schools like Harvard, Yale, the University of Chicago, the University of California. At the same time, university faculties and students have usually been white, the custodians black. The universities have concerned themselves primarily with the needs and interests of the white upper middle and upper classes, and have viewed the lower classes, and especially blacks, as objects of study rather than of service. In this sense, they have, willy-nilly, been institutionally "white racist."

In the following pages we will examine the available data on white attitudes toward black Americans. There we will see that although there have been some favorable changes in the past twenty years, a considerable amount of racial hostility and opposition to integration remains. To understand the sources of this opposition, we will examine the social characteristics of those whites most opposed to racial change, and we will consider psychological studies which examine prejudice in the individual personality. In the final section, on the widening racial gap, we will examine the disparity between white and black perception of racial issues, including the perception of causes and consequences of riots. This disparity is typified by the responses of black Americans to the same April, 1968, opinion survey in which white Americans rejected the view that white racism was responsible for the riots: by a 58 to 17 percent majority, blacks agreed with the contention that the 1967 riots were brought on by white racism. Also in the concluding section we will examine an opinion gap that may be even more important and ominous than black-white differences. That is the discrepancy between public willingness and congressional unwillingness to enact programs guaranteeing significant improvement in jobs, housing, and education in the black ghetto.

Decline in Prejudice

Since the early 1940's, survey research organizations such as the National Opinion Research Center in Chicago have, at repeated intervals, asked a series of standardized racial attitude questions of representative samples of the U.S. population. The immediately apparent trend of responses to these questions is a decline in the verbal expression of anti-Negro prejudice and a striking reduction in support for discrimination and segregation.[3] Thus the percentage of white Americans who express approval of integration when asked, "Do you think white students and Negro students should go to the same schools or to separate schools?" was 30 percent in 1942, 48 percent in 1956, and 60 percent in 1968. Support for residential integration as measured by responses to the question, "If a Negro with the same income and education as you moved into your block, would it make any difference to you?" exhibit a similar pattern. In 1942, only 35 percent of American whites would not have objected to a Negro neighbor of their own social class. By 1956, 51 percent and, by 1968, 65 percent would accept such a neighbor. Similar trends can be observed in decreasing support for segregation in transportation facilities and increasing support for equality of employment opportunity.

Chárt V-1: Percent of White Americans Who Say White Students and Negro Students Should Go to the Same Schools

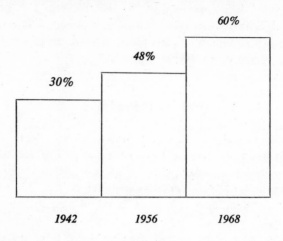

Data furnished courtesy of the National Opinion Research Center.

Chart V-2: Percent of White American Who Do Not Object to Residential Integration

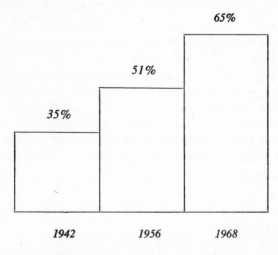

Data furnished courtesy of the National Opinion Research Center.

The Validity of Racial Attitudes Surveys

Several critics have questioned whether these changes in poll responses represent "real" reductions in prejudice as opposed to a mere decline in the respectability of prejudice. Even if we accept this skeptical explanation of the positive trends, however, there are grounds for optimism. At the very least, the reported shifts signify a change in perceived racial norms, which in itself creates a climate of opinion more favorable to interracial understanding. It is true that any attempt to assess white attitudes toward black Americans is subject to numerous pitfalls. A person's "true" racial beliefs and feelings cannot be measured directly but can only be inferred from what he says and does. For a variety of reasons an individual may not wish to reveal his true attitudes, and indeed he may be only dimly aware of them. Several students of race relations have argued, in fact, that overt discriminatory actions, rather than verbal reports of feelings, are the appropriate indices of prejudice. However, this suggestion overlooks the fact that people can lie with behavior as well as with words.[4] Under the pressure of economic gain or social expectations, a racially intolerant person may accept desegregation, while the opposite pressures may lead to discriminatory behavior on the part of tolerant individuals.

With regard to social policy implications, the chief justification for studying *attitudes* of intolerance and exclusiveness is the fact that racist attitudes are *among* the important causes of racist behavior. There are several grounds for believing that racial opinion survey responses do reflect genuine beliefs and feelings. Several experiments have demonstrated a clear relationship between the standard measures of racial attitudes used in public opinion polls and more direct measures of autonomic or "gut-level" emotional responses.[5] Others have shown a positive relationship between verbal measures of attitudes toward minority groups and actual behavior in interaction with members of the minority group.[6] The positive relationship between attitudes and behavior has not been demonstrated only in experimental studies of interracial behavior. Preelection surveys have also shown that attitudes, when properly measured, are predictive of complex social behavior.

Several grounds for believing that the polls are tapping genuine feelings and evaluations have been suggested by Thomas Pettigrew.[7] For example, the remarkable consistency of the results of surveys of white attitudes toward blacks reported by different polling agencies using a wide variety of questions would be difficult to explain if the respondents in such surveys were merely attempting to appear respectable or to gain the approval of the interviewers. As Pettigrew points out, rapport in the polling situation is unusually good, and most survey critics underestimate what a good confidant an attentive stranger makes, who is interested in your personal views. Perhaps most compelling of all, the data reported in this chapter on regional differences in verbal expressions of negative attitudes toward black Americans, and the general trend over time of a sharp national reduction, but not elimination, of anti-Negro prejudice, are completely consistent both with the persisting regional differences in segregation and discrimination and with the national reduction in social and legal sanctions in support of segregation.

The Elusive White Blacklash: Increased Acceptance of Goals, Continued Rejection of Means

Another question raised by the preceding data on changing racial opinions concerns the widely discussed "white backlash." Have recent hardenings and reversals of white attitudes nullified the gains of the past? The answer to this question is surprisingly complex. As we shall see, there has been no overall white backlash in the sense of a reversal of attitudes on the part of previously tolerant whites. Nor has there been a decline in white support for the broadly defined goals of equality of opportunity. But to suggest that the term "backlash" may be a misnomer is not to deny that white racism continues to be a powerful force in American life. The events of the 1960's have made race more salient for all white Americans, especially for the lower-middle and working class white Northerner, whose latent anti-Negro feelings could now emerge with political force, and for the white liberal, whose sympathy for the broad goals of equality were put to the test by specific policies such as the bussing of schoolchildren and increased demands for black autonomy.

The several post-riot studies of immediate white reactions to riots do not lend much support to the view that formerly sympathetic whites have suddenly shifted to an anti-Negro stance because of the riots. Those whites who reacted most negatively to the Watts riot, for example, were those who initially disliked Negroes, favored segregation, and opposed the civil rights movement.[8] However, one can find scattered evidence in the poll data to support the assertion that there has been an overall negative reaction to the riots. An August, 1967, Gallup poll found that almost a third of all white persons nationally say they have a lower regard for Negroes because of the riots. But the same poll demonstrates that basic white attitudes toward integration in housing have undergone no significant negative change. Gallup reports the following shifts in white attitudes toward housing integration during the period of ghetto riots and the presumed "white backlash":

Chart V-3: Responses of White Americans to the Question: "If colored people came to live next door, would you move?"

	1963	1965	1966	1967
Yes, definitely	20%	13%	13%	12%
Yes, might	25	22	21	23
No	55	65	66	65

From *Gallup Report* press releases. Furnished courtesy of the American Institute of Public Opinion.

Chart V-4: Responses of White Americans to the Question: "Would you move if colored people came to live in great numbers in your neighborhood?"

	1963	1965	1966	1967
Yes, definitely	49%	40%	39%	40%
Yes, might	29	29	31	31
No	22	31	30	29

From *Gallup Report* press releases. Furnished courtesy of the American Institute of Public Opinion.

Thus, there is little in the available opinion data to support the notion of white backlash, if backlash is defined as increased opposition to the *goals* and aspirations of Negro Americans. The trend toward greater acceptance of interracial goals by white Americans was merely slowed, not reversed. When one looks at white attitudes toward the *means* employed by groups protesting inequality of opportunity for black Americans, a somewhat less sympathetic picture emerges. In a survey conducted by the National Opinion Research Center in April of 1968, it was found that even though 40 percent of the white Americans interviewed said that they have become more favorable toward racial integration in recent years (as opposed to 33 percent who report becoming less favorable and 25 percent who say their attitudes have not changed), almost two out of three said they think the actions Negroes have taken have *hurt* their cause more than they have helped it.

The tentative acceptance of the goals of black Americans, particularly for equal treatment by the law and for equal educational opportunities, coupled with a rejection of the means employed by action groups striving for equality of opportunity, has long characterized white attitudes. Throughout the 1960's, whites have consistently opposed civil rights demonstrations. Whites opposed, by close to a two to one majority, the lunch counter sit-ins in 1960, the Freedom Rides of 1961, the civil rights rally in Washington, D.C., in 1963, the student-run Negro voter registration project in Mississippi in the summer of 1964, and more generally "actions Negroes have taken to obtain civil rights." [9]

Much of the argument for the existence of white backlash has been based upon an increase in opposition to the *pace* of social change. The evidence for the desire for a slowdown is supplied primarily by the changes in response to the following question:

Chart V-5: Responses of Representative Samples of Americans to the Question: "Do you think the Johnson administration is pushing integration too fast, or not fast enough?"

Percent Saying "Too Fast"

February, 1964	30
April, 1965	34
July, 1966	46
September, 1966	52
August, 1967	44
April, 1968	39
October, 1968	54

From *Gallup Report* press releases. Furnished courtesy of the American Institute of Public Opinion.

Although there has been a great deal of fluctuation, the general trend appears to have been toward an increased resistance to the pace of racial change.

In a recent study, however, Professor Michael Ross of the University of California at Santa Barbara has cast doubt upon this interpretation.[10] Ross's data suggest that during the Kennedy and Johnson administrations there was a cyclic quality to public reactions to the pace of racial change, and that shifts in public opinion about the rate at which integration is proceeding constitute not an overall hardening of white attitudes, but simply highly volatile but temporary reactions to recent events. The Ross analysis suggests that responses to the question about the pace at which the administration is pushing integration are influenced by the general popularity of the administration, *independent* of racial issues.

The results of a survey conducted by Louis Harris for *Newsweek* magazine in the summer of 1967 fit the pattern of increased acceptance of goals, coupled with continued rejection of means. Though the Harris survey showed that whites were somewhat more inclined to admit to stereotyped views regarding anti-Negro prejudice than they had been in the immediate past, a clear majority were "ready to approve even the most drastic federal programs to attack the root causes of violence in the ghettos." [11] (Notably, by 1968 the acceptance of negative stereotypes had generally declined to below the 1963 level.) In sum, then, during the 1960's assertive attempts to achieve political, social, and economic equality of opportunity for Negroes have met with the disfavor of a majority of white Americans. Only moderate legislation receives the approval of more than half of the whites in this country. At the same time, over the past twenty years, and despite some minor short-term fluctuation, there has been a steady increase in white support for the goals of integration and equality of opportunity for black Americans. Nevertheless it is abundantly clear that a great deal of resistance to racial change remains.

To understand the sources of this resistance, we must know more about the characteristics of those who oppose integration and who accept negative stereotypes of black Americans. Who are the prejudiced and the opponents of racial change, and how do they differ from their more tolerant countrymen? Both social structure and individual personality are involved in the causes of prejudice, and thus the answer to this question will be given in two parts. We will examine first the differences in white racial attitudes among population subgroups, and then the psychological characteristics associated with racial prejudice.

Subgroup Difference in White Attitudes Toward Blacks

Numerous studies of the relationships between prejudice and such variables as age, education, and socioeconomic status are in agreement on at least one point: no single social characteristic can completely account for patterns of ethnic hostility.[12] Nevertheless, in a number of studies, small but consistent differences in prejudice have been shown to be associated with certain social groups. In the United States, the greatest differences in attitudes toward racial integration are regional. Surveys conducted by the National Opinion Research Center in 1963 show white Northerners overwhelmingly more favorable toward integration in schools, housing, and public transportation than white Southerners, by a difference ranging from 19 percent in the case of housing integration to 38 percent on the issue of integration in public transportation.[13] Clearly, historical effects continue to exert their influence on white Southern racial opinion. Nevertheless these regional differences are declining, and Southern attitudes have undergone drastic changes from their earlier baseline of a total rejection of integration.

Another population variable which is related to prejudice,

though less strongly than region, is urbanization. Sheatsley [14] found that residents of the ten largest metropolitan areas obtained the highest and most favorable scores on a "pro-integration scale" consisting of responses to questions dealing with equality of employment opportunity for Negroes, racial integration in schools, housing, and public transportation, and approval or disapproval of white-Negro social interaction. Those who reside in rural areas had the lowest and least favorable scores on the pro-integration scale. These rural-urban differences in racial exclusiveness are perhaps in keeping with the widely held view of the city-dweller as more cosmopolitan, and tolerant of diversity in traits and behavior.

In keeping with another commonly held view, several studies have shown marked age differences in anti-Negro prejudice, with the oldest age groups expressing the most intolerance. This difference may be related to the long-term trend in white attitudes; it is possible that part of this long-term trend reflects the replacement of an older, more intolerant generation by a newer and less prejudiced one. However, until adequate long-term studies of the *same* individuals become available (as opposed to age-grading of a sample interviewed at one point in time), this must remain a tentative hypothesis. It is logically possible, as Bettelheim and Janowitz have pointed out,[15] that as a person grows older his attitudes become less tolerant. A disturbing exception to the age and prejudice relationship is the finding in several recent surveys that the very youngest Southern respondents interviewed, i.e., those in their early twenties, are somewhat *less* tolerant than those in their thirties. It has been suggested that this difference may reflect the impact of the post-1954 controversy over school desegregation upon the formation of racial attitudes during the adolescence of these young Southerners.[16]

In sociological research, socioeconomic status is often defined in terms of three closely related variables: education, income, and occupational status. Both separately and in combination, these three components of socioeconomic status are clearly related to anti-Negro prejudice. The higher an individual's socioeconomic status, the less likely it is that he will express intolerant pro-segregationist attitudes toward black

Americans. Of the three, education bears the strongest and most consistent inverse relationship to anti-Negro prejudice. In fact, the previously discussed relationship of age to prejudice is complicated by the important role of education. Young people are not only likely to have more education than older Americans (in terms of years of schooling), but the quality of education that young people receive is more likely to stress values and perspectives incompatible with racism. Thus the relationship between age and prejudice is at least partly attributable to the more basic relationship between education and prejudice.

These findings should prove encouraging to those who view the transmission of democratic values as one of the important functions of education in a free society. However, certain qualifications must be made regarding the presumed increase in tolerance as a function of education. First of all, as Bettelheim and Janowitz pointed out, "the very fact that a significant portion of college graduates still hold stereotypes and support discrimination reflects the limits of the educational system in modifying attitudes." [17] In addition, Stember has shown that education brings both positive and negative changes.[18] The better educated are less likely to accept traditional stereotypes or to reject casual contacts with minority group members, and they are opposed to formal discriminatory policies. However, better educated people develop their own "idiosyncratic" and derogatory stereotypes, and they may be more likely to favor informal discrimination and to reject intimate contact with minority groups. Thus, while the overall effect of education is undoubtedly to reduce at least the most blatant and obvious varieties of prejudice and discrimination, education as it is presently offered in our society is not completely incompatible with bigotry and intolerance.

A variable that bears a more complex relationship to prejudice than any mentioned so far is religion. Several studies show that Jewish respondents are considerably less intolerant of Negroes than are Protestant and Catholic respondents, though this may be due in part to differences in level of education and urbanization. The data on church attendance are especially interesting and perhaps somewhat surprising. Numerous studies have shown that church attenders are, on the average, *more* prejudiced than nonattenders. This finding is particularly disturbing in view of the fact that the teachings of all the world's major religions have stressed brotherly love and humanitarian values. That Americans who attend church are more intolerant than those who do not seems to suggest that Christian religious denominations have failed to communicate the values of brotherly love and humanitarianism.

Social psychologists Gordon Allport and Michael Ross [19] have suggested a possible resolution of this paradox. Since intolerance and discrimination conflict with religious principles, a person for whom religion is intrinsically valuable, and who has internalized the teachings of his religion, should be particularly unlikely to direct hostile sentiments and actions toward others. On the other hand, prejudiced attitudes would not necessarily be dissonant for the casually religious person for whom religion, instead of being valued for its own sake, serves instrumental needs such as getting along in the community. If we can assume that frequency of church attendance is positively associated with devoutness and intrinsic religiosity, then the Allport-Ross interpretation receives some support from recent studies which have asked more detailed questions about frequency of church attendance. Several such studies have demonstrated a curvilinear relationship between prejudice and church attendance, with the casual infrequent attender being more prejudiced than either the nonattender or the person who attends church very frequently. Studies of the relationship between attitudinal religious orientation and prejudice provide even more direct support for Allport's distinction between instrumental and intrinsic religiosity.[20]

In sum, a composite profile of the racially intolerant individual emerges: He (or she) is most likely to be a poorly educated, older, rural Southerner, with a poor-paying, low-status job. Though he is nominally a Christian, he attends church irregularly. His more tolerant countryman is most likely to be a well-educated, highly paid resident of a large Northern city, with a high-status occupation. If he professes allegiance to any religious denomination, he is most likely to be Jewish or, if he is a Christian, a devoutly religious person who attends religious services frequently.

Personality and Prejudice

Although such social factors as urbanization, region, and education account for much racial prejudice, these forces do not exert their effects directly upon intolerance and discrimination. They are mediated through the personality, beliefs, and feelings of individuals.

White racism may serve three general needs or functions for those who subscribe to it. [21] One psychological function of prejudice which has received a great deal of attention in many studies is the externalization of inner conflict. A person who is insecure about his own personal or social status may attempt to maintain his own sense of worth by disparaging others. Influenced by the writings of Sigmund Freud, a number of authors have argued convincingly that, for many individuals, their own unacceptable and unconscious impulses and desires may be an important cause of prejudice. Sexual and aggressive feelings, which the individual would rather not acknowledge to himself, may be projected outward and attributed to minority groups. This refusal to acknowledge negative characteristics of oneself or one's own group, coupled with a tendency to project the unacceptable characteristics onto "out-groups," has been labeled the "authoritarian personality" and may result from child-rearing practices in which the expression of sexuality and aggression is met with severe parental sanctions.[22] Such a person is most comfortable with rigid and clear-cut systems of authority and status. He tends to be unusually submissive to those above him in such hierarchies and unusually aggressive toward those he perceives as below him. The authoritarianism or "F" (for fascism) scale developed by the personality researchers has been used in hundreds of studies, most of which have found a clear relationship between authoritarianism and prejudice. Authoritarian personalities are not necessarily "sick" or "neurotic." Indeed where authoritarian and racist social and political institutions exist, such personalities may be happier and "better-adjusted" than the more ambivalent and more consciously conflicted egalitarian personalities.

Externalization of inner conflict is not the only psychological need that prejudice may serve. Obviously, intolerant attitudes may receive continual support from the social environment. Most individuals, needing the approval of their families, friends, and work or business associates, do not readily dissent from their views.[23] In a study contrasting the psychological sources of anti-Negro prejudice in the North and the South, Thomas Pettigrew found that the externalization of inner conflict, as measured by the authoritarianism scale, played an equally important role as a cause of prejudice in both regions: in both the North and South, the authoritarians were more anti-Negro than the nonauthoritarians. That authoritarianism was not the sole cause of prejudice, however, was demonstrated by the fact that, though the level of authoritarianism was the same in the Northern and Southern samples, the level of anti-Negro prejudice was much higher among the Southern respondents. Pettigrew found that in the South, but not in the North, those who were most attuned to and concerned about adhering to local social customs were most prejudiced.

In addition to the functions of social adjustment and externalization of inner conflict, prejudiced attitudes may serve a reality testing function for some people, helping them to "size up" objects and events in the environment.[24] The cognitive advantages of "prejudgment" in terms of culturally acquired beliefs and evaluations are numerous and immediately apparent. For example, reports of political turmoil in the emerging African nations are quickly categorized by the bigot as yet another illustration of "innate Negro inferiority" and the need for white leadership and dominance of black people. This saves him the mental effort of considering the complex historical, political, and economic factors involved in these and similar problems. By helping him make sense of the world, these borrowed stereotypes become more firmly fixed, and he becomes convinced of the accuracy of his socially acquired definition of "reality."

A great deal of contemporary social psychological research has supported the general proposition that there is a strain toward consistency and "balance" in people's beliefs and evaluations. We feel more comfortable when the groups and people that we like are associated with "good" characteristics and actions, and similarly we expect those we dislike to have negative qualities and to engage in "bad" activities. If we become aware of inconsistencies and contradictions in our beliefs, we feel uncomfortable and tend to change them so as to eliminate or at least reduce the inconsistency.[25]

The contradiction between American values of fair play and equality of opportunity on the one hand, and racial discrimination on the other, are potential sources of "cognitive dissonance." Does this mean that communications which directly attack this potential conflict will result in less prejudice? In a public opinion survey, sociologist Frank Westie [26] first asked people to indicate their agreement or disagreement with general American creed statements, such as "Everyone in America should have equal opportunities to get ahead," and "Under our democratic system people should be allowed to live where they please if they can afford to." Most respondents agreed with the general items. They were then asked for their opinions on *specific* social policy questions related to the general values, such as "I would be willing to have a Negro as my supervisor in my place of work," or "I would be willing to have a Negro family live next door to me." A smaller percentage of people were willing to support values such as equality of opportunity in employment and housing when these values were expressed in the form of specific and personal reactions to a Negro supervisor or a Negro neighbor than when they were expressed in general terms. At this point, Westie's interviewers asked the respondents to compare their responses to the two related sets of questions. When they had been inconsistent, most of the respondents recognized the dilemma, and of those who responded to the inconsistency, 82 percent changed their anti-democratic answers to the specific questions in the direction of their democratic answers to the general questions. For example, upon seeing the conflict between his endorsement of equal employment opportunity and his rejection of the idea of a Negro as his supervisor, a respondent might say, "Well, I guess it might be all right for a Negro to be supervisor if he were unusually qualified." Perhaps this finding lends support to Myrdal's prediction that in the long run the general tenets of the American creed will win out over the contradictory valuations defining American race relations. However, it is clear that historical and situational factors will also play a decisive role.

Selecting the Target for Prejudice: Racial Differences or Belief Differences?

A source of prejudice that is related to the reality testing and cognitive balance functions of attitudes is illustrated by Milton Rokeach's recent research on "perceived belief dissimilarity." [27] In a series of studies, Rokeach and his associates have contended that when a person is racially prejudiced he is not really bothered by racial difference so much as by a feeling that beliefs and values differ from his own. When given a choice, whites prefer to associate with persons of other races who hold similar beliefs, e.g., a white Christian with a black Christian rather than with a white atheist. These results were obtained not only in experimental studies in which students completed questionnaires but also in very realistic work situations in which newly hired janitors and hospital attendants chose work partners on the basis of similarity in beliefs rather than on the basis of race. This general principle must be qualified in the case of intimate social contact. In interpersonal forms of behavior such as one's own dating or marriage or that of a member of one's family, race is a more important consideration than beliefs. Although this seems to contradict Rokeach's general formulation, the contradiction may be more apparent than real. Though discrimination tends to occur along visible lines of language, color, religious affiliation, and ethnicity, according to Rokeach, these visible characteristics indicate to most people the existence of important differences in beliefs, interests, and values.[28] Even when we learn that for at least some important religious or political values he is similar to us, we apparently assume that in other realms he will probably differ from us more than a person who has similar views *and* is of our own race. Thus, even the slight preference for persons of the same race and same belief, over persons of a different race but same belief, may really represent attributed differences and similarities in beliefs and values in realms *other* than those in which the beliefs have been made public. At the very least, we can probably conclude that for most people it is not color per se that produces intolerance, but rather the differences in beliefs, values, and behavior that are assumed to be associated with differences in color.

The ethnocentric preference for in-group members and dislike for those who are "not our kind" varies from one individual to another and from one population subgroup to another. One important consequence of the experiences and widening psychological horizons that accompany urbanization and industrialization appears to be an increased tolerance for other people and for other ways of doing things. Not only does intergroup contact provide an opportunity for learning about existing similarities of the out-group to the in-group, but such contact may also work indirectly to reduce prejudice by increasing behavioral and attitudinal similarities between groups.[29] Nevertheless, enclaves of provincialism remain in even the largest cities, particularly in homogeneous ethnic neighborhoods, where social interactions may be almost entirely limited to members of one's ethnic group.

To summarize, prejudice may serve to externalize psychic conflict, or it may enhance adaptation to an already prejudiced group, or it may offer the mental stability that comes with stereotypical thinking. Related to the reality testing or stereotyped thinking function, recent research demonstrates that perceived dissimilarities in beliefs and values are important determinants of the selection of a target for prejudice. That there are varying bases for prejudice has implications for action programs designed to reduce intergroup tension. For maximum effectiveness, a campaign to reduce prejudice should be applied to the motivational bases of prejudice. An "information" campaign which tries to destroy old stereotypes and stresses qualities held in common by the in-group and the out-group will have little effect if antipathy toward the out-group is deeply rooted in local customs and norms. In such a situation, prejudice helps the individual adjust to his own group, and information about the disliked minority is irrelevant to the needs his antipathy serves. Statements by highly respected leaders, together with legislation prohibiting discrimination, may be more helpful than information campaigns in undermining the social adjustment basis of racial hostility. But neither information nor statements from respected and admired leaders is likely to affect the prejudices of those for whom racial hostility serves as an expression of deep social and personal frustration.

Social Change and Prejudice

In order to predict future changes in white attitudes toward black Americans, we must consider the impact of certain social changes upon individual beliefs and values. The effects of modernization upon prejudice are neither entirely positive nor entirely negative. We shall begin by discussing some positive effects.

As a nation we are becoming increasingly more urban, more affluent, and better educated. At the same time white attitudes toward black Americans become increasingly favorable. Does this mean that the social changes taking place in the United States are inimical to dogmatic ethnocentrism? Such is the conclusion arrived at by William Brink and Louis Harris after their analysis of white racial attitudes: "The thrust of education, mobility, and rising incomes will produce fewer backlash whites and far more affluent whites. . . . The impact of education and rationalism is having a telling effect on white society in America." [30]

The manner in which the social changes accompanying modernization and industrialization increase tolerance has been suggested by the sociologist Samuel Stouffer. Stouffer found that youth, more education, higher status occupation, and urban residence were associated with tolerance for political nonconformity, a result that corresponds with the findings of studies of racial tolerance. Stouffer suggests:

> Great social, economic, and technological forces are working on the side of exposing ever larger proportions of our population to the idea that "people are different from me, with different systems of values, and they can be good people." [31]

In the light of Rokeach's studies of perceived differences in beliefs as a source of prejudice, it appears that, in addition to this "tolerance through familiarity" effect, a related process may be occurring in which urbanization, education, and the mass media bring real and vicarious contact with other groups. Through this contact people learn that other groups are *not* so different from themselves as they had imagined.

In general, then, the total effect of urbanization, education, and widening social contacts should eventually undermine the belief that "our way is the one true way." Perhaps this is best exemplified by the process of education. Ideally, college students should not only acquire information in their courses that conflicts with a belief in innate racial inferiority or superiority, they should also acquire a questioning, skeptical outlook that is incompatible with the ethnocentric assumption that all good resides in the in-group, while the out-group has nothing but bad qualities.

Age differences in anti-Negro prejudice among whites provide still another reason for optimism. Even though it is logically possible that aging will bring a hardening of racial attitudes, the fact that young people, particularly well-educated young people, express more support for integration than their elders may be a harbinger of the direction of change in American race relations.

Unfortunately several important qualifications must be added to this optimistic picture. For one thing, the available evidence suggests that higher education does not *automatically* reduce prejudice. Years spent attending college do not, in themselves, serve to eliminate racist beliefs and attitudes, unless the quality of the educational experience is incompatible with such beliefs and attitudes. In a study done for the Kerner Commission, Campbell and Schuman found that college education has a positive effect upon racial attitudes only for those who received their college education after World War II.[32]

A convincing proof that education and industrialization are not in themselves foolproof immunization against prejudice and ethnocentrism is given by Nazi Germany. In that instance, advanced scientific achievements simply increased the efficiency with which the ultimate genocidal conclusion of racism was carried out. These all too recent horrors, along with continuing racial intolerance in America, have led several social scientists to examine the sources of strain in our society that may generate intergroup hostility. Paradoxically, certain aspects of those very democratic institutions and values in which we take most pride may under certain circumstances cause an increase in anti-democratic attitudes. Bettelheim and Janowitz point out: "In an advanced industrial society where individualistic values predominate, those sociological variables that tend to weaken ethnic hostility have some limits and may even generate counter-trends." [33]

One such counter-trend is an inordinate concern with status and with social and personal identity. Historian Richard Hofstadter has remarked: "Because, as a people extremely democratic in our social institutions we have had no clear, consistent and recognizable system of status, our personal status problems have an unusual intensity." [34] Thus the rootlessness and heterogeneity of American life produce in some of us an anxious desire to secure an identity and to escape from the freedom of a democratic, loosely structured, rapidly changing social system.[35] The results of several studies indicate that those who are most concerned about status tend also to be most prejudiced,[36] and that status concern is associated with child-rearing practices that result in authoritarianism and prejudice in children.[37] Concern for status seems to produce a preference for hierarchical orderings, in which the prestige that accrues to one's own group is derived at least in part from the fact that there are groups below it on the totem pole of prestige. Social changes that appear to have adverse effects upon the relative standing of his own group are particularly distasteful to the individual whose personal identity is derived to a large extent from his social standing. That politicians are aware of this reaction is indicated by their explicit appeal in the 1968 campaign to the "forgotten men" of the lower-middle and working class—the whites who feel that their relative standing is threatened by the social and economic gains of black Americans.

A consequence of our fluid and changing social structure that is closely related to anxiety over the status of one's own group relative to other groups is the social mobility of individuals. Inevitably there are losers as well as winners in a striving, competitive, achievement-oriented society. The losers are the "downwardly mobile"—those who experience declines in socioeconomic status within the spans of their own work careers or whose socioeconomic status is lower than that of their parents. After reviewing a series of studies on the attitudinal consequences of social mobility, Bettelheim and Janowitz conclude that downward mobility typically increases prejudice, and while slightly upward mobility may have little effect or may reduce prejudice slightly, extremely upward mobility may also increase prejudice.[38] The effect of downward mobility seems readily understandable: a visible and vulnerable minority group makes a likely scapegoat for the bitterness and frustration caused by a loss in status. But additional mechanisms may be operating to produce a relationship between mobility and prejudice.

One of the negative consequences of mobility is a disruption of interpersonal relationships with family, friends, and work associates. Because of his social origins, the mobile individual is ill-at-ease with those of his present social rank and also with those whose origins are similar to his. This breakdown in social integration may result in a loosening of the normative constraints which are naturally exerted upon the individual by ·the everyday, face-to-face groups to which he belongs. The absence of a restraint upon the mobile person's prejudices may lead to a more blatant manifestation of his racial hostility. In some cases, the slightly upwardly mobile individual may successfully compensate for the disruption of his relationships with primary, face-to-face groups by increased participation in formal voluntary organizations in his community. This is apparently less likely to occur in the case of the downwardly mobile or the extremely upwardly mobile.

"Vertical" mobility, or change in socioeconomic status, is not the only prejudice-inducing disruption that is endemic to life in Western industrial democracies. "Horizontal," i.e., geographical, mobility may also increase alienation and rootlessness. One in every five Americans moves annually. In an as yet unpublished study of white voters in Gary, Indiana, Thomas Pettigrew and Robert Riley found that George Wallace's strongest supporters in 1968 were Protestants of small town origin who *did not* grow up in Gary.[39] Whatever the nature of the underlying mechanisms, research has demonstrated that both a subjective feeling of social isolation [40] and an objective absence of social participation [41] are associated with increased prejudice.

Isolation, anxiety over status, and downward social mobility, with their unfortunate personal and social consequences, appear to be inevitable by-products of American democracy. They are part of the price we pay for a free and open society in which rewards are based upon individual achievement. Whether or not we believe that the price is too high, these consequences are likely to remain with us. We must therefore understand and somehow cope with the consequences of alienation and status anxiety if we are to avert their potential resolution in the authoritarian and racist social movements which attract and appeal to the "dispossessed." [42]

The Widening Racial Gap: Social Perception in the "Two Societies"

White Resistance and Black Insistence

The National Advisory Commission on Civil Disorders concluded that "our Nation is moving toward two societies, one black, one white—separate and unequal." There are several senses in which this largely unheeded warning accurately depicts continuing trends in American society. Most obviously there are the demographic changes described by the Kerner Commission: ". . . central cities are becoming more heavily Negro while the suburban fringes around them remain almost entirely white." But perhaps even more ominous than the white suburban "noose" around the black ghetto is the growing psychological gulf separating black Americans from white Americans. Although there has been a gradual increase in white acceptance of racial integration and equality of opportunity, a sizable portion of the white population still resists these goals. Some surveys show increasing white opposition to the pace of racial change as well as continuing opposition to most of the means that have been used in attempts to achieve integration and equality of opportunity, including peaceful demonstrations and voter registration drives. In sharp contrast to the mixture of gradualism and resistance that characterizes white racial opinions in the United States, black Americans are increasingly insistent in their demands for an end to discrimination and inequality. This polarization and conflict between white gradualism and the black revolution of rising expectations and demand for immediate change manifests itself in many ways.

Happiness and Satisfaction with Life

The results of several studies indicate that Negroes are generally less content than whites with the existing conditions in their lives. Black Americans experience a large gap between aspirations and achievements. One quantitative measure used by pollsters which provides an index of the degree of personal happiness or dissatisfaction is the "Self-Anchoring Striving Scale" developed by social psychologist Hadley Cantril.[43] In this procedure, the interviewer first asks the respondent to describe the best and worst possible future lives for himself. After obtaining these descriptions of personal hopes and fears, the interviewer shows the respondent a picture of an eleven-step ladder numbered from zero to ten, and asks:

> Suppose we say that the top of the ladder represents the best possible life for you and the bottom represents the worst possible life for you. Where on the ladder do you feel you personally stand at the present time? Step number _____ ?

The ladder rating obtained in response to this question provides a measure of the individual's feeling of gratification or deprivation *relative* to his own conception of the ideal life for himself. In several surveys in which this ladder rating question was asked of representative samples of black and white Americans, the former assigned themselves a significantly lower position than did the latter, indicating a greater feeling of deprivation relative to their goals and aspirations.

The results of a survey of more than 5,000 Negroes and whites conducted in early 1968 in fifteen major American cities provides more specific information concerning the sources of discontent among urban Negroes. Campbell and Schuman found that, as compared to urban whites, Negro city dwellers express more dissatisfaction with public services in their neighborhoods, complain more about the prices and the quality of goods in neighborhood stores, and are both less satisfied with the protection they receive from the police and more likely to report unfavorable experiences in their personal contacts with the police.[44]

A recent study shows that blacks are far more critical of the police than are whites. On the one hand, blacks see the police as less effective in giving protection to citizens: 17 percent of nonwhite males in the $6,000 to $10,000 income range felt the police did a "very good" job in protecting people in their neighborhoods, as opposed to 51 percent of the white males of similar income.[45] On the other hand, blacks are considerably less confident than whites about police honesty, and considerably less satisfied with the treatment they received from the police. Only 36 percent of nonwhite males in the $6,000 to $10,000 income bracket thought police in their neighborhoods were "almost all honest," while 21 percent felt they were "almost all corrupt"; the corresponding percentages for white males of the same income bracket were 65 percent and 2 percent.[46] Only 31 percent of the non-whites, as opposed to 67 percent of the whites felt the police did a "very good" job of being respectful to people like themselves.[47]

To many white Americans, the discontent that black people more and more vociferously express is surprising and unjustified. Distinguished commentators rarely fail to point out that a great deal of "progress" has been made in the past several decades, and particularly in the past few years, in the social and economic conditions of nonwhite Americans. However, as Thomas Pettigrew has suggested, what appear at first glance to be "real gains" for Negro Americans fade into "psychological losses" when they are compared with the standards of the more affluent white majority.[48] Pettigrew's "real gains–psychological losses" analysis is as applicable in 1969 as it was in 1963, despite some progress during the past six years in reducing the disparity between white and nonwhite life-styles. Thus a 1968 publication of the Bureau of Labor Statistics entitled *Recent Trends in Social and Economic Conditions of Negroes in the United States* provide figures demonstrating that black Americans have made gains in income, education, occupational status, and other areas in recent years. To many white Americans, such figures apparently suggest that Negroes should be happy with the progress that is being made. After all, the statistics show, for example, that for the first time the number of Negroes moving into well-paying jobs has been substantial: since 1960 there has been a net increase of 300,000 nonwhite professional and managerial workers. To a black American, however, the more important statistics may be those demonstrating that a nonwhite is still almost three times as likely as a white man to be in a low-paying job as a laborer or service worker. A white defender of the status quo may point out that 27 percent of nonwhite families in 1967 had a total income above $8,000—double the 1960 proportion, even when the figures are placed in constant 1967 dollars. For black people, it may be more relevant that in 1967 the annual family income of Negroes was only 59 percent of the median annual white family income.

Furthermore, it is misleading to focus only on gains for blacks in general. While various indices. *do* show increasing gains for blacks as a group, the situation of the black ghetto dweller is less promising. Department of Labor figures clearly indicate that "social and economic conditions are getting worse, not better, in slum areas." [49] In many ghetto areas, housing conditions are deteriorating rather than improving; in South Los Angeles, for example, the percentage of substandard housing units increased from 18 percent to 34 percent between 1960 and 1965, while median rents *also* increased, from $69 to $77.[50] In 1966, the unemployment rate of nonwhite boys aged 14 to 19 in urban poverty areas stood at 31 percent; of nonwhite girls, 46 percent. Comparable rates for whites in poverty areas were 20 percent lower for boys and 10 percent lower for girls.[51] Overall figures for nonwhite youth unemployment are similarly discouraging. The jobless rate for nonwhite males aged 16 to 17 was 9.4 percent in 1948 and 24.7 percent in 1968; for white youths of the same age, the rate was 2.2 percent in 1948 and 10.9 percent in 1968.

Further, even where blacks have entered higher levels of the economic ladder, they have not yet attained significant decision-making influence. A study of Negroes in policy-making positions in Chicago—where some 28 percent of the population in 1965 was black—makes this clear:

> The whitest form of policy-making in Chicago is in the control of economic enterprises. Out of 6838 positions identified in business corporations, Negroes held only 42 (six-tenths of 1 percent). Thirty-five of these were in insurance, where Negroes occupy 6 percent of the 533 posts. But all 35 were in two all-Negro insurance firms. The other seven positions were in four smaller banks. In banks in general, Negroes occupied three-tenths of 1 percent of the policy posts. There were no Negro policy-makers at all in manufacturing, communications, transportation, utilities, and trade corporations.
>
> Out of 372 companies we studied, the Negro-owned insurance companies were the only ones dominated by blacks. And if we had used the same stringent criteria for banks and insurance companies that we used for nonfinancial institutions, there would have been no black policy-makers in the business sector at all.
>
> Now, amazingly enough, Chicago has proportionately more Negro-controlled businesses, larger than neighborhood operations, than any other major city in the North. Therefore, similar surveys in other Northern Metropolitan areas would turn up an even smaller percentage of Negro policy-makers in the business world.[52]

Protests and the Pace of Change

Public opinion surveys conducted by Louis Harris and others have shown that the gradualist racial sentiments of most whites conflict with the increasingly urgent demands of black Americans for their share of the affluence of America. This gap has manifested itself on issues such as the causes of riots, the pace of racial change, and the propriety of various means for achieving integration and equality. For example, a 1966 Gallup poll found that while 58 percent of white Americans thought that the Johnson administration was pushing integration too fast, only 5 percent of the black Americans interviewed shared this opinion.

The pattern of approval or disapproval of protests and demonstrations is similar to the observed differences regarding the appropriate speed of integration. In a 1965 Harris poll, a representative sample of Americans was asked whether they felt that demonstrations by Negroes had helped or hurt the advancement of Negro rights. While two out of three white respondents said that the demonstrations had hurt more than they helped, two out of three Negro respondents expressed the opposite view. For the most part, responses to more specific questions about protests and demonstrations reveal the same racial gap. Thus the Harris survey found that, in May of 1968, 80 percent of the Negro interviewees but only 29 percent of the whites approved of the Poor People's March in Washington, D.C. Only with regard to riots and the use of violence do the majority of both races agree in expressing disapproval, and even here the level of white disapproval is considerably higher than that of Negro disapproval.

Riots: Their Causes and Cures

An especially profound discrepancy exists between black and white perception of the *causes* of riots. In their 1968 survey of opinions in fifteen large U.S. cities, Campbell and Schuman found:

> Negroes and whites do not perceive the riots in the same terms. Most Negroes see the riots partly or wholly as spontaneous protests against unfair conditions, economic deprivation, or a combination of the two. . . . The white population in the 15 cities is more divided on the nature of riots. A large segment, roughly a third on several questions, takes a viewpoint similar to that of most Negroes, viewing the disturbances as protests against real grievances, which should be handled by removing the causes for grievance. Approximately another third see the riots in very different terms, however, emphasizing their criminal or conspiratorial character, their origin in a few men of radical or criminal leaning, and the need to meet them with police power. The balance of the white population in the 15 cities mix both views in various combinations.[53]

Comparable results were obtained in a Harris opinion survey, conducted in the summer of 1967, on the perceived causes of riots. The racial differences in opinion shown in Chart V-6 clearly support the Harris assertion that white and black views on the causes of riots are "eerily out of register."

Chart V-6: Most Frequent Spontaneously Mentioned Causes of Negro Rioting by White and Negro Adults [54]

	White	Negro
Outside agitation	45%	10%
Prejudice—promises not kept, bad treatment	16	36
Lack of jobs–unfair employment	10	29
Poverty—slums, ghetto conditions	14	28
Negroes are too lazy to work for their rights	13	5
Uneducated people—don't know what they are doing	11	9
Teen-agers looking for trouble	7	7
Law has been too lax	7	0.5

In view of their assessment of their situation, it is small wonder that Negroes feel alienated from American society and government. In April of 1968, 56 percent of the Negro respondents told Harris interviewers that they agreed with the statement, "I don't have nearly as good a chance to get ahead as most people." Only 17 percent of the white interviewees expressed such a belief in limited opportunity. In the same poll, 52 percent of the Negroes and 39 of the whites agreed with the statement, "People running this country don't really care what happens to people like me." Similarly, blacks are more critical than whites of government at the federal, state, and local levels.[55] The most disturbing aspect of the political alienation of black people is the rapid growth of such feelings in the past few years. From 1966 to 1968 there was a 20 percent increase in the number of black Americans who express a feeling of powerlessness to influence the government.

Congressional Backlash

Although black and white Americans disagree about the causes of riots and have different beliefs about their abilities to influence the government, according to both Gallup and Harris polls, they are in substantial agreement on the crucially important question of steps the government should take to prevent future racial outbreaks. Clear majorities of both whites and Negroes support federal programs to tear down the ghettos and to give jobs to all the unemployed.[56] The Campbell and Schuman fifteen-cities survey substantiates this conclusion:

> There is majority support in the white sample for government action to provide full employment, better education, and improved housing in parts of cities where they are now lacking. . . . Support for such programs declines somewhat but remains at a majority level even when the proviso is added for a ten percent rise in personal taxes to pay the costs.[57]

Apparently the level of public support for proposals such as those recommended by the Kerner Commission has been underestimated by congressmen and others in political office. Perhaps the press has oversold the notion of a white backlash and has placed too little emphasis upon public approval for massive federal spending to overcome racial inequities. Perhaps although the minority of white Americans who have received a disproportionate amount of attention from the press oppose such programs, the preponderance of American public opinion would support a war on poverty that goes far beyond any of the measures seriously considered by recent Congresses. Thus, on the issue of public spending, the more important gap appears to be between public willingness and congressional unwillingness to initiate and support federal programs in jobs, housing, and education. The American public, black and white, appears apprehensive and fearful about the future well-being of the neighborhood, the city, the country in general. Most blacks tend to give different weight to the nature and causes of the problems of America than most whites. But each group would apparently support a strong effort at the federal level to reduce intergroup hostility, and neither views the remedy primarily in terms of establishing "law and order." The popularly reported, but misnamed "white backlash" phenomenon has served to rationalize our timidity in making bold and imaginative inputs toward the solution of our urban problems.

The minority of whites who radically oppose the aspirations of the black community is a matter of considerable concern, and their organization into militant groups poses at least as much a threat to public order and safety as the activities of groups already discussed. In analyzing anti-war, student, and black protest, we have perhaps misleadingly brought together groups with varying potential for action. In the present section of this report, we have attempted to distinguish between white attitudes and white actions. The next chapter therefore considers the nature and roots of militant white action in contemporary America, and the role of the militant white in American history.

Chapter VI

White Militancy

THE IDEA of "militancy" suggests the activities of blacks, students, anti-war demonstrators, and others who feel themselves aggrieved by the perpetuation of old, outworn, or malignant social institutions. The historical record, however, indicates that considerably more disorder and violence have come from groups whose aim has been the preservation of an existing or remembered order of social arrangements, and in whose ideology the concept of "law and order" has played a primary role. There is no adequate term to cover all of the diverse groups who have fought to preserve their neighborhoods, communities, or their country from forces considered alien or threatening. The lack of a common term for Ku Klux Klansmen, Vigilantes, Minutemen, Know-Nothing activists, and anti-Negro or anti-Catholic mobs reflects the fact that these and other similar groups have different origins, different goals, and different compositions, and arise in response to specific historical situations which repeat themselves, if at all, only in gross outline.

Still, certain patterns stand out in the history of white militancy. In the past, the white militant was usually—though not always—an Anglo-Saxon Protestant, and the targets of his protest included other white ethnic groups. Today, while the WASP remains a major figure in the overall picture of white militancy, much of the white protest, especially in the urban North, comes from ethnic groups—especially Southern and Eastern European—which were themselves former targets of nativist agitation. Another change is more subtle. Until recently, the violent white militant acted, very frequently, with the assistance, encouragement, or at least acquiescence of more "stable" elements of the population, and quite often in concert with the militant and nativist aims of the American political and legal order. Today this is considerably less true. With the exception of some areas of the country—notably parts of the South—the violent white militant has become a minority, and operates beyond the pale of the law and the polity, both of which he tends to distrust in proportion to his lack of political efficacy or influence.

This chapter attempts to put white militancy in social and historical perspective. The first section considers the characteristic form of violent white militancy in history—vigilantism—in its interplay with the general thrust of a militantly nativist society. The following sections deal with contemporary white militancy in the South, the urban North, and among white paramilitary "anti-Communist" groups.

Vigilantism and the Militant Society [1]

American society has a lengthy tradition of private direct action to maintain order, coupled with a certain disdain for legal procedure and the restraints of the orderly political process. At the same time, American institutions have had a long history of nativism and racism. The interplay of these two traditions has resulted in vigilante violence most often expressed in racist and nativist channels.

Every social order is maintained, at some level, by actual or implicit sanctions of violence. An important aspect of the American experience has been the degree to which private groups have taken it upon themselves to administer or threaten such sanctions. Some of these groups, perceiving the formal enforcement of law and administration of justice as weak or inefficient, have acted to "take the law into their own hands." In practice, however, private enforcement of the "law" has tended to mean a rejection of *mere* law in the name of a presumably overarching conception of "order" rooted inevitably in group interest.

The nature of the American frontier produced the rationale for the extralegal enforcement of law which came to be known as vigilantism. This pragmatic approach to the genuine crises of order, occurring in areas where settlement had preceded the establishment of effective social control, was deeply rooted in American traditions of self-help. The roots of that tradition, in turn, are a number of national experiences and predilections, including the Puritan heritage of collective responsibility for the preservation of the moral order and a traditional distrust of government regulation and intervention. Perhaps more important than collective tradition was the immediate problem of danger and insecurity in areas where the formal agencies of law had barely penetrated or had atrophied in periods of intense disorder. Not infrequently, vigilante justice brought a crude kind of order to these sparsely settled areas. This was the context of the pre-Revolutionary War South Carolina Regulators, the Law and Order, Regulator, and Anti-Horsethief Societies of the Eastern and Middle Western states, the vigilantes of the Western frontier, and the popular tribunals of the mining camps.

In most of these private law enforcement ventures, the aims were simple and unambitious. There was no attempt to create new legal forms or to promote a new vision of the social order. Rather, the aim was the establishment of mechanisms for order patterned, so far as possible, on familiar models. In the absence of formal institutions of social control, voluntary associations sprang up to get done those things which needed doing.

Beneath the pragmatic zeal for order, understandable enough in the light of frontier conditions, lay a series of dangerous precedents. The self-help tradition largely sidestepped the restraints which a developed legal system imposes on the quest for order. Consequently, voluntary enforcement of the "law" tended to lean inevitably toward the enforcement of order, with or without law. Private violence, sometimes in conjunction with constituted authority and sometimes not, came to be used as an instrument for enforcing a threatened, or presumably threatened, system of social, political, economic, and cultural arrangements against the claims of those groups standing outside the system whose actions—or, sometimes, whose very existence—were seen as threatening.

Doubtless the first "alien" group to feel the combined assault of private and official violence was the American Indian. Regarded as wholly alien and wholly exterminable, Indians were subject to massive private violence which—like the massacre of over two hundred, largely women and children, which took place on Indian Island in California in 1860—more often than not took place under the tacit auspices of the American government. With regard to the Indian, "Many Americans cherished a conviction that they were waging what came to be called a 'war of extermination,' and they waged it with determination and hardly disguised enjoyment." [2]

The San Francisco Vigilance Committee of 1851 and the Great Committee of 1856 are the best known of the Western vigilante organizations. These committees were, on the whole, composed of leading citizens whose aim was the seizure of the administration of justice and the development of such means of subsidiary control, including standing armies, as were necessary in order to function without interference. They sought neither legislative change nor the reform of existing institutions, but rather the punishment of criminals and undesirables whom the courts had "allowed" to escape. They sought, in short, to act as a substitute for a judicial process which they saw as weak and inefficient. These committees had counterparts in all states west of the Mississippi. In practice, the rough justice of the vigilance committees was slanted toward nativist aims, and worked hardest against foreigners and minority groups, especially Mexicans and Chinese. The pursuit of "law and order" meant—as it apparently does today—a special effort against minority groups considered dangerous to constituted order, moral values, and racial hegemony.

In this effort the vigilante groups were not alone. Rather, private violence against minority groups in the West was only the leading edge of an endemic regional nativism supported by large segments of the population and in time elevated into the laws of the land. Ten Broek and his associates suggest this mixture of the formal and the informal, the legal and the criminal, in the treatment of the Orientals in California:

> The long agitation against the Oriental in California, to be seen in proper perspective, must be set against a background of violence and conflict involving the dominant white majority and the dark-skinned minorities; a heritage of hatred which had its inception in the fiercely competitive environment of gold-rush mining camps, was institutionalized in local ordinance and state law, and came to constitute a primary cause of some of the worst outbreaks of criminal lawlessness in California history.[3]

Private violence in California was encouraged by state law, which prohibited Chinese from testifying in cases involving whites. With this protection, militant Californians were officially allowed to slaughter Chinese with relative impunity. As in other instances of nativist agitation, there tended to develop a division of labor between "respectable" elements who utilized legislation—such as that resulting in the act of 1882 banning further Chinese immigration into the country—and mobs who looted, burned, and murdered men, women, and children in the Chinese quarters of the West Coast. This is not to suggest that a majority condoned mob violence. But the movement for social and political exclusion of the Chinese effectively withdrew legal protection against this kind of action. In the context of official denial of Chinese rights, the preservation of "order" meant in practice that virtually any pretext was sufficient for massive violence against them. In Los Angeles, after a white was killed during a tong war, mobs invaded the Chinese quarter, looting and "killing twenty-one persons—of whom fifteen, including women and children, were hanged on the spot from lamp-posts and awnings."[4]

A similar combination of public and private action has characterized the expression of white militancy in the South, where the Ku Klux Klan has intermittently arisen in the context of a social order which has given official and widespread approval to the exploitation and subordination of the black population. The Klan arose in the aftermath of the Civil War, when emancipation, the Fourteenth Amendment, and the ravages of the war itself had disrupted the traditional caste order and weakened, to some extent, the effectiveness of black subordination. To many white Southerners, the limited gains of the Southern blacks represented a state of fearful disorder. Woodward has described this atmosphere and the early legislation aimed at reestablishing social control along caste lines:

> The temporary anarchy that followed the collapse of the old discipline produced a state of mind bordering on hysteria among southern white people. The first year a great fear of black insurrection and revenge seized many minds, and for a longer time the conviction prevailed that Negroes could not be induced to work without compulsion. Large numbers of temporarily uprooted freedmen roamed the highways, congested in towns and cities, or joined the federal militia. In the presence of these conditions the provisional legislature established by President Johnson in 1865 adopted the notorious Black Codes. Some of them were intended to establish systems of peonage or apprenticeship resembling slavery.[5]

After the Black Codes were struck down, the Klan emerged to drive the freedmen out of politics and restore power and control to the dominant white leadership. The night-riding assaults on blacks, Northerners, and their Southern sympathizers were justified as "the necessary effort to prevent crime and uphold law and order." [6] The first Imperial Wizard of the Klan, General Nathan B. Forrest, explained the need for the Klan in these terms:

> Many Northern men were coming down there, forming Leagues all over the country. The Negroes were holding night meetings; were going about; were becoming very insolent; and the Southern people . . . were very much alarmed . . . parties organized themselves so as to be ready in case they were attacked. Ladies were ravished by some of these Negroes. . . . There was a great deal of insecurity.[7]

While Klan leadership was often held by men of substance,

the rank-and-file Klansman was most often a poor white fearful of black economic competition. Klan violence, like Western vigilantism, more often than not received support from significant segments of the dominant population: "Acts of violence were usually applauded by the conservative press and justified then, and afterwards, by the always allegedly bad reputation of the victims." [8]

The typical weapon of the Reconstruction Klan and subsequent white terrorists was lynching. The Tuskegee Institute has kept a record of lynchings in the United States since 1882 which gives an indication of the extent of white violence and serves as a reminder that the white militant has been the single most violent force—outside of war—in American history. For the period 1882–1959, Tuskegee has recorded a total of 4,735 lynchings, of which 73 percent were of Negroes and 85 percent of which took place in the Southern and border states.[9]

Again, it should be stressed that terrorist violence was only the leading edge of Southern anti-Negro militancy, which, in an important sense, was itself only the most blatant element of an endemic national racism and nativism. The revived Ku Klux Klan of the 1920's, which mixed anti-Negro, anti-Semitic, and anti-Catholic agitation, spread throughout the country and rose to a membership of several million. It was deeply entwined with several local and state governments.

> Klan violence in California was as brutal as anywhere in the South, and in the town of Taft, in Kern County, the police and best citizens turned out to watch an evening of torture in the local ball park. When an anti-Klan candidate won the Republican primary in Oregon, the Klan jumped to the Democratic Party and helped capture the governorship and enough of the legislature to outlaw all parochial schools. In Colorado, the Klan, with business support, elected two U.S. Senators and swept the state. When the Grand Dragon, a Denver doctor, was accused of having forced a high-school boy into marriage by threatening him with castration, the governor appointed the Klan leader aide-de-camp, as a show of confidence.[10]

In part, the rise of the later Klan was influenced by D. W. Griffith's racist epic, *Birth of a Nation,* which portrayed the

early Klan as a romantic defender of Southern white woman-
hood against the ravages of the freed blacks. Such nostalgia
was not confined to the poor, the uneducated, and the paro-
chial. Woodrow Wilson, on seeing the picture, was reported
to have been much impressed: " 'It is like writing history
with lightning,' he said, 'and my only regret is that it is all so
terribly true.' " [11]

In addition to the resurgence of the Ku Klux Klan, the era
during and after the First World War saw an eruption of vigilante activity against numerous groups, often backed by
constituted authority or the highly placed. During a wave of
agitation against German-Americans during the war, Theodore Roosevelt advocated shooting or hanging any German-
American who proved to be disloyal.[12] A private organization
called the American Protective League, operating as a kind
of quasi-official adjunct to the Department of Justice, engaged in various acts of physical force against German-Americans, unionists, and draft evaders.[13] Vigilante violence against
IWW organizers in the Pacific Northwest took place in the
context of a judicial system explicitly hostile to unions and
largely controlled by business interests.[14] In some of the postwar race riots, like that in Washington in 1919, police and
the military joined with other militant whites in assaults on
the Negro community.[15] Where nativist violence was not
officially sanctioned, whole communities sometimes rose up
against "alien" elements:

> During the night of August 5, 1920, and all through the
> following day hundreds of people laden with clothing and
> household goods filled the roads leading out of West Frank-
> fort, a mining town in Southern Illinois. Back in town their
> homes were burning. Mobs bent on driving every foreigner
> from the area surged through the streets. Foreigners of all
> descriptions were beaten on sight, although the Italian popu-
> lation was the chief objective. Time and again the crowds
> burst into the Italian district, dragged cowering residents
> from their homes, clubbed and stoned them, and set fire to
> their dwellings. The havoc went on for three days, although
> five hundred state troops were rushed to the scene.[16]

The militant violence of white vigilantes, then, has not operated as a peripheral phenomenon in isolation from the

major currents of American history. Rather, vigilantism represented the armed and violent wing of national tendencies toward racism, nativism, and strident Americanism which have been present since the nation's beginnings. With sporadic acceptance by a dominant, largely Anglo-Saxon and Protestant population in substantial control of much of the American political, military, and legal apparatus, private violence was a significant factor in thwarting the democratic aspirations of minorities.

Today, the violent or potentially violent white militant tends to speak from a position of relative political impotence, and his militancy must be seen as in large part a protest against that impotence and the insecurity which accompanies it. Nevertheless, in some instances, the militant white receives at least qualified support from—and sometimes achieves influence in—local or regional political structures. In other instances, white militants have adopted American political rhetoric and used it to structure the expression of their own discontents. On the other hand, national politics has seemingly adopted some of the rhetoric of white militancy. In all instances, the fabric of American social and political institutions has created the context in which contemporary white militancy flourishes. All of these phenomena are evident in the contemporary South.

The South

The advancement of the nigra can be solely attributed to the sincerity of the Southerner.

—ROBERT SHELTON

In 1928, a leading historian characterized the South as "a people with a common resolve indomitably maintained—that it shall be and remain a white man's country." [17] Despite a number of social and economic changes, on balance the South remains distinct in the degree to which it remains committed to the preservation of the "white man's country," and in many areas of the South official politics and private violence interact to make the South the great regional fortress of white racism.

The flourishing white violence in the South must be seen against the background of major social and economic changes which have produced in many areas of the region a dispossessed and insecure class of marginal whites. Increasing industrialization has shifted the center of influence to a rising middle class, frequently Republican and increasingly affluent. At the same time, industrialization has effectively begun to undermine the caste order in the economic realm, a process noted by students of the South some years ago.[18] Jobs formerly "white" have been entered by Negroes, especially in the burgeoning area of the Southern economy composed of industries working in part on government contracts.[19] At the same time that caste controls over black economic competition are crumbling under the impact of economic rationalization, a pervasive economic insecurity exists throughout much of the still essentially underdeveloped region. Coupled with a decreasing effectiveness of white sanctions over black social and political behavior—resulting partly from urbanization and industrialization and partly from civil rights activity—these events have accentuated a traditional sense of powerlessness and insecurity on the part of those marginal whites who historically have owned little else than their white skin and controlled little more than the local behavior of blacks.

The plight of the marginal white reflects a more general marginality and primitivism characteristic of large areas of the entire region. Culturally, parts of the South remain shot through with a strident fundamentalism and distrust of everything foreign; politically, parts of it remain dominated by self-serving cliques whose power rests primarily on the traditional political exclusion of blacks; its economic stagnation in many areas combines with its politics to produce in several places a depressingly high rate of malnutrition, infant mortality, and disease. These conditions affect both poor black and poor white. It is in this context that white terrorists, abetted in some areas by an affluently racist middle class and a political and legal order committed to the maintenance of caste domination, have perpetrated repeated violence against blacks, civil rights workers, and others.

It should be stressed that in the South it is particularly difficult to separate the phenomena of official and private violence. Southern police have traditionally condoned private violence in many areas. In other areas, white vigilante groups have drawn considerable membership from police forces.

Much of the militant white violence in the South has come from organizations such as the several Ku Klux Klans and the National States Rights Party, although considerable violence has been done by apparently unaffiliated whites, such as the Florida group who recently kidnapped a young black who was "beaten to an unrecognizable pulp" with a machete on the mistaken belief that he had had sexual relations with a white girl.[20] There is some evidence that the militant white organizations differ in the degree to which they have espoused or participated in violent action.

The National States Rights Party, with headquarters in Birmingham and a membership in several non-Southern states, is, like the Klan, anti-Semitic as well as anti-Negro. It is an outgrowth of an earlier guerrilla group in Georgia called the Columbians, which in the late 1940's organized an armed plot to overthrow the Georgia state government. Though small, the NSRP has been extremely active in Southern racial violence.[21]

The largest of the Klan organizations, the United Klans of America, headed by Robert Shelton of Tuscaloosa, Alabama, has striven for a respectable image, and Shelton has reportedly discouraged the use of violence by members. Nevertheless, Klan ideology and organizational structure are neither oriented toward nor capable of control over the activities of local groups and individuals. The murders of Lemuel Penn in Georgia and of Mrs. Viola Liuzzo in Alabama were the by-product of relatively disorganized patrolling efforts by such local units. Further, even the "official" advocacy of nonviolence is qualified in view of the Klan's conception of the imminent danger which black gains pose to Southern order. "We don't want no violence," Shelton has said, "but we ain't gonna let the niggers spit in our face, either." [22]

The unaffiliated Mississippi White Knights of the Ku Klux Klan have been the source of much of the violence against civil rights workers in the state. The group arose during, and in response to, the intensive civil rights activity in Mississippi, after a long period in which Klan activity in the state had been dormant. Thirty-six White Knights have recently been arrested on charges of terrorism, including suspicion of at least seven murders. Much of this terrorist activity took place during the "long hot summer" of 1964. The group has been held responsible for the killing of three civil rights workers in Neshoba County, Mississippi, during that summer; and its leader, Sam Bowers, along with Neshoba Deputy Sheriff Cecil Price, is now appealing federal conviction. The involvement of the Neshoba Sheriff's Department in the murders indicates the degree to which the Mississippi Klan has drawn membership and support from law enforcement. No state charges were ever brought against the Neshoba group.

The Mississippi White Knights have remained in the forefront of white violence. In 1966, the head of the Hattiesburg chapter of the NAACP was killed in a shooting and firebombing attack on his home by carloads of White Knights. In 1967, the head of the NAACP's Natchez chapter was blown to bits when a bomb was planted in his car. The White Knights are suspected of burning some seventy-five churches, a fact that contrasts peculiarly with the group's justification of violence in terms of Christian duty:

> As Christians we are disposed to kindness, generosity, affection and humility in our dealings with others. As militants, we are disposed to the use of physical force against our enemies. How can we reconcile these two apparently contradictory philosophies, and at the same time, make sure that we do not violate the divine law by our actions, which may be held against us when we face that last court on the Day of Judgement? The answer, of course, is to purge malice, bitterness and vengeance from our hearts. To pray each day for Divine Guidance, that our feet shall remain on the Correct Path, and that all of our acts be God's will working through our humble selves here on earth.[23]

The White Knights have stressed that the major source of their effectiveness is favorable public opinion. "As long as they are on our side," Bowers has written, "we can just about do anything to our enemies with impunity." [24] As a general rule, Klan success throughout the South has come primarily in those areas where state and local leaders and police have been most militant in resisting civil rights activity. In the

Klan's center of strength in Alabama, a square in the center of the state including Tuscaloosa, Birmingham, Anniston, and Montgomery, the tacit encouragement of police and political leaders has signficantly abetted Klan violence.

> When it came down to bombings and beatings, the Negroes of Birmingham claimed, it was sometimes difficult to distinguish between the Klansmen and the deputies. Also within the Klan's charmed geographical quadrilateral was the governor's mansion in Montgomery where Alabama governors John Patterson and George Wallace refrained from giving the impression that pro-segregation violence was completely distasteful.[25]

Local and state juries and courts have acquired an impressive record of failing to indict or convict in crimes against civil rights workers. For that matter, the federal government was not overly quick to step in against white violence until the summer of 1964.[26] There are signs, however, that the attitude of many elements of the South is in transition. New civil rights laws, Supreme Court decisions, and increased FBI surveillance have combined with local resistance to Klan violence. The convictions brought by an all-white federal jury in the Neshoba case are one such indication; another is the increasing pressure by Mississippi police against the terrorist activity of the White Knights of the Ku Klux Klan.[27]

The Klan and other militant white groups, both organized and ad hoc, have operated as the "dirty workers" of a system of caste domination. In an important sense, Southern racism has successfully channeled the political protest of the marginal white into expressions which support the existing political and social arrangements of the South. In the process, the actual sources of the grievances of the marginal white have gone uncorrected. Klan violence represents the thwarted and displaced political protest of whites acting from a context of economic insecurity, threatened manhood, and inability to influence local and national political structures.

A study of Klan membership in the late 1950's described it as largely composed of marginal white-collar, small business, and skilled workers occupying an intermediate position between clear-cut blue-collar and clear-cut white-collar positions.[28] An assessment of present Klan membership would not show much change. Among the recent leadership of various state and national Klan organizations are numbered a truck driver, a crane operator, a barber, a former rubber plant worker and later salesman, a former bricklayer and lightning-rod salesman, a machinist, a paint sprayer, and several evangelical ministers. The seven Klansmen convicted in the Neshoba County slayings included three truck drivers, one trailer salesman, a chemical plant worker, a deputy sheriff, and a vending-machine distributor. In contrast to the middle- and upper-middle-class membership of the vigorously racist Citizens' Councils of the Black Belt South,[29] the typical rank-and-file Klansman is subject to the vicissitudes of Southern economic insecurity and to a large degree excluded from the benefits of industrialization accruing to the new middle class.

In addition to economic insecurity and marginality, the grievances of the rank-and-file Klansman include a strong sense of diminished manhood. The rhetoric of Southern white militancy, like that of black militants, is suffused with a sense of the decline of male effectiveness and the restorative functions of militant action: "Step out from behind the petticoat and be a man." [30]

Klan rhetoric reflects the strong sense of distributive injustice common to the marginal Southern white. Klansmen have criticized the extent of federal anti-poverty funds given to blacks in the face of white poverty, and complain that riots have brought blacks federal largesse while the law-abiding poor white must work and receives no federal attention. "Health, education, and welfare is nigger health, nigger education, and nigger welfare; they have done nothing about yours." [31] The Grand Dragon of the North Carolina Klan has complained that "the only contact with the federal government is the FBI bug," and that the government has never approached him to discuss constructive measures for poor whites.[32] Another Klan complaint has been that those whites who advocate integration are those who are able to afford to send their children to private schools, thus shifting the burden of accommodation to the poor white.[33]

The racist thrust of Southern white protest has largely obscured the genuine grievances which have indeed been largely ignored, on both local and federal levels. For some areas of the South, it may be the case that, as one critic has suggested, "The establishment fears war between the races less than an alliance between them." [34] In any case, under present political conditions in many areas, the channeling of the marginal white protest into anti-Negro directions serves to buttress a system of political and economic stagnation in which the poor of both races lose. Whether this condition can be altered is largely dependent on the sensitivity of efforts to deal with the grievances of the poor white. For the moment, the white protest remains at the level of a crude racism, well expressed in one of the Klan's recordings:

> You have to be black to get a welfare check
> and I'm broke
> No joke
> I ain't got a nickel for a coke
> I ain't black you see
> so Uncle Sam won't help poor nigger-hating me.[35]

The Urban North

They have learned from the black people that the squeaky wheel gets the grease, so they're going to squeak, too.
—TONY IMPERIALE

It should be abundantly clear that violent white militancy has not been confined to the South. At present, although there has been relatively little private violence by whites in the North, the potential exists for a substantial amount of urban violence directed against blacks. There are a number of indications that militancy is increasing among some segments of the population of the Northern and Western cities. The immediate precipitants seem to have been black civil rights activity, the ghetto riots, and a perception of the increasing danger of black criminality; but the increasing militancy of these groups reflects a larger problem that has received less attention than its importance warrants—the situation of the working-class and lower-middle-class white living in what may be called the white ghettos of the cities.

The leading edge of the growing Northern militancy lies in the largely working-class, generally ethnic neighborhoods of the cities. Given a national context in which the representatives of all three major political parties felt compelled to issue remarkably similar demands for "law and order," it is not surprising that a similar, but more strident, demand is made by those who are most directly threatened by the disorder attendant on contemporary social change. In short, the new militancy of the urban working class must be seen in proper perspective. The militancy of those in the white ghettos differs principally in being more urgent.

This urgency is anchored in a set of real and pressing problems. As Robert Wood of HUD has put it:

> Let us consider the working American—the average white ethnic male:
> He is the ordinary employee in factory and in office. Twenty million strong, he forms the bulk of the nation's working force. He makes five to ten thousand dollars a year; has a wife and two children; owns a house in town—between the ghetto and the suburbs, or perhaps in a low-cost subdivision on the urban fringe; and he owes plenty in installment debts on his car and appliances.
> The average white working man has no capital, no stocks, no real estate holdings except for his home to leave his children. Despite the gains hammered out by his union, his job security is far from complete. Layoffs, reductions, automation, and plant relocation remain the invisible witches at every christening. He finds his tax burden is heavy; his neighborhood services, poor; his national image, tarnished; and his political clout, diminishing . . . one comes to understand his tension in the face of the aspiring black minority. He notes his place on the lower rungs of the economic ladder. He sees the movement of black families as a threat to his home values. He reads about rising crime rates in city streets and feels this is a direct challenge to his family. He thinks the busing of his children to unfamiliar and perhaps inferior schools will blight their chance for a sound education. He sees only one destination for the minority movement—his job.[36]

As has been the case historically, American social and political institutions have not found ways of accommodating both the legitimate grievances of aspiring minorities and the grievances of those who feel the threat of displacement. Nor have those institutions succeeded in substantially lessening the dangers of physical violence or criminal victimization which accompany life on the fringes of the slums. The result has been a pervasive insecurity for the white urban dweller, which, while frequently exaggerated, nevertheless has a basis in the rather grim realities of contemporary urban life. Under present conditions, property values may indeed be threatened when blacks move in numbers into white areas; whites living near black ghettos do have to cope directly with the problem of "crime in the streets"; and the failure of American institutions to commit themselves decisively to the eradication of racial injustice means that the root causes of white insecurity as well as black discontent are likely to remain with us. It is in the context of these conditions that urban white militancy is nourished. Politically ineffective, educationally limited, and uncommitted to the finer distinctions regarding civil liberties and minority rights, the urban white of ethnic working-class background is increasingly disposed to resistance.

One indication of the depth of the new militancy is the body of evidence showing that a sizable segment of the urban population is willing to use violence to defend itself against black disorder. Not only do many Northern whites organize in support of harsh police measures against rioters, many urban whites express a willingness to use private violence. A Harris poll taken in September, 1967, indicated that 55 percent of a sample of white gun owners said they would use their gun to shoot other people in case of a riot; [37] a later Harris survey in March, 1968, found the same question answered affirmatively by 51 percent of white gun owners.[38] In the 1967 survey, 41 percent of whites with incomes under $5,000 expressed the fear that their own home or neighborhood would be affected in a riot, as compared with 34 percent of all whites. A study of white reaction to the Los Angeles riot of 1965 indicates that the willingness to use guns and personal fear of the riot are related. Twenty-three percent of a sample of whites said that they had felt a great deal of fear for themselves and their families during the riot, and 29 percent said that they had considered using firearms to protect themselves or their families. However, nearly half of those who had considered the use of firearms were also among those who had felt a great deal of fear.[39] Willingness to use guns was highest in lower-income communities and in integrated communities at all income levels; among whites living in close proximity to Negroes; among men, the young, the less-educated, and those in three occupational categories —managers and proprietors, craftsmen and foremen, and operatives.[40]

In general, these findings support the conception of the white working and lower-middle class on the ghetto fringe as the most violence-prone wing of the growing white militancy, but the fact that higher-income whites living close to blacks express a high degree of willingness to use violence empha- sizes the point that it is the situation—rather than the charac- ter or culture of the working class—which is critical. The perception of threat appears to be a great equalizer of class distinctions.

Expressing willingness to use guns in the face of a riot, of course, is not the same as actually doing so. Since the recent riots have been contained within the black ghettos them- selves, no information exists which directly matches white be- havior with white opinion of the use of guns. However, the Los Angeles study found that 5 percent of their sampled whites did in fact buy firearms or ammunition during the riot to protect themselves and their families.[41] In Detroit, more than twice as many guns were registered in the first five months of 1968—following the riot in August of 1967—than in the corresponding five months in 1967, prior to the riot, and a similar trend is evident in Newark.[42] It must be re- membered that white neighborhoods were not significantly threatened during these riots. Speculation on what might re- sult if white areas were directly threatened is not reassuring.

Further light on the potential for white violence is shed by a study prepared for the Kerner Commission which at- tempted to pinpoint the "potential white rioter." A sample of whites was asked whether, in case of a Negro riot in their city, they should "do some rioting against them" or leave the matter for the authorities to handle. Eight percent of male whites advocated counterrioting. Suburban whites were slightly less inclined to advocate a counterriot than were city whites. Less-educated whites tended to support counterrioting, and there was a striking degree of advocacy of counterrioting by teen-age males, 21 percent of whom agreed that they should riot against Negroes. This percentage was slightly higher than the percentage of Negro teen-agers who said they would join a riot if one occurred in their city.[43]

Again, the degree to which these attitudes are, or might be, expressed in behavior is not clear. Nevertheless, studies of recent riots indicate that a significant number of "riot-related" arrests of whites have taken place. Occasionally, as in the Detroit riot of 1967, whites have been arrested on charges of looting, apparently in cooperation with blacks. More frequently, however, white males have been arrested beyond or near the perimeters of riot areas for "looting outside the riot areas, riding through the area armed, refusing to recognize a police perimeter, shooting at Negroes." [44] Such incidents were particularly apparent in the New Haven, Plainfield, Dayton, and Cincinnati riots of 1967. The white counterriot, of course, has historical precedent; most of the Northern race riots before 1935 involved pitched battles between whites and blacks, with working-class white youth particularly in evidence.[45]

The historically prominent role of youth in militant white violence has received less attention than it deserves. A similar pattern has been evident in more recent years, as the foregoing figures would suggest. Participation of white workingclass youth in violence against civil rights activity and against blacks moving into white neighborhoods has been noted in many Northern cities. In Chicago, for example, white youth were especially prominent in the Trumbull Park housing disturbances of the late 1950's, the assault on civil rights activists attempting to integrate South Side beaches in the early 1960's, and the violence accompanying Martin Luther King's West Side campaign in 1966. Militant white youth have been active in several racially troubled areas of Chicago in 1968. In Blue Island, for example, sixty-seven white youths were arrested after harassing and beating Negroes following an incident in which two young whites were shot.[46] Schools in many areas have been disrupted by conflict between black and white youth. The new militancy of black high school students is being countered in some areas by a corresponding

white student militancy. In Trenton, New Jersey, for example, militant white high school students, many carrying signs
reading "White Power," boycotted classes protesting incidents
of "roughing-up" by black students.[47]

Although youth have been prominent in relatively disorganized instances of militant white violence, the major efforts
at organized militancy have been made by the adults who
comprise the leadership of the various neighborhood defense
organizations which have appeared in the North and West.
Some of these, like the "Breakthrough" organization in Detroit, urge members to "study, arm, store provisions and
organize"; a similar group called "Fight Back" in Warren,
Michigan, argues that "The only way to stop them is at the
city limits." [48] Others focus less on arms training and storage,
concentrating on community patrols to discourage black intrusion. The most significant of these urban vigilante groups
is the North Ward Citizens Committee of Newark, whose
leader, Anthony Imperiale, has recently been elected to the
Newark City Council.

Newark's North Ward is a primarily Italian-American
neighborhood with a large and growing black population, adjacent to the predominantly black Central Ward, which was
the scene of the Newark riot of 1967. The strident nativism
of the North Ward Citizens Committee reflects the ironies of
the process of ethnic succession in America. Not too long
ago,

> The Italians were often thought to be the most degraded of
> the European newcomers. They were swarthy, more than
> half of them were illiterate, and almost all were victims of a
> standard of living lower than that of any of the other promi-
> nent nationalities. They were the ragpickers and the poorest
> of common laborers; in one large city their earnings averaged
> forty percent less than those of the general slum-dweller.
> Wherever they went, a distinctive sobriquet followed them.
> "You don't call an Italian a white man?" a West Coast con-
> struction boss was asked. "No sir," he answered, "an Italian
> is a Dago." Also, they soon acquired a reputation as blood-
> thirsty criminals. Since Southern Italians had never learned to
> fight with their fists, knives flashed when they brawled among
> themselves or jostled with other immigrants. Soon a penolo-
> gist was wondering how the country could build prisons
> which Italians would not prefer to their own slum quarters.

On the typical Italian the prison expert commented: "The knife with which he cuts his bread he also uses to lop off another 'Dago's' finger or ear . . . he is quite as familiar with the sight of human blood as with the sight of the food he eats." [49]

Today, of course, the situation has shifted considerably, and the North Ward Italians feel themselves beleaguered by a horde of criminal blacks, instigated by radicals. The North Ward Citizens Committee operates patrols of the neighborhood, and members train in karate. Their militant quest for law and order is rooted in a set of severe insecurities attendant on life in Newark, where all the problems of the urban white North exist in extreme form. Newark is over half black; it leads all cities of its size in crime rates. It was the scene of one of the most disastrous episodes of black disorder and violent official response in the sixties. The sense of fear pervading the white ghetto is reflected in Imperiale's words: "When is it gonna stop? Everybody says, 'don't bother 'em now. Leave 'em alone, and they'll calm down.' Well, it took riots that burned down half of a town before we learned." [50]

Accompanying the fear of black violence is a strong sense of relative injustice. The citizens of the North Ward, conscious that their own neighborhood is deteriorating, strongly resent the concentration of state and federal monies being poured into the black community.

> Are there no poor whites? But the Negroes get all the anti-poverty money. When pools are being built in the Central Ward, don't they think the white kids have got frustration? The whites are the majority. You know how many of them come to me, night after night, because they can't get a job? They've been told, we have to hire Negroes first.[51]

The sense of special and unjust treatment for whites with grievances is compounded by what Imperiale regards as unfair discrimination against his organization:

> The Mayor says he is going to try to get funds to start civilian patrols in the Central Ward. He claims this should be done for the so-called ghetto area. I went to Washington to get federal funds to set up a civilian patrol program in the North Ward and the other areas of the city, black as well as

the white, and I was pushed from pillar to post. It is all right
for the Central Ward but not for the North Ward where I
am called a para-military organization.[52]

In August, Imperiale's headquarters were bombed, and Imperiale has been highly critical of the lack of response by the
law and city officials. "What makes me mad is that if the
bombing had happened in the Central Ward, there would
have been all kinds of FBI agents and authorities. When we
get bombed, neither the mayor, the governor nor anyone else
said it was a bad thing to have happened. No statement what-
soever was made in the papers." [53]

This sense of injustice and of exclusion from political concern could lead to a heightened political alienation. The citizens of Newark's North Ward are largely correct in feeling
that the polity has ignored them. At present, the Imperiale
organization remains involved in traditional political action
through the electoral process. Imperiale has insisted on this:
"The Anti-Vigilante bill will do nothing because I am not a
Vigilante. I am one-hundred percent for a para-military law
because that would outlaw people dressed in uniforms getting
together and practicing sabotage and overthrow of the government. I love the government and am trying to save it." [54]
Should legitimate politics bear few significant results in terms
of the grievances of the white ghetto, the North Ward Citizens Committee and similar groups may feel driven beyond
politics. If this were to happen, the protest of the working-
class urban white could take a new and ominous form, whose
outlines are best indicated by the white paramilitarism examined below.

White Paramilitarism

Groups willing to use violence to defend presumably
threatened "American" values are not new in this country's
history. Nevertheless, the state of thinking and information
on these groups are undeveloped. This is doubtless partly due
to their frequently illegal and usually conspiratorial nature. It
is due also to a certain amorphous character of the groups
themselves. Paramilitary groups are constantly fragmenting,

dissolving, undergoing rapid membership turnover, and forming and breaking alliances with other groups, both illicit and aboveboard. Their disorganized character is an important index of the nature of these groups and of their relation to the larger social and political structure. As one observer has suggested, "The Minutemen are more a frame of mind than an organization or movement." [55] Put differently, these groups could be said to represent a frame of mind in search of an organization, and having little success in finding one. "Patriotic" paramilitary groups are composed of men whose grievances are not well articulated and who are unable to organize themselves into a coherent political force, partly because of their own ideology and background and partly as a result of the response of the polity to them. Consequently the source of their grievances remains unaltered, while they are driven farther and farther away from normal political life.

"Paramilitarism" here refers to the activities of a group that prepares for coordinated, violent action in order to restore, defend, or create general values, having a technological capacity for collective violence, and existing outside formal legal or military institutions. [56] A number of the groups previously discussed have paramilitary aspects, including some black organizations. This section focuses on groups that are almost pure types of the paramilitary organization, in the sense of dissociation from legitimate political structures and a considerable degree of armament. One such group, the Minutemen, is the largest and best organized of the type, and will serve here as a model.

The contemporary Minutemen organization was founded in 1961 out of several local guerrilla-style groups which had arisen during the years 1957 to 1960, at a time when the sense of threat from a growing and ostensibly monolithic international Communism pervaded the country's psyche, conditioned its foreign policy, and dominated its rhetoric. This Cold War atmosphere must be kept in mind in order to recognize that the Minutemen, like other white militant groups of a violent nature, are not so distant from the more respectable elements of the larger society as it appears on the surface. Rather, the original aim of the Minutemen—to provide guerrilla training in case of an armed invasion of the

United States by Soviet forces—may be interpreted as a logical extension of the national security policies of the American government and of a populace that took seriously the issue of whether it was better to be dead or Red.

It was not entirely unnatural, therefore, that when the image of a sharply dichotomized world altered considerably— especially as a result of new perceptions of differences among various Communist nations—some of those with a deeper stake in the earlier image began to ask whether there was not some kind of internal subversion of American commitment, whether in fact "Communists" or their allies had substantially taken control of the American polity. This became the theme of the Minutemen soon after their origin, and remains so today.

Minutemen believe that Communists are in substantial control of American politics, education, and communication; that liberals and fellow travelers are working hand in hand, knowingly or otherwise, with the hard-core in preparation for a total Communist take-over of the country. This will occur in the near future at an unspecified date referred to as "The Day," at which time patriotic Americans will have to take to countryside, armed, in defense of the country.

Minutemen refer to themselves as "America's last line of defense against Communism" and see violence as justified in view of the depth of the threat to American principles: "When our constitutional form of government is threatened we are morally justified in resorting to violence to discourage Communists and their fellow travelers." [57] They view the use of armed force as an explicitly counterrevolutionary measure in the face of a thirty-year, largely nonviolent, bureaucratic left-wing revolution which has been taking place in this country.

An informed estimate of active Minutemen membership as of 1968 puts it at eight to ten thousand nationally, with heaviest concentrations on the West Coast, especially around Los Angeles and Seattle; the Southwest; and the Midwest, especially the St. Louis–Kansas City area, with a sizable pocket in New York.[58] That the Minutemen are capable of much violence is undisputed. Recent Minutemen-linked events have included an attempted bank robbery, complete with dynamiting of police and power stations, near Seattle; [59] an assault on a peace group in Connecticut; and an attempted assault on three left-wing camps in the New York area. In the last incident, some twenty Minutemen were arrested and a sizable amount of weaponry confiscated. The weapons included the following:

> 125 rifles, single or automatic; ten pipe bombs; five mortars; twelve .30 calibre machine guns; twenty-five hand guns; twenty sets of brass knuckles with knives attached; 220 knives of various sorts; one bazooka; three grenade launchers; six hand grenades; fifty 80 mm. mortar shells; one million rounds of ammunition of all kinds; chemicals for preparing bomb detonators, including picric acid; thirty walkie-talkies and various other communication devices including short-wave equipment capable of intercepting police bands; fifty camouflage suits with boots and steel helmets; and a crossbow.[60]

Minutemen train for guerrilla operations and conduct seminars on weapons use, making of explosives, and so on.[61] A considerable amount of effort is spent on gathering intelligence on potential targets—communications centers, power stations, arms supplies—and this effort includes an attempt to infiltrate police and National Guard units. This has apparently been partly successful. Minutemen infiltration of the New York State Police netted considerable information on police radio communications.[62]

Effort is also devoted to a campaign of psychological warfare oriented to the harassment of liberals. The following Minutemen message, printed on stickers and postcards, has become well-known:

Traitors Beware

See the old man at the corner where you buy your papers? He may have a silencer equipped pistol under his coat. That extra fountain pen in the pocket of the insurance salesman who calls on you might be a cyanide gas gun. What about your milk man? Arsenic works slow but sure. Your auto mechanic may stay up nights studying booby traps. These patriots are not going to let you take their freedom away from them. They have learned the silent knife, the strangler's cord, the target rifle that hits sparrows at 200 yards. Traitors beware. Even now the crosshairs are on the back of your necks.

MINUTEMEN

In addition to their own potential for violence, the Minutemen represent what may be the clearest example of a kind of political alienation which could conceivably come to characterize a wider and wider range of groups in American society. Lacking sufficient data, an analysis of their source and future is at best tentative and exploratory. Still, several facts are illuminating.

The Minutemen membership is largely composed of marginal whites. The founder and leader, Robert DePugh, is a Midwestern small entrepreneur with a history of business failure, who now operates a small, largely family-owned veterinary drug concern. The former Midwest Coordinator of the group, now head of a smaller but similar group called the Counter-Insurgency Council, owns and operates a small machine shop and gunsmithy in a small Illinois town.[63] The group arrested in Redmon, Washington, in connection with the attempted bank robbery included a longshoreman, a grocery clerk, a church maintenance man, a ship's oiler, a civilian driver for an army base, and a draftsman.[64] Those arrested in the New York camp episode included a landscape artist, two truck drivers, a cab driver, a heavy equipment operator, a milkman, a draftsman, a mold-maker, an airport steward, a gardener, a horse groom, a bus driver, a New York City fireman, a plasterer, two mechanics, and a clerk.[65] Most of these were young, between the ages of eighteen and thirty-one. A close student of the Minutemen describes their membership as predominantly male, of Western European ancestry and at least nominal Christianity; at least one-half blue-collar workers, few professionals or salaried white-collar workers, and an overrepresentation of small proprietors.[66] It is noteworthy that this distribution parallels to a considerable extent estimates of contemporary Klan membership. This fact may indicate a similar set of conditions underlying the rise of the two groups, as well as offering an explanation for the failure of the Minutemen to recruit Southern membership.[67]

This distribution also approximates the traditional social base of fascist movements.

The standard explanations of "right-wing" militancy in the United States have relied heavily on the notion that such militancy represents a form of "status politics" accompanying the strains of prosperity.[68] This kind of explanation clearly applies fairly well to groups such as the John Birch Society, whose membership tends to be suburban and relatively affluent.[69] But in the case of "patriotic" organizations as well as organized Southern racism, a certain division of labor is apparent, based on class or at least occupational lines. Just as the Citizens' Councils represent a higher-income membership than the Klans, the Birch Society represents the prosperous and at least quasi-respectable arm of the radical "anti-Communist" movement. At the level of the Minutemen, a different kind of analysis may be required.

While the problem of "status" is doubtless great for the marginal white, his grievances run much deeper. In an important sense, the small-time, small-town businessman, the urban clerk, or worker has been overwhelmed by social developments beyond his capacity to understand or to control. It can be argued that the source of his complaint is not "Communism" at all; rather, it is a form of capitalism which has been imposed upon him from outside—not the classical entrepreneurial capitalism of early America, which he cherishes, but the newer, bigger, corporate capitalism of contemporary America. The new capitalism, while creating new opportunities and new security for large business and for much of organized labor, and extending an at least rudimentary welfare state apparatus to the poor, has largely passed by those in the various occupational backwaters which the Minutemen membership represents. The advantages—tax loopholes, government contracts, controlled markets, and the like—accruing to large-scale corporate capitalism are not available to them; nor for many are the benefits of organized labor. Increasingly left behind in the thrust of these developments, the marginal white feels all of the strains of modern life without most of its benefits.

This situation is strongly reflected in Minutemen ideology, which, while "anti-Communist" on the surface, is actually much more complex. To begin with, the nature of "Communism" for the Minutemen is considerably blurred, as it is for many extreme right-wing groups: "No matter what the name by which this collective ideology is known; commun-ism, social-ism, liberal-ism, progressiv-ism or welfare-ism, it still adds up to the same thing; it is the antithesis of individualism, it is the enemy of freedom." [70] In a real sense, the "enemy" is a complexity and centralization which goes well beyond the meaning of "Communism." For that matter, Minutemen ideology explicitly renounces contemporary capitalism in its espousal of the classical variant; DePugh argues that there is a "great difference between theoretical capitalism (the free enterprise system) and capitalism as a power structure." [71] And again, ". . . the 'power elite' is indeed a strange combination of monopoly capitalism and world communism." [72] These facts are congruent with evidence of the populist character of certain other right-wing phenomena; for example, a study of support for Senator Joseph McCarthy found his support highest among small businessmen who opposed both labor unions and big corporations.[73]

The content of Minutemen ideology leads to the strong suspicion that the agitation against "Communism" represents primarily a muddled political awareness of the nature of a "New Industrial State" [74] in which certain groups have been effectively cut off from appreciable influence. The sense of persecution by an organized conspiracy is heightened by their political exclusion and finds its mode of expression in the ideological preoccupations of the larger society.

Political impotence leads the Minutemen to a sense that orderly political activity is not feasible, and the Minutemen—like many militants on the left—renounce existing political parties and call for political purism: "Throughout history all major political changes, violent and nonviolent, have been made by minorities. Logically, then, the patriots must cooperate only with their own kind, not in coalitions with members of the vested bureaucracy, either Democratic or Republican." [75] In 1966, the Minutemen organized their own political party, the Patriotic Party. This reflects the growing politicization of the group and an attempt, if not to influence the political order substantially, at least to promote a recognition of the political, rather than criminal, character of the group. The Minutemen have insisted on their political identity in the face of numerous criminal prosecutions. "We are not criminals," wrote DePugh while fleeing indictment in connection with the Seattle bank robbery, "we are political refugees in our own land." [76]

The Minutemen have been unable to organize themselves for political action in an effective sense. They remain a loose collection of armed guerrilla bands. Their attempts at alliance with other groups have met with little success. They were allied with the Birch Society until DePugh was expelled from that organization in 1964. Informal affiliation remains; some of the Minutemen arrested in the New York incident were also Birch members. Individual Minutemen have had connections with the American Nazi Party and the Klan; the National States Rights Party cut off its support of the Minutemen in 1964 on the ground that the Minutemen had "gone too far." [77] The lack of enduring alliances among such groups is traditional, but in the case of the Minutemen more specific factors may be involved, including the lack of anti-Semitic or anti-Negro elements in Minuteman ideology. The Minutemen's highly individualistic ideology and their loose control over membership severely hinder more effective collective organization. At the same time, the lack of strong organizational control may increase the potential for localized violence by individual members and units.

Lack of effective organization furthers the Minutemen's political impotence. Their effective exclusion from politics in turn influences their perception of the nature of the "power structure" and forces them further into a political limbo where violence becomes increasingly seen as the only effective activity. As Hofstadter has suggested, this kind of political exclusion serves to confirm preexisting conceptions of the polity as being in the hands of a malignant force:

> The situation becomes worse when the representatives of a particular political interest—perhaps because of the very unrealistic and unrealisible nature of their demands—cannot make themselves felt in the political process. Feeling that they have no access to political bargaining or the making of decisions, they find their original conception of the world of power as

omnipotent, sinister, and malicious fully confirmed. They see
only the consequences of power—and this through distorting
lenses—and have little chance to observe its actual machinery.[78]

Conclusion

For decades, violent white militancy represented the rough
edge of a wider national nativism aimed at excluding immigrants and blacks, Indians and foreigners, from full participation in American life. Official policy today, except in some
areas of the South and the more hard-bitten sections of the
North, repudiates these aims. Still, a significant minority of
white Americans feel driven to the use or contemplation of
violence in support of similar aims. Their protest reflects the
failure of American society to eradicate the underlying causes
of the disaffection of both blacks and whites. On the one
hand, the failure to deal with the roots of racism has meant
the rise of violent black protest in the cities, which the working-class white fears will spill over into his own neighborhood
along with rising crime and sinking property values. On the
other hand, the failure to deal with the institutional roots of
white marginality has left many whites in a critical state of
bitterness and political alienation as they perceive the government passing them by.

For the Minutemen, the Klan, and similar groups, adrift
and overwhelmed by the processes of the modern corporate
state, the language of racism or anti-Communism structures
all discontents and points to drastic solutions. Politically im-
mature groups define the source of their problems in terms
provided for them. This should not obscure the fact that their
problems are genuine.

Continued political exclusion and organizational fragmentation render such groups increasingly prone to violence as a
last political language. An effective response to these groups
must transcend mere surveillance and condemnation, which
can only aggravate their frame of mind without providing redress of their situation.

For the most part, the political response to white militancy
has been either repressive or self-servingly encouraging. The
current emphasis on "law and order" partakes of both ele-

ments. A continued repressive response to the militancy of both blacks and whites could conceivably lead to a state of guerrilla warfare between the races. There are precedents for such warfare in some of the race riots of the first half of the century, and in recent clashes between armed black and white militants in the South.

Of more immediate importance is the growing militancy among white policemen, as evidenced by the recent activity of the Law Enforcement Group in New York, the beating of black youths by policemen in Detroit, and the revelation of Ku Klux Klan activity in the Chicago police force. The new militancy of the police has obvious and ominous implications for the American racial situation, indeed for the future character of all forms of group protest in America. The policing of protest takes on a new aspect when the policeman carries with him the militant white's racist and anti-radical world-view. The following chapter analyzes the sources and direction of the increasing protest of the police.

Chapter VII

The Police in Protest

The Police and Mass Protest:
The Escalation of Conflict, Hostility, and Violence

ONE CENTRAL fact emerges from any study of police encounters with student protesters, anti-war demonstrators, or black militants: there has been a steady escalation of conflict, hostility, and violence.

The Black Community

Writing in 1962, three years before the Watts riots and almost the distant past in this respect, James Baldwin vividly portrayed the social isolation of the policeman in the black ghetto:

> . . . The only way to police a ghetto is to be oppressive. None of the Police Commissioner's men, even with the best will in the world, have any way of understanding the lives led by the people; they swagger about in twos and threes patrolling. Their very presence is an insult, and it would be, even if they spent their entire day feeding gumdrops to children. They represent the force of the white world, and that world's real intentions are, simply, for that world's criminal

profit and ease, to keep the black man corralled up here, in his place. The badge, the gun in the holster, and the swinging club, make vivid what will happen should his rebellion become overt. . . .

It is hard, on the other hand, to blame the policeman, blank, good-natured, thoughtless, and insuperably innocent, for being such a perfect representative of the people he serves. He, too, believes in good intentions and is astounded and offended when they are not taken for the deed. He has never, himself, done anything for which to be hated—which of us has? And yet he is facing, daily and nightly, the people who would gladly see him dead, and he knows it. There is no way for him not to know it: There are few things under heaven more unnerving than the silent, accumulating contempt and hatred of a people. He moves through Harlem, therefore, like an occupying soldier in a bitterly hostile country; which is precisely what, and where he is, and is the reason he walks in twos and threes.[1]

Today the situation is even more polarized. There have been riots, and both black Americans and police have been killed. Black anger has become more and more focused on the police: the Watts battle cry of "Get Whitey" has been replaced by the Black Panther slogan: "Off the pigs." The black community is virtually unanimous in demanding major reforms, including police review boards and local control of the police. According to the Kerner Commission [2] and other studies,[3] conflict with the police was one of the most important factors in producing black riots. In short, anger, hatred, and fear of the police are a major common denominator among black Americans at the present time.

The police return these sentiments in kind—they both fear the black community and openly express violent hostility and prejudice toward it. Our review of studies of the police revealed unanimity in findings on this point: the majority of rank and file policemen are hostile toward black people.[4] Usually such hostility does not reflect official policy, although in isolated instances, as in the Miami Police Department under Chief Headley, official policy may encourage anti-black actions.[5] Judging from these studies, there is no reason to suppose that anti-black hostility is a new development brought on by recent conflicts between the police and the black community. What appears to have changed is not police attitudes, but the fact that black people are fighting back.

The Harlem Riot Commission Report of 1935 reserved its most severe criticism for the police:

> The police of Harlem show too little regard for human rights and constantly violate their fundamental rights as citizens. . . . The insecurity of the individual in Harlem against police aggression is one of the most potent causes for the existing hostility to authority. . . . It is clearly the responsibility of the police to act in such a way as to win the confidence of the citizens of Harlem and to prove themselves the guardians of the rights and safety of the community rather than its enemies and oppressors.[6]

And William A. Westley reported from his studies of police in the late forties:

> No white policeman with whom the author has had contact failed to mock the Negro, to use some type of stereotyped categorization, and to refer to interaction with the Negro in an exaggerated dialect, when the subject arose.[7]

Students of police seem unanimous in agreeing that police attitudes have not changed much since those studies. In a study done under a grant from the Office of Law Enforcement Assistance of the United States Department of Justice, and submitted to the President's Commission on Law Enforcement and the Administration of Criminal Justice in 1966, Donald J. Black and Albert J. Reiss, Jr., found overwhelming evidence of widespread, virulent prejudice by police against Negroes.[8] The study was based on field observations by thirty-six observers who accompanied police officers for a period of seven weeks in the summer of 1966 in Boston, Chicago, and Washington, D.C. It was found that 38 percent of the officers had expressed "extreme prejudice," while an additional 34 percent had expressed "considerable prejudice" in front of the observers. Thus, 72 percent of these policemen qualified as prejudiced against black Americans. It must be remembered that these views were not solicited, but were merely recorded when voluntarily expressed. And it seems fair to assume that some proportion of remaining 28 percent were sophisticated enough to exercise a certain measure of restraint when in the presence of the observers. Also, examples presented by Black and Reiss make it clear that their observers found intense and bitter hatred toward blacks. Moreover, these are not rural Southern policemen, and our investigation has shown that their views are typical of those in most urban police forces.

Concrete examples of this prejudice are not hard to find. For example, the Commission's Cleveland Study Team found that prejudice had been festering in the Cleveland police force for a long time but suddenly bloomed into virulent bigotry following the July, 1968, shoot-out between police and black militants. When white police were withdrawn from the ghetto for one night to allow black community leaders to quell the rioting, racist abuse of Mayor Carl B. Stokes, a Negro, could be heard on the police radio. And posters with a picture of the Mayor under the words "WANTED FOR MURDER" hung in district stations for several weeks after the shoot-out. Elsewhere our interviews disclosed the fact that nightsticks and riot batons are at times referred to as "nigger knockers." [9] Robert Conot writes that "LSMFT"—the old Lucky Strike slogan—has slipped into police argot as: "Let's Shoot a Mother-Fucker Tonight." [10]

Police actions often reflect these attitudes. In recent years there have been numerous allegations by Negro and civil liberties groups of police insulting, abusing, mistreating, and even beating or murdering blacks. Studies of the police by independent bodies tend to support these allegations. For instance, the 1961 Report on Justice, by the United States Civil Rights Commission, concluded that "Police brutality . . . is a serious problem in the United States." [11] Without presently recounting specific additional instances and varieties of misconduct, suffice it to say that this conclusion finds support throughout the literature on police. [12]

The problem has become even more acute with the emergence of increased black militancy. Reports in numerous cities, including Detroit, [13] San Francisco, [14] New York, [15] and Oakland, [16] indicate that police officers have attacked or shot members of the black community, often Black Panthers, at offices, social events, and even courthouse halls. Indeed, it appears that such incidents are spreading and are not isolated in a few police departments.

Moreover, difficult to document, it seems clear that police prejudice impairs the capacity of the police to engage in impartial crowd control. If anything, the behavior that typifies day-to-day policing is magnified in riot situations. The report of the Kerner Commission indicates that, for example, police violence was out of control during the 1967 riots,[17] and similar findings are seen elsewhere,[18] including the study of the commission's Cleveland Study Team.

Protesters: Student and Anti-War

Conflict has been escalating not only between the police and the black community; bad feeling and violence between the police and students and peace groups has also increased.

The earliest peace marches were treated much like ordinary parades by the police, and the protesters, many of whom accepted nonviolence as their guiding principle, seldom baited the police or expressed hostility toward them. But slowly incidents began accumulating, until by the spring and summer of 1968 protest marches frequently became clashes between protesters and the police.

As discussed in our chapter on anti-war protest, the escalation of the war led to growing frustrations and greater militancy on the part of protesters. Yet the police handling of protesters was often unrestrained and only increased the potential for violence—in the immediate situation and for the future. Predictably, the escalation continued. Protesters grew bitterly angry; and as anger against the police became a major element in protest meetings and marches, the police grew to hate and fear the protesters even more. Numerous respected commissions, among them the Cox Commission,[19] which studied the student uprising at Columbia University, and the Sparling Commission,[20] which studied the April, 1968, peace march in Chicago, found that the police used uncalled-for force, often vindictively, against protesters, often regardless of whether the latter were "peaceful" or "provocative."

The extent of violence in police-protester confrontations

was most clearly shown to the nation by the media coverage of the 1968 Democratic National Convention in Chicago. What was shown and reported confirmed what some people already thought, confused others, but probably changed few minds. However, the investigation of this commission's Chicago Study Team documents "unrestrained and indiscriminate police violence on many occasions."

> During the week of the Democratic National Convention, the Chicago police were the targets of mounting provocation by both word and act. It took the form of obscene epithets, and of rocks, sticks, bathroom tiles and even human feces hurled at police by demonstrators. Some of these acts had been planned; others were spontaneous or were themselves provoked by police action. Furthermore, the police had been put on edge by widely published threats of attempts to disrupt both the city and the Convention.
> That was the nature of the provocation. The nature of the response was unrestrained and indiscriminate police violence on many occasions, particularly at night.
> That violence was made all the more shocking by the fact that it was often inflicted upon persons who had broken no law, disobeyed no order, made no threat. These included peaceful demonstrators, onlookers, and large numbers of residents who were simply passing through, or happened to live in, the areas where confrontations were occurring.
> Newsmen and photographers were singled out for assault and their equipment deliberately damaged. Fundamental police training was ignored; and officers, when on the scene, were often unable to control their men. As one police officer put it: "What happened didn't have anything to do with police work." [21]

Significantly, the violent police actions seen on television were less fierce than the brutality they displayed at times or places where there were no television cameras present.[22]

What is truly unique about Chicago, however, is not the occurrence of police violence; rather, it is the extent and quality of media coverage given to the actual events, the fact that a respected commission with sufficient resources chose to find out what happened, and the extent and quality of media coverage of the report of those findings. Similar violence has occurred in many places, including New York, San Francisco, and Los Angeles.

For example, in March, 1968, in New York's Grand Central Station, while demonstrators engaged in typical Yippie tactics, police suddenly appeared and, without giving the crowd any real chance to disperse, indiscriminately attacked and clubbed demonstrators.[23] A similar outburst occurred a month later in Washington Square; [24] and, of course, the police violence that spring at Columbia, described in Chapter III, is by now a matter of common knowledge. The dispersal of a march of thousands to Century City in Los Angeles during the summer of 1967 is also a case in point. There, as reported in *Day of Protest, Night of Violence,* a report prepared by the American Civil Liberties Union of Southern California, dispersal was accompanied by similar police clubbing and beating of demonstrators, children, and invalids.[25] It should be emphasized that the decision to disperse that march was at best questionable, since the protesters were not a violent, threatening crowd. Moreover, the report finds that the paraders did not violate the terms of their parade permit, and thus "the order to disperse was arbitrary, and served no lawful purpose." [26]

The point that the Chicago convention violence is not unique is highlighted by considering that in April, 1968, four months earlier, similar violence occurred between police and protesters during another peace march in Chicago. An investigation was conducted by an independent committee which was chaired by Dr. Edward J. Sparling, president emeritus of Roosevelt University, and whose membership included such persons as Professor Harry Kalven, Jr., of the Chicago Law School, and Mr. Warren Bacon, Vice President of the Inland Steel Corporation. To quote from the report of this committee:

On April 27, at the peace parade of the Chicago Peace Council, the police badly mishandled their task. Brutalizing demonstrators without provocation, they failed to live up to that difficult professionalism which we demand.

Yet to place primary blame on the police would, in our view, be inappropriate. The April 27 stage had been prepared by the Mayor's designated officials weeks before. Administrative actions concerning the April 27 Parade were designed by City officials to communicate that "these people have no right to demonstrate or express their views." Many acts of brutal police treatment on April 27 were directly observed (if not commanded) by the Superintendent of Police or his deputies.[27]

What happened during the Chicago convention, therefore, is not something totally different from police work *in practice*. Our analysis indicates that the convention violence was unusual more in the fact of its having been documented than in the fact of its having occurred. The problem most definitely is not one unfortunate outburst of misbehavior on the part of a few officers, as the report of the Chicago administration alleged.[28]

In closing this section, it is instructive to note two facts: First, the behavior of most police, most of the time, is not necessarily represented by their actions in situations involving protest. In protest situations their own political views often seem to control their actions. Second, a violent response by police to protesters is not inevitable. For example, recently a major London demonstration protesting the Vietnam War and the politics of the "Establishment" resulted in no serious violence, and one serious attempt to provoke trouble was avoided by a superbly disciplined and restrained team of policemen. According to the *New York Times:*

> . . . the police never drew their truncheons and never showed anger. They held their line in front of the embassy until, as the attackers tired, they could begin to push the crowd down South Audley Street and away from the square.
>
> Americans who saw the Grosvenor Square events could not help drawing the contrast with the violence that erupted between the Chicago police and demonstrators at the Democratic Convention in August.[29]

More recently, in the United States, during the inaugural ceremonies for President Nixon, the Washington, D.C. authorities and city police received a complimentary reaction from all sides. David Dellinger called the police performance "beautiful" and added that, "at key points the Mayor and other people stepped in to prevent (violence) from escalating." The *Washington Daily News,* in an editorial of January 22nd, 1969, described the conduct of the police as "a superb demonstration of discipline—a new, professional police force awesome in its strength and self-control." In the materials that follow, we shall attempt to analyze those features of the police role in society that contribute to a breakdown of discipline and self-control, when it occurs.

The Predicament of the Police

The significance of police hostility, anger, and violence need hardly be stressed. Yet any analysis along this line runs the risk of being labeled anti-police, and it is often argued that such analyses demand more of the police than of other groups in society. However, this criticism may both be true and miss the point.

In some senses we do demand more of the police than we do of other groups—or more accurately, perhaps, we become especially concerned when the police fail to meet our demands. But this *must* be the case because it is to the police that we look to deal with so many of our problems, and it is to the police that we entrust the legitimate use of force. Moreover, unnecessary police violence can only exacerbate the problems police action is used to solve. Protesters are inflamed, and a cycle of greater and greater violence is set into motion—both in the particular incident and in future incidents. More fundamentally, the misuse of police force violates basic notions of our society concerning the role of police. Police are not supposed to adjudicate and punish; they are supposed to apprehend and take into custody. To the extent to which a nation's police step outside such bounds, that nation has given up the rule of law in a self-defeating quest for order.

So it becomes especially important to explore *why* the police have become increasingly angry and hostile toward blacks and protesters and why they are inclined to overreact violently when confronting such persons. The necessary starting point is a careful examination of what it is like to be a policeman today.

The predicament of the police in America today can scarcely be overstated, caught as they are between two contradictory developments: their job is rapidly becoming much more difficult (some say impossible), while at the same time their resources—morale, material, and training—are deteriorating. No recent observer doubts that the police are under increasing strain largely because they are increasingly being given tasks well beyond their resources.

The Policeman's Job

The outlines of the growing demands upon the police are well known and require but brief review here. Increasingly, the police are required to cope with the problems that develop as conditions in the black community remain intolerable and as black anger and frustration grow. Yet all intelligent police observers recognize that the root causes of black violence and rebellion are beyond the means or authority of the police. As a former Superintendent of the Chicago Police Department, O. W. Wilson, commented on riots in a recent interview:

> I think there is a long-range answer—the correction of the inequities we're all aware of: higher educational standards, improved economic opportunities, a catching up on the cultural lag, a strengthening of spiritual values. All of these things in the long run must be brought to bear on the problem if it is to be solved permanently, and obviously it must be solved. It will be solved, but not overnight.[30]

Since the publication of the Kerner Commission Report there is no longer much reason for anyone not to understand the nature of the social ills underlying the symptomatic violence of the black ghettos. But while we all know what needs to be done, it has not been done. The American policeman as well as the black American must therefore suffer daily from the consequence of inaction and indifference.

James Baldwin's characterization of the police as an army of occupation, quoted earlier, requires more and more urgent consideration. The police are set against the hatred and violence of the ghetto and are delegated to suppress it and keep it from seeping into white areas. Significantly, no one knows this better than the police who must try to perform this dangerous and increasingly unmanageable and thankless task. Throughout our interviews with members of major urban police forces, their despair and anger in the face of worsening violence and impending disaster were evident. No recent account about the police by scholars and journalists reports evidence to the contrary. As the *Saturday Evening Post* recently wrote of the police in St. Louis: "To many policemen, the very existence of [an emergency riot mobilization] plan implies that it will be used, and it is this sense of inevitability, this feeling that events have somehow slipped out of their control, that unnerves and frustrates them. . . ." [31]

And, of course, the police are correct. Events are slipping out of their control and they must live, more than most people, with the threat of danger and disaster. As one patrolman told a *Post* reporter, "the first guys there [responding to the riot plan]—they've had it. I've thought of getting myself a little sign saying 'expendable' and hanging it around my neck." [32] When the temperatures rise above 100 degrees in the ghetto and tenements overrun with people, rats, hopelessness, and anger, it is the police who are on the line; and any mistake can bring death. A New York policeman interviewed by our task force put the widespread apprehensions of the police simply: "Yeah, I'm scared. All the cops are. You never know what's going to happen out there. This place is a powder keg. You don't know if just putting your hand on a colored kid will cause a riot."

Similarly, the police can do little to ameliorate the reasons for student and political protest. Many demands of the protesters—moral political leadership, peace, and reform of the universities—lie outside the jurisdiction of the police. But when protesters are met with police, protest becomes a problem for the police.

Protest, moreover, poses an *unusual* problem for the policeman. Although policemen are characteristically referred to as law enforcement officers, more than one student of police has distinguished between the patrolman's role as a "peace officer" concerned with public order [33] and the policeman's role as detective, concerned with enforcing the law. As a peace officer, the patrolman usually copes with his responsibilities by looking away from minor thefts, drunkenness, disturbances, assaults, and malicious mischief. "[The] normal tendency of the police," writes James Q. Wilson, "is to under-enforce the law." [34]

In protest situations, however, the police are in the public eye, and frequently find themselves in the impossible position of acting as substitutes for necessary political and social reform. If they cope with their situation by venting their rage on the most apparent and available source of their predicament—blacks, students, and demonstrators—it should occasion no surprise. The professional restraint, compassion, and detachment oftentimes displayed by police are admirable. Under pressure and provocation, however, the police themselves can pose serious social problems.

The Resources of the Police

As the job of the policeman has become more important and sensitive, society has neglected the police in quite direct ways. From our study of the police in many cities it is apparent that law enforcement as an occupation has declined badly.

The Problem of Manpower: Quantity and Quality

It is hard to say why men join the police force, but the evidence we have indicates that police recruits are not especially sadistic or even authoritarian, as some have alleged. On the contrary, the best evidence that we have been able to accumulate from the works of such police experts as Niederhoffer [35] and McNamara [36] suggests that the policeman is usually an able and gregarious young man with social ideals, better than average physical prowess, and a rather conventional outlook on life, including normal aspirations and self-interest.

One outstanding problem of the police is a decline in pay relative to comparable occupations.[37] Correspondingly, the prestige of the occupation in the estimate of the general public has fallen sharply, and there has been a sharp decline in the quality and quantity of new recruits.[38] Most departments have many vacancies. In New York City, for example, according to a study conducted by Arthur Niederhoffer,[39] more than half of the recruits to the New York City police in June, 1940, were college graduates. During the last decade, on the other hand, the proportion of recruits with a college degree has rarely reached 5 percent. Neiderhoffer attributes this change to a decline in the relative financial rewards for being a policeman.[40] He notes: "In the 1930's . . . top-grade patrolmen in New York City earned three thousand dollars a year. They owned houses and automobiles; they could afford the luxuries that were the envy of the middle class; and they were never laid off. In the panic of the Depression, the middle class began to regard a police career pragmatically." [41] However, as the affluence of the country has risen in general, the relative rewards of police work have lagged badly. "Patrolmen's pay in major cities now averages about $7,500 per year—33% less than is needed to sustain a family of four in moderate circumstances in a large city, according to the U.S. Bureau of Labor Statistics." [42] Even though a top-grade patrolman in New York now earns about $9,000, this is less than a skilled craft-worker, such as an electrician or plumber, earns in New York.[43] Meanwhile, we have encouraged police to aspire to a middle-class life style. To achieve this, many police "moonlight" on a second job and have wives who work. Others—we do not know what percentage—engage in graft and corruption, which, in some cities, has been described as "a way of life." [44]

Thus a decline in the relative salary of the police profession is at least partly to blame for the fact that, while we have increasingly become committed to professionalism among the police, in many of our great cities the quality of recruits has actually been declining. In fact, matters are worse than they might appear, for while the average level of education among police recruits has been declining, the average level of educational achievement in the population has been increasing rapidly. Thus, new police recruits are being taken from an ever-shrinking pool of undereducated persons; increasingly it is such people who find being a policeman a "good job." [45]

In many urban departments today the older policemen are better educated and qualified than are the young policemen —a reversal of the trend operating in almost every other occupation in America. As an Oakland police captain with twenty-seven years on the force described changes in his department to our interviewer:

> We are not getting the type of college people in the department that we were before. The guys that we're getting now have had a high school education, have gone into the army for a couple of years and have come out and are looking to get in the police department because of the good pay. Oakland is a relatively high-paying department, but still does not get educated recruits. We're not getting one twentieth of the people out of the junior colleges that we should get. What we're going to have to do is subsidize the education of these people.

Even more bleak is the picture painted by Dr. Maurice Mensh, a physician who cares for the Washington, D.C., police: "This is an uneducated group. You should read some of the essays they write. They can hardly write. . . . And you put them on the street and ask them to make decisions that are way beyond their capacity." [46] Moreover, such situations exist even in what are considered to be the most elite, competent, and·educated police forces in the country. For example, in Berkeley, California, there has recently been a sharp decline in the educational level of recruits.[47]

Alongside problems of recruitment are problems of retention. For example, the *San Francisco Chronicle* reported on November 12, 1968, that 195 officers of the San Francisco Police Department had suddenly put in for early retirement. This was approximately 11 percent of the force, which, like most urban departments, chronically operates at about 5 percent below authorized strength for lack of suitable applicants. The mass of retirement applications followed the June passage of a ballot proposition to improve policemen retirement benefits and permit retirement at an earlier age. The purpose of the new program was to aid the department in recruiting new officers. Ironically, its results thus far have been to increase retirement applications.

What reasons did these policemen give for quitting the force at the earliest possible moment? One veteran inspector said, "It's a dog's job. It's a job the average man wouldn't take. It doesn't have to be, but it is." Another inspector explained his decision this way: "We're running scared. . . . If there are social injustices, that's society's bag. We can't cure them. All we can do is make arrests. . . ." In the judgment of Captain Charles Barca, the men leave because "It's just an ugly, difficult, uncomfortable way to make a living and will continue to be that way until the general public develops more appreciation for officers and more respect for them." [48]

Although the San Francisco episode was striking because a change in the law produced a sudden mass retirement, reports from urban departments across the nation show that the majority of officers retire as soon as they are eligible.

Even more troubling is the fact that many urban departments report massive resignation rates—often nearly 20 percent per year—among officers short of retirement. According to our interview with Berkeley Police Chief William Beall, Berkeley officers quit the force at all stages of their career. "We lose many veteran officers with ten to fifteen years on the force, men who are at the peak of their efficiency." Almost none of these men take law enforcement jobs elsewhere —Berkeley is one of the highest paying and most admired departments in the nation—but take up other occupations. "The men who find these opportunities are our best, as you would expect," Chief Beall told our interviewer. Thus for many policemen the way to cope with the predicament of modern policing is simply to get out.

One obvious consequence of all this has been a shortage of manpower on police forces. An examination of the Uniform Crime Reports of the Federal Bureau of Investigation shows that the number of full-time police employees per 1,000 population in America's cities has gone virtually unchanged since 1960, while the number of complaints handled by the police has increased enormously. [49] A corollary is, of course, the tendency to overwork and overextend our police.

Training: Deterioration in the Face of New Needs

Perhaps an even more significant effect of pressing manpower needs is the tendency to allow existing training programs to deteriorate because of the pressure for immediate manpower. There is considerable evidence that the new recruits are receiving less adequate training from within departments than in the recent past.[50] However, this deterioration has largely gone unnoticed outside the police. While police academies have undoubtedly been upgraded in many cities, and while their curricula have been immeasurably improved, frequently new recruits are not given the benefit of these improvements. Because of the overwhelming need for manpower, recruits often are hustled out of their training period and onto the streets before they have been adequately instructed. To appreciate the severity of this problem, one need only consider the following excerpts from our interviews with New York policemen about officer training. We select New York because it is the largest police department in the nation and is generally regarded as a police department with outstanding training practices.

A patrolman on a Brooklyn beat:

> There is no professionalization in this department. We're getting a bunch of dummies on this job now. We've got guys out on the street who haven't had any training outside of three or four days in the academy. We had one class that graduated in December and it had three weeks of training and we had another class that was in June for only I think it was two days, and they were put out on the street. The Mayor says we've got to have more policemen; so we put these guys out, and they shouldn't be there. And they keep saying, we'll send them back to the academy for their training later, and they've said this half a dozen times now and the guys are still out on the street. You know, they aren't even training these guys to shoot. . . . The way it stands now, we're putting uniforms on guys and calling them cops, but they're not cops; they don't know anything.

A sergeant:

> I was an instructor at the police academy last year and I know I had one of my classes turned out on the street after about three weeks. They're supposed to come back to work one day a week at the academy for what they missed, but it never happened. They're out there working now with just three weeks training. Last night I had a couple of young officers who had just a very short time on the job and only a few weeks in the academy and something happened and one of the detectives fired his revolver and one of these young guys couldn't resist, he fired too. I'm really afraid of what's

going to happen with these young guys. They're all eager to get in and do what they think is real police work, but they just don't have the training.

A patrolman:

We had a young officer killed about two days ago, and I went and checked on his record myself, so I know this to be a fact. He had been out of the academy for a few months now and he had never had any training on how to handle a gun.

Indeed, according to a story in the *New York Times* more than 2,000 new policemen had been assigned to duty during the first eight months of 1968 without being cleared by the background investigation which "normally precedes appointment to the force." [51] The reason given by city officials was the urgent need to obtain new policemen.

Deterioration of existing training programs is particularly unfortunate at a time when new and vastly improved methods of training are needed if the police are adequately to deal with demonstration, protest, and confrontation. In dealing with crowds, police are required to exhibit teamwork, impersonality, and discipline seldom demanded in their routine work. In fact, certain characteristic features of police training may hinder men from operating properly in crowd control situations. As the National Advisory Commission on Civil Disorders observed:

Traditional police training seeks to develop officers who can work independently and with little direct supervision. But the control of civil disturbances requires quite different performance—large numbers of disciplined personnel, comparable to soldiers in a military unit, organized and trained to work as members of a team under a highly unified command control system. No matter how well-trained and skilled a police officer may be, he will be relatively ineffectual to deal with civil disturbances so long as he functions as an individual.[52]

Thus one National Guard commander complained after viewing the police utilization of Guard units during the Detroit riot of 1967:

They sliced us up like baloney. The police wanted bodies. They grabbed Guardsmen as soon as they reached the armories, before their units were made up, and sent them out, two on a fire truck, this one on a police car, that one to guard some installation. . . . The Guards simply became lost boys in the big town carrying guns.[53]

Perhaps no more dramatic illustration of the shortcomings of police crowd control techniques can be offered than the Detroit riot of 1967. Responsibility for riot control was divided between U.S. Army paratroopers on one side of town and a combination of Detroit police and the National Guard on the other. The Guard proved as untrained and unreliable as the police; and between the two, thousands of rounds of ammunition were expended and perhaps thirty persons were killed while disorder continued. Yet in paratrooper territory, only 201 rounds of ammunition were fired, mostly in the first several hours before stricter fire discipline was imposed, only one person was killed, and within a few hours quiet and order were restored in that section of the city.[54]

The Police View of Protest and Protesters

Faced with the mounting pressures inherent in their job, the police have naturally sought to understand why things are as they are. Explanations which the police, with a few exceptions, have adopted constitute a relatively coherent view of current protests and their causes. The various propositions making up this view have nowhere been set out and made explicit, but they do permeate the police literature. We have tried to set them out as explicitly as possible.

As will be seen, this view functions to justify—indeed, it suggests—a strategy for dealing with protest and protesters. Like any coherent view of events, it helps the police plan what they should do and understand what they have done. But it must also be said that the police view makes it more difficult to keep the peace and increases the potential for violence. Furthermore, police attitudes toward protest and protesters often lead to conduct at odds with democratic ideals of freedom of speech and political expression. Thus the police often view protest as an intrusion rather than as a contribution to our political processes. In its extreme case, this may result in treating the fundamental political right of dissent as merely an unnecessary inconvenience to traffic, as subversive activity, or both.

The "Rotten Apple" View of Man

What is the foundation of the police view? On the basis of our interviews with police and a systematic study of police publications,[55] we have found that a significant underpinning is what can best be described as a "rotten apple" theory of human nature. Such a theory of human nature is hardly confined to the police, of course. It is widely shared in our society. Many of those to whom the police are responsible hold the "rotten apple" theory, and this complicates the problem in many ways.

Under this doctrine, crime and disorder are attributable mainly to the intentions of evil individuals; human behavior transcends past experience, culture, society, and other external forces and should be understood in terms of wrong choices, deliberately made. Significantly—and contrary to the teachings of all the behavioral sciences—social factors such as poverty, discrimination, inadequate housing, and the like are excluded from the analysis. As one policeman put it simply, "Poverty doesn't cause crime; people do." (And as we discuss later, the policeman's view of "crime" is extremely broad.)

The "rotten apple" view of human nature puts the policeman at odds with the goals and aspirations of many of the groups he is called upon to police. For example, police often relegate social reforms to the category of "coddling criminals" or, in the case of recent ghetto programs, to "selling out" to troublemakers. Moreover, while denying that social factors may contribute to the causes of criminal behavior, police and police publications, somewhat inconsistently, denounce welfare programs not as irrelevant *but as harmful* because they destroy human initiative. This negative view of the goals of policed communities can only make the situation of both police and policed more difficult and explosive. Thus, the black community sees the police not only as representing an alien white society but also as advocating positions fundamentally at odds with its own aspirations. A recent report by the Group for Research on Social Policy at Johns Hopkins University (commissioned by the National Advisory Commission on Civil Disorders) summarizes the police view of the black community:

> The police have wound up face to face with the social consequences of the problems in the ghetto created by the failure of other white institutions—though, as has been observed, they themselves have contributed to those problems in no small degree. The distant and gentlemanly white racism of employers, the discrimination of white parents who object to having their children go to school with Negroes, the disgruntlement of white taxpayers who deride the present welfare system as a sinkhole of public funds but are unwilling to see it replaced by anything more effective—the consequences of these and other forms of white racism have confronted the police with a massive control problem of the kind most evident in the riots.
>
> In our survey, we found that the police were inclined to see the riots as the long range result of faults in the Negro community—disrespect for law, crime, broken families, etc. —rather than as responses to the stance of the white community. Indeed, nearly one-third of the white police saw the riots as the result of what they considered the basic violence and disrespect of Negroes in general, while only one-fourth attributed the riots to the failure of white institutions. More than three-fourths also regarded the riots as the immediate result of agitators and criminals—a suggestion contradicted by all the evidence accumulated by the riot commission. The police, then, share with the other groups—excepting the black politicians—a tendency to emphasize perceived defects in the black community as an explanation for the difficulties that they encounter in the ghetto.[56]

A similar tension sometimes exists between the police and both higher civic officials and representatives of the media. To the extent that such persons recognize the role of social factors in crime and approve of social reforms, they are viewed by the police as "selling out" and not "supporting the police."

Several less central theories often accompany the "rotten apple" view. These theories, too, are widely shared in our society. First, the police widely blame the current rise in crime on a turn away from traditional religiousness, and they fear an impending moral breakdown.[57] Yet the best recent evidence shows that people's religious beliefs and attendance neither reduce nor increase their propensity toward crime.[58]

But perhaps the main target of current police thinking is permissive child-rearing, which many policemen interviewed by our task force view as having led to a generation "that thinks it can get what it yells for." Indeed, one officer interviewed justified the use of physical force on offenders as a corrective for lack of childhood discipline. "If their folks had beat 'em when they were kids, they'd be straight now. As it is, we have to shape 'em up." While much recent evidence, discussed elsewhere in this report, has shown that students most concerned with social issues and most active in protest movements have been reared in homes more "permissive," according to police standards, than those who are uninvolved in these matters, it does not follow that such "permissiveness" leads to criminality. In fact the evidence strongly suggests that persons who receive heavy corporal punishment as children are more likely to act aggressively in ensuing years.[59]

The police also tend to view perfectly legal social deviance, such as long hair worn by men, not only with extreme distaste but as a ladder to potential criminality. At a luncheon meeting of the International Conference of Police Associations, for example, Los Angeles patrolman George Suber said:

> You know, the way it is today, women will be women—and so will men! I got in trouble with one of them. I stopped him on a freeway after a chase—95, 100 miles an hour. . . . He had that hair down to the shoulders.
> I said to him, "I have a son about your age, and if you were my son, I'd do two things." "Oh," he said, "what?" "I'd knock him on his ass, and I'd tell him to get a haircut."
> "Oh, you don't like my hair?" "No," I said, "you look like a fruit." At that he got very angry. I had to fight him to get him under control.[60]

Nonconformity comes to be viewed with nearly as much suspicion as actual law violation; correspondingly, the police value the familiar, the ordinary, the status quo, rather than social change. These views both put the police at odds with the dissident communities with whom they have frequent contact and detract from their capacity to appreciate the reasons for dissent, change, or any form of innovative social behavior.

Explaining Mass Protest

It is difficult to find police literature which recognizes that the imperfection of social institutions provides some basis for the discontent of large segments of American society. In addition, organized protest tends to be viewed as the conspiratorial product of authoritarian agitators—usually "Communists"—who mislead otherwise contented people. From a systematic sampling of police literature and statements by law enforcement authorities—ranging from the Director of the Federal Bureau of Investigation to the patrolman on the beat —a common theme emerges in police analyses of mass protest: the search for such "leaders." Again, this is a view, and a search, that is widespread in our society.

Such an approach has serious consequences. The police are led to view protest as illegitimate misbehavior, rather than as legitimate dissent against policies and practices that might be wrong. The police are bound to be hostile to illegitimate misbehavior, and the reduction of protest tends to be seen as their principal goal. Such an attitude leads to more rather than less violence; and a cycle of greater and greater hostility continues.

The "agitational" theory of protest leads to certain characteristic consequences. The police are prone to underestimate both the protesters' numbers and depth of feeling. Again, this increases the likelihood of violence. Yet it is not only the police who believe in the "agitational" theory. Many authorities do when challenged. For example, the Cox Commission found that one reason for the amount of violence when police cleared the buildings at Columbia was the inaccurate estimate of the number of demonstrators in the buildings:

> It seems to us, however, that the Administration's low estimate largely resulted from its inability to see that the seizure of the building was not simply the work of a few radicals but, by the end of the week, involved a significant portion of

the student body who had become disenchanted with the operation of the university.[61]

In line with the "agitational" theory of protest, particular significance is attached by police intelligence estimates to the detection of leftists or outsiders of various sorts, as well as to indications of organization and prior planning and preparation. Moreover, similarities in tactics and expressed grievances in a number of scattered places and situations are seen as indicative of common leadership.

Thus Mr. J. Edgar Hoover, in testimony before this commission on September 18, 1968, stated:

> Communists are in the forefront of civil rights, anti-war, and student demonstrations, many of which ultimately become disorderly and erupt into violence. As an example, Bettina Aptheker Kurzweil, twenty-four year old member of the Communist National Committee, was a leading organizer of the "Free Speech" demonstrations on the campus of the University of California at Berkeley in the fall of 1964.
>
> These protests, culminating in the arrest of more than 800 demonstrators during a massive sit-in, on December 3, 1964, were the forerunner of the current campus upheaval.
>
> In a press conference on July 4, 1968, the opening day of the Communist Party's Special National Convention, Gus Hall, the Party's General Secretary, stated that there were communists on most of the major college campuses in the country and that they had been involved in the student protests.[62]

Mr. Hoover's statement is significant not only because he is our nation's highest and most renowned law enforcement official, but also because his views are reflected and disseminated throughout the nation—by publicity in the news media and by FBI seminars, briefings, and training for local policemen.

Not surprisingly, then, views similar to Mr. Hoover's dominate the most influential police literature. For instance, a lengthy article in the April, 1965, issue of *The Police Chief,* the official publication of the International Association of Chiefs of Police, concludes, referring to the Berkeley "Free Speech Movement":

One of the more alarming aspects of these student demonstrations is the ever-present evidence that the guiding hand of communists and extreme leftists was involved.[63]

By contrast, a "blue-ribbon" investigating committee appointed by the Regents of the University of California concluded:

We found no evidence that the FSM was organized by the Communist Party, the Progressive Labor Movement, or any other outside group. Despite a number of suggestive coincidences, the evidence which we accumulated left us with no doubt that the Free Speech Movement was a response to the September 14th change in rules regarding political activity at Bancroft and Telegraph, not a pre-planned effort to embarrass or destroy the University on whatever pretext arose.[64]

And more recently, the prestigious Cox Commission, which was headed by the former Solicitor General of the United States and investigated last spring's Columbia disturbances, reported:

We reject the view that describes the April and May disturbances primarily to a conspiracy of student revolutionaries. That demonology is no less false than the naive radical doctrine that attributes all wars, racial injustices, and poverty to the machinations of a capitalist and militarist "Establishment."[65]

One reason why police analysis so often finds "leftists" is that its criteria for characterizing persons as "leftists" is so broad as to be misleading. In practice, the police may not distinguish "dissent" from "subversion." For example, listed in *The Police Chief* article as a "Communist-linked" person is a "former U.S. government employee who, while so employed, participated in picketing the House Committee on Un-American Activities in 1960."[66] Guilt by association is a central analytical tool, and information is culled from such ultra-right publications as *Tocsin* and *Washington Report*. Hostility and suspicion toward the civil rights movement also serve as a major impetus for seeing Communist involvement and leadership. *The Police Chief* found it significant that black civil rights leaders such as James Farmer, Bayard Rustin, John

Lewis, James Baldwin, and William McAdoo were among "the swarm of sympathizers" who sent messages of support to the FSM.[67]

Some indication of how wide the "communist" net stretches is given by a December, 1968, story in the *Chicago Tribune*. The reporter asked police to comment on the Report of this commission's Chicago Study Team:

> While most district commanders spoke freely, many policemen declined to comment unless their names were withheld. The majority of these said the Walker report appeared to have been written by members of the United States Supreme Court or Communists.[68]

Supplementing the problem of police definition and identification of leftists is a special vision of the role that such persons play. Just as the presence of police and newsmen at the scene of a protest does not mean they are leaders, so the presence of a handful of radicals should not necessarily lead one to conclude that they are leading the protest movement. Moreover, our chapter on student protest as well as other studies of student protest—including the Byrne Report on the Free Speech Movement and the Cox Report on the Columbia disturbances—indicate that "the leadership," leaving aside for the moment whether it is radical leadership, is able to lead only when events such as administration responses unite significant numbers of students or faculty. For example, the FSM extended over a number of months, and the leaders conducted a long conflict with the university administration and proposed many mass meetings and protests, but their appeals to "sit-in" were heeded by students only intermittently. Sometimes the students rallied by the thousands; at other times the leadership found its base shrunken to no more than several hundred. At these nadir points the leaders were unable to accomplish anything significant; on their own they were powerless. Renewal of mass support for the FSM after each of these pauses was not the work of the leadership, but only occurred when the school administration took actions that aroused mass student feelings of betrayal or inequity. The "leadership" remained relatively constant in its calls for support—and even then had serious internal disputes—but the students gave, withdrew, and renewed their support independently, based on events. Clearly, the leaders did not foment student protest on their own; and whatever the intentions or political designs of many FSM leaders, they never had the power to manufacture the protest movement.

One special reason for this kind of police analysis of student protest may derive from police unfamiliarity with the student culture in which such protests occur. When this culture is taken into account, one need not fall back upon theories of sinister outside organizers to explain the ability of students to organize, plan, and produce sophisticated leaders and techniques. Even at the time of the Free Speech Movement in 1964, many of the students, including campus leaders, had spent at least one summer in the South taking part in the civil rights struggles. Moreover, everyone had read about or seen on television the "sit-ins" and other nonviolent tactics of the civil rights movement. Also, while the police in Berkeley saw the use of loudspeakers and walkie-talkies as evidence of outside leadership, the former had long been standard equipment at student rallies and meetings, and the latter were available in nearby children's toy stores (and were largely a "put-on" anyway). Finally, with the intellectual and human resources of thousands of undergraduates, graduate students, and faculty at one of the most honored universities in the world, one would hardly expect less competent organization and planning.

A similar analysis may be made of conspiracy arguments relying on similarities in issues and tactics in student protests throughout the nation; explanations more simple than an external organizing force can be found. There is no question that there has been considerable contact among student protesters from many campuses. For example, students who are undergraduates at one university often do graduate work at another. And television news coverage of protest, student newspapers, and books popular in the student culture have long articulated the grievances and tactics around which much unrest revolves. Thus, when it is also considered that students throughout the country do face similar circumstances, it is hardly surprising for similar events to occur widely and to follow a recognizable pattern. Interestingly, collective actions, such as panty raids, have spread through the student subculture in the past without producing sinister conspiracy theories.

A related problem for police is sorting among certain types of claims from and statements about radical movements. Chicago prior to and during the Democratic National Convention is a case in point. To quote from the report of the commission's Chicago Study Team:

> The threats to the City were varied. Provocative and inflammatory statements, made in connection with activities planned for convention week, were published and widely disseminated. There were also intelligence reports from informants.
>
> Some of this information was *absurd,* like the reported plan to contaminate the city's water supply with LSD. But some were *serious;* and both were strengthened by the authorities' *lack of any mechanism for distinguishing one from the other.*
>
> The second factor—*the city's response—matched in numbers and logistics, at least, the demonstrators' threats.*[69]

Surely it is unsatisfactory not to distinguish the absurd from the serious.[70] And just as surely, the incapacity to distinguish can only result in inadequate protection against real dangers, as well as an increased likelihood of unnecessary suppression and violence. Again, this illustrates some of the problems of the police view when confronted with modern mass protest. The police are more likely to believe that "anarchist" leaders are going to contaminate a city's water supply with LSD than they are to believe that a student anti-war or black protest is an expression of genuine, widespread dissatisfaction. Moreover, some radicals have increasingly learned to utilize and exploit the power of the media in order to stage events and create scenes, to provoke police into attacking peaceful protesters, and the police have played an important role in assuring their success.

An interesting footnote to this discussion of police ideas about protest may be added by noting that, if the standards used by leading police spokesmen to identify a conspiracy were applied to the police themselves, one would conclude that police in the United States constitute an ultra-right wing conspiracy. For example, one would note the growing police militancy with its similar rhetoric and tactics throughout the nation, and the presence of such outside "agitators" as John Harrington, president of the Fraternal Order of Police, at the scene of particular outbursts of militancy. We hasten to add that we do not feel that this is an adequate analysis of the situation. Police, like students, share a common culture and are subject to similar pressures, problems, and inequities; the police across the country respond similarly to similar situations because they share common interests, not because they are a "fascist"-led conspiracy.

Militancy as a Response to the Police Predicament: The Politicization of the Police

Traditional Political Involvement of Police

Political involvement of the police is not per se a new phenomenon. Indeed, it is well known that in the days of the big city political machines the police were in politics in a small way. They often owed their jobs and promotions to the local alderman and were expected to cooperate with political ward bosses and other sachems of the machines. In Albany, writes James Q. Wilson, "The . . . Democratic machine dominates the police department as it dominates everything else in the city." [71] In some cities under such domination, police were expected or allowed to cooperate with gamblers or other sources of graft. Wilson comments, however, that "there is little evidence that this is the case in Albany." [72] Still, they played relatively minor roles in active politics. As Wilson writes, "The police are in all cases keenly sensitive to their political environment without in all cases being governed by it." [73] Their political concerns are ordinarily reserved for those decisions affecting their careers as individual members of a bureaucracy.

Yet there was traditionally another, perhaps more significant, way in which the police were political—as the active arm of the status quo. For decades the police were the main bulwark against the labor movement: picket lines were roughly dispersed, meetings were broken up, organizers and activists were shot, beaten, jailed, or run out of town. Such anti-union tactics are unusual today when national labor leaders are firm figures of the establishment, but most of these same men experienced encounters with the police in their youth. While these days have passed for the unions—except perhaps for those having a large Negro membership—participants in the new protest movements of the sixties also have come to see the police as enforcers of the status quo. Civil rights workers, first in the South and then in the North, and subsequently student and anti-war protesters, have met with active police opposition, hostility, and force. In addition, as we have discussed elsewhere, minority communities, especially black and Spanish-speaking, have come to regard the police as a hostile army of occupation enforcing the status quo.

While these types of political involvement pose serious questions, recent events point to a new and far more significant politicization of the police. This politicization exacerbates the problems inherent in, for example, using the police to enforce the status quo against minority groups; but, more significantly, it raises questions that are at the very basis of our conception of the role of the police in our society.

The Role of the Police

The importance of police to our legal processes can hardly be overestimated. The police are the interpreters of the legal order to the population; indeed, for many people, they are the sole source of contact with the legal system. Moreover, police are allowed to administer force—even deadly force. Finally, the police make "low visibility" decisions; the nature of the job often allows for the exercise of discretion which is not subject to review by higher authorities. Styles of enforcement vary from place to place, and informality often prevails.[74] So what the policeman does is often perceived as what the law is, and this is not an inaccurate perception.[75]

At the same time, and because he is a law enforcement officer, the policeman is expected to exhibit neutrality in the enforcement of the criminal law, to abide by standards of due process, and to be responsible to higher officials. The concept of police professionalization connotes the further discipline that a profession imposes; and while the police have not yet achieved all of these standards, it is useful to list some of them. For example, one expects a professional group to have a body of specialized knowledge and high levels of education, training, skills, and performance. The peer group should enforce these standards, and elements of state control may even be interjected (as is true, for instance, of doctors and attorneys).

Complicating matters, however, is the policeman's perception of his job, for this may conflict with these demands and expectations. For example, the policeman views himself as an expert in apprehending persons guilty of crimes. Since guilty persons should be punished, he often resents (and may not comply with) rules of procedural due process, seeing them as an administrative obstacle. So also when a policeman arrests a suspect, he most likely has made a determination that the suspect is guilty. Thus it may appear irrational to him to be required to place this suspect in an adjudicatory system which presumes innocence.[76] Moreover, there is a tendency to move from this position to equating "the law" with "the police." One commentator has noted the following:

> In practice, then, the police regard excessive force as a special, but not uncommon, weapon in the battle against crime. They employ it to punish suspects who are seemingly guilty yet unlikely to be convicted, and to secure respect in communities where patrolmen are resented, if not openly detested. And they justify it on the grounds that any civilian, especially any Negro, who arouses their suspicion or withholds due respect loses his claim to the privileges of law abiding citizens.[77]

Thus the policeman is likely to focus more on order than on legality and to develop a special conception of illegality.[78] These tendencies are accentuated by and contribute to the growing police frustration, militancy, and politicization.

Police Militancy and Politicization: An Overview

The insufficient resources available to the police and a view that attributes unrest to "malcontents" who illegitimately "agitate" persons, in combination with the growing stresses inherent in the policeman's job, led to greater and greater police frustration. And this frustration has increased as the police perceive that some high police and governmental officials and the courts do not accept their prescriptions for social action (such as "unleashing" the police), let alone their demands for more adequate compensation and equipment. In response, the police have become more militant in their views and demands and have recently begun to act out this militancy, sometimes by violence but also by threatening illegal strikes, lobbying, and organizing politically.

This militancy and politicization have built upon an organizational framework already available: guild, fraternal, and social organizations. These organizations—especially the guilds—originally devoted to increasing police pay and benefits, have grown stronger. The Fraternal Order of Police, for example, now has 130,000 members in thirty-seven states.[79] Moreover, these organizations have begun to challenge and disobey the authority of police commanders, the civic government, and the courts and to enter the political arena as an organized, militant constituency.

Such developments threaten our long tradition of impartial law enforcement and make the study of "police protest" essential to an understanding of police response to mass protest. Moreover, many of the manifestations of this police activism bring the police themselves into conflict with the legal order —they may act in a manner inconsistent with their role in the legal order, or even illegally. Yet much of this activity is justified in the name of law and order.

The issues raised by the growing police militancy and politicization may at times be made especially difficult and complex because tension exists between our idea of free expression and some of the demands we must place on the police. In what follows, however, we shall argue that the role of police in a democratic society places special limits on police activism and that, although exact limits are hard to define, in several respects police activism has exceeded reasonable bounds.

It is important to note at this point that not all of our expectations with regard to police behavior are, or should be, reflected in statutes, regulations, or court decisions. We may well expect police to act in ways which would be inappropriate—even impossible—to define in terms of legality and illegality. The issues raised are not necessarily "legal issues," except in the sense that they affect the legal system.[80] Moreover, even where legal issues are involved, it cannot be stressed too much that the solution to problems is not going to be found merely in "strict enforcement" of the law: *solutions* to the problems necessarily will lie in more fundamental sorts of action. Similarly, it is important to understand that the courts in fact can be little more than a generator of ideals. The real problem comes in devising means to infuse these ideals within the administrative structure of police organization. To assert that the courts are an effective check upon police misconduct is often to overlook that misconduct in our desire to affirm the adequacy of our judicial procedures.

Activism in Behalf of Material Benefits

Growing activism is seen both in the issues to which the police address themselves and in the means employed to express these views. A traditional area of police activism is the quest for greater material benefits. Police have long organized into guildlike organizations, such as the Fraternal Order of Police, whose aims include increased wages, pensions, and other benefits. However, difficulties arise when police increase the militancy of their demands. The growing phenomenon of "police protest" is itself a form of mass protest which in many ways directly affects the police response to other protesting groups.

An example of such increased militancy is the threat of a police "strike" in New York by John Cassese, President of the Patrolmen's Benevolent Association.[81] This is not solely a "police issue," but instead is related to the issue of the rights of all government employees. One hardly needs to be reminded of the strikes of transit workers, sanitation workers, teachers, and so forth to realize that the right of government employees to strike is still a disputed issue—in fact, if not in law. Regardless of the merits of the arguments on this general question, it is clear that a police strike is among the most difficult to justify, for the police are clearly in that category of government employment where continued service is necessary not only in the public interest but for the public safety.

And even then the policeman is different; we have seen that, as a law enforcement officer, his role is peculiarly important and sensitive. Thus when police demands for higher material benefits are expressed in a manner defiant of the law, such as illegal strikes, unique problems arise. First, the law enforcement apparatus is placed in the incongruous position of one part having to enforce a law against another part. Even if vigorous enforcement does occur, this is hardly a way to improve the morale and efficiency of the system. Second, efforts to encourage the public to respect and obey laws are seriously undermined. To more people than ever, the law is made to seem arbitrary, subject to the policeman's whim, and lacking in moral force.

Less explicit forms of "strikes" raise related problems. One such tactic is known as the "blue flu." In Detroit last year, for example, according to newspaper accounts, an

> aggressive police association steamrollered city hall into acceptance of one of the most generous salary scales in the nation by the classic trade-union device of "job action" and "blue flu," police vernacular for phony illnesses that keep police off the job as a display of power.[82]

Ray Girardin, then the police commissioner, was quoted as saying, "I was practically helpless. I couldn't force them to work."[83] "Blue flu" has also been reported elsewhere.[84]

Even more significant, perhaps, is the tactic of varying the enforcement of the criminal law as a means of exerting pressure. In Detroit the police combined a slowdown in ticket writing with their "blue flu" campaign.[85] New York has experienced this tactic also (although over the issue of one-man patrol cars).[86] Overenforcement of the criminal law can also be used as a tactic of police pressure. Long Island police, for example, are reported to have given unprecedented numbers of traffic tickets in unprecedented circumstances—for such things as exceeding the speed limit by one mile per hour.[87] Even when such conduct stays within the letter of the law, it is correctly perceived by citizens as a nonneutral, political abuse of police power. In this sense it is an even more direct assault on norms of due process and illustrates even more graphically that when the police abuse the law we are left without the machinery to "police the police."

Activism in the Realm of Social Policy

A second substantive area of growing militancy involves broader questions of social policy, including which type of conduct should be criminal, societal attitudes toward protest, the procedural rights of defendants, and the sufficiency of resources allocated to the enforcement of the criminal law. On each of these issues the police are likely to consider themselves expert; after all, they deal in this area day after day.

Police Violence

The most extreme instances of police militancy are seen in confrontations between police and other militant groups, whether they be students, anti-war protesters, or black militants. The police bring to these confrontations their own views on the substantive issues involved, on the character of the protesting groups, and on the desirability and legitimacy of dissent—in other words, the view discussed previously. In numerous instances, including the recent Democratic National Convention in Chicago, the nature of the police response, to quote the commission's Chicago Study Team, has been "unrestrained and indiscriminate police violence." [88] The extent of this violence has previously been described in some detail.

To understand how it happens one must consider that the police view these other militants as subversive groups who inconvenience the public and espouse dangerous positions. Perhaps some flavor of this feeling is given by the following excerpt from the tape of the Chicago Police Department radio log at 1:29 A.M. Tuesday during the convention:

Police Operator: "1814, get a wagon over at 1436. We've got an injured hippie."

Voice: "1436 North Wells?"
Operator: "North Wells."
In quick sequence, there are the following remarks from
five other police cars:
"That's no emergency."
"Let him take a bus."
"Kick the fucker."
"Knock his teeth out."
"Throw him in a wastepaper basket." [89]

Similarly, columnist Charles McCabe tells of returning to the
lower East Side of New York, his childhood home, and meeting a childhood friend who was now a policeman:

> We went to a corner saloon, together with a couple of
> buddies and we talked—mostly about cops.
> It was really terrifying. These guys, all about my age, had
> been to Manhattan and Fordham and St. John's. They had
> brought up decent families. But they had become really quite
> mad in their work. On the subject of hippies and black mili-
> tants, they were not really human.
> Their language was violent. "If I had my way," said one,
> "I'd like to take a few days off, and go off somewhere in the
> country where these bastards might be hanging out, and I'd
> like to hunt a couple of them down with a rifle." The other
> cops nodded concurrence. I could only listen.[90]

When these attitudes are coupled with a local government
that is also hostile to the protesting group and with provoca-
tions by that group, unrestrained police violence is not surprising. Indeed, the police may develop the expectation that
such conduct, if not expected, will at least go unpunished.
Such may well have been true of the Chicago convention,
where the Mayor's negative attitude toward police restraint
during the April racial disorders was well known [91] and
where discipline against offending police officers was thought
unlikely.[92]

Another striking instance of police militancy carried into
action is found in the growing number of police attacks on
blacks—attacks entirely unrelated to any legitimate police
work. Police attacks on members of the militant Black Panther Party are a case in point. In Brooklyn it was reported
that off-duty police, plus an undetermined number of other

men, attacked several Panthers in a court building where a hearing involving the Panthers was taking place.[93] And in Oakland after the Huey P. Newton trial, two policemen were reported to have shot up a Black Panther office.[94] Moreover, in other cities, including Detroit [95] and San Francisco,[96] off-duty police officers have attacked or shot members of the black community. Accounts of such incidents could continue, but the point is clear; these are isolated episodes only in the trivial sense of being especially clear-cut and well-publicized atrocities.

The Revolt Against Higher Authority

Attempts by higher officials to avoid occasions for such outbursts of militancy illustrate the severity of that problem and place in perspective another manifestation of police militancy—the revolt against higher authority. A well-documented example of this phenomenon has been provided by the commission's Cleveland Investigative Task Force.

The task force has found that, in the wake of the July 23 shoot-out, police opposition to Mayor Carl Stokes and his administration moved toward open revolt. When police were withdrawn from ghetto duty for one night in order to allow black community leaders to quell the rioting and avoid further deaths, police reportedly refused to answer calls, and some sent racist abuse and obscenities against the Mayor over their radios. Officers in the fifth district refused to travel in two-man squads, one white and one black, into the East Side. For several weeks after the riot, posters with the picture of Mayor Stokes, a Negro, under the words "Wanted for Murder" hung in district stations. Spokesmen for the police officers' wives organization have berated the Mayor; the local Fraternal Order of Police has demanded the resignation of Safety Director Joseph F. McNanamon; and many have reportedly been privately purchasing high-powered rifles for use in future riots, despite official opposition by police commanders.

Similar revolts against higher police and civic authority over similar issues have occurred elsewhere. For example, in New York on August 12, 1968, Patrolmen's Benevolent Association President John Cassese instructed his membership, about 99 percent of the force, that if a superior told them to ignore a violation of the law, they should take action notwithstanding that order.[97] Thus if a superior ordered that restraint be used in a particular area of disorder (because, for example, shooting of fleeing looters would create a larger disturbance with which his men could not deal), policemen were to ignore the orders. According to Cassese, this action stemmed from police resentment both of directives to "cool it" during disturbances in the wake of Dr. Martin Luther King's assassination and of restraints during demonstrations the following summer. Cassese charged that the police had been "handcuffed" and were ready for a "direct conflict" with City Hall to end such interference.[98] Police Commissioner Howard R. Leary countered with a directive of his own reasserting the authority of the departmental chain of command and promising disciplinary action against any officer who refused to obey orders.[99] Thus far the dispute has remained largely rhetorical, and no test incident has yet arisen.[100]

Cassese's position may understate the extent of militancy in the New York police force. According to anonymous sources quoted by Sylvan Fox, *New York Times* reporter and former Deputy Commissioner in Charge of Press Relations for the New York Police Department, Cassese took the steps outlined above in an effort to head off a grass-roots, right-wing revolt within his own organization.[101] "He responded just like the black militants to the guys coming up from below," Fox quotes one informant. "This was an attempt by a union leader to get out in front of his membership." This militant challenge was from the Law Enforcement Group (LEG), some of whose members are alleged to have beaten Black Panthers outside a Brooklyn courtroom.[102] In fact, it would appear that Cassese was not able to appease these new young militants by his actions. The group has become more and more prominent—the first of the militant, young, right-wing policemen's groups to attract nationwide attention.

Clearly such militancy is outside any set of norms for police behavior; indeed, it is the antithesis of proper police behavior. Moreover, the implications of such conduct for the political and legal system are profound. The immediate problem, of course, is to find to whom one can turn when the police are outside the law. A corollary is that illegal police behavior will encourage a similar lack of restraint in the general population. Moreover, within the police department itself, the effects of the erosion of authority have untold consequences. A graphic illustration of the loss of discipline and authority that can occur within a police force was recounted by this commission's Chicago Study Team: "A high-ranking Chicago Police commander admits that on occasion (during the convention disorders) the police 'got out of control.' This same commander appears in one of the most vivid scenes of the entire week, trying desperately to keep an individual policeman from beating demonstrators as he screams, 'For Christ's sake, stop it!'" [103]

Activism and Politicization

A form of police militancy that may raise somewhat different problems is what we have called the politicization of the police—the growing tendency of the police to see themselves as an independent, militant minority asserting itself in the political arena. Conduct in this category may be less extreme than the police lawlessness discussed previously in the sense that it may not necessarily be in violation of the law or departmental orders. On the other hand, the issues it raises are, if anything, more complex and far-reaching. Moreover, it exacerbates the problems previously discussed.

Before turning to the more controversial forms of police politicization, we shall focus on the organized police opposition to civilian police review boards, for this experience foreshadowed the later politicization of the police.

Police Solidarity and the Civilian Police Review Board

The police see themselves, by and large, as a distinct and often deprived group in our society:

> To begin with, the police feel profoundly isolated from a public which, in their view, is at best apathetic and at worst hostile, too solicitous of the criminal and too critical of the patrolman. They also believe that they have been thwarted by the community in the battle against crime, that they have been given a job to do but deprived of the power to do it.[104]

One result of this isolation is a magnified sense of group solidarity. Students of the police are unanimous in stressing the high degree of police solidarity. This solidarity is more than a preference for the company of fellow officers, esprit de corps, or the bonds of fellowship and mutual responsibility formed among persons who share danger and stress. It often includes the protective stance adopted regarding police misconduct.[105] A criticism of one policeman is seen as a criticism of all policemen, and thus police tend to unite against complaining citizens, the courts, and other government agencies. Students of police feel that this explains both the speedy exoneration of police when citizen complaints are lodged, and the paucity of reports of misconduct by fellow officers. It seems clear, for example, that the officers who took part in the famous Algiers Motel incident did not expect to get into trouble and that the presence of a state police captain did not deter them.[106]

Because of this situation many government officials and citizens have demanded that a means of reviewing police conduct be established and that it be external to the police department. The civilian police review board is one such recommendation. It, however, is anathema to the police, and fights against these boards marked one of the earliest exertions of political power by the police.

Both because it served as an example for police elsewhere and because of its role in the evolution toward militancy of the police involved, the most significant single case is the civilian review board battle in New York City.[107] There, in 1966, the largest police force in America, led by the Patrolmen's Benevolent Association, successfully appealed to the public to vote a civilian review board out of existence.

On July 7, 1966, Mayor Lindsay fulfilled campaign promise by appointing a review board made up of three policemen and four civilians. The PBA placed a referendum on the November ballot to abolish the board. From then until the election the PBA conducted one of the most hard-fought and bitter political campaigns in New York City's history. According to a number of accounts policemen campaigned hard while on duty: patrol cars and wagons bore anti-review board signs, police passed out literature, and even harassed persons campaigning on the other side. Many have claimed that at the height of the campaign cars with bumper stickers supporting civilian review were flagrantly ticketed, while an anti-review sticker seemed to make autos almost ticket-proof. Billboards, posters, and ads were heavily exploited, and the campaign was heavily financed by the PBA and private sources. One poster depicted damaged stores and a rubble-strewn street and read: "This is the aftermath of a riot in a city that *had* a civilian review board." Included in the text was a statement by J. Edgar Hoover that civilian review boards "virtually paralyzed" the police. Another poster showed a young girl fearfully leaving a subway exit onto a dark street: "The Civilian Review Board must be stopped! . . . Her life . . . your life . . . may depend on it." On November 8, 1966, election night, the civilian review board was buried by a landslide of almost two to one.

Similar battles have since been waged in cities throughout the nation.[108] Our review of printed material circulated by police organizations, articles in police magazines, and speeches by prominent police spokesmen indicates a frequent theme which is fairly represented by the following:

> No matter what names are used by the sponsors of the so-called "Police Review Boards" they exude the obnoxious odor of communism. This scheme is a page right out of the Communist handbook which says in part, ". . . police are the enemies of communism, if we are to succeed we must do anything to weaken their work, to incapacitate them or make them a subject of ridicule." [109]

At the outset, it was the distrust by minority group members of internal police review procedures which caused the demands for civilian review boards; the militant opposition of the police has only heightened this distrust. Thus, as might be anticipated, a cycle of greater and greater polarization has been set in motion.

An example of this polarization was seen in St. Louis in September, 1968.[110] The five-man civilian police board suspended one policeman for thirty days and another for ten and sent a letter of reprimand to four others for use of excessive force in a highly controversial arrest and detention of two black militant leaders. While the black community and pro-civil rights whites called this merely a "slap on the wrist," it produced an angry rebellion among rank-and-file police. More than 150 police officers attended an initial protest meeting. A second meeting produced a petition signed by more than 700, one third of the total force, demanding the resignation of the police board and saying police no longer had any confidence in the board. Subsequently, the city has rapidly been polarized. Civil rights and student groups, the ACLU, and others have come to the support of the board. Meanwhile the police have built a powerful coalition with unions, neighborhood clubs, political associations, the American Legion, civic groups, and various ad hoc committees. In the words of *Los Angeles Times* correspondent D. J. R. Bruckner, the polarization of the community "is a frightening situation."

Beyond the Review Board

Perhaps the most significant impact of these struggles, aside from further polarizing an already polarized situation, has been to give the police a sense of their potential political power. Their overwhelming victories in review board fights have given them, as one distinguished law professor interviewed by a task force member put it, "a taste of blood." Indeed, many experts believe the American police will never be the same again. Police organizations such as the Patrolmen's Benevolent Association, conceived of originally as combining the function of a trade union and lobbying organization for police benefits, are becoming vehicles for the political sentiments and aspirations of the police rank and file, as well as a rallying point for organized opposition to higher police and civilian authority. We call this phenomenon the politicization of the police.

On issues concerning the criminal law and its enforcement, the police traditionally have asserted their views by communications within the existing police structure and by testimony before legislative and executive policy-making bodies. Today, as a result of their growing politicization, the police are more likely to resort to activist forms of expression such as lobbying and campaign support for measures and candidates conforming to their ideology. Indeed, at a time when they are becoming more and more disenchanted with the decisions reached by our political process, the police perceive no sharp line dividing traditional activities from more partisan political issues such as choices among candidates for local or national office.

One example of partisan political involvement was found in the last two Presidential campaigns. During the 1964 campaign a number of departments had to issue special directives in order to curtail policemen from wearing Goldwater buttons on their uniforms and putting Goldwater stickers on their patrol cars. Moreover, this past fall there were reports that police in Washington, D.C., and other cities were passing out Wallace-for-President literature from police patrol cars.[111]

But perhaps the most significant political action is seen on the local level, and this political activity is far from the traditional seeking of higher benefits. According to Michael Churns, one of the founders of the Law Enforcement Group in New York, his group is more interested in "constitutional and moral" issues than "the purely monetary considerations. We're for better conditions in the country."[112] A survey of police in five cities found that police "are coming to see themselves as the political force by which radicalism, student demonstrations, and Black Power can be blocked."[113]

This activity takes many forms, one of which is campaign support. The following excerpt from a story in the *San Francisco Chronicle* reveals a practice which is becoming more common across the nation:

Plans were announced yesterday to have policemen from all communities in Alameda County sell $10-a-person tickets for a testimonial dinner for Robert Hannon, Republican candidate for State Senate.

Detective Sergeant Jack Baugh of the Alameda County Sheriff's Department, co-chairman of the dinner, said the record of Democratic State Senator Nicholas Petris is "repulsive to a police officer."

Baugh said tickets would be sold by police outside of their working hours and in civilian clothing.[114]

Police are also discovering that as a lobby they can have great political power. Mayor John Lindsay has seen this power in New York. When he tried to have police cadets take over traffic patrol duties in New York, the Patrolmen's Benevolent Association lobbied against him in the state legislature and won.[115] On other issues, such as the use of one-man squad cars and the consolidation of precincts, the Mayor has had to back down.[116] Indeed, the PBA may well be one of the most powerful lobbies in the New York State Legislature. The scale of its activities is indicated by a reception held in March of 1968 for members of the State Legislature.[117] More than five hundred people were entertained in the Grand Ballroom of the DeWitt Clinton Hotel in Albany by three bars, a live orchestra, and other trappings. The success of PBA lobbying is seen, again, in the fact that, after a bitter fight, the New York State Legislature, at the urging of the PBA, broadened the areas in which police may use deadly force.

A powerful police lobby is not unique to New York. In Boston, for example, the PBA lobbied vigorously against Mayor Kevin White's decision to place civilians in most jobs occupied by traffic patrolmen, a move that would have freed men for crime work. The City Council, which had to approve the change, sided with the police.[118] The Mayor then went to the State Legislature, but the police lobby again prevailed and White lost. In November, 1968, the PBA again prevailed over the Mayor when the City Council substantially altered the police component of White's Model Cities Program. Changes included the removal of a plan to allow citizens to receive (not judge) complaints against the police and the deletion of references to the need to recruit blacks to the police force.[119]

In a West Coast city in which we conducted interviews, a graphic example of police lobbying was described. According to a policeman on the board of the local Police Officers Association, the practice has been to put "pressure" on City Council members directly through phone calls, luncheons, and the like. So far the local POA leaders are uncertain how far this has gotten them. As one POA board member told a task force interviewer: "[We have gotten very little] although we have tried to wine and dine them and even blackmail the members of the City Council. But they are too stupid to understand what the Association is trying to do."

Militant tactics similar to those used by students, anti-war protesters, and blacks have also found their way into police activism. For example, New York police have marched on City Hall, and Detroit police have shown up in uniform at a City Council hearing in what some councilmen are reported to have felt was a blatant attempt at intimidation.[120] Moreover, because they are law enforcement officers, police can avail themselves of tactics beyond those available to most dissident groups—and of even more questionable legitimacy. The examples of slowdowns in ticket writing and overenforcement of the criminal law have already been discussed. In addition, an extraordinary tactic has been reported in a confrontation between Philadelphia Police Commissioner Frank L. Rizzo and the city's school board over the stationing of police in unruly, predominantly black schools. Rizzo is said to have told the school board that the police performed many duties of which the public was unaware—for example, keeping "dossiers" on a lot of people, including "some of you school people." [121] The threat was implicit. Similarly, a private Los Angeles group called "Fi-Po," the Fire and Police Research Association, maintains dossiers on individuals and groups, compiled from "open sources." During the 1968 campaign Fi-Po is reported to have passed the word that the son of a candidate for a major California political office had once been arrested on a narcotics charge.[122]

One of the more militant police groups in New York is "LEG," the Law Enforcement Group. Its activism is not only political but is often directed against the courts. The hostility of police to the United States Supreme Court—and their disregard of some of its rulings—is widely known.[123] LEG, however, directs much of its attention to lower courts. Indeed, it came into existence with a petition calling for the removal of Criminal Court Judge John F. Furey from the bench because LEG alleged that he permitted unruly conduct in his court during the arraignment of two members of the Black Panther Party.[124]

As pointed out previously, the police tend to view themselves as society's experts in the determination of guilt and the apprehension of guilty persons. Because they also see themselves as an abused and misunderstood minority, they are particularly sensitive to what they perceive as challenges to "their" system of criminal justice—whether by unruly Black Panthers or "misguided" judges.

LEG's current political activities are varied. They are demanding a grand jury investigation of "coddling" of criminals in the courts.[125] And moving more explicitly into the realm of partisan politics, LEG announced a campaign to support United States senators who will prevent "another Warren Court" by blocking the appointment of Abe Fortas as Chief Justice.[126] But perhaps LEG's most extraordinary tactic is its system of court watchers. Off-duty members attend court sessions and note "misbehavior" by judges, prosecutors, probation officers, and others involved in the judicial process. Lieutenant Leon Laino, one of the founders of LEG, described this program to a task force interviewer:

> The courts have a lot to do with the crime rate—the way they handle people, let them out on bail or without bail so that they can commit the same crime two or three times before coming to trial. Nowadays the courts let people get away with anything. Even disrespectful conduct while in court. But since we have instituted a policy of court watchers . . . we have noticed a change in the behavior of these judges.

LEG has already singled out several judges as "coddlers" of criminals.[127] Especially where judges must stand for reelection, the potential for further police intervention into the judicial and electoral process appears clear.

Although the politicization of the police is recent and thus difficult to assess, one thing is clear—police political power in our large cities is both considerable and growing. The police are quite consciously building this power, and its impact is being felt throughout the political system. An example is given by an observer in New York:

> In fact, there's a growing danger of disagreeing with the cops. On precinct consolidation, for example, councilmen, rabbis, state senators privately would say, "It doesn't sound

like a bad idea, but the police are getting everybody so hot, I don't see how we could go with it."

See, these [issues like precinct consolidation] are not the exciting issues and a lot of people don't feel like taking on a political force like the cops.[128]

Some police spokesmen rate this power even higher:

We could elect governors, or at least knock 'em off. I've told them [the police] if you get out and organize, you could become one of the strongest political units in the commonwealth.[129]

And in cities, including New York [130] and Boston,[131] there is talk that police spokesmen may run for public office.

Thus the growing police politicization, combined with the disruptive potential of other forms of police militancy, make the police a political force to be reckoned with in today's city. Indeed at times they appear to dominate. For example, aides to New York Mayor John Lindsay are reported to feel that the Mayor's office has lost the initiative to the police, who now dominate the public dialogue.[132] And some observers feel that ultimate political power in Philadelphia resides in Police ·Commissioner Frank L. Rizzo, not the Mayor.[133] The implications of this situation are pointed to by Boston Mayor Kevin White: "Are the police governable? Yes. Do I control the police, right now? No." [134]

The Military Analogy

Political involvement of the police—even apart from its contribution to more radical forms of police militancy—raises serious problems. First, aside from the military, the police have a practical monopoly on the legal use of force in our society. For just such a reason our country has a tradition of wariness toward politicization of its armed forces, and thus both law and custom restrict the political activities of members of the military. Similar considerations obviously apply to the police.

In some senses the police are an even greater source of potential concern than the armed forces because of their closeness to the day-to-day workings of the political process and their frequent interaction with the population. These factors make police abuse of the political process a more immediate prospect. For example, bumper stickers on squad cars, political buttons on uniforms, selective ticketing, and similar contacts with citizens quickly impart a political message.

A second factor which has led to restrictions on members of the armed forces is the fear that unfettered political expression, if adopted as a principle, might in practice lead to political coercion *within* the military. Control over promotions and disciplinary action could make coercion possible, and pressure might be exerted on lower-ranking members to adopt, contribute to, or work for a particular political cause. Thus, again, regulation (and sometimes prohibition) of certain political activities has been undertaken. For example, superiors are prohibited from soliciting funds from inferiors, and many political activities are prohibited while in uniform or on duty. Such considerations, again, apply to the police.

The Judicial Analogy

Even where coercion of the populace (or fellow force members) does not exist in fact, politicization of the police may create the appearance of such abuses. This can affect the political process and create both hostility toward the police and disrespect for the legal and political system.

Moreover, lobbying, campaigning, and the like, in and of themselves, tend to make the policing function itself appear politically motivated and nonneutral. Since the policing function is for so many people so central and important a part of our legal mechanisms, the actual or apparent politicization of policing would carry over to perceptions of the entire legal system. Such perceptions of politicization would be contrary to society's view that the system should be neutral and nonpolitical. And such a situation would, of course, have adverse consequences for confidence in and thus reliance on its legal system to resolve disputes peacefully. And this is most true of those groups—students, anti-war protesters, and blacks—who perceive the police political position as most hostile to their own aspirations and who are also among the most heavily policed. Moreover, the legal system would in turn be exposed to even greater political pressures than is presently the case.

So, while the police may be analogous to other government employees or to members of the armed forces, they are also, and perhaps more importantly, analogous to the judiciary. Each interprets the legal order to, and imposes the laws on, the population, and thus the actions of each are expected to be neutral and nonpolitical. In the case of the judiciary, there is a strong tradition of removing them from the partisan political arena lest their involvement impede the functioning of the system.

It may be useful in this connection to illustrate just how strong are our societal norms concerning judicial behavior and to note that these norms often demand standards of conduct higher than what is legally required. For example, even when judges run for reelection, it is widely understood that the election should not be political in the usual sense. Moreover, at various times in our history there has been public uneasiness about justices of the Supreme Court advising Presidents of the United States. Perhaps even more to the point, however, is the fact that whereas justices have from time to time informally advised Presidents, it is unthinkable that they would take to the stump or engage in overt political activity in their behalf.

Conclusion

Thus we find that the policeman in America is overworked, undertrained, underpaid, and undereducated. His difficulties are compounded by a view expounded at all law enforcement levels—from the Director of the Federal Bureau of Investigation to the patrolman on the beat. This view gives little consideration to the effects of such social factors as poverty and discrimination and virtually ignores the possibility of legitimate social discontent. Typically, it attributes mass protest instead to a conspiracy promulgated by agitators, often Communists, who misdirect otherwise contented people. This view, disproven so many times by scholars and distinguished commissions, tends to set the police against dissident groups, however lawful.

Given their social role and their view, the police have become increasingly frustrated, alienated, and angry. These feelings are being expressed in a growing militancy and political activism.

In short, the police are protesting. Police slowdowns and other forms of strike activity, usually of questionable legality, are employed to gain greater material benefits or changes in governmental policy (such as the "unleashing of the police"). Moreover, direct police challenges to departmental and civic authority have followed recent urban disorders, and criticisms of the judiciary have escalated to "court watching" by police.

These developments are a part of a larger phenomenon— the emergence of the police as a self-conscious, independent political power. In many cities and states the police lobby rivals even duly elected officials and influence. This poses serious problems, for police, just as courts, are expected to be neutral and nonpolitical; even the appearance of partiality impairs public confidence in the legal system. Thus, difficult though it may be to articulate standards for police conduct, the present police militancy seems to have exceeded reasonable bounds.

Moreover, this police militancy is hostile to the aspirations of other dissident groups in our society. Police view students, the anti-war protesters, and blacks as a danger to our political system, and racial prejudice pervades the police attitudes and actions. No government institution appears so deficient in its understanding of the constructive role of dissent in a constitutional democracy as the police.

Thus, it should not be surprising that police response to mass protest has resulted in a steady escalation of conflict, hostility, and violence. The police violence during the Democratic National Convention in Chicago was not a unique phenomenon—we have found numerous instances where violence has been initiated or exacerbated by police actions and attitudes. Such police violence is the antithesis of both law and order. It leads only to increased hostility, polarization, and violence—both in the immediate situation and in the future. Certainly it is clear today that effective policing ultimately depends upon the cooperation and goodwill of the policed, and these resources are quickly being exhausted by present police attitudes and practices.

Implicit in this analysis is a recognition that the problems discussed in this chapter derive from larger defects. Their importance reflects the urgent need for the fundamental reforms discussed elsewhere in this report—reforms leading, for example, to more responsive political institutions and an affirmation of the right to dissent.

Police spokesmen, in assessing their occupation, conclude that what they need is more money and manpower and less interference by the civic government and the courts. As this chapter has indicated, the latter recommendation is mistaken, and the former does not say enough. What is needed is a major transformation of the police culture by, for example, bringing a greater variety of persons into police work and providing better training. Because of time limitations, this task force has not developed specific proposals for legislative or executive action. We have, however, given thought to such proposals, and in what follows we shall discuss the types of action we feel should be taken.

A first step is a thorough appraisal by the Department of Justice of the role played by the federal government in the development of the current police view of protest and protesters. This would require several efforts, including examining and evaluating literature distributed by the federal government to local police agencies and examining all programs sponsored by the federal government for the education of police. Moreover, an attempt should be made to create an enlightened curriculum for police training concerning the role of political activity, demonstration, and protest in a constitutional democracy.

A second step toward a meaningful transformation of the police culture would be the establishment of a Social Service Academy under the sponsorship of the United States government. This academy should be governed by an independent board whose members would be selected for their eminence in such fields as criminology, sociology, and psychology—in a manner analogous to that used for the selection of members of the National Science Board of the National Science Foundation.[135] Like the military academies, this institution would provide a free higher education to prospective police, social workers, and urban specialists who, after graduation, would spend a minimum of three or four years in their chosen specialty. Internships would be arranged during one or more summers, and police graduates would undoubtedly be considered qualified to enter police departments at an advanced level. The academy would provide the prospective policeman an opportunity for the equivalent of a college education. Moreover, it would attract a larger variety of people into police work—and help bring a desirable flexibility in dominant police culture. This suggestion might be supplemented within existing universities by a federally financed program of scholarships and loans to persons who commit themselves to a period of police, social welfare, or urban work after graduation (or a foregiving of educational loans to persons who in fact enter such occupations). Indeed, this nation has in the past adopted analogous programs,[136] when the need in question was national defense.

Accompanying the creation of a Social Service Academy should be the development of a system of lateral entry in police departments. This has been recommended numerous times in the past,[137] and we can only urge that consideration be given to a program of federal incentives to achieve this end. Generally speaking, across the country one police department cannot hire a man from another police department unless that man starts at the bottom.[138] The only exception is in the hiring of police chiefs. This situation is analogous to a corporation which filled its executive positions exclusively with persons who had begun their careers with that corporation. One can imagine how dismal the corporate scene would be if inbreeding were the fundamental and unshakable norm in the acquisition of personnel. This is the situation in most police departments.

The combination of these two programs would no doubt lead to increased pay for police. Lateral entry itself would tend, though the market mechanism, to drive wages up, and the insertion of academy-trained recruits into the labor pool would have the same result. The quality of people and training which we envision should go a long way toward making policing a profession, in the full sense of that term. As this result is approached, substantial increases in police pay would be necessary and desirable, and these increases should be significantly more than the 10 or 15 percent usually mentioned.

The impact of these changes will be felt only over a period of perhaps ten years. Yet a short-run means to alleviate the problems discussed is a necessity. Several possibilities exist. First, the lack of police manpower is in part due to a problem of definition. Certain functions the police now perform, such as traffic control, could be performed by other civil servants. Other writers and commissions have recommended such a redefinition of the "police function," and we concur.

In need of similar reexamination is the definition of "crime." This is not the best of all possible worlds, and resources are limited. Thus even disregarding the philosophical debate over legislation in the area of "private morality," a rational allocation of police resources might well remove certain conduct from the purview of the criminal law.[139] Not only would such action free police resources for more important uses, but it would also remove one source of police corruption and public disrespect for law.

If communities are to be policed adequately—and this concept includes the community's acceptance of the policing as well as the quality of the policing—the principle of community control of the police seems inescapable. Local control of the police is a fairly well-established institution in the suburbs, and it may well be a necessity in the central cities. We recognize that the implementation of this policy is a complex matter—that different plans would be appropriate in different urban situations and that different types of control for different police functions may be desirable. We feel, however, that the principle is sound and that alternative models should be developed and utilized.

Finally, institutionalized grievance procedures are badly needed, especially in our large cities. It is clear that effective machinery should be external to any offending governmental agency if it is to be effective *and* be perceived as effective.[140] Ideally, the police should not be singled out for such treatment, but it is imperative that they be included. We suggest that models for a federal grievance procedure be explored.

Chapter VIII
Judicial Response in Crisis

THE ACTIONS of the judicial system in times of large-scale mass protest—and especially civil disorder—are an important, if severe, test of a society's judicial system and its capacity to protect the rights and liberties of its citizens.[1] This chapter is a study of the judicial system and its response to mass protest. Because of the breadth of this topic—ranging from anti-war protest to black militancy and from the nature of political justice to the mechanics of processing thousands of cases during civil disorders—we have chosen to focus our inquiry more narrowly. So we begin this chapter with a survey of the actions of courts during the recent urban disorders. We then indicate some of the causes and implications of these actions, focusing primarily on themes that we feel have been developed inadequately elsewhere. In so doing we also indicate the broader implications of our analysis for the legal system and its functioning during periods of social unrest and mass protest, whether that be black militancy, student unrest, or anti-war protest.

To undertake even the study of the judicial response to the recent urban disorders, however, is far from easy, for there is little in the way of data. Indeed, there are far fewer studies in depth about even the *routine* operations of judges, prosecutors, and other court officials in the lower criminal courts than, for example, about police. Furthermore, judges are not as uniform in their views as police, and they are not organized into guild organizations that have a sharp ideological character. So it is more difficult to generalize about judicial attitudes and actions.

Moreover, early governmental investigations of riots include few explicit comments on the operation of the judicial system. Reports of the 1919 Chicago riot, the 1935 Harlem riot, the 1943 Detroit riot, and the 1965 Watts riot offer, at most, cursory generalizations, without data on case processing, bail, or counsel. These early commissions evidently did not consider judicial actions as having any great importance; they were more or less taken for granted. This view was equally shared by government agencies and academics—even such classical studies of urban race relations as DuBois' study of *The Philadelphia Negro* [2] and Drake and Cayton's *Black Metropolis* [3] evaluated criminality without addressing its judicial context.

Official reports of riots during 1968, however, have given more attention to the judicial system. Undoubtedly this is in part because of an increased sensitivity in recent years to standards of judicial due process, largely because of the lead of the Supreme Court. Another reason for this recent concern is, of course, that during the urban disorders of the 1960's persons have been arrested in the thousands, straining the capacity of the courts to process and adjudicate cases in an orderly fashion. Almost 4,000 persons were arrested in Watts in August, 1965; [4] more than 7,200 persons were arrested in Detroit in a nine-day period in 1967; [5] 1,500 were arrested during a five-day riot in Newark; [6] in April, 1968, following the death of Martin Luther King, [7] over 3,000 persons were arrested in Chicago within a three-day period; during the week following Dr. King's death, 7,444 were arrested in Washington, D.C., and over 5,500 in Baltimore. [8] Thousands of other persons, including lawyers and media personnel, were, in the process, brought into contact with the lower criminal courts, persons who would not otherwise have been exposed to or even had secondhand knowledge about them. Responses ranged from anger at the injustices and callousness of the judicial system during periods of civil emergency to praise for overworked officials who did their best under trying conditions.

In these circumstances, it is not surprising that official attention has turned to assessing the administrative competence of the courts to cope with the volume of cases generated by civil disorders. The Kerner Commission Report devoted a chapter to problems of criminal justice during crises,[9] and the Chicago Riot Study Committee included a chapter on the courts in their report of August, 1968.[10] Other investigations have specifically focused on the courts; a District of Columbia committee reported on the courts in May, 1968; [11] a Baltimore committee reported in the same month; [12] a New York committee presented recommendations to Mayor Lindsay for court procedures during emergencies in August, 1968; [13] and the American Bar Association reviewed the problems of courts during civil disturbances in the spring issue of the *American Criminal Law Quarterly*.[14] We shall draw on these reports, as well as our own interviews and other materials, to describe judicial operations during civil disorders.

The Lack of Preparation: An Overview

The first major urban riot of the 1960's—in the Watts section of Los Angeles—was unanticipated by the judicial system, which understandably experienced severe administrative pressures. But even after the development of "emergency contingency plans" in some cities judicial systems continued to be unprepared for and overwhelmed by civil disorders.

The lack of preparation had an immediate practical impact. In Detroit, within two days of the beginning of the riot, 4,000 were incarcerated in makeshift jails. William Bledsoe, an Assistant State's Attorney General assigned to the Civil Rights Commission, reported that prisoners were "standing where there wasn't enough room to lie down. Or at least, people would take turns lying down. If you did find a place, you didn't dare get up. . . . Men and women were housed under these conditions together, without sanitary facilities, with perhaps one or two bologna sandwiches a day, if that. . . ." [15] In Newark, a large proportion of those arrested were held in an armory without proper food, water, and toilet or medical facilities until detention pressures finally forced authorities to release defendants on lower bails.[16]

Despite the Kerner Report's publication of lucid recommendations concerning the administration of justice in crisis, only New York had formulated a comprehensive emergency plan for the judicial system by April, 1968. Even in Washington, D.C., where the judicial system responded more fairly and efficiently than any other urban jurisdiction, "advance planning had been confined to discussion, making plans that were not operational by the time of the riot, or the drawing up of isolated plans that did not really resolve the central problems of mass arrest and detention." [17]

And in Chicago, for example, the Bar Association's Special Committee on Civil Disorders, which had been established almost ten months before the riot in April, 1968, had made no practical recommendations either to its constituency or the courts.

Thus, it is not so surprising that in Washington, D.C., cells built for eight were at times crowded with up to sixty persons.[18] And in Chicago, whose jail handles on an average day some fifty arrestees, on the weekend of the riots following Dr. King's death there were over five hundred cases per day without any corresponding increase in clerical and administrative personnel.[19]

In all cities studied, there was a serious shortage of professional and administrative personnel. The lack of a centralized and efficient record-keeping system meant that families and lawyers could not quickly locate defendants, nor could they always find an official who would accept bond.

These practical difficulties, which might have been predicted, often were aggravated by inflexible and hostile policies of court and correction officials. In Chicago and Baltimore, defendants were initially prevented from making phone calls to their families on the grounds that the security risk would be too great. In Detroit, men who were absent from their homes for as long as ten days could not be located by families or employers. In Baltimore, defendants were arraigned in courtrooms guarded by armed and helmeted soldiers. When lawyers were available there was little opportunity for lawyers to advise their clients, and some judges even refused to allow lawyers in their courtroom during the arraignment procedures. "The writ of habeas corpus," commented one Detroit defense lawyer, "was suspended and for several days there was a sign on the door of the Wayne County Jail that stated that no attorneys, either assigned or retained, could see their clients." [20]

The indignities to prisoners caught up in mass arrests were aggravated by the imposition of high bail, amounting to preventive detention, inadequate representation, and minimal observance of due process requirements.

The Role of Lawyers in Crisis

An important factor in shaping the judicial response was the absence of adequate defense lawyers in criminal court. During riots, the lack of experienced criminal lawyers becomes a major crisis, for the adversary system of justice depends upon defense attorneys to maintain its impartiality and integrity. When lawyers are either untrained, uninterested, or unavailable, the adversary system becomes a fiction and defendants are forced to rely on the good sense, professionalism, or benevolence of the courts—an outcome particularly undesirable in the stressful situation accompanying mass disorders.

One of the most severe deficiencies in the administration of justice under normal conditions is its failure to provide skilled defense counsel for defendants. Though lawyers are qualified to help strengthen the dignity, self-assertiveness, and power of the poor and disaffiliated, they have only recently begun to show organized interest in this task.[21] This becomes especially clear in times of civil disorders. The Kerner Commission found that the most serious legal problem during civil disorders is the "shortage of experienced defense lawyers to handle the influx of cases in any fashion approximating individual representation." [22] With the possible exception of some special interest groups, such as the American Civil Liberties Union and neighborhood legal agencies, the response by the organized bar to such emergencies has been, with very few exceptions, slow, insufficient, and ineffective. To make matters worse, the judiciary has at times restricted participation by volunteer groups, as in Detroit and Newark in 1967 and Chicago in 1968, where lawyers were denied access to courtrooms and jails.[23]

In Detroit, volunteer lawyers found it difficult to contact clients, and the organized bar made little effort to represent prisoners at arraignment, though they later responded after the riot was brought under control. According to a local law professor, "the legal profession in Detroit did not check the court of justice throughout most of the week in which the riot occurred. In fact, the profession was paralyzed." [24] By the middle of the second week of preliminary examinations it was difficult to secure the volunteer services of lawyers, since only 10 to 15 percent of the members of the Detroit Bar Association had offered their services.[25] While the bar associations in Chicago, Baltimore, and Washington, D.C., responded more quickly to the civil disorders in 1968, the results were by no means adequate. Little had been done to implement the Kerner Commission's recommendation that "the bar in each community undertake mobilization of all available lawyers for assignment so as to insure early individual legal representation to riot defendants." [26] Washington was the only city where the organized bar and judiciary cooperated in quickly recruiting and directing volunteer lawyers. In Chicago, the Bar Association offered assistance to the Chief Judge and Public Defender, who declined on grounds that extra resources were not needed. This response was taken at face value. The Bar Association refrained from criticizing the courts' actions during the riots, preferring instead to act as a broker between the courts and various legal defense organizations.[27] This was seen by representatives of these organizations as quiescent support of the courts' policies. Volunteer help was also initially refused by the Public Defender, who resented the interference of "outsiders" and regarded with suspicion their lack of experience in criminal courts.[28]

During the riots, courts in various cities often become armed camps, and some lawyers were intimidated by police and troops in and around the courtrooms. According to one volunteer in Detroit, "going into the court building was a devastating experience. It was surrounded by armed guards with machine guns. The building was practically a tomb and prisoners were being processed by some method I couldn't fathom." [29] In Chicago, lawyers were initially turned away from the courts by police guards. Those that demanded and received entry were ignored and, in some cases, met with hostility from bailiffs and court officials. At first, they were not allowed to enter the "bullpens" to interview prisoners. Even members of the Public Defender's Office were turned away from the jail by nervous sheriff's deputies. "I'm surprised that no one got shot there," commented an assistant public defender. "I remember walking up the steps [of the jail] with my public defender card in front and saw the Sheriff's police with a machine gun, with the safety off, pointed at me. . . ." [30]

Moreover, even when volunteer lawyers were present, they were all too often unfamiliar with criminal court practices. According to a survey in Detroit, 67 percent of the lawyers had spent less than 5 percent of their time in criminal court. [31]

Without organization or leadership, most volunteer lawyers found themselves facing chaotic situations in which they spent many frustrating hours waiting, petitioning officials, and wasting their considerable skills and resources. In Washington, D.C., according to Ronald Goldfarb:

> Lawyers converged on the Courthouse. Being unfamiliar with General Sessions, they groped for several hours trying to figure out the system. After doing so, they sat around, in many cases, waiting for appointments that were slow in coming because of the breakdown in the papering process. [32]

In Detroit and Washington, D.C., however, experienced criminal lawyers and law school interns established a briefing course for the volunteers. [33] There was no time for organization of similar programs in Chicago or Baltimore. Many inexperienced volunteers quickly left the courts out of feelings of frustration and incompetence.

With the exception of Chicago, black lawyers and criminal court "regulars" were generally absent from the ranks of volunteers. In Washington, the president of the predominantly black Washington Bar Association claimed that Negro defense lawyers had been purposely bypassed by the courts in favor of "uptown" lawyers.[34] In Chicago, the city's black Bar Association mobilized its members after the riot was over, held emergency meetings, and made public statements criticizing the court's expedient policies. This pressure helped to prod the court into holding bail hearings. In addition, these actions demonstrated sympathy by black lawyers with the "brothers on the street" and also helped to "reinstitute faith" in both black lawyers and the legal process.[35]

In general, riots have underlined the fact that the great majority of lawyers have little interest or experience in the legal problems of the poor. Bar associations have taken at best only a charitable interest in the criminal courts. This problem is compounded during riots by court officials who rarely extend cooperation to volunteers and maintain a veil of secrecy over proceedings. Legal agencies with special interest in judicial reforms also find that their efforts during a civil disorder tend to be frustrated in the interest of efficient rather than just proceedings. In Detroit and Chicago, members of the Lawyers' Guild and ACLU openly expressed their frustration with the courts. "We lent dignity to it last time by participating," said a spokesman for the Detroit Civil Liberties Union. "It was a farce." [36]

High Bail as Preventive Detention

Another serious problem in the judicial response to riots is found in bail. We have put together a city-by-city survey of bail practices during civil disorder in Detroit, Newark, Washington, D.C., Baltimore, and Chicago. The evidence is clear: the constitutional right to bail was almost invariably replaced by what in effect was a policy of preventive detention. This was particularly unfortunate. Not only did it work great hardships on the individuals involved—such as loss of employment because of absence—it also gave these persons an especially unfavorable experience with the practical workings of "the rule of law," an experience that was unlikely to persuade anyone of the merits of "working within the system for orderly change." In this way, the functioning of the judicial system during disorders may have contributed to the very grievances that lie at the roots of such disorders. Moreover, the implicit justification (if there was one) for these practices —that without preventive detention persons arrested would return to rioting—ignores two most important points. First, no evidence exists that this is true as a general proposition; indeed, it is surely untrue with respect to a great many of riot-related arrests—because of either the circumstances of the area or of the arrest, or the normal lapse of time involved in processing an arrested person. Thus, the "feedback to riot" justification for holding *large* numbers in custody is wholly lacking in evidence; and furthermore, it seems implausible to believe that following a court appearance, an arrestee charged with looting would return to the riot area, especially if his promise not to return was made a condition of his release. Second, the Kerner Commission correctly pointed out that alternatives exist to incarceration and suggested:

> That communities adopt station house summons and release procedures (such as are used by the New York City Police Department) in order that they be operational before emergency arises. All defendants who appear likely to return for trial and not to engage in renewed riot activity should be summoned and released.

In fact, all too often the constitutional right to bail seemed irrelevant. According to Judge Crockett of the Recorder's Court in Detroit:

> . . . hundreds of presumably innocent people, with no previous record whatever, suddenly found themselves separated from their unknowing families and jobs and incarcerated in our maximum security detention facilities . . . ; and all of this without benefit of counsel, without an examination, and without even the semblance of a trial.[38]

Whether this was because the courts were too overcrowded or because the courts intended to aid other public agencies in quelling the disturbances or were expressing distaste and fear of the participants in the disturbances, the effect was the same: punishment was applied before trial.

Detroit: In Detroit the use of bail as preventive detention was explicitly acknowledged by the judiciary. The twelve Recorder's Court judges met on the second day of the riot (Monday, July 27) and agreed to set bonds averaging $10,000; some were set as high as $200,000.[39] The *Detroit Free Press* noted that as a result of the decision, hundreds of persons were "railroaded through Recorder Court Sunday . . . night and Monday, slapped with high bonds and stashed away to await trial." [40] The high bail policy was applied uniformly—ignoring the nature of the charge, family and job status of those arrested, the prior record, and all other factors usually considered in the setting of bail. In response to criticism from black leaders, this policy was defended by one Recorder's Court judge: "We had no way of knowing whether there was a revolution in progress or whether the city was going to be burned down or what." [41] With the exception of one judge who gave individualized hearings but later said that even he had set bail too high, the judges of Recorder's Court carried out the high bail policy from July 23 to 30.

The impact of this policy was immediate. The detention facilities became severely overcrowded. The Wayne County Juvenile Home, with a capacity for 160 boys, housed more than 650 boys who could not make bond. Judge Lincoln, a Juvenile Court judge, dealt with this problem by declaring that "in spite of all the pressures, there has not been one boy released back to feed this riot." [42] Adult prisoners were incarcerated in maximum security prisons and police garages as the County Jail became overcrowded. Prisoners able to post bond were not always released. The overcrowded conditions did not prevent the Sheriff of the County Jail from refusing release of prisoners if he felt that the bond was "too low." The Sheriff claimed that the Executive Judge of the Recorder Court had ordered him to refuse release until the original judge reviewed the bail to see if it had been set too low.[43]

According to Judge Crockett, the situation had gotten so "far out of control that there was justifiable fear that if there were no riot then the Recorder Court's actions would surely have started one. We had hundreds of people in buses on Sunday for eighteen hours using a manhole as a latrine. This was prior to arraignment." [44] A week after the start of the riot, judges released hundreds of prisoners. Over 1,000 were released on their own recognizance. Yet, by Monday of the second week, 2,000 people were still confined, and on August 4, the end of the second week, 1,200 remained. Judge Crockett commented later that "even now there is [no real appreciation] of the full extent of the injustices we committed by our refusal to recognize the right to immediate bail and our objection to fixing reasonable bail." [45]

The arbitrariness of Detroit's high bail policy is further supported by a study made of 1,014 arrestees who were being detained awaiting trial in the Michigan State Prison.[46] Forty-four percent of those awaiting trial were married, and 86 percent had resided at the same address for one to five years. Eighty percent were employed, and 41 percent were employed at a major auto company. Moreover, 49 percent of those employed had worked at the same place for one to five years, and 14 percent had had the same employer for five to ten years. There was no consistent prior record. Sixty-seven percent had *no* prior convictions, 19 percent had one prior conviction, and 14 percent had previously been convicted two or more times. Thus from these statistics, one would have expected *less* stringent bail policies than usual; in fact the contrary was true.

Furthermore, the amount of bond showed little relation to the severity of the crime charged. The study concluded that "arrestees who were married, employed and without prior criminal records were treated virtually the same as were defendants who were single, unemployed, and had previous convictions and/or arrests." [47] Moreover, there are grounds to believe that future bail policies will have a similar effect. A former judge of Michigan's Supreme Court, for example, feels that the only lesson the Recorder's Court is likely to draw from the events is that "$15,000 to $20,000 bonds were unnecessary—next time bond will be $2,000 or so—to accomplish the same objective but to avoid the exposure. $2,000 bonds will keep them off the streets." [48]

Newark: In the summer of 1967, Newark courts employed a similar high bail-preventive detention policy until detention pressures forced a complete reversal. A "Release on Recognizance" program was initiated in the last days of the riot, with half of those arrested being interviewed and 65 to 80 percent of those being released. As in Detroit, public statements by high judicial officials showed a distinct lack of concern for those affected by a high bail policy. At the height of the riot, according to the *Newark Evening News* (July 14, 1967), the Chief Magistrate commented, "If they can't afford it, let them stay in jail." [49]

Chicago: In the April, 1968, disorders following the assassination of Dr. Martin Luther King, Chicago evidently took no notice of the Kerner Report's recommendations that

> . . . communities and courts plan for a range of alternative conditions to release, such as supervision by civic organizations or third party custodians outside the riot area, rather than to rely on high money bail to keep defendants off the streets. The courts should set bail on an individual basis and provide for defense counsel at bail hearings. Emergency procedures for fast bail review are needed.[50]

No emergency plans were made for release in a mass arrest situation. Rather, the courts continued the use of high bail to keep people off the streets. This policy had results similar to those in Detroit and Newark: detention facilities were overwhelmed and individualized justice was abandoned.

Yet the response of the Chicago courts to the April, 1968, disorders was consistent with plans made *after* Newark and Detroit. Soon after the disorders in those cities, the Chief Judge for the Circuit Court met at the Chicago Bar Association with the State's Attorney, Public Defender, Corporation Counsel, and representatives of the Chicago Bar and Legal Aid Society. They met to discuss "what lessons to draw from Newark and Detroit." At that meeting, the Chief Judge announced a high bail policy that would be followed in Chicago with the explicit intention of keeping those arrested off the streets during a riot.[51]

The April, 1968, riots were not the first time such a policy had been employed. In late January, 1967, Chicago experienced a snowstorm which immobilized the whole city, including the police. During this period, acts of looting and vandalism broke out on the predominantly black West Side. The courts responded to this crisis by imposing high bail on "looters." When the Chief Judge of the Circuit Court, John Boyle, was asked about the constitutionality of using high bond to keep a defendant in jail rather than to guarantee appearance at trial, he replied, "What do you want me to do—cry crocodile tears for people who take advantage of their city? Didn't I read . . . all about President Johnson's 'war on crime'?" [52] The Public Defender, in response to criticism from the ACLU that he was not challenging the courts' bail policies, commented that he was "not going to start fighting with judges because they set some bond that some people think is too high." [53]

According to an ACLU study in Chicago, the average bail for the charge of burglary under "normal" conditions is $4,300. Bail for the winter "looting" cases ranged from $5,000 to $30,000, with an average of $14,000. Bond hearings, as reported in official transcripts, typically took the following form: [54]

The Clerk:	Sam B.
The Court:	Branch 46. 1-31.
The Clerk:	Bond, Mr. State's Attorney?
The Court:	Bond for B . . . ?
State's Attorney:	On Sam B . . ., your Honor, the State will recommend a bond of $20,000.
The Court:	$20,000.

And in another case:

The Court:	What do you do for a living, son?
Defendant:	Sir, I work for the post office and for . . . two jobs.
The Court:	Can you afford to hire a lawyer?
Defendant:	Yes, I could, your Honor.
The Court:	All right. You hire yourself a good lawyer, sir. We will continue this case.
Defendant:	Your Honor, I have a wife and three kids and I only left them with twelve dollars in the house. Could I possibly get . . .
The Court:	Twelve dollars.
Defendant:	But I get paid from the post office this coming Thursday and I get my check at the other job, your Honor.

The Court:	You should have been on the job instead of out on the corner that night.
Defendant:	I had to get milk for my baby. I avoided this crowd as far as I could and then I was afraid they would rob me, your Honor; and my baby was crying. He is only 9 months old and I was going to—I was two blocks from my house avoiding these crowds because I am afraid they would rob me, but, your Honor, I got there and the police I saw—I could only see the top of the police car. Then I wasn't afraid any more because I thought the police wouldn't bother me. Then when the police got close the people went out of the store and dropped goods all over the ground.
The Court:	Someday you'll learn how order is in Chicago.
Defendant:	Sir, may I please have a personal bond?
The Court:	No, sir.
State's Attorney:	Motion State, February 20, 1967.
The Court:	I will not interfere with the bond. February 20, Bailiff.

Counsel was not permitted to represent defendants at the time bail was set, and the preliminary hearings were continued by the court for at least three weeks. This meant that defendants held under unusually high bail were incarcerated for three weeks before the court would even consider if there was probable cause to hold them. Almost all of the arrestees remained in custody unable to make bond. The city's judicial policies with respect to "looting" were well expressed by Magistrate Maurice Lee: "This type of crime during a citywide emergency is comparable to grave-robbing." [55]

It is perhaps not surprising, then, that the April, 1968, disorders found Chicago courts ready to impose bails which, though actually not "exorbitant," were nevertheless sufficiently high to prevent the immediate release of most prisoners. Moreover, there was no official mechanism for notifying families of the detention or amount of bond required for the release of those arrested. And volunteers were required to put tremendous pressure on the courts even to participate in such matters as notification during the bond hearings.

Problems of actually posting bail were endless. In most cases, the family of an arrested person knew only that he did not return home. The records department of the jail was closed in the evenings and, when open, rarely had information on the location of prisoners. Many prisoners who had money when arrested were initially unable to post bond since no bond clerks were available. At the jail and House of Correction, hundreds of concerned relatives were milling around with little idea of how to proceed. Several Sheriff's deputies guarded the jail, pointing their guns at the waiting crowd. Law students and legal aid lawyers performed the tasks that clerks should have performed if they had been assigned to the bond office.[56]

The bail policy was later justified by the Chief Judge of the Municipal Division. "When a man is sitting on the bench and he's looking out the window and he sees the city afire, big blazes here and there and everywhere, and he sees the people who are supposedly involved, it's very difficult for him to make a real considered judgment." [57] This inability to make a "considered judgment" inevitably favored the police over defendants. About 800 defendants were given bonds of $1,000 or over. Release-on-own-recognizance bonds were restricted for the most part to curfew violators, indicating that the gravity of the allegation tended to dictate the amount of bond. In determining bond, the courts paid little attention to such criteria as the background of those accused, despite the fact that over 70 percent of the defendants had never been previously arrested, 83 percent had never been previously convicted, and about 50 percent were arrested within six blocks of their homes. At least 37 percent of the arrestees spent over four days in jail pending the disposition of their cases. Ten days after the riot began, there were still over 200 people in jail who could not make bond.[58]

Baltimore: In Baltimore, according to a local blue-ribbon committee, bail for curfew violations was invariably set at $500, and few, if any, bondsmen were available at the courts. "Very few defendants were released on their own recognizance, and rarely was there time or inclination on the part of the judge to hear a defense plea for a bail geared to the circumstances of the individual defendant." [59] Of 345 curfew defendants who were not tried immediately, only 99 managed to make bail.[60] A significant number of curfew violators stood trial immediately under a stipulated prosecution; many reportedly pleaded guilty because of the "threat of incarceration implicit in the bail systems." [61] Of the 3,500 persons charged with curfew violations, all but 345 had been tried and sentenced during the riot:

> The mass trials of many defendants took place in an atmosphere akin to martial law. The disorders and the administration of the curfew generally made detention of defendants an incommunicado detention. Contact with those who might help in posting bail was problematic at best. Thus there was considerable pressure on defendants to agree to be tried summarily.[62]

Washington, D.C.: Bail policy in Washington, D.C., varied considerably. Compared with policies in other cities, it was certainly less oppressive and less arbitrary. Nevertheless, some judges set bond during the first two days of the riot with the express purpose of keeping defendants off the streets.[63] Other judges strictly adhered to the provisions of the Bail Reform Act, releasing many prisoners on their own recognizance and cooperating with volunteer lawyers to facilitate immediate release of their clients. Even so, fewer defendants were released on personal recognizance than is usually the case under normal conditions. According to Ronald Goldfarb:

> A check of Bail Agency records, and interviews with Bail Agency personnel, defense lawyers and prosecutors leads to one inescapable conclusion: defendants arraigned during the riot had more stable family ties, better employment records and far less serious criminal records than does the regular criminal defendant in the Court of General Sessions. . . . It is clear that many judges effectively discarded the liberal policies of the Bail Reform Act during the riot.[64]

Some Causes and Implications of Judicial Response

Routine Justice and Riot Justice

It is clear from the foregoing that the courts are ill prepared to cope with the volume of cases encountered in civil emergencies. When we ask why, the reason that is often given is strain—the added caseload simply is too much for the courts to handle. Any operating system, from a washing machine to a government bureau, breaks down from overload. Yet the "strain" explanation suggests an implicit assumption we believe to be unfounded: that the courts ordinarily offer services that are consonant with ideals of due process of law under an adversary system. By contrast, the evidence points to a direct relation between the way courts function during emergency situations and the way they function normally, and it is important that persons concerned with the shortcomings of the courts during emergencies not lose sight of the similar day-to-day shortcomings. Reform of the former necessarily should embrace the latter.

The courts are ordinarily understaffed and ill equipped; and the actions of courts during civil disorders may be seen as ordinary practices writ large, given public attention, and made vivid. In this section, we will examine routine justice as it proceeds in the same areas discussed previously. The similarities, we believe, will become evident.

It is in the lower courts that the quality of criminal justice must be measured, for as many as 90 percent of the criminal cases in this country are settled at this level.[65] Though the Supreme and Appeal Courts set precedents and receive wide publicity, it is the municipal courts that are the judicial system of most relevance for the vast majority of accused persons. It is thus of great significance that the President's Commission on Law Enforcement and the Administration of Justice found:

> It is clear that the lower courts are generally manned by less competent personnel than the courts of general jurisdiction. There are judges, attorneys and other officers in the lower courts who are as capable as their counterparts in more prestigious courts, but the lower courts regularly do not attract such persons. [66]

And the President's Commission on Crime in the District of Columbia recently observed that "abbreviated trials, disregard for witnesses, inadequate and shabby facilities—all contribute to an appearance of justice which weakens respect for law and order." [67] Again, according to the President's Commission on Law Enforcement and Administration of Justice:

> Every day in the courthouses of metropolitan areas the inadequacies of the lower courts may be observed. There is little in the process which is likely to instill respect for the system of criminal justice in defendants, witnesses or observers. [68]

Bail

If a defendant is charged with a noncapital offense, he generally has the right to be released on bail. Apart from the Eighth Amendment guarantee that bail cannot be "excessive," there are no strict guidelines, though the Supreme Court has ruled that the function of bail must be limited to guaranteeing the appearance of the defendant at subsequent proceedings; [69] thus it cannot be based on a desire to protect society from subsequent criminal conduct. In reality, however, the practices prevailing during riots also prevail in day-to-day bail-setting. Usually there is no evaluation of the factors, such as the accused's family and community ties, which may affect the likelihood of escape; more often bail is used *against* a defendant to "teach him a lesson," or to "protect the community," just as it is during a civil disorder. [70] The practical result of the system is that persons with money or access to money are able to obtain release on bail, while poor persons, who often cannot meet even the bondsman's fee, remain incarcerated.

A study of the administration of bail in Philadelphia showed that over 50 percent of persons held in lieu of bail were eventually released after trial, either through acquittal or on suspended sentence or probation. [71] Moreover, several studies have demonstrated that accused persons released on bail are able to put together a better defense and generally make a better appearance before the court, since they are able to get fresh clothes and do not enter the courtroom as prisoners. [72] The results of these opportunities are dramatic: persons released on bail are less likely to be convicted, and if convicted are more likely to receive shorter or suspended sentences. [73] Moreover, because the judge need not take account of this "dead time" in sentencing, the period awaiting trial often places pressure on the accused to plead guilty.

Ironically, then, the overcrowding of detention facilities during periods of civil crisis may work to the advantage of those so detained, as compared to the situation of the average poor arrestee charged with a felony. Overcrowded detention facilities put pressures on judges to release early—within a few days or a week—as compared to the weeks or months of jail time not uncommonly experienced in routine justice.

Counsel

Though the Supreme Court has held that the accused must be informed of his constitutional guarantees and his right to obtain or have counsel appointed, in day-to-day situations— just as in civil disorder situations—judges generally bypass or give little emphasis to these requirements.

> In theory the judge's duty is to advise the defendant of the charges against him and of his right to remain silent, to be admitted to bail, to retain counsel or to have counsel appointed, and to have a preliminary hearing. But in some cities the defendant may not be advised of his right to remain silent or to have counsel assigned. In others he may be one of a large group herded before the bench as a judge or clerk rushes through a ritualistic recitation of phrases, making little or no effort to ascertain whether the defendants understand their rights or the nature of the proceedings. In many jurisdictions counsel are not assigned in misdemeanor cases; even where lawyers are appointed, it may not be made clear to the defendant that if he is without funds he may have free representation.[74]

In Detroit, for example, counsel is rarely provided at the arraignment stage in Recorder's Court and, according to one expert, "ordinarily the accused is not informed that he has a right to have counsel 'appointed,' or that he can exercise this right 'immediately.' " [75] For the many who have been inadequately advised of their right to attorney, their first appearance in court is also likely to be their last. Most plead guilty without consultation, often under the implied threat of an additional stay in jail if a further hearing for a plea is required.

Even if an accused citizen obtains counsel, the reality of

what "counsel" means differs markedly from the abstraction envisioned in such Supreme Court decisions as *Gideon v. Wainwright* (1963), *Escobedo v. Illinois* (1964), *Miranda v. Arizona* (1966), and *In re Gault* (1967). In theory the right to counsel is perhaps the most important of rights because the presence of counsel should assure procedural regularity and the implementation of related principles. In fact, however, we find few defense attorneys who give to the role the attitude that Francis Allen has suggested as the mark of the qualified defense attorney: "a constant, searching, and creative questioning of official decisions and assertions of authority at all stages of the process." [76]

Studies of criminal defense lawyers suggest that "legal service" is characteristically too little and too late. The relatively few private lawyers available to the poor tend to be the least well trained and most inclined to violate the profession's code of ethics.[77] Criminal lawyers are predominantly general practitioners, unaffiliated with law firms, who make their livings from "small fee" cases and do a great deal of trial work.[78] According to Ladinsky, solo lawyers (most of whom handle the criminal matters of the poor) more often than firm lawyers come from lower-class backgrounds and from families having minority status. They "have quantitatively inferior education when compared to firm lawyers." [79] It is not surprising, then, that criminal lawyers on the average earn less from their work and outside sources than civil lawyers.[80]

Since most persons who appear in the lower courts are poor, where a defendant has counsel (and, again, a large proportion of defendants, particularly in misdemeanor cases, are not represented at all) that counsel is generally appointed without charge by the court. The quality of defense work by state-appointed attorneys is often even less distinguished than that by small-fee criminal lawyers.

Moreover, even in large cities the criminal bar is small and tends, along with the Public Defender's Office—which is usually more competent than appointed attorneys—to constitute a closed system. Given the pressures of the system to process vast numbers of cases, cooperation and accommodation are highly valued, with the result that most cases are negotiated on the basis of informal norms developed in response to administrative needs rather than legal principles:

> Most cases are disposed of outside the traditional trial process, either by a decision not to charge a suspect with a criminal offense or by a plea of guilty. In many communities one third to one half of the cáses begun by arrest are disposed of by some form of dismissal by public prosecutor, or judge. When a decision is made to prosecute, it is estimated that in many courts as many as 90% of all convictions are obtained by guilty pleas.[81]

Defense counsel is intimately involved in this process; his work comes to depend on cooperation with other officials in the system. The mass of clients may not be adversely affected. Yet the individual case may not be considered solely on its merits.[82] Moreover, there is no judicial review as to the fairness of the bargain, no guarantee that the defendant will receive what he has bargained for, and no control over the degree of pressure used to elicit acceptance of the bargain.[83] In this pretrial, publicly invisible method of dispensing justice, the defendant's guilt is generally assumed, a burden that ideally at least should be carried by the state.[84] The process comes to look less rational—subject to chance factors, to undue pressure, and sometimes to the hint of corruption.[85]

Faced with enormous caseloads, lacking financial and technical resources, and lacking especially the interest of the organized bar, the lower criminal courts should not be expected to generate a quality of distinction during emergencies that is fundamentally absent in its routine operations. Moreover, recommendations for improving the performance of courts during emergencies will be lacking unless they also address the problems found in these routine operations.

The Lower Court as an Agency of Law Enforcement

Although one may liken the functioning of the judicial system during mass disorders to its routine functioning, obviously something more dramatic is occurring. Not only are the problems faced during riots more severe than those confronted in the routine administration of justice; in addition, more varied and intense outside pressures are brought to bear on the courts.

During riots there is fear in the wider community, the courts come under scrutiny by the news media, and judicial authorities are in constant communication with political leaders. Under these circumstances, judicial actions and statements indicate that the courts usually cooperate by employing their judicial authority in the service of riot control, becoming, in effect, an agency engaged in nonjudicial forms of law enforcement.

In Detroit, for example, the Chief Judge of Recorder's Court made it clear in press releases that high bonds would be used to keep "rioters" off the street and that he would not release "thugs who would help to further [a] 'takeover-by-violence' plan." [86] The courts in Detroit refused to release prisoners until they were assured by the Mayor, a federal representative, and local military commanders that the city was secure.[87] The executive may tend to perceive judicial action as his responsibility. Regarding the Newark riot, the Governor proclaimed that "New Jersey will show its abhorrence of these criminal activities, and society will protect itself by fair, speedy and retributive justice." [88] The judges and magistrates in Newark were responsive to the Governor's direction that "the strength of the law . . . be demonstrated." [89] In Chicago, where the judicial system is routinely under tight political control, the courts cooperated with the Mayor's office and city prosecutors in detaining "rioters" until the emergency was declared over. The Chief Judge of Chicago's Municipal Division accurately reflected the political perspective of city hall: "I have seen tremendous progress for this particular minority group. They have come up so far and are progressing except for these civil disorders. Civil disorder . . . is the worst thing for the black race. It's bad; it's creating a cleavage in our society against them." [90]

In response to, and usually in agreement with, a desire for a quick restoration of order, the courts adopt a law enforcement perspective on riot control. Such a perspective may be summarized as follows: (1) civil disorders represent a time of extreme and dangerous emergency, requiring extraordinary measures of control and resistance; (2) the efforts of the police, military, fire department, and other public agencies must be actively supported to restore order as quickly as possible; (3) the presumption of guilt of defendants is made necessary by the presence of troops in the city, the sight of "fires on the horizon," and a common-sense appreciation of the danger and inherent criminality of a "riot" or "uprising"; (4) high bail is required to prevent rioters returning to the riot; (5) the nature of the emergency and the overwhelming number of defendants preclude the possibility of observing the niceties of due process; (6) due process will be restored as soon as the emergency has been terminated.[91] Both the courts and the police seek to prevent growth of the disorder, to distinguish the leaders, and to control the mob. The courts attempt to control the mob by detaining rioters until order is restored, by displaying power and resolve in the processing of defendants, by observing strict security precautions (having troops and police in court buildings and courtrooms, limiting access to prisoners, and checking credentials of lawyers), and by coordinating policies with other public agencies.

We have already suggested that the need for eliminating due process has not been documented. The evidence suggests that most "rioters" will not necessarily return to the riot area following a court appearance.[92] Moreover, when during crisis courts do become an instrument of order, rather than of law, communities find themselves without a tribunal for impartial judgment. This conclusion has two important consequences. First, as we have already noted, since the guilt of the accused is assumed, the adversary system and its attendant guarantees of due process are further eroded. Second, while there is ordinarily little control over the police and other agencies of government by courts, during riots there is active cooperation.

The criminal courts do more than arraign and try accused persons and sentence the guilty. When they operate properly, the courts insist on lawful standards of operation from other agencies of government. We do not have in mind here suits brought against governmental agencies, but rather what happens in the course of the routine criminal process. The courts have the responsibility to bring legal standards to bear on prosecutors, probation officers, police, lawyers, and other persons and agencies involved in law enforcement. In doing so, the courts are presumed to constrain these persons and agencies to adhere to law.

In order to perform this supervisory task, however, courts must in some degree be independent of other parts of the criminal justice system. The necessity for such independence —for a capacity to be both part of the law enforcement apparatus and in some degree stand apart from it—has long been recognized, for there are strong pressures on the criminal courts to be uncritical of other agencies of law enforcement. Recent Supreme Court decisions concerning the proper use of police power reflect an awareness of this tendency to erode the insulation between the criminal courts and other agencies of law enforcement. Under normal conditions, this tendency is occasionally halted by appellate court decisions and by professional standards of propriety. During periods of civil emergency, however, even stronger pressures are generated for expedient action, and the courts surrender much of what remains of their supervisory function; law enforcement agencies are encouraged, at least implicitly, to exert control by any means necessary. Moreover, the court's own actions— such as preventive detention through high bail—may be in violation of law. By condoning and following such policies, the courts contribute to the "breakdown of law" and to the establishment of an "order" based on force without justice. The implications of this situation are far-reaching. Some have been discussed earlier. To fully appreciate their gravity, however, one must examine the unique role that the courts play in our governmental system and the stresses that our legal system is undergoing in this time of widespread dissatisfaction and protest.

Disenchantment with Law

The criminal courts, like all legal institutions, are "political" in the sense that they engage in formulating and administering public policies.[93] The ties and differences between the political and judicial systems, however, are complex, and we must not overlook their distinctive characters.

The judicial system is tied to the political system in several obvious ways. Judicial personnel are sometimes elected; even more often they are appointed by political officeholders. Also, the enforcement of judicial decisions is often left to political officials. Finally, the laws the judiciary is empowered to interpret and apply are created and can be changed through political processes. In general, the closeness of the courts to the political system does much to ensure the flexibility of our legal system, its openness to change.

At the same time the judicial system is relatively insulated from politics. The selection of judicial personnel is guided in some measure by standards developed according to legal rather than political competence, and tenure arrangements have developed to protect judges from political interference. Moreover, judges are expected, and in considerable degree expect themselves, to be constrained by constitutional, statutory, and case law and by general principles of legality, in their assessment of evidence and their decisions. Such constraints are intended both to protect individuals against arbitrary state action and to prevent the courts from usurping powers more properly exercised by legislative and executive agencies.

In a constitutional democracy, then, the judiciary ideally functions as an impartial arbiter of conflict, relatively free from partisan interests—whether they be social, economic, or political. Our society recognizes that departures from that ideal are inevitable. However, it also views them with deep suspicion; for when the judiciary assumes a partisan role, the ideal of legality may seriously be undermined and the resolution of conflict reduced to the distribution and availability of force.

The evidence presented with respect to judicial behavior during the recent urban riots indicates a readiness by courts to lend their support to a system of preventive detention, to become an instrument of political needs relatively unrestrained by considerations of legality.[94] In the process, they undermine their own reputation as impartial arbiters of social disputes. Such actions lead to disaffection among those who have come into contact with a partisan judiciary, or who think they have. The importance of this cannot be underestimated, for the courts are our model for the "rule of law" to which we urge rioters to adhere. And lawlessness is precisely what we condemn in such dissidents.

Riot situations, however, are not the first instance of such disaffection. Yet the fact remains that the conduct of courts during riots reinforces the cynicism that many feel toward the legal system and converts others to similar views.

Because such disaffection decreases the likelihood of widespread acceptance of appeals to the "rule of law," it is important to examine briefly how this disaffection developed, prior to and after the recent urban disturbances. While it may be argued that much of this disaffection is due to naive and unreal demands made of the courts by the disaffected, it must be emphasized that the courts—and other branches of government—have themselves contributed to the decline of legal authority and, in some instances, to strengthening the resolve of dissenting groups. To the extent that this is true, the courts, like the police, may aggravate collective outbursts.

Political activity in the civil rights and anti-war movements was the first experience for many persons, both black and white, with the legal apparatus. In the early stages of the civil rights movement, especially in the South during the 1950's, the legitimacy of the legal system was assumed. People intentionally violated local laws, but they did so in the name of higher federal laws, which they believed would prevail in the courts. They had implicit faith in the justice of the legal system, if only it could be made to operate according to its own stated ideals.

The trouble was that even in theory, but especially in practice, the ideals of a federal system are ambiguous. Civil rights activists saw "the law" as federal law, the Constitution, the Supreme Law of the Land. White Southerners, at least those in political power, defied the federal law and interposed state law. Thus a paradox appeared: though federal law was declared by federal courts to be supreme, the hegemony of local laws and government—based on white supremacy—prevailed in practice. State judicial systems often actively partipated in this erosion of legality. Moreover, federal courts, especially the lower federal courts, often facilitated or acquiesced in this process, or at best were powerless—whether for legal or political reasons—to do anything about it. As a result, the stature of all law—state and federal, legislative and executive and judicial—suffered. As Tom Hayden testified before this commission on October 23, 1968:

> The major issue that shaped our political outlook . . . was domestic policy and particularly the problem of civil rights in the South which came to the attention of northern students in 1960 through the direct action of voter registration campaigns. . . . Working in the South brought us face to face for the first time with the reality that we had never known, the direct reality of the police state. . . . The crucial discovery of that experience for many students, however, was that the South was not an isolated and backward region but was an integral part of the whole country. . . .
> An elementary lesson began to dawn on us, a lesson that never was taught us in our civics classes, and that lesson was simply that law serves power. . . .[95]

Although the importance of experiences in the South cannot be overestimated, disaffection was not merely a product of the civil rights struggle in the South.

Two points are of particular importance in this respect. First, lower-class blacks, whether in the North or South, have always been skeptical of the courts' capacity to administer fair and equal criminal justice.[96] As long ago as 1903, W. E. B. DuBois noted that "the Negro is coming more and more to look upon law and justice, not as protecting safeguards, but as sources of humiliation and oppression."[97] In recent years, most militant blacks have come to believe, along with one SNCC leader, that "the legal system is bankrupt. There is no such thing as justice for black folks in this country."[98] Thus, the Kerner Commission was correct in concluding that "civil disorders are fundamental governmental problems, not simply police matters."[99] We will enlarge on that perspective in our concluding chapter.

Second, among protesters outside the South there was also a deterioration of respect for the legal system. To understand why this occurred, one must examine (1) the expectations of these protesters, and (2) the suitability of the courts for the role they are forced to play in protest situations.

In the early 1960's, students, blacks, and civil rights workers had much faith in the courts, and early experiences in the civil rights movement at least held out the hope that the judiciary might be a progressive governmental ally. Indeed, the courts were often far ahead of the other branches of government in upholding the notion of legality. Moreover, legality —with its corollaries of consistency and impartiality—was often found to coincide with justice, and this nurtured the expectation that some element of "social justice" could and would emerge through the judicial process. Even when civil rights activists became disillusioned with the legal system and the courts in the South and began to focus their attention on the North, they still had faith in the legal processes in the North—after all, it was not the South. Profound disillusionment, however, soon occurred in the North also.

An extensive literature exists on the role that courts play in our democracy. Some of this has already been sketched, but the functioning of courts is obviously much more complex than this. The importance of precedent, the doctrine of "political questions," the scope of appellate review, the distinction between "pure speech" and "conduct," the roles of the jury and the judge, and similar nuances—which often prevent. courts from reaching the "just" result or even from deciding a case on its substantive, as opposed to procedural, merits— are all important to a sophisticated evaluation of the courts. However, for better or worse, it is a fact that the vast majority of our citizens—and protesters—do not have such refined notions concerning the courts.

Thus at least some of the disillusionment with the legal system might have been avoided if a more "sophisticated" appreciation of our judicial and governmental system had existed. Such an appreciation would have recognized the limitations "inherent" in the judicial process and would not have been disappointed by actions of courts which were consistent with a strict standard of "neutrality" and "legality" but did not meet broader notions of social justice. Indeed, it would have been recognized that, in other contexts (such as the South), judicial neutrality had been thought desirable.

However, such understanding of the limitations of the judiciary was not widespread in the civil rights movement (as Tom Hayden's testimony suggests), and increasingly courts were perceived as and resented for acting in a manner contrary to the movement's conceptions of social justice. For example, the Chief Judge of the Court of General Sessions in Washington, D.C., has defended "neutrality" and "objectivity" by saying:

> When faced with a mass civil disorder, there will be great pressure to disregard the particular violation—especially if the activity is nonviolent; especially when it is in support of a cause which is obviously just; and especially when you happen personally to agree with some of the basic aims of the demonstrators. We, the judges, cannot afford to succumb to that kind of temptation.[100]

So, activists soon perceived "neutrality"—at least a strict judicial interpretation of it—as an obstacle to social justice. Ironically, even those with "more sophisticated" views are likely to agree with such a short-run analysis. They, however, point to the long-run necessity of a neutral judiciary. It is this point that the disenchanted activists either did not see or rejected on grounds that social needs were too urgent.

But that was only part of the problem. An authority can manage a claim of "neutrality" provided it is also consistent. Yet an increased exposure to the courts, especially the lower courts, seemed to those involved to reveal inconsistency. An observer of civil rights activity in San Francisco in the summer of 1964 commented:

> Scores of defendants all accused of the same crime are being tried by different departments of one system. There are variations in rulings on the admissibility of evidence, variations in the attitudes of judges toward the cases and, most importantly, great variations in outcome. Some jurors have complained that attempts have been made to "gag" them in the deliberation process. I know of one instance of three boys who alleged that they were sitting together that night at the Sheraton Palace. One of the boys was acquitted, one of the boys was convicted, and one of the boys will be tried again because of a hung jury. The boys expressed in amazement to me: "And we were sitting side by side!" [101]

Clearly, the reality was out of line with expectations. Defendants are less likely than officials to view the system in overall terms.[102]

As important, perhaps, was the fact that students more and more tended to view the courts as enforcers of rules that were themselves arbitrary. For example, students during the

1964 Free Speech Movement at the University of California challenged the administration's attempt to end a long tradition of political activity near Sather Gate. Judge Robert Kroninger, when faced with sentencing students arrested during the Free Speech Movement, made the following evaluation: "Resistance to the rule of law whether active or passive is intolerable, and to describe criminal conduct as civil disobedience is to make words meaningless." [103] Yet from the perspective of the student protesters, *merely* to describe their civil disobedience as criminal conduct is equally meaningless. As they saw it the alternative was to acquiesce to an administration which, according to the report of its own prestigious investigative committee, had "displayed a consistent tendency to disorder in its own principles." [104]

Similarly, the courts have come to be seen as enforcing laws that are technicalities either designed or used to suppress dissent. Such a view in many instances was not without factual basis. For example, after the April, 1968, peace march in Chicago, a distinguished commission reached the following conclusion:

> By attempting to discourage protest by withholding [parade] permits, the City invites disaster at some time when it may have constitutional reasons for prohibiting a particular assembly. . . . The First Amendment is meaningless unless dissenting individuals attempt to take advantage of the rights it affords. If such individuals do not make the attempt, it is true that there is no violence, no conflict, no overt repression of speech; there is also no freedom. . . . In a democracy, it should not require courage to defy authorities in order to express dissenting views.[105]

Moreover, congressional enactment and judicial enforcement of a law specifically aimed at draft card burning—after this was already used as a means to voice dissent—was widely seen as a blatant attempt to stifle dissent, as were many of the policies promulgated by General Hershey, Director of the Selective Service System. Finally, anti-war protestors and blacks have seen themselves charged with criminal offenses—often of an omnibus nature such as "mob action"—to which police actions have contributed.

It is obviously true that the courts, as such, should not be the object of blame in many of the foregoing instances; under any realistic theory of judicial responsibility they had no option open to them. At the same time, however, it is true that judicial enforcement of these laws heightened the bitterness of protesting groups and lessened their respect for the legal system. Perhaps, then, any lessons to be drawn from this experience should be addressed to the other branches of government. And central to any such lesson is the recognition that during periods of protest the legal and social system, fragile in the first place, is by definition undergoing unusual stress, precisely because of the importance of the issues involved and depth of feelings involved. To the extent that the courts are required to enforce laws that are not particularly necessary or which place unnecessary stress on the legal system, the legal system itself suffers.

Related to this is another manner in which the recent escalation of protest has resulted in an enormous burden on traditional disciplinary and criminal procedures and thus contributed to the growing disenchantment with the legal system. This derives not so much from the larger number of cases, but rather from the courts being asked to perform tasks for which they are inherently unsuited. And this becomes increasingly true as protest increases, and it becomes more difficult to draw lines between dissent and criminality.[106]

The criminal process is based on the implicit assumption that crime, by and large, is an individual enterprise, or at most an enterprise encompassing only a small proportion of any community. The lower criminal courts are designed to handle a large volume of misdemeanor cases in which most defendants plead guilty and do not contest the authority and legitimacy of the courts. Moreover, the process assumes that those activities defined as "crimes" are disapproved of by a large proportion of the community. This, however, is not true of contemporary mass protest, if the community in which the protest occurs is taken to be the most relevant.

Often a significant segment of the protesting community is involved in protest "crimes"—as, for instance, in Watts, Detroit, Berkeley, and Columbia—and a large proportion do not define the activity as "crime." Moreover, protesters do not accept the court's authority to decide the disputes. This situation is one in which even further disenchantment and erosion of the concept of legality are likely; as such it presents a crisis for the courts and the legal system. By being required to pass judgment over communities that do not support the judgment, courts are placed in an extremely difficult political and thus legal situation.

The federal courts have faced this type of situation in the South; municipal courts in the North face what is perhaps an even more difficult situation with respect to the black communities. The black communities are black, and they are segregated as a result of a history of white domination going back to slavery. So perhaps more accurate than this analogy to the South is one to the colonial court, for the black communities of America—segregated communities providing the maids and janitors and carwashers for more affluent whites—come close to being internal colonies. And to the extent that a lack of political and social change forces the courts to deal with these problems, the legal system itself is placed in a difficult and dangerous position.

Recommendations

To those who seek recommendations for improving the performance of the courts during civil crises, we can offer no simple—or even difficult—*solutions*. When the courts become a central political forum, it seems reasonable to infer that the traditional political machinery is malfunctioning. For the courts, the fundamental problem is that they are organized to do one sort of task—adjudicating—and that in civil disorders they are asked to deal with the outcome of political conflict as if it were *only* a criminal matter. Under such conditions, they often become and are perceived as an instrument of power rather than of law.

Given the fact that the courts will probably continue to be burdened with the responsibility of handling mass protests, every effort should be made to improve the ability of the courts to administer justice efficiently and fairly, with full regard to the civil liberties of defendants. Several reforms are needed in this respect:

1. The criminal courts are in serious need of thorough re-

organization so that they may be capable of meeting even minimal standards of justice, decency, and humanity under normal conditions. Such reorganization would help to eliminate some of the more flagrant abuses of legal rights during a civil disorder. More significantly, it would help to eradicate one of the causes of such emergencies, for there is good reason to believe that injustice and the ensuing loss of faith in the authority of the law may move rational persons toward extralegal action. It is especially tragic that those who have most reason to be disenchanted with our society—particularly the poor and ethnic minorities—are treated most unjustly by the courts. Our criticism is not primarily aimed at court officials, for in an important sense the personal competence of such officials is the least of our problems. Much more important is the fact that we have not furnished the courts with financial, administrative, and jurisprudential resources commensurate with their importance in a society aspiring to constitutional democracy.

2. The actions of the courts during a civil disorder should be lawful, sympathetic, and respectful. It seems clear from the evidence that during periods of civil crisis pressures on the courts for expedient action are inevitable. Despite these pressures, the courts must make every effort to encourage the *lawful* operation of the entire law enforcement system, including the police and prosecutors, as well as themselves. The Kerner Report made several important suggestions with respect to this problem. Among its recommendations are:

> That communities adopt station house summons and release procedures (such as are used by the New York City Police Department) in order that they be operational before emergency arises. All defendants who appear likely to return for trial and not to engage in renewed riot activity should be summoned and released.
>
> That recognized community leaders be admitted to all processing and detention centers to avoid allegations of abuse or fraud and to reassure the community about the treatment of arrested persons.
>
> That the bar in each community undertake mobilization of all available lawyers for assignment so as to insure early individual legal representation to riot defendants through disposition and to provide assistance to prosecutors where needed.

Legal defense strategies should be planned and volunteers trained in advance. Investigative help and experienced advice should be provided.

That communities and courts plan for a range of alternative conditions to release, such as supervision by civic organizations or third-party custodians outside the riot area, rather than to rely on high money bail to keep defendants off the streets. The courts should set bail on an individual basis and provide for defense counsel at bail hearings. Emergency procedures for fast bail review are needed.

That no mass indictments or arraignments be held and reasonable bail and sentences be imposed, both during or after the riot. Sentences should be individually considered and pre-sentence reports required. The emergency plan should provide for transfer of probation officers from other courts and jurisdictions to assist in the processing of arrestees.[107]

We support these recommendations of the Kerner Commission, which were adopted in detail by the District of Columbia and other Committee reports, with the following reservation. Clearly some emergency measures are needed to permit the courts to operate in an orderly fashion during a civil crisis. The danger is that such "temporary" measures may become permanent and "emergencies" become routine. We are especially concerned with the trend toward devising "emergency measures" which are not addressed to needed fundamental reforms in the routine criminal justice system. For example, recent official investigations of the operation of the courts in crisis have sought new laws and new judicial techniques for controlling "rioters." Thus, many cities are presently exploring the possibility of preventive detention legislation,[108] and a blue-ribbon commission in Baltimore has recommended the passage of a "scavenging" law in anticipation of future riots.[109] Moreover, these trends lead us to believe that preparations are being made to deal efficiently with future civil disorders while little is being done to remedy the social and political grievances that motivate such disorders. This is a fundamental error.

Finally, we believe that a number of assumptions, both in social psychology and in official conceptions, have served to obscure and undermine the political character of contemporary protests. In our concluding chapter, we intend to assess those assumptions.

Part Four
Conclusion

Chapter IX
Social Response to Collective Behavior

THROUGHOUT THIS report we have concentrated on showing the difficulty of determining what causes and what prevents violence, such as it is, in several protest movements. A common theme has emerged from the analysis of these movements. We have argued that they represent forms of political protest oriented toward significant change in American social and political institutions. In this concluding chapter we consider some of the implications of this perspective for public policy. In doing so, we narrow our focus to the question of the meaning of riots and civil disorder. We believe that conventional approaches to the analysis and control of riots have inadequately understood their social and political significance, and need to be revised.

In the first section of this chapter we examine the perspective on riots developed in social-scientific theories of collective behavior. This is not merely an academic exercise. At least since the 1919 Chicago Commission on Race Relations,[1] these perspectives have influenced the assumptions underlying official responses to civil disorders. Even where direct influence is unclear, it remains true that there has been a remarkable similarity between academic and official views on the nature, causes, and control of civil disorder. In the second section, we consider some of the themes in the official conception of riots in the light of historical and contemporary evidence. In the final section, we consider the implications of our findings for conventional approaches to the social control of disorder.

Theories of Collective Behavior

"Common sense" sees riots as threatening, irrational, and senseless. They are formless, malign, incoherent, and destructive; they seem to raise to the surface those darker elements of the human character that are ordinarily submerged. Most of all, they are something others do: the lower classes, disadvantaged groups, youth, criminals. By and large, this conventional view of riots has been adopted in the development of the study of collective disorder, although some of the most recent work in social science has come to perceive the relative and definitional aspects of such terms as "order," "violence," and "crime." As William Kornhauser has recently written, "The readiness to assimilate all politics to either order or violence implies a very narrow notion of order and a very broad notion of violence . . . what is violent action in one period of history becomes acceptable conflict at a later time." [2] It is this more recent perspective that we attempt to apply to the analysis of collective behavior, especially in our consideration of social response.

The "Crowd"

The modern study of collective behavior has its origins in the nineteenth-century European writers on the "crowd." In the work of Gabriel Tarde, Gustave Le Bon, and others, the emergence of the "crowd" was identified with the rise of democracy. It was seen as both the catalyst and symbol of the decline of everything worthy in European civilization during and after the French Revolution. In becoming part of a crowd, wrote Le Bon, "a man descends several rungs in the ladder of civilization." [3] Unlike civilized behavior, crowd behavior was impulsive, spontaneous, and uninhibited, rather than the product of reason, established tradition, and the restraints of civilized life. Ideas spread in the crowd through processes of contagion and suggestion. In this view, the crowd developed like a highly infectious disease; the crowd represented a pathological state.[4] Like others after him, Le Bon had little to say about the origins of crowds; while exhaustively discussing their nature, he left the conditions of their emergence obscure. In this way, the "pathological" and "destructive" behavior of crowds was dissociated from its environmental and institutional framework. Finally, Le Bon and other early writers tended to lump together indiscriminately what we today regard as distinct phenomena; in their aristocratic assault on the crowd, they included parliamentary bodies and juries as manifestations of "crowd behavior." [5] This approach, while perhaps useful in discrediting the aspirations of rising social classes in a democratizing age, seriously undermined the analysis of specific instances of collective behavior.

Transplanted to American sociology and social psychology, the preconceptions of European theorists underwent considerable modification.[6] Lacking a feudal tradition, American society was not receptive to the more explicitly anti-democratic biases represented in European theories of the crowd. The irrational behavior of crowds was no longer, for the most part, linked to the rise of democratic participation in government and culture. The simplistic disease model of collective behavior was for the most part replaced by a new perspective which, while discarding some of the older themes, retained many of their underlying premises.[7]

The major change invoked in more recent analyses of collective behavior is toward greater interest in the *causes* of disorder. At the same time, early conceptions of the *nature* of riots have largely been retained.

The Nature of Riots

Social scientists usually place riots under the heading of "collective behavior," a broad concept which, in most treatments, embraces lynchings, panics, bank runs, riots, disaster behavior, and organized social movements of various kinds.[8] Underlying this union of apparently diverse phenomena is the idea that each in some sense departs from the more routine, predictable, and institutionalized aspects of social life. Collective behavior, in the words of a leading social psychology text, is not only "extraordinary" and "dramatic," but also "likely to be foolish, disgusting, or evil." [9]

The crucial element of "collective behavior" is not that it is collective—all group interaction is—but that it is qualitatively different from the "normal" group processes of society. Smelser, for example, acknowledges that although patriotic celebrations may erupt into riot, they are not to be considered as illustrative of collective behavior:

> True, they are based often on generalized values such as the divine, the nation, the monarchy or the *alma mater*. True, they are collective. True, they may release tensions generated by conditions of structural strain. The basic difference between such ceremonials and collective behavior—and the reason for excluding them—is that the former are institutionalized in form and context.[10]

"Collective behavior" is thus conceived as nonconforming and even "deviant" group behavior. Under this conception, the routine processes of any given society are seen as stable, orderly, and predictable, operating under the normative constraints and cumulative rationality of tradition. The instability, disorder, and irrationality of "collective behavior," therefore, are characteristic of those groups that are experiencing "social strain"—for example, "the unemployed, the recent migrant, the adolescent." [11] As such, "collective behavior" is characteristically the behavior of outsiders, the disadvantaged and disaffected. Sometimes, however, "collective behavior" becomes the property of the propertied, as when businessmen and bankers "panic" during a stock-market crash or the failure of a monetary system. Yet since the propertied rarely experience such "social strain," they likewise rarely inherit the derogation "panicky" and "crazy." When they do they are also relegated to the status of social outcasts, even though a bank run may in fact be an illustration of rational self-interest, narrowly conceived. Usually, however, "panicky" and "crazy" are terms reserved for social movements and insurrections, collective behavior theorists suggesting that a fundamentally similar departure from reasonable and instrumental concerns underlies all of them.

According to a recent theorist, what such phenomena have

in common is their organization around ideas which, like magical beliefs, distort reality and "short-circuit" the normal paths to the amelioration of grievances.[12] This distorted outlook is held responsible for the "crudeness, excess, and eccentricity" of collective behavior.[13]

Related to this conception of collective behavior as irrational is an implicit notion that collective behavior is—particularly in its more "explosive" forms—inappropriate behavior. Just as many bewildered observers tend to view a riot in the same terms as a temper tantrum, so a social scientist categorizes collective behavior as "the action of the impatient."[14] Implicit in this perspective is the application of different premises to collective as opposed to "institutionalized" behavior. To define collective behavior as immoderate, and its underlying beliefs as exaggerated, strongly implies that "established" behavior may be conceived as both moderate and reasonable, barring direct evidence to the contrary. Needless to say, such an approach has important political implications, which ultimately renders much of collective behavior theory an ideological rather than analytical exercise. This inherently judgmental aspect of collective behavior theory is made all the more damaging by being unexpressed; indeed, many of the theoretical traditions represented in current work on collective behavior stress the need for a "value-free" social science.

It should be emphasized that theories of collective behavior are not all of a piece, nor are they necessarily as internally consistent as this overly brief analysis implies. Several theorists, for example, recognize the potentially constructive character of collective behavior: all, however, remain deeply rooted in the tradition of viewing collective behavior as distinct from "orderly" social life.[15]

Whereas much of modern social science remains close to its early forerunners in its assessment of the nature and quality of collective behavior, it departs from the traditional view in recognizing that the origins of collective disorder are neither mysterious nor rooted in the dark side of human personality.[16] Rather, modern social theory usually focuses on two social sources of collective behavior: a condition of social "strain" or "tension," leading to frustration and hostility on the part of marginal or disadvantaged groups; and a breakdown of normal systems of social control, in the sense of both widespread social disorganization and the inability of local authorities to maintain order in the face of emergent disorder. When contemporary theorists attempt to deal with the causes of riot, one or both of these factors is generally invoked. On balance the latter factor—i.e., the breakdown of social control on a global or local level—predominates in these discussions. A major text in the sociology of collective behavior stresses as determinants of collective behavior both "social disintegration" and the failure of those occupying positions of social control to effectively perform their functions.[17] Another, while stressing the importance of "frustration" as one kind of strain leading to "hostile outbursts," [18] also argues that firmness in the "agencies of social control" may play a role in preventing outbursts.[19] This perspective is affirmed in a recent work directed specifically at the causes and control of ghetto disorders, where it is argued that while "social tensions" clearly underlie riots, they amount to only a partial explanation; "a key element in the outbreak of riots is a weakness in the system of social control." [20]

Specifically, the failure of social control is said to be involved in a number of ways, and at a number of stages, in the emergence of ghetto riots. On one level, the breakdown of social control means the existence of "a moral and social climate that encourages violence," especially through the mass media.[21] On another level, it means the failure of law enforcement agencies to stop the process of "contagion" [22] through which riots spread. Left inadequately controlled, the riot escalates into widespread destruction and extensive sniper fire.[23] Similarly, modern riot control manuals stress that riots are triggered by "social contagion," and "the level of mob frenzy . . . is reinforced and augmented by seeing others who are equally excited and also rioting." [24]

The retention of the concept of contagion illustrates the degree to which most theories of collective disorder remain bound by earlier perspectives. The conception of the "escalated riot" involving heavy sniper fire illustrates the reciprocal relation between an inadequate theoretical framework and an inadequate attention to questions of fact, for, as the Kerner

Commission exhaustively demonstrated, the existence of "heavy sniper fire" in the ghetto riots of the 1960's was largely mythical.[25] It is the kind of myth, however, that fits very well the theoretical presuppositions dominating much collective behavior theory. It is also the kind of myth that may turn out to be self-confirming in the long run.

We find conventional theories of riots open to challenge on the following counts:

1. They tend to focus on the destructive behavior of disaffected groups while accepting the behavior of authorities as normal, instrumental, and rational. Yet established, thoroughly institutionalized behavior may be equally destructive as, or considerably more so than, riots. No riot, for example, matches the destructiveness of military solutions to disputed political issues.[26] Further, available evidence suggests both that (a) armed officials often demonstrate a greater propensity to violence against persons than unarmed civilians; and (b) these actions often escalate the intensity of the disorder and comprise a good part of the "destructiveness" of riots, especially in terms of human deaths and injuries. Furthermore, as the reports of our Chicago, Cleveland, Miami, and San Francisco study teams well illustrate, riots are not unilaterally provoked by disaffiliated groups. Collective protest involves interaction between the behavior of "rioters" and the behavior of officials and agents of social control. Each "side" may on close inspection turn out to be equally "riotous." The fact that the behavior of one group is labeled "riot" and that of the other labeled "social control" is a matter of social definition.[27]

2. They tend to describe collective behavior as irrational, formless, and immoderate. As we will demonstrate in the next section, less emotional scrutiny of riots indicates that they show a considerable degree of structure, purposiveness, and rationality.[28] Nor is "established" behavior necessarily guided by rational principle. While the beliefs underlying a riot may frequently be inaccurate or exaggerated, they are not necessarily more so than, for example, commonly held beliefs about racial minorities by dominant groups, the perception of foreign threats to national security, of the causes of crime, of threats to internal security, and so forth. A

measure of irrationality, then, is not a defining characteristic of collective behavior generally or of riots in particular; rather, it is an element of many routine social processes and institutions *and* forms of collective behavior. The more significant difference may be that established institutions are usually in a more advantageous position from which to define "rationality."

The "inappropriateness" of riots is clearly variable, depending on the availability of alternative modes of action. Only by neglect of the relevant institutional setting can "inappropriateness" be considered a definitive characteristic of riots. Historically, riots have been used as a form of political bargaining in the absence of other channels of effective action. Where such channels are atrophied, nonexistent, or unresponsive, the riot may become a quasi-established, relatively standard form of political protest.[29]

Hans W. Mattick, a consultant to the Kerner Commission, has described the underlying political character of recent urban riots:

> The content of the riot is reciprocal, like a broken bargain. It consists of claims and denials made in the substance and conceptions of life, liberty, and the pursuit of happiness. The parties to the bargain are the Negro community and the white majority, living under the rule of law, at some level of social accommodation. In process of time the predominant social forces come to shape the law in accordance with the differential distribution of power between the white majority and the black minority. Such consolidations of power are reinforced with irrational myths about black inferiority and white supremacy, and supported by discriminatory behavior patterns and prejudicial attitudes. As a result the Negro community experiences unfair treatment at the hands of the white majority and grievances accumulate. When claims of grievance are made, they are denied, minimized, and rationalized away. When legal attacks are made on discriminatory patterns, the formal law is changed in a grudging, rearguard action and represented as progress. Meanwhile informal procedures are devised to subvert the formal changes in the law. Grievances continue to accumulate and soon the grievance bank of the Negro community is full: almost every aspect of social life that has a significant effect on the life chances of Negroes seems blocked. The progress of the law has been too little and too late. At this juncture of history, after a series of

prior incidents of similar character, the final incident takes place and violence erupts.

Any attempt to understand the nature of a riot based on final incidents is, more frequently than not, to deal with symptoms rather than causes. Indeed, final incidents are routine and even trivial. They are distinguished in retrospect because they happen to have been the occasion for the eruption of violence; otherwise they resemble ordinary events.[30]

Beyond this, it is questionable whether there exists any necessary correlation between appropriate or moderate behavior and the use of established means. A strong preference for "normal channels" is discernible in many of the critiques of disorderly protest, black or otherwise. However, in human history, witches have been burned, slaves bought and sold, and minorities exterminated through "normal" channels. The "rioters" in Prague, for example, may not be "senseless" in believing that the Soviet Union is attempting to crush Czechoslovakian aspirations for democracy; nor are they necessarily "irrational" in perceiving unresponsiveness in "normal channels." The propriety—and to a large degree the rationality—of disorderly behavior is ultimately determined by historical outcomes, in the light of existing alternatives. Further, an assessment of the existing alternatives to disorderly protest must concern itself with the actual as well as the ideal, with substance as well as form. To suggest, for example, that disorderly protest has no justification in a society organized on democratic principles may obscure the fact that the society historically has offered less equality of political participation than its stated form would suggest. Which, of course, is not to suggest disorderly protest is always justified. Our point is that such labels as "normal channels" or "protest" do not automatically attach themselves to "goodness" or "badness" and that particular demands and grievances should be considered on their merits.

3. Finally, it is insufficient to analyze riots in terms of "tension" and "frustration." It is not that this perspective is wrong, but that it tells at once too little and too much. Too little, because the idea of "tension" or "strain" does not encompass the subjective meaning or objective impact of subordinate caste position or political domination. Too much, because it may mean almost anything; it is a catchall phrase

that can easily obscure the specificity of political grievances. It is too broad to explain the specific injustices against which civil disorders may be directed; nor does it help to illuminate the historical patterns of domination and subordination to which the riot is one of many possible responses.

The difficulty with most traditional collective behavior theory is that it treats protest and riots as the "abnormal" behavior of social groups and derives many of its conceptual assumptions from psychological rather than from political premises. It may well be asked what remains of the idea of collective behavior if a political perspective is adopted. Does such a perspective imply that there is no such phenomenon, or that there is not a "carnival" element or "contagion" element in riots that have political roots? Such an implication is not intended. We recognize that there may well be an element of "fun" in being caught up in a collective episode, whether race riot or panty raid. (Some years ago, it was customary for Yale students to overturn trolley cars after football victories.) We also recognize that individual participants in disorders may have their share of disturbance or ignorance. What we object to is the *substitution* of a psychological analysis for a political one and, especially, the one-sided application of psychological premises to collective protest. We see no analytical justification for an arbitrary classification of *some* forms of political action as based, wholly or in part, on the cognitive or emotional inadequacies of the participants. We do not object to collective behavior theories that attempt to generalize about interaction and development in a nonjudgmental fashion. By contrast, we are most critical of those theories that are inherently ideological and that inadvertently use ostensibly "neutral" concepts and "scientific" language to discredit political action. From the point of view of a political analysis, the question has to be asked, "Why did Yale students move from overturning trolley cars to engaging in peace marches?" Collective behavior theory, as presently developed, does not offer adequate answers to that question, or to similar ones.

We have discussed collective behavior theories of riot to indicate how widespread and dominant certain assumptions concerning riots are. These assumptions sometimes spill over into analyses of less violent forms of collective protest, although this tendency to generalize has not been widespread. But it has been true that the view of riots as pathological has been adopted by officials who have analyzed riots. The next section deals specifically with these official views, and contrasts them with historical and contemporary evidence supporting the view that riots represent a form of instrumental political action.

Official Conceptions of Riot

In Chapter IV, we discussed evidence indicating that the ghetto riots of the 1960's were participated in by a cross section of the ghetto communities, and given wide sympathy or support by those communities. Given these facts, few serious official treatments of riots now attempt to explain the resulting violence purely in terms of a criminal or "riffraff" element. Nevertheless, some official commissions, while generally appreciating that riots attract some popular support and participation, argue that riots are invariably aggravated or instigated by the criminal activities of a small group of provocateurs who take advantage of human weakness and transform basically nonviolent individuals into an irrational mob.

Thus, riots are widely characterized as outlets for pent-up frustrations and grievances sparked by a few. In Chicago, according to the 1919 report, even "normal-minded Negroes" exhibited a "pathological attitude to society which sometimes expresses itself defensively in acts of violence and other lawlessness." [31] The Harlem riot also drew upon the participation of "normal" citizens:

> [Neither] the threats nor the reassurances of the police could restrain these spontaneous outbursts until the crowds had spent themselves in giving release to their pent up emotions. . . . Negro crimes result from the fact that normal individual impulses and desires are often forced to express themselves in a lawless manner in a disorganized social environment.[32]

The Watts riot was characterized as an "insensate rage of destruction," a "spasm," and a "formless, quite senseless, all but hopeless violent protest." [33] Similarly, the riots of 1968 were viewed as the product of a "sense of rage" and "years of frustration born and bred in poverty." [34]

Implicit in this concept of frustration-aggression is the idea that riots are without purpose or direction. Though it is granted that "rioters" have some objective justification for their unhappiness and anger, it is also argued that they tend to exaggerate the importance of underlying grievances. According to the recent Chicago Commission, for example, "There is a conviction on the part of a clear majority of our black citizens that [political] representation is entirely unsatisfactory and must be improved. This conviction, *whether or not or to what extent it is true* [our emphasis], is of critical importance to the continued health of our city." [35]

The essential problem with this perspective is that it neglects the intrinsically political and rational aspects of collective protest and fails to take seriously the grievances that motivate riots. Looting, for example, which distinguishes the riots of the 1960's, is a form of group protest and not merely individualistic or expressive action. Looting is widespread, collective, public, and undertaken by a cross section of local residents whose behavior is perceived by most of the community as a legitimate form of protest. The instrumental nature of looting is evident in its selective character: stores and supermarkets with a reputation for discrimination and exploitation are usually singled out by looters.[36] It is not accurate, therefore, to conceive of looting as merely random or senseless violence.

Finally, the emphasis on the irrational and "hypnotic" [37] aspects of rioting tends to obscure the interactional nature of riots. It is misleading to ignore the part played by social control agencies in aggravating and sometimes creating a riot. It is not unusual, as the Kerner Commission observed, for a riot to begin *and* end with police violence.

Abnormality

Almost every official riot commission has pointed out that riots are abnormal and useless:

The problem will not be solved by methods of violence.[38]

The avenue of violence and lawlessness leads to a dead end.[39]

[There] can be no justification in our democratic society for a resort to violence as a means of seeking social justice.[40]

[Unless] order is fully preserved, . . . no meaningful, orderly, and rational physical, economic or social progress can occur.[41]

Violence cannot build a better society.[42]

This "violence doesn't pay" argument is misleading on two counts. First, it refers only to the domestic violence of disaffected groups, while ignoring the fact that systematic official violence for social ends is widely upheld in other spheres. Thus, the commissions of 1919, 1943, and 1968 do not even mention the possibility of a connection between war and domestic violence. It is a matter of moral judgment to attribute "normality" to one kind of violence—such as overseas war—but not to another. And it may be a glaring example of motivated obtuseness to ignore the possible connection between the public celebration of heroic military violence "over there" and the sporadic appearance of rebellious violence "back home." The breakdown of peaceful restraint during periods of war is among the most firmly established findings of social science.

Second, whether or not violence is "useless" is a problem for historical analysis, not a certainty. In any event, rioting has not been a particularly novel or unusual technique for expressing grievances. Instances of such rioting by both the respectable and disreputable poor in eighteenth- and nineteenth-century Europe have been well documented by historians.[43] As Hobsbawm has noted, the preindustrial city mob "did not merely riot as a protest, but because it expected to achieve something by its riot. It assumed that the authorities would be sensitive to its movements, and probably also that they would make some sort of immediate concession." Like the modern riot, the classical mob was composed of a cross section of "the ordinary urban poor, and not simply of the scum." [44] Moreover, one need not be fond of revolutions to observe that riots are sometimes the preface to an even more organized overthrow of existing arrangements with the substitution of new regimes. And one need not admire the consequence of the Russian Revolution to appreciate those of

America or France. All three began with rioting. There is no intention here of making dire predictions. Our only point is that the viewpoint that holds that rioting is "useless" lacks a certain foundation in reality. At the same time, rioting is a "primitive" form of political action, which may lead to consequences undesired by the rioters.

Collective violence by powerless groups acts as a "signaling device" to those in power that concessions must be made or violence will prevail.[45] Hobsbawm gives the example of the Luddites, whose "collective bargaining by rioting was at least as effective as any other means of bringing trade union pressure, and probably *more* effective than any other means available before the era of national trade unions."[46] Similarly, Rimilinger notes that those involved in the development of European trade unionism were "convinced of the righteousness not only of their demands but also of the novel means proposed to enforce them."[47]

The available evidence, then, suggests that contemporary urban riots are participated in by a predominantly youthful cross section of the lower-class black community, that they are supported (usually passively) by other segments of that community, that they are often instrumental and purposive, and that they are not a historically unique form of social protest.

Social Control of Riots

Official and academic conceptions of riots have strongly influenced the assumptions underlying governmental response to civil disorders in the past. We have argued that these conceptions seriously misconstrue the meaning of riots on several counts. It follows that riot-control efforts based on these conceptions may be inadequate and often self-defeating.

No recent treatment advocates a purely repressive approach to riot control. On the contrary, official conceptions of riots have usually been translated into recommendations combining a program for the reduction of social tensions with a call for the development of strategy and technology to contain disruption. On its face, this dual approach seems both reasonable and feasible. It suggests sympathetic response to legitimate grievances, and at the same time it offers the prospect of sophisticated, measured, and controlled force to protect civic order. After considerable analysis, however, we have come to question whether this two-pronged approach is ultimately workable.

Prospects of Support

First, implicit in the two-pronged theory is the assumption that, in practice, reform measures have about the same prospect of gaining executive and legislative support as control and firepower measures. Historical experience, however, suggests no such parity. On the contrary, commissions from the Chicago Commission of 1919 to the Kerner Commission have adopted the dual approach and have lived to observe control recommendations being implemented without concomitant implementation of social reform measures. Although it has generally been recognized that riots are motivated in part by legitimate grievances, the ensuing political response clearly reveals that order has been given priority over justice. After the Harlem riot in 1935, it was reported that "extra police stand guard on the corners and mounted patrolmen ride through the streets. . . . To the citizens of Harlem they symbolize the answer of the city authorities to their protest. . . . It offers no assurance that the legitimate demands of the community for work and decent living conditions will be heeded." Yet the Harlem Commission warned that riots would recur so long as basic grievances were not answered.[48] Over thirty years later, the Kerner Commission reported a similar finding that "in several cities, the principal official response has been to train and equip the police with more sophisticated weapons." [49] Following the Kerner Commission, there has been considerable development of riot-control weapons and programs in urban areas,[50] without similar efforts, recommended by the Commission, to meet underlying and legitimate grievances. From the evidence, it appears that it has been found more expedient to implement recommendations for control than recommendations for altering the social structure. There is little evidence that a call for social reform, on the one hand, and for the development of sophisticated riot-control techniques and weaponry, on the other, will not suffer the same fate today.

We may suggest as a general rule that a society which must contemplate massive expenditures for social control is one which, virtually by definition, has not grappled with the necessity of massive social reform. There are various possible levels of social reform, ranging from merely token and symbolic amelioration of fundamental problems to significant changes in the allocation of resources—including political power. We feel that contemporary efforts at reform in this country remain largely at the first level. Precisely because society leaves untouched the basic problems, the cycle of hostility spirals: there is protest, violence, and increased commitment to social control: as we spiral in this direction, the "need" for massive social control outstrips the capacity of democratic institutions to maintain both social order and democratic values. Little by little, we move toward an armed society which, while not clearly totalitarian, could no longer be called consensual.

We need to reverse the spiral. A genuine commitment to fundamental reform will have positive effects, both reducing the need for massive social control and altering the quality and character of social control. We do not, of course, suggest that every demand of every protester or protest group be met. We do suggest, however, that a distinction be drawn between *demands* and *underlying grievances* and that grievances be considered on their merits. Too often attention is paid to disruption, but not to the reasons for it.

Law enforcement should be taken seriously. By this we mean to suggest that policing should take place within the framework of due process of law, using the minimum force required to effect the establishment of order. When actual crimes are committed, suspects should be arrested, charged, and tried in a court of law, not beaten in the streets. As suggested in Chapter VII, we should support reform of control agencies, not simply the addition of weaponry. The reduction and reformation of control should also occasion positive benefits by reducing polarization and hostility; that, in turn, should decrease disaffection, thus decreasing the need for force, and so forth. Only if the roots of disorder are attacked can the spiral be reversed and the problem of social order rendered manageable within a democratic framework.

The ramifications of reducing force and reforming the social structure, including the established policing services, are evident if we examine the connection between anti-war, student, and black protest. For example, a reduction of military spending and involvement overseas would reduce the level of anti-war and student protest, freeing resources that could then be used to combat the problems of the black communities. A greater understanding of black problems by control agents—a sympathetic understanding—would, in turn, also reduce the need for massive force.

Strategies of Control

The escalation of violence is related to strategies of social control. Our evidence suggests that a diversion of resources into domestic force and away from redress of social grievances is not only costly but self-defeating, since the heightening of force is likely to be a factor in creating still more violence. The ultimate result of force will probably *not*, in the long run, be to "channel the energy of collective outbursts into more modest kinds of behavior"; [51] the eventual effects may be directly contrary.

Because the police are received with hostility in the black communities of America (for reasons discussed in Chapters IV and VII), the introduction of more and better-armed police will, we believe, only aggravate the situation. The contemporary ideology and behavior of police across America make it difficult to think otherwise. Furthermore, the introduction of sophisticated weaponry will likely be seen by protesting groups as evidence of governmental duplicity. The development of "nonlethal" weapons, for example, will not be perceived by the young man in the ghetto as a humane response to his condition; to him they will still be weapons—aimed at him—and will be viewed with hostility. Finally, as we have developed at length, the police, the military, and other agents of social control may themselves be implicated in triggering riots and in building up long-term grievances.

The Political Significance of Riots

The conventional approach underestimates the political significance of riots. Even given the possibility of efficient

short-term control of riots, and ignoring its immediate destructive effects, the political nature of riots suggests that
forceful riot-control techniques may channel expressive protest
into more organized forms of political violence, thus requiring greater military and paramilitary force with its inescapable monetary and social costs. Thus it is not surprising that
one expert finds that riots may be "giving way to more specific, more premeditated and more regularized uses of
force." [52] What is surprising, however, is his conclusion that
"only surveillance and covert penetration supplies an effective
technique of management." [53]

We have learned from the Vietnam War that power and
covert surveillance may well have the unanticipated effect of
increasing resistance. Indeed, the literature of guerrilla warfare stresses that revolutionaries are made through violence.
So, too, the young man who encounters the hostile actions of
a policeman is likely to increase his hostility toward the society and to be attracted to groups that express such hostility.[54]
Moreover, in measuring the consequences of escalating
domestic force, we must add the political and social dangers
of depending on espionage as an instrument of social control,
including its potential for eroding constitutional guarantees of
political freedom.

For these reasons, we question the conventional two-
pronged approach to contemporary American protest. An approach that gives equal emphasis to force and reform fails to
measure the anticipated consequences of employing force;
and it fails to appreciate the political significance of protest.
If American society concentrates on the development of more
sophisticated control techniques, it will move itself into a destructive and self-defeating position. A democratic society
cannot depend upon force as its recurrent answer to long-
standing and legitimate grievances. This nation cannot have it
both ways: either it will carry through a firm commitment to
massive and widespread political and social reform, or it will
develop into a society of garrison cities where order is enforced without due process of law and without the consent of
the governed.

Appendix

Witnesses Appearing at Hearings Conducted by the Task Force on "Violent Aspects of Protest and Confrontation" on October 23, 24, 25, 1968

First Day

I. **Anti-war and Student Movements**

    A. HENRY MAYER, Student Co-Chairman of Faculty-Student Committee after 1966 strike at University of California, Berkeley.

    B. TOM HAYDEN, author of *Rebellion in Newark* and former officer of Students for a Democratic Society.

    C. KINGMAN BREWSTER, President, Yale University.

    D. SAM BROWN, organizer, Eugene McCarthy campaign.

    E. IRVING LOUIS HOROWITZ, Professor of Sociology, Washington University, St. Louis; Editor of *Trans-action*.

Second Day

II. **Responses of the Social Order**

    A. Police

        1. GORDON MISNER, Visiting Associate Professor of Criminology, University of California, Berkeley.

2. JOHN HARRINGTON, President, Fraternal Order of Police.

3. DAVID CRAIG, Public Safety Commissioner of Pittsburgh.

B. Majority Group and Judicial Responses

1. DAVID GINSBURG, Executive Director, National Advisory Commission on Civil Disorders.

Third Day

III. Black Militancy

A. LOUIS MASOTTI, Director, Civil Violence Research Center, Case Western Reserve University.

B. HERMAN BLAKE, Assistant Professor of Sociology, University of California, Santa Cruz.

C. STERLING TUCKER, Director of Field Services, National Urban League.

D. PRICE COBBS, M.D., San Francisco psychiatrist, co-author of *Black Rage*.

NOTES

Chapter I

1. Amitai Etzioni, *Demonstration Democracy* (Washington, D.C.: Center for Policy Research, 1968), p. 10.
2. See, in general, reports of Chicago, Cleveland, and Miami Study Teams. Also, Etzioni, pp. 36–41.
3. National Advisory Commission on Civil Disorders, *Report* (Washington, D.C.: U.S. Government Printing Office, 1968), p. 2. Hereafter cited as *Kerner Report*.
4. Etzioni, p. 10.
5. George F. Kennan, *Democracy and the Student Left* (New York: Bantam Books, 1968), pp. 8–9.
6. Robert F. Kennedy, quoted in Irving L. Horowitz, "Kennedy's Death—Myths and Realities," *Trans-action*, V, No. 8, July/August, 1968, p. 3.
7. Gallup Poll, September, 1968.
8. Unless otherwise noted, the material in this section is drawn from an unpublished paper by Richard Rubenstein, "Mass Political Violence in the United States," prepared for this commission, 1968.
9. Clifford Geertz, "Is America by Nature a Violent Society?" *New York Times Magazine*, April 28, 1968, p. 25.
10. Some of the better known works of this "consensus school" are: Daniel Boorstin, *The Genius of American Politics* (Chicago: University of Chicago Press, 1953); Louis Hartz, *The Liberal Tradition in America* (New York: Harcourt, Brace, 1955); Daniel Bell, *The End of Ideology* (New York: Free Press, 1960); Seymour Martin Lipset, *Political Man: The Social Basis of Politics* (Garden City, New York: Doubleday, 1960). In a brief summary it is impossible to do descriptive justice to the complexity and diversity of these

thinkers. It is worth noting, in particular, that not all consensus scholars jumped from the perception of consensus to its celebration; this is particularly true of the work of Louis Hartz.

11. This seems to have been an underlying assumption of the *Kerner Report*. Chapter 6 of the Report is limited to a discussion of Negro history. Chapter 9, comparing Negroes with European immigrants, suggests one similarity between the two group experiences—the length of time needed to escape from urban poverty (three generations). It does not recognize, however, that domestic groups other than Negroes resorted to mass violence as a method of group advancement.

12. Hartz, p. 58.

13. The focus on insurgent groups in the succeeding paragraphs may seem to imply that political violence originated with these groups, or that they were the aggressors. On the contrary, these revolts were generally conceived as defensive responses to outside aggression, a conception with some basis in fact. See note 16.

14. Quoted in Martin Gruberg, *Women in American Politics* (Oshkosh, Wisconsin: Academia Press, 1968), p. 4.

15. Gruberg, p. 6.

16. There is no definitive work on political violence in the United States, and very little comparative work has been done in this field. See Orville J. Victor, *History of American Conspiracies,* 1863; Lamar Middleton, *Revolt U.S.A.* (New York: Stackpole Sons, 1938); Bennett Milton Rich, *The Presidents and Civil Disorder* (Washington, D.C.: The Brookings Institution, 1941); Daniel Aaron, ed., *America in Crisis* (New York: Knopf, 1952); Richard Hofstadter, *The Paranoid Style in American Politics* (New York: Knopf, 1966). The following works of broader scope will also repay study: on Indians, Oscar Handlin, *Race and Nationality in American Life* (Boston: Little, Brown, 1957), and Roy Pearce, *The Savages of America* (Baltimore: Johns Hopkins Press, 1965); on Southern nationalism, Jesse T. Carpenter, *The South as a Conscious Minority* (reissued New York: New University Press, 1963), and William R. Taylor, *Cavalier and Yankee* (New York: G. B. Braziller, 1961); on Reconstruction violence, Stanley F. Horn, *Invisible Empire* (Boston: Houghton Mifflin, 1939), and Kenneth Stampp, *The Era of Reconstruction* (New York: Knopf, 1965); on slave revolts, Herbert Aptheker, *American Negro Slave Revolts* (New York: International Publishers, 1939), and William Styron, *The Confessions of Nat Turner* (New York: Random House, 1967); on nativism, John Higham, *Strangers in the Land* (New Brunswick, N.J.: Rutgers University Press, 1955); on vigilantism, David W. Chalmers,

Hooded Americanism (Chicago: Quadrangle, 1968); on labor-management warfare, Louis Adamic, *Dynamite* (reissued Gloucester, Mass.: P. Smith, 1963), Robert F. Hoxie, *Trade Unionism in the United States* (reissued New York: Russell and Russell, 1966), Graham Adams, Jr., *Age of Industrial Violence* (New York: Columbia University Press, 1966); on black-white violence, Arthur I. Waskow, *From Race Riot to Sit-In* (Garden City, New York: Doubleday, 1966).

17. Daniel Bell, "Crime as a Way of Life," in Bell, Chap. 10.
18. Quoted in Middleton, *Revolt*, p. 141.
19. From an unpublished paper by Irving L. Horowitz, "The Struggle Is the Message: An Analysis of Tactics, Trends, and Tensions in the Anti-War Movement," prepared for this commission, 1968.
20. *New York Times*, September 12, 1967, p. 1; September 30, 1968, p. 1.
21. *New York Times*, January 5, 1967, p. 5.
22. *New York Times*, October 23, 1968, p. 46.
23. John V. Lindsay, "Law and Order," *Life*, September 2, 1968, pp. 32–33.
24. Colin Miller, "Press and the Student Revolt," in *Revolution at Berkeley*, eds. Michael V. Miller and Susan Gilmore (New York: Dial Press, 1967), p. 347.
25. *Harris Poll*, June 10, 1968.
26. *Harris Poll*, March 27, 1967.

Chapter II

1. See Willard A. Heaps, *Riots U.S.A.—1765–1965* (New York: Seabury Press, 1966); and Lawrence Lader, "New York's Bloodiest Week," *American Heritage*, June, 1959, pp. 44–49, 95–98.
2. See Twain's polemical writings, "To the Person Sitting in Darkness," and "On the Killing of 400 Moros." For a scholarly development of such policies and attitudes see Walter La Feber, *The New Empire: An Interpretation of American Expansion 1860–1898* (Ithaca, New York: Cornell University Press, 1963).
3. Cited in Raymond Leslie Buell, *Cuba and the Platt Amendment*, Foreign Policy Association, New York, April, 1929, p. 52.
4. On May 2, 1965, President Johnson first alluded to an international conspiracy in the Dominican crisis, by announcing, "We will defend our nation against all those who seek to destroy not only the United States but every free country in the hemisphere" (*New York Times*, May 3, 1965, p. 10). On May 5, the United States government released its fa-

mous list (later revised downwards) of 54 "Communist and Castroist" leaders in the Bosch forces. Referring to these elements, Under-Secretary of State Thomas Mann claimed that "left-wing totalitarians that are members of the Communist apparatus are not really indigenous forces. These are, rather, instruments of Sino-Soviet military power." (*New York Times,* May 9, 1965, IV, p. 3.)

5. *New York Times,* March 9, 1968, p. 2.

6. *London Daily Mirror,* July 4, 1965.

7. President Johnson, speaking in New York, August 12, 1964, as quoted in Theodore Draper, *Abuse of Power* (New York: Viking Press, 1967), p. 66. See also the President's speeches of August 29 and September 28, 1964 (*loc. cit.,* p. 67).

8. *U.S. Department of State Bulletin,* August 31, 1964, p. 299.

9. All pertinent articles and the final declaration of the conference are reprinted in *Vietnam: History, Documents and Opinions on a Major World Crisis,* ed. Marvin E. Gettleman (Greenwich, Conn.: Fawcett, 1965). The entire text can be found in George McTurnan Kahin and John W. Lewis, *The United States in Vietnam* (New York: Dial Press, 1967).

10. Discussions to work out arrangements for elections throughout Vietnam in 1956 were scheduled by the Geneva Agreements to begin after July 20, 1955, between "the competent representative authorities of the two Zones."

"As legal successor to the French, Diem was either bound by the terms of this armistice, politically as well as militarily, or obliged to turn authority in the South back to French until the elections were held. . . . The Eisenhower Administration was advised of this logical conclusion at the SEATO meeting in February 1955. There the United States was cautioned by its allies that SEATO would not function if a South Vietnamese refusal to hold the required elections resulted in an attack from the North. . . . Nevertheless, backed by Washington, Diem declared on September 21 that '. . . there can be no question of a conference, even less of negotiations' with the Hanoi Government [*Times* (London), September 22, 1965]. Diem adamantly held to his position. The election date of July 1956 passed with Diem still refusing even to discuss the possibility of sitting down with Vietminh representatives to discuss the modalities of such elections. In this stand he continued to receive warm American encouragement and the fullest American diplomatic backing." (Kahin and Lewis, *op. cit.,* p. 82; cf. Philippe Devillers, "Ngo Dinh Diem and the Struggle for Reunification in Vietnam," in Gettleman, *op. cit.,* pp. 210–21.)

For a fuller study of this period, consult F. Weinstein, *Vietnam's Unheld Elections* (Cornell University South East Asia Program Data Paper No. 60, 1966).

American responsibility for Diem's intransigence has sometimes been denied, by pointing to Secretary of State Dulles' statement on June 28, 1955, that "We are not afraid at all of elections, provided they are held under conditions of general freedom which the Geneva armistice agreement calls for. If these conditions can be provided we would be in favor of elections." *American Foreign Policy: Current Documents 1950–1955,* II, 2404.)

As, however, the Dulles notion of general freedom was unlikely to prevail in North Vietnam, it was quite consistent for him to agree with Diem, in their meeting of March 14, 1956, "that present conditions would not permit free elections as provided in the 1954 Geneva armistice agreement for Vietnam" (*New York Times,* March 15, 1956, p. 12). On June 1, 1956, Assistant Secretary of State for Far Eastern Affairs Walter S. Robertson publicly ridiculed the notion of "so-called 'free elections,'" using the argument of the State Department's Blue Book in 1961. (See note 11.)

Meanwhile North Vietnam, the Soviet Union, and mainland China repeatedly and vigorously protested Diem's failure to hold consultations or a general election (cf. e.g. *New York Times,* May 13, 1956, p. 38; July 18, 1956, p. 5). The efforts in 1965 of William Bundy and other government spokesmen to blame North Vietnam for the failure to hold elections contributed not a little to the growing alienation of college students and their awareness of a "credibility gap."

11. "It was the Communists' calculation that nationwide elections scheduled in the Accords for 1956 would turn all of Viet-Nam over to them. . . . The authorities in South Viet-Nam refused to fall into this well-laid trap. . . . The Government in the South had never signed the Geneva Accords and was not bound by their provisions. It refused to take part in a procedure that threatened its country with absorption into the Communist bloc." ("A Threat to the Peace: North Viet-Nam's Effort to Conquer South Viet-Nam," U.S. Department of State Publication 7308, Far Eastern Series 110, December, 1961, pp. 3–4.)

12. The government's claim that the guerrillas were directed from Hanoi was based on the claim that, according to *U.S. News and World Report* (October 7, 1963, p. 56), "Between 5 and 10 per cent of the so-called 'hard core' guerrillas were *trained* in Communist North Vietnam. . . . Most of these are southern-born Vietnamese who were taken to the North by their pro-Communist families" (in accordance with the military provisions of the 1954 Agreements). The hard-core guerrillas were estimated to comprise between 20 and 25 percent of the total number. The claim of Hanoi's leadership amounted therefore to the contention that between 1 and 2.5 percent of their numbers had received training in North Vietnam, the majority of whom had been

regrouped there from their native South Vietnam in 1954 as part of the Geneva Accords.

13. *New York Times,* October 23, 1966; cf. February 10, 1966.

14. *Vietnam: Lotus in a Sea of Fire* (New York: Hill and Wang, 1967), p. 68.

15. President Johnson himself voiced this theory in his famous "unconditional discussions" speech of April 7, 1965:

"Over this war—and all Asia—is another reality: the deepening shadow of Communist China. The rulers in Hanoi are urged on by Peiping. This is a regime which has destroyed freedom in Tibet, which has attacked India, and has been condemned by the United Nations for aggression in Korea. It is a nation which is helping the forces of violence in almost every continent. The contest in Vietnam is part of a wider pattern of aggressive purposes." ("Pattern for Peace in Southeast Asia," U.S. Dept. of State Publication 1872, April, 1965, p. 3.)

Yet when the President uttered these words it was already clear that Chinese military support for the war was strictly limited; and the State Department had already received numerous reports that in contradistinction to the more intransigent Chinese position, the North Vietnamese were prepared to envisage a reconvening of the 1954 Geneva Conference. The theme of Chinese instigation recurs in many of President Johnson's speeches, e.g. July 28, 1965.

16. Appendix D to the White Paper listed the captured enemy-manufactured weapons in an 18-month period as 72 rifles, 64 submachine guns, 15 carbines, 8 machine guns, 5 pistols, 4 mortars, 3 recoilless 75-mm rifles, 3 recoilless 57-mm guns, 2 bazookas, 2 rocket launchers, and 1 grenade launcher. According to Pentagon figures obtained by I. F. Stone from the Pentagon press office, in the three years 1962–64 the guerrillas had captured 27,400 weapons, while giving up 15,100 weapons, or an average of 7,550 for each 18 months. This roughly constituted only 2.5 percent of the weapons captured in the same period (during which 23,500 American troops were introduced into Vietnam). Much of the remaining 97.5 percent, presumably, was of American origin (*I. F. Stone's Weekly,* March 8, 1965). The estimate that only 2.5 percent of captured Viet Cong weapons were Communist-manufactured is confirmed by an earlier U.S. estimate of 2 percent (*Baltimore Sun,* October 14, 1963) and by the statement of an unnamed senior U.S. military adviser in Saigon that 90 percent of Viet Cong weapons came from the United States (*New York Times,* June 18, 1964, p. 5).

17. The U.S. government's arguments for the legality of its intervention are summarized in "The Legality of United States Participation in the Defense of Viet-Nam," Memorandum from the Department of State, Office of the Legal Adviser, March 4, 1966 (reprinted in *Congressional Record,* March 10, 1966, pp. 5503–9). This memorandum is contained as

Appendix I in the answering document prepared by the Lawyers Committee on American Policy Towards Vietnam, *Vietnam and International Law: The Illegality of United States Military Involvement* (New York: O'Hare Books, 1967), pp. 113–30. The extensive legal debate is usefully summarized, with relevant citations, by John H. Messing, "American Actions in Vietnam: Justifiable in International Law?" *Stanford Law Review,* XIX (1966–67), pp. 1307–36. Among the more recent law review articles which bear on the same subject are J. K. Andonian, "Law and Vietnam," *American Bar Association Journal,* LIV (May, 1968), pp. 457–59; "Political Settlement for Vietnam: the 1954 Geneva Conference and its Current Implications," *Virginia Journal of International Law,* VIII (December, 1968), p. 4; E. P. Deutsch, "Legality of the War in Vietnam," *Washburn Law Journal,* VII (Winter, 1968), pp. 153–86; L. R. Velvel, "War in Vietnam: Unconstitutional, Justiciable, and Jurisdictionally Attackable," *Kansas Law Review,* XVI (June, 1968), pp. 449–503e.

18. *Why Vietnam,* U.S. Government Publication, August 20, 1965, p. 5.

19. See President Eisenhower's letter to Diem of October 23, 1954, emphasizing the dependency of any economic aid on forthcoming "assurances" and "performance" in the area of "needed reforms." No mention is made of military assistance in *Department of State Bulletin,* XXXI, November 15, 1954, p. 735f.

20. It is truè, however, that the SEATO treaty, drawn up at Secretary Dulles' urging in the wake of Dienbienphu and the American sponsorship of Diem, does envision the defense of South Vietnam against aggression. The American government attached a special statement clarifying its understanding that "aggression" was to apply "only to Communist aggression." See *Background Information Relating to Southeast Asia and Vietnam* (Report of the U.S. Senate Committee on Foreign Relations, 89th Congress, 1st Session, Revised, June 16, 1965).

21. Nicholas Katzenbach, *Senate Congressional Record,* September 11, 1967, S12758.

22. Quoted in *New York Times,* August 6, 1964, p. 8.

23. Senator Gaylord Nelson, *Congressional Record,* September 18, 1967, S25834–35.

24. *Washington Post,* February 25, 1968, p. 1.

25. See, for example, *I. F. Stone's Weekly,* December 5, 1966; I. F. Stone in *New York Review of Books,* March 28, 1968; and the lead item and editorial in the *Washington Post,* February 25, 1968.

26. See *New York Times,* June 3, 1964, pp. 1 and 3; November 2, 1967; and the editorial of May 20, 1966, p. 46. See also

Charles Roberts, *LBJ's Inner Circle* (New York: De La Conte, 1965), pp. 20–22.

27. Two sets of government figures for 1962, for example, convey the impression that 15,000 enemy guerrillas sustained 30,000 casualties. See Arthur M. Schlesinger, Jr., *A Thousand Days: John F. Kennedy in the White House* (New York: Houghton Mifflin, 1965), p. 982.

28. James Reston, "Washington: Ships Passing in the Night," *New York Times,* February 9, 1966, p. 38.

29. President Johnson first attacked "nervous nellies" in his speech of May 17, 1966 (*New York Times,* May 18, 1966, p. 8).

30. Robert S. Elegant, "New War Policy—Truth," *San Francisco Chronicle,* February 14, 1969, p. 15.

31. *New York Times,* April 2, 1968, p. 1. The stock market resurgence of April 1, 1968 involved sales of 17.7 million shares, surpassing the former volume record of 16.4 million shares which had been set on "Black Tuesday," October 26, 1929.

32. *New York Times,* April 2, 1968, p. 63.

33. *New York Times,* February 9, 1968, p. 12.

34. The revised estimate of ARVN desertions in 1965 was, according to official ARVN figures, 113,000. For the first six months of 1966 it was 67,000. Viet Cong defections were put at 11,000 in 1965, 20,242 in 1966 (*New York Times,* February 24, 1966, p. 1; January 4, 1967, p. 3).

35. *New York Times,* February 9, 1968, p. 12.

36. 50 U.S.C. App. S. 456(j). The concept "Supreme Being" has been broadly interpreted by the Supreme Court, thus liberalizing the restrictions on "religious training and belief." See *U.S. v. Seeger,* 380 U.S. 163.

37. The implementation of this recommendation was struck down by the U.S. Court of Appeals, Second Circuit, in *Wolff v. Selective Service System Local Board No. 16,* 372 F. 2d 817, wherein it was decided that the local boards exceeded their jurisdiction in so complying: "no regulation authorizes a draft board to declare a registrant delinquent or to reclassify him for such action," 372 F. 2d at 821.

In *Oestereich v. Selective Service System Local Board No. 11,* the Supreme Court held that the Selective Service System uses regulations governing delinquency, "to deprive registrants of their statutory exemption, because of various activities and conduct and without any regard to the exemptions provided by law," and described the board's activity as "basically lawless," 37 Law Week 4054.

38. *New York Times,* January 15, 1968, p. 5.

39. Martha Gellhorn, "Suffer the Little Children . . . ," in *Ladies Home Journal,* January, 1967, p. 108.

40. Richard E. Perry, "Where the Innocent Die," in *Redbook*, CXXVIII, No. 3, January, 1967, p. 103.

41. Quotations from Allied Control Law No. 10, promulgated in 1945 for the trial of war criminals.

42. International Military Tribunal, Charter, Art. VIII; in *Trial of the Major War Criminals* (Nuremberg, 1947), I, 12; quoted also in Whiteman, *Digest of International Law,* XI, p. 883. For discussions of the legal validity of this principle, see Y. Dinstein, *The Defense of Obedience to Superior Orders in International Law* (Leyden, 1965); I. Brownlie, *International Law and the Use of Force by States* (Oxford, 1963), p. 192; A. von Knieriem, *The Nuremberg Trials* (1959), pp. 247 ff. The bearing of the Nuremberg principle on the court-martial of Captain Howard Levy is discussed in a note by Martin Redish, *Harvard International Law Journal,* IX (1968), pp. 169–81.

43. *New York Times,* September 5, 1965, p. 4E.

44. *New York Times,* August 15, 1965, p. 3.

45. A.P. Report, January 15, 1967.

46. A.P. Report cited by Noam Chomsky, *Ramparts,* September, 1967, p. 18.

47. *Air War—Vietnam* (New York: Bantam Books, 1967). Mr. Harvey, an aviation correspondent, visited Vietnam for fifty-five days while compiling an article for the magazine *Flying.* "Because of his credentials, he was allowed and encouraged to fly every kind of mission being flown. . . . At the outset Harvey intended to do no more than record, as clearly as possible, every aspect of the air war. . . . He decidedly was not looking for damaging material, but . . . he found it" (Robert Crichton, *New York Review of Books,* January 4, 1968, p. 3).

48. *Air War—Vietnam.*

49. David Perlman, "U.S. Starving Wrong People in Vietnam," in *San Francisco Chronicle,* January 23, 1967, p. 8.

50. *Science,* February 9, 1968, p. 613.

51. *Science,* May 10, 1968, p. 600.

52. Editorial in *New York Times,* March 24, 1965, p. 42.

53. The United States is a party to the Hague Convention No. IV of 18 October 1907, Respecting the Law and Customs of War on Land (36 Stat. 2277; Treaty Series 539), and the Annex thereto, embodying the Regulations Respecting the Laws and Customs of War on Land (36 Stat. 2295; Treaty Series 539). According to Article 23, par. (a) of the Annex, "It is especially forbidden . . . to employ poison or poisoned weapons." However, as the old War Department Basic Field Manual (FM 27-10, 1940, Sect. 8) noted succinctly (while prohibiting "the wanton destruction of a district"): "The practice of recent years has been to regard the prohibition

against the use of poison as not applicable to the use of toxic gases."

The variance between international agreements and United States practice with respect to poisons and toxic gases is conveniently summarized by the U.S. Department of the Army Field Manual FM 27-10, *The Law of Land Warfare*, 1956, Sects. 37–38, pp. 18–19:

"37. Poison

"a. *Treaty Provision.*

"It is especially forbidden . . . to employ poison or poisoned weapons. [Hague Convention No. IV, Annex, Par. 23(a)]

"b. *Discussion of Rule.* The foregoing rule does not prohibit measures being taken to dry up springs, to divert rivers and aqueducts from their courses, or to destroy, through chemical or bacterial agents harmless to man, crops intended solely for consumption by the armed forces (if that fact can be determined).

"38. Gases, Chemicals, and Bacteriological Warfare

"The United States is not a party to any treaty, now in force, that prohibits or restricts the use in warfare of toxic or nontoxic gases, of smoke or incendiary materials, or of bacteriological warfare. A treaty signed at Washington, 6 February 1922, on behalf of the United States, the British Empire, France, Italy, and Japan *(3 Malloy, Treaties 3116)* contains a provision (art. V) prohibiting 'The use in war of asphyxiating, poisonous or other gases, and all analogous liquids, materials, or devices,' but that treaty was expressly conditioned to become effective only upon ratification by all the signatory powers, and, not having been ratified by all of the signatories, has never become effective. The Geneva Protocol 'for the prohibition of the use in war of asphyxiating, poisonous, or other gases, and of bacteriological methods of warfare,' signed on 17 June 1925, on behalf of the United States and many other powers *(94 League of Nations Treaty Series 65)*, has been ratified or adhered to by and is now effective between a considerable number of States. However, the United States Senate has refrained from giving its advice and consent to the ratification of the Protocol by the United States, and it is accordingly not binding on this country.

For a fuller discussion of the various international agreements with respect to asphyxiating gases, see G. H. Hackworth, *Digest of International Law* (Washington, 1943), VI, 269–71.

54. Editorial, *New York Times,* October 11, 1966, p. 46.
55. George McT. Kahin, "The NLF Terms for Peace," *New Republic,* October 14, 1967, p. 17.
56. Fred Emery, "Vietnam's Other War Moves Slowly," *London Times,* March 10, 1967, p. 13.
57. *San Francisco Chronicle,* October 9, 1967, p. 12. Representative Ford was attacking the Americanization of the South Vietnamese economy: "This is just the opposite of our declared purpose. This trend should be immediately reversed."

58. *New York Times,* September 1, 1965, p. 36.
59. Speech of April 28, 1966, cited in *New York Times,* April 29, 1966, p. 32.
60. "Beyond Vietnam," speech of April 4, 1967. Reprinted in J. Grant, ed., *Black Protest* (Greenwich, Conn.: Fawcett Premier Books, 1968), p. 419.
61. Secretary Rusk, *Congressional Record,* August 25, 1966, U.S. Congress, Senate Committee on Armed Services, p. 9.
62. *San Francisco Chronicle,* August 9, 1967, p. 1.
63. Gerald Moore, speaking of Gary, Indiana, reported that "Surprisingly many [Wallace supporters] say they would have voted for Robert Kennedy (and did in the May primary)" ("Microcosm of the Politics of Fear," *Life,* September 20, 1968, p. 40).
64. *New York Review of Books,* February 23, 1967, p. 16.
65. See Chapter III of this report.
66. William Sloane Coffin, Yale University Chaplain, was indicted along with Dr. Benjamin Spock for abetting draft resisters. Dr. Robert McAfee Brown, Professor of Religion at Stanford University, participated in a ceremonial mailing of draft cards to General Hershey in January, 1968. In October, 1967, the Rev. Philip Berrigan and others poured duck blood on Selective Service files in Baltimore, and in May, 1968, he and his brother, Rev. Daniel Berrigan, a Jesuit, were arrested for the burning of 600 draft records in Catonsville, Maryland. Martin Luther King, during a December, 1967, visit to those imprisoned after the October Stop-the-Draft Week demonstrations in Oakland, California, replied to a question from a young black draft resister that he encouraged him to stand by his decision of conscience.
67. *New York Times,* December 5, 1965, p. 1.
68. An early and significant example of black anti-war protest was the leaflet circulated in McComb, Mississippi, and printed in the Mississippi Freedom Democratic Party newsletter of McComb on July 28, 1965. The leaflet set forth "five reasons why Negroes should not be in any war fighting for America." It is reprinted in J. Grant, ed., *Black Protest,* pp. 415–16.
69. Martin Luther King, Jr., "Beyond Vietnam," in *Black Protest,* p. 419.
70. James Ridgeway, "Freak-out in Chicago: The National Conference of New Politics," *New Republic,* September 16, 1967, p. 11.
71. For the Hershey incident, see *New York Times,* March 22, 1967, p. 13. For Eartha Kitt at the White House, *New York Times,* January 19, 1968, p. 1. For the forty-three black soldiers at Fort Hood who on the night of August 24, 1968, refused orders to go to Chicago for possible riot-control duty, see *New York Times,* September 8, 1968, p. 47.

72. *New York Times,* March 6, 1964, p. 11.

73. See, for example, *San Francisco Chronicle,* November 13, 1968, p. 10.

74. For a detailed narrative of the permit negotiation for the August events, see Daniel Walker, *Rights in Conflict,* a report prepared for this commission, November 18, 1968, pp. 31–42.

75. See *New York Times,* April 22, 1968, p. 16; Dave Dellinger, "Lessons from Chicago," *Liberation,* October, 1968; and the investigation by civic leaders called *Dissent and Disorder: A Report to the Citizens of Chicago on the April 27 Peace Parade.*

76. An early example was the failure of the Oakland police to interfere with the Hell's Angels who violently attacked the Vietnam Day Committee march of October 16, 1965. Their strange passivity is indicated by the *New York Times* report that "The attackers carried off a big banner and took it back to the Oakland police line to shred it. Then they charged in again" (*New York Times,* October 17, 1965, p. 43). It should be noted that the Berkeley police (the incident occurred at the Berkeley-Oakland city limits) moved in to end the violence and arrested six Hell's Angels. In doing so one Berkeley police officer suffered a fractured leg.

77. The *New York Times* account of the San Francisco incident makes it clear that "A *few* of the demonstrators threw bricks, bottles, and balloons filled with animal blood" (January 12, 1968, p. 9; emphasis added). Some fifty specially trained police, "provoked by the missiles," then indiscriminately attacked the 400-odd demonstrators with clubs, in accordance with a prearranged strategy. "At least 60 persons were arrested."

78. The flag-lowering incident is summarized as follows in Walker, *Rights in Conflict,* p. 24: "Some of those present claim that the actual flag lowering was the work of police undercover agents. The *Chicago Tribune* reported that Robert L. Pierson, who as 'Big Bob' Lavin served in an undercover capacity as Jerry Rubin's bodyguard, was 'in the group which lowered an American flag in Grant Park.' Pierson has said, however, that he had no part in lowering the flag.

79. Walker, November 18, 1968, p. 4.

80. Walker, November 18, 1968, pp. 1–30.

81. For other examples of attempted self-immolation see *New York Times,* November 12, 1965, p. 3; April 11, 1966, p. 4; August 20, 1967, p. 31; October 16, 1967, p. 11; and December 4, 1967, p. 20.

82. For the Catonsville incident of May 17, 1968, see *Facts on File,* 1968, p. 263. For the Milwaukee incident of September 24, 1968, see *New York Times,* September 25, 1968, p.

5. In the first incident 600 draft files were burned; in the second, considerably more.

83. Sée a Selective Service System Memorandum, *Channeling* (Washington, D.C.: National Headquarters, Public Information for Selective Service, July, 1965).

84. See, for example, Nicholas Von Hoffman, "The Class of '43 Is Puzzled," *The Atlantic*, October, 1968.

85. See Archibald Cox, *Crisis at Columbia* (New York: Vintage, 1968).

86. *Boston Globe*, September 8, 1968.

87. See "Chaplain Coffin Explains His Position," *Yale Alumni Magazine*, March, 1967.

88. See, for example, *New York Times*, April 24, 1966, p. 3; November 12, 1966, p. 7; February 23, 1967, p. 24; and May 31, 1967, p. 12.

89. "The University and the Multiversity," *New Republic*, April 1, 1967, p. 17.

90. Douglas F. Dowd, "American Fouls Its Dream," *The Nation*, February 13, 1967, p. 200.

91. "Intellectuals and the War," *Viet-Report*, October, 1966, p. 29.

92. "Lessons from Chicago," *Liberation*, October, 1968, p. 11.

Chapter III

1. Data supplied by Legal Rights Desk, U.S. National Student Association; also, see Richard E. Peterson, *The Scope of Organized Student Protest in 1967–68* (Princeton: Educational Testing Service, 1968).

2. See the discussion in *Newsweek*, February 24, 1969, pp. 22–23.

3. *Fortune*, January, 1969, p. 68.

4. *Crisis at Columbia: Report of the Fact-Finding Commission Appointed to Investigate the Disturbances at Columbia University in April and May 1968* (New York: Vintage Books, 1968), p. 4.

5. Relevant studies of the personality and background of student activists include the following: Richard Flacks, "The Liberated Generation," *J. Social Issues*, XXIII (1967), pp. 52–75; J. Katz, *The Student Activist* (United States Office of Education, 1967); P. Heist, "Intellect and Commitment; The Faces of Discontent" (Berkeley, Center for the Study of Higher Education, 1965); K. Mock, "The Potential Activist and His Perception of the University" (Berkeley, Center for the Study of Higher Education, 1968); D. Westly and R. G. Braungart, "Class and Politics in the Family Backgrounds of Student Political Activists," *American So-*

ciological Review, XXXI (1966), pp. 690–92; C. Weissberg, "Students Against the Rank" (unpublished M.A. essay, Department of Sociology, University of Chicago, 1968); W. A. Watts and David Whittaker, "Free Speech Advocates at Berkeley," *Journal of Applied Behavioral Science,* II (January-March, 1966); S. Lubell, "That Generation Gap," *The Public Interest* (Fall, 1968), pp. 52–61; C. Derber and R. Flacks, "Values of Student Activists and Their Parents" (University of Chicago, 1967), mimeo; R. Flacks, "Student Activists—Result, Not Revolt," *Psychology Today* (October, 1967); N. Haan et al., "The Moral Reasoning of Young Adults" (Berkeley: Institute for Human Development, 1967); Lamar E. Thomas, unpublished dissertation research (Committee on Human Development, University of Chicago, 1968).

6. The following sources provide a theoretical and empirical foundation for our discussion of the "classical" student movement in "transitional societies": S. Eisenstadt, *From Generation to Generation* (New York: Free Press, 1966); P. Altbach, "Students and Politics," in *Student Politics,* ed. S. M. Lipset (New York: Basic Books, 1967), pp. 74–93; J. Ben-David and R. Collins, "A Comparative Study of Academic Freedom and Student Politics," *ibid.,* pp. 148–95; S. M. Lipset, "University Students and Politics in Underdeveloped Countries," *ibid.,* pp. 3–53; D. Matza, "Position and Behavior Patterns of Youth," in *Handbook of Modern Sociology,* ed. R. Faris (Chicago: Rand McNally, 1964), pp. 191–215; E. Shils, "The Intellectuals in the Political Development of New States," *World Politics,* April, 1960, pp. 329–68; A. Yarmolinsky, *Road to Revolution* (New York: Collier, 1962); R. Lifton, "Youth and History: Individual Change in Postwar Japan," *Daedalus,* November, 1962, pp. 172–91; J. P. Worms, "The French Student Movement," in Lipset, *Student Politics,* pp. 267–79; Walter Lacqueur, *Young Germany* (New York: Basic Books, 1962); Frank Pinner, "Tradition and Transgression: Western European Students in the Postwar World," *Daedalus* (Winter, 1968), pp. 137–55. The discussion of current student rebellion in Latin America, France, West Germany, and Czechoslovakia has been greatly aided by conversations with Mario Machado, Martin Verlet, Wolfgang Neitsch, and Tomas Kohut—all active participants in the student movements of their respective countries.

7. Quoted in the *New York Times,* February 16, 1968.

8. S. M. Lipset, "Student Activism," *Current Affairs Bulletin,* XLII, No. 4 (July 15, 1968), p. 58.

9. *Ibid.,* pp. 52–53.

10. The standard history of American higher education is Fred-

erick Rudolph, *The American College and University* (New York: Vintage, 1965).

11. See, for example, Kenneth Keniston, *The Uncommitted: Alienated Youth in American Society* (New York: Harcourt, Brace, 1965).

12. Studies of political activity and student attitudes at Berkeley prior to the Free Speech Movement include: D. Horowitz, *Student* (New York: Ballantine Books, 1962); H. Selvin and W. O. Hagstrom, "Determinants of Support for Civil Liberties," in *The Berkeley Student Revolt*, eds. S. M. Lipset and S. Wolin (New York: Anchor, 1965), pp. 494 ff.; M. Heirich and Sam Kaplan, "Yesterday's Discord," in Lipset and Wolin, pp. 10 ff.

13. J. O'Brien, "The New Left's Early Years," *Radical America* (May-June, 1968); H. Zinn, *SNCC: The New Abolitionists* (Boston: Beacon, 1964); J. Newfield, *A Prophetic Minority* (New York: New American Library, 1966).

14. The most important of these journals were *New University Thought, Studies on the Left, The Activist, Root and Branch,* and the English journal, *New Left Review.*

15. Richard E. Peterson, *The Scope of Organized Student Protest in 1967–68* (Princeton: Educational Testing Serice, 1968).

16. *Life,* October 18, 1968.

17. SDS's initial policy strategy is best described in the *Port Huron Statement* (Chicago: Students for a Democratic Society, 1966). The early history of SDS is discussed in O'Brien, in Newfield, and in Paul Jacobs and Saul Landau, *The New Radicals* (New York: Vintage, 1966). The early political orientation of SDS is reflected in articles published in Mitchell Cohen and Dennis Hale, *The New Student Left: An Anthology* (Boston: Beacon, 1966). SDS's changing orientation toward the university is described and documented in Richard Flacks, "Student Power and the New Left; the Role of SDS" (Berkeley: Center for the Study of Higher Education, 1968), mimeo.

18. R. Rothstein, "ERAP: Evolution of the Organizers," *Radical America* (March-April, 1968), pp. 1–18; also the essays by Gitlin, Flacks, Moody, Davis, Wittman and Hayden in Cohen and Hale, pp. 120–220.

19. Elizabeth Sutherland, ed., *Letters from Mississippi* (New York: McGraw-Hill, 1965).

20. Tom Hayden, "SNCC, the Qualities of Protest," *Studies on the Left* (Winter, 1965).

21. *SDS Bulletin* (August, 1965).

22. Letter from Dean of Students Katherine Towle to student organizations, dated September 14, 1964.

23. Sutherland; Bruce Payne, "SNCC: An Overview, Two Years

Later," and Mario Savio, "An End to History," both in Cohen and Hale.

24. Although it is difficult to assess the size of SDS accurately because the majority of its adherents do not pay dues, the following figures demonstrate its growth rate: In 1962, SDS had 10 functioning chapters and about 200 paid members; by September, 1964, there were 25 chapters and 1,000 members; by April, 1966, there were at least 150 chapters and 5,000 dues-paying members (see Newfield). SDS leaders now claim 7,000 dues-paying members and 300 chapters, and they believe there are 35,000 other students who participate regularly in SDS activities (*Life,* October 18, 1968). Richard Peterson's recent survey based on reports of university administrators indicates that these may be underestimates.

25. Student radical debates over tactics concerning the Vietnam War are reflected in the pages of *New Left Notes,* the SDS weekly newsletter, during 1965–67.

26. The University of Chicago sit-in and its aftermath are described in Vern Visick, "The Rank Protest of 1966–67" (University of Chicago Divinity School, 1967), mimeo.

27. The new SDS strategy was enunciated in Carl Davidson, "A Student Syndicalist Movement," *New Left Notes,* September 9, 1967, p. 2.

28. For a review of the implications of these protests for SDS's strategic outlook, see Carl Davidson, "Toward Institutional Resistance," *New Left Notes,* November 13, 1967, p. 1.

29. The following discussion is based on interviews with student movement leaders and local activists, observation of student meetings and protest activity, and review of the student radical press during the years in question by various members of and consultants to the task force. Some published material may be singled out as particularly indicative of changing attitudes within the movement.

On the impact of the civil rights movement on white student radicals: Hayden, "SNCC," A. Kopkin, ed., *Thoughts of Young Radicals* (*New Republic,* Harrison-Blaine, 1966).

On the poverty program and the organization of the poor: Robert Kramer and Norm Fruchter, "An Approach to Community Organizing," *Studies on the Left* (March-April, 1966).

On the university: Savio, "End to History"; "Davidson Outlines Four-Pronged Strategy," *National Guardian,* November 11, 1967, p. 9; "SDS Meeting Probes Theory of Social Change," *National Guardian,* March 4, 1967, p. 6; *Columbia Liberated* (New York: Columbia Strike Coordinating Committee, 1968); Clark Kerr, *The Uses of the University* (New York: Harper, 1963); North American Congress on Latin America, *Who Rules Columbia* (New York:

NACLA, 1968); Hal Draper, "The Mind of Clark Kerr," *New Politics,* III (1965), pp. 51–61; S. Weissman and D. Tuthill, "Freedom and the University," *Motive* (October, 1965), pp. 4–14.

On the war and United States foreign policy: Carl Oglesby, "Let Us Shape the Future," *Liberation* (January, 1966); Hans Morgenthau, "What Ails America," *New Republic* (October 28, 1967); L. Menashe and R. Radosh, *Teachins USA* (New York: Praeger, 1967); Oglesby and R. Shaull, *Containment and Change* (New York: Macmillan, 1967).

On military penetration of education: Sol Stern, "NSA: CIA," *Ramparts* (March, 1967); "The Universities and the War," *Viet-Report,* January, 1968; R. J. Samuelson, "War on Campus: What Happened when Dow Recruited at Harvard," *Science* (December 8, 1967).

On the draft: Alice Lynd, *We Won't Go* (Boston: Beacon, 1968); "A Call to Resist Illegitimate Authority" (Boston: Resist, 1967); Richard Flacks et al., "On the Draft," in *The Triple Revolution,* eds. R. Perucci and M. Pilisuk (Boston: Little, Brown, 1968).

On the psychology of radicalization see Kenneth Keniston, *Young Radicals* (New York: Harcourt, Brace, 1968).

On the psychological bases of legitimacy see Richard Flacks, "Social Psychological Perspectives on Legitimacy" (University of Chicago, 1968), mimeo. Norman Mailer's two recent books, *The Armies of the Night* (New York: New American Library, 1968), and *Miami and the Siege of Chicago* (New York: New American Library, Signet Book, 1968), contain excellent expressions of the attitudes of youthful rebels toward national authority and the police at the present time.

30. Quoted in *The Saturday Evening Post* (September 21, 1968).

31. "Columbia and the New Left," *The Public Interest* (Fall, 1968), p. 81.

32. On the rationale for resistance and confrontation tactics: informal interviews and conversations were conducted with the following new left leaders: Thomas Hayden, Rennard Davis, Todd Gitlin, Carl Davidson, Paul Potter, Clark Kissinger, Michael Rossman, Steve Halliwell, Frank Bardacke; public speeches by Mark Rudd, Michael Klonsky; conversations with Staughton Lynd and David Dellinger; a systematic monitoring of the following "new left" periodicals: *New Left Notes, The Movement, San Francisco Express Times, The Guardian, The Rat, Village Voice, Liberation.* Particularly helpful writing on the issues raised in our discussion frequently appears in these publications, especially in articles by the following persons: Julius Lester, Robert

Allen, Jack Smith, Carl Davidson, Greg Calvert (*The Guardian*); Marvin Garson (*Express Times*); Michael Klonsky, Les Coleman (*New Left Notes*); interviews with Tom Hayden and Jerry Rubin (*The Movement*, October, November, 1968).

We have participated in and observed numerous meetings and informal group discussions among students.

On the growing "alienation," pessimism and radicalism of students on the campus, a recent study of campus opinion at Columbia: A. Barton, "The Columbia Crisis: Campus, Vietnam and the Ghetto" (Bureau of Applied Social Research, Columbia University, July, 1968). A pilot study just completed by Richard Flacks, of student attitudes toward the "movement" at the University of Chicago, shows a similar pattern of disillusionment with the political system, but also a strong pattern of hostility toward SDS because of its "revolutionary" posture.

On the spontaneity of major campus confrontations: Berkeley—Max Heirich, *The Free Speech Movement at Berkeley* (New York: Columbia University Press, forthcoming); Columbia—Cox; Brooklyn College—Interview with Professor Norman Weissberg, Department of Psychology, Brooklyn College.

On the police as a provocative force: Cox, "Tactics for Handling Campus Disturbances," *College and University Business,* August, 1968, pp. 54–58.

33. In Chapter IV we consider black high school protest in some detail.

34. James Forman, *Sammy Younge, Jr.: The First Black College Student to Die in the Black Liberation Movement* (New York: Grove Press, 1968).

35. This commission has appointed a special task force to investigate the disturbances at San Francisco State: their report will deal with those issues in greater detail.

36. *The Culture of the University: Governance and Education,* Report of the Study Commission on University Governance (University of California, Berkeley, January 15, 1968), p. 9.

37. The following material is adapted from Rodney T. Hartnett, *College and University Trustees: Their Backgrounds, Roles, and Educational Attitudes* (Princeton, New Jersey: Educational Testing Service, 1969).

38. Kerr, *The Uses of the University.*

39. For a description of this change see Christopher Jencks and David Riesman, *The Academic Revolution* (Garden City, New York: Doubleday, 1968), ch. 1.

40. Seymour Lipset and Phillip Altbach, "Student Politics and Higher Education in the United States," *Comparative Education Review,* X (June, 1966), pp. 326–29.

41. For an influential study of local faculty contrasted to

cosmopolitan professors see Alvin W. Gouldner, "Cosmopolitans and Locals: Toward an Analysis of Latent Social Roles," *Administrative Science Q.*, II (1957–58), pp. 281–306, 444–80.

42. James Trent and Judith Craise, "Commitment and Conformity in the American Culture," *Journal of Social Issues*, XXIII (July, 1967), pp. 34–51.

43. Frederick Rudolph, "Changing Patterns of Authority and Influence," in *Order and Freedom on the Campus*, eds. Owen Knorr and W. John Minter (Boulder, Col.: Western Interstate Commission for Higher Education, 1965), pp. 1–10.

44. Morris B. Abram, "The Eleven Days at Brandeis—as Seen from the President's Chair," *New York Times Magazine*, February 16, 1969, p. 116.

45. For one thorough analysis, see Study Commission on University Governance, *op. cit.*

46. David Riesman and Christopher Jencks, "The Viability of the American College," in Nevitt Sanford, ed., *The American College* (New York: Wiley, 1962), p. 109.

47. See the account of the role of students in policy-making and discipline at the University of California, Berkeley, at the turn of the century in C. Michael Otten, "From Paternalism to Private Government: The Patterns of University Authority over Students" (Unpublished Ph.D. dissertation, Department of Sociology, University of California, Berkeley, 1968).

48. See Study Commission on University Governance, *op. cit.*, pp. 57–64 for an extensive discussion of law in the campus community. Our formulation here of the need for a transition from "discipline" to "due process" is a shorthand phrase for a complex problem. Beyond the problem of implementing due process, moreover, is the problem of the development of legal mechanisms for dealing with political conflict—a problem which, as we indicate in Chapter VIII of this report, remains unresolved in the legal order as a whole.

49. Bell, *op. cit.*, p. 95.

50. Quoted in *Newsweek*, February 24, 1969, p. 23. This should not be taken as a blanket endorsement of the University of Chicago's handling of recent conflict.

51. The response of outside authorities to recent campus disorders typically ranges widely, from the reasonable to the ludicrous: we do not intend to suggest that it is all of a piece. Few authorities, for example, would agree with the recent suggestion of a California State Assemblyman concerning disorder on California campuses: "Wouldn't we be money ahead in the long run to put walls around our campuses and have a Checkpoint Charley and make people show their cre-

dentials?" Quoted in the *San Francisco Chronicle,* February 21, 1969, p. 12.

52. "The Case of the Columbia Gym," *The Public Interest,* No. 13 (Fall, 1968).

Chapter IV

1. Chicago Commission on Race Relations, *The Negro in Chicago: A Study of Race Relations and a Riot* (Chicago: University of Chicago Press, 1922); The Mayor's Commission on Conditions in Harlem, *The Negro in Harlem* (New York, 1935); Governor's Committee to Investigate the Riot Occurring in Detroit, June 21, 1943, *Report* (Michigan, 1943); Governor's Commission on the Los Angeles Riots (1965), *Violence in the City—An End or a Beginning* (Los Angeles: College Book Store, 1965); National Advisory Commission on Civil Disorders, *Report* (New York: Bantam, 1968); and Chicago Riot Study Committee, *Report* (Chicago, 1968).

2. National Advisory Commission on Civil Disorders, p. 16.

3. Frederick Douglass, quoted in Charles E. Silberman, *Crisis in Black and White* (New York: Vintage, 1964), p. 218.

4. Malcolm X, *The Autobiography of Malcolm X* (New York: Grove Press, 1966), p. 394.

5. Lerone Bennett, *Confrontation: Black and White* (Chicago: Johnson Publishing Co., 1965), p. 19; and *Black Protest,* ed. Joanne Grant (Greenwich, Conn.: Fawcett Premier, 1968), p. 8.

6. For example, Glazer's contention that the situation of black Americans has evolved into one of "economic well-being and political despair" is considerably oversimplified. Nathan Glazer, "America's Race Paradox," *Encounter,* XXXI (October, 1968), pp. 9–18.

7. See Harvey Wish, "American Slave Insurrections Before 1861," *Journal of Negro History,* XXII, July, 1937, pp. 299–320; see also Herbert Aptheker, *American Negro Slave Revolts* (New York: Columbia University Press, 1943).

8. Bennett, p. 48; and David Walker, "An Appeal to the Coloured Citizens of the World," in *Black Protest,* ed. Joanne Grant, pp. 84–89.

9. Quoted in *Black Protest,* p. 65.

10. *Malcolm X Speaks,* ed. George Breitman (New York: Grove Press, 1966), p. 116.

11. Garveyism refers to Marcus Garvey's Universal Negro Improvement Association, a nationalist and separatist movement which gained a wide following in the United States in the 1920's. See Edmund D. Cronon, *Black Moses* (Madison,

Milwaukee, and London: University of Wisconsin Press, 1955).

12. *Shelly v. Kraemer,* 68 Sup. Ct. 836 (1948).

13. *Brown v. Board of Education,* 347 U.S. 483 (1954).

14. Bennett, pp. 169–170.

15. Bennett, pp. 38–65.

16. Bennett, pp. 150–151.

17. *Black Protest,* p. 10.

18. See generally Arthur I. Waskow, *From Race Riot to Sit-In: 1919 and the 1960's* (Garden City, New York: Doubleday Anchor, 1966).

19. James Farmer, "The New Jacobins and Full Emancipation," in *Black Protest,* pp. 377–82.

20. Martin Luther King, Jr., "Nonviolence and the Montgomery Boycott," in *Black Protest,"* pp. 281–82.

21. See Sally Belfrage, "Freedom Summer," in *Black Protest,* pp. 393–402.

22. James Forman, *Sammy Younge, Jr.* (New York: Grove Press, 1968), pp. 252–253.

23. *Southern Justice,* ed. Leon Freedman (New York: Random House, 1965).

24. *Black Protest,* p. 399.

25. John Lewis, "March on Washington," in *Black Protest,* pp. 375–77.

26. Howard Zinn, "The Limits of Nonviolence," in *Freedomways,* IV, First Quarter, 1964, pp. 143–48, and reprinted in *Black Protest,* pp. 312–17; see also Lewis, note 25.

27. Lewis, pp. 375–77.

28. Zinn, p. 315.

29. *Black Protest,* p. 369.

30. Zinn, p. 314.

31. Lewis, pp. 375–77.

32. Stokely Carmichael and Charles Hamilton, *Black Power: The Politics of Liberation in America* (New York: Vintage Books, 1967).

33. Loren Miller, "Farewell to Liberals," in *Black Protest,* p. 434.

34. Lee Rainwater and William L. Yancey, *The Moynihan Report and the Politics of Controversy* (Cambridge, Mass.: M.I.T. Press, 1967).

35. Fred Ferretti and Martin G. Berck, "Harlem Riot, 1964," in *Black Protest,* pp. 349–56.

36. Belfrage, p. 399.

37. Quoted in *Black Protest,* pp. 415–16.

38. Quoted in *Black Protest,* pp. 416–17.

39. The following discussion has been informed by the work of Robert Blauner.

40. Jean Paul Sartre, Preface in Frantz Fanon, *The Wretched of the Earth* (New York: Grove Press, 1963), p. 7.

41. George L. Shepperson, "Notes on Negro American In-

370

fluences on the Emergence of African Nationalism," in *Black History,* ed. Melvin Drimmerced (Garden City, New York: Doubleday, 1968), p. 499.

42. LeRoi Jones, *Home* (New York: Morrow, 1966), p. 203.
43. Fanon, p. 174.
44. Ronald Segal, *The Race War* (New York: Bantam, 1966), p. 38.
45. Immanuel Wallerstein, *Africa: The Politics of Independence* (New York: Vintage, Random House, 1961), p. 12.
46. Rupert Emerson and Martin Kilson, "The American Dilemma in a Changing World: The Rise of Africa and the Negro American," in *Daedalus* (Fall, 1965), pp. 1061–62.
47. Melville J. Herskovits, *The Myth of the Negro Past* (Boston: Beacon Press, 1958), p. 298.
48. Wallerstein, p. 68.
49. Emerson and Kilson, p. 1067.
50. Albert Memmi, *The Colonizer and the Colonized* (Boston: Beacon Press, 1967), p. 120.
51. Memmi, p. 123.
52. Wallerstein, p. 50.
53. Malcolm X, *Autobiography,* p. 321.
54. Malcolm X, *Autobiography,* p. 324.
55. Malcolm X, *Autobiography,* p. 369.
56. *Malcolm X Speaks,* pp. 46–47.
57. Emerson and Kilson, pp. 1066–67.
58. Segal, p. 253.
59. Harold Isaacs, *The New World of Negro Americans* (New York, 1963), Chapter 1.
60. Emerson and Kilson, p. 1060.
61. Malcolm X, *Autobiography,* p. 350.
62. Malcolm X, *Autobiography,* pp. 346–47.
63. Malcolm X, *Autobiography,* p. 347.
64. Georges Balandier, "Political Myths of Colonization and Decolonization in Africa," trans. Jean-Guy Vaillancourt from *Cahiers Internationaux de Sociologie,* XXXIII, July-December, 1962, pp. 85–96 and cited in *State and Society,* ed. Reinhard Bendix (Boston: Little, Brown, 1968), p. 476.
65. See E. U. Essien-Udom, *Black Nationalism* (New York: Dell, 1962).
66. Wallerstein, p. 59.
67. Fanon, p. 191.
68. See, generally, the work of Herskovits and Harold Cruse.
69. Fanon, pp. 54 and 104.
70. Fanon, p. 48.
71. Fanon, p. 73.
72. Memmi, p. 127.
73. Fanon, especially pp. 121–38.
74. Fanon, p. 104.

75. Harold Cruse, *The Crisis of the Negro Intellectual* (New York: Morrow, 1967).

76. Tucker, testimony before this commission, October 25, 1968, p. 2131.

77. The "riffraff" theory is fully described and criticized by T. M. Tomlinson and David O. Sears, *Los Angeles Riot Study: Negro Attitudes Toward the Riot* (Los Angeles: Institute of Government and Public Affairs, University of California, 1967); see also Robert M. Fogelson and Robert B. Hill, "Who Riots? A Study of Participation in the 1967 Riots," in *Supplemental Studies for the National Advisory Commission on Civil Disorders* (Washington, D.C.: U.S. Government Printing Office, July, 1968), pp. 221–22.

78. Federal Bureau of Investigation, *Prevention and Control of Mobs and Riots* (Federal Bureau of Investigation, U.S. Department of Justice, 1967), p. 31.

79. Governor's Committee to Investigate the Riot Occurring in Detroit, Part III, pp. 1–3; Governor's Commission on the Los Angeles Riots, p. 1; Chicago Riot Study Committee, p. 3; and *Interim Riot Report to Mayor of Pittsburgh*, Summer, 1968, p. 3.

80. Chicago Riot Study Committee, p. 28.

81. Mayor's Commission on Conditions in Harlem, p. 11.

82. David O. Sears and John B. McConahan, *Los Angeles Riot Study: Riot Participation* (Los Angeles: Institute of Government and Public Affairs, University of California, 1967), pp. 20–21.

83. Nathan E. Cohen, ·*Los Angeles Riot Study: Summary and Implications for Policy* (Los Angeles: Institute of Government and Public Affairs, University of California, 1967).

84. Fogelson and Hill, pp. 221–48.

85. T. M. Tomlinson and David O. Sears, *Los Angeles Riot Study: Negro Attitudes Toward the Riot*, p. 33.

86. Cohen, p. 4.

87. Fogelson and Hill, p. 243.

88. Richard Komisaruk and Carol Pearson, "Children of the Detroit Riots," *Journal of Urban Law*, XXXXIV, Spring and Summer, 1968, pp. 599–626.

89. William H. Grier and Price M. Cobbs, *Black Rage* (New York: Basic Books, 1968), p. 211.

90. Eldridge Cleaver, *Revolution in the White Mother Country and National Liberation in the Black Colony* (Oakland, California, Ministry of Information Black Paper, Black Panther Party for Self-Defense, 1968), p. 1.

91. Martin Luther King, Jr., "Beyond Vietnam," in *Black Protest*, p. 419.

92. *Ibid.*

93. *Black Protest*, p. 21.

94. John Dollard, *Caste and Class in a Southern Town* (Garden City, New York: Doubleday, Anchor, 1949).

95. See generally Waskow.

96. Robert F. Williams, "Negroes with Guns," in *Black Protest*, pp. 340–44; see also Cruse.

97. Williams, p. 342.

98. Charles R. Sims, "Armed Defense," in *Black Protest*, pp. 357–65.

99. Harold Nelson, "The Defenders: A Case Study of an Informal Police Organization," *Social Problems*, XV, No. 2 (Fall, 1967), pp. 127–47.

100. Malcolm X, *Autobiography*, p. 366.

101. From a staff interview with Huey P. Newton.

102. Newton interview.

103. *New York Times*, September 11, 1968, p. 37.

104. *New York Times*, September 5, 1968, pp. 1 and 94.

105. President's Commission on Law Enforcement and the Administration of Justice, *Task Force Report: The Police* (Washington, D.C.: U.S. Government Printing Office, 1967), Chapter VI.

106. President's Commission, *Police,* Chapter VI.

107. Cleaver, p. 4.

108. Newton interview.

109. See generally an unpublished manuscript by Richard Rubenstein, "Mass Political Violence in the U.S.," prepared for this task force, 1968; and Chapter VI of this report.

110. From a staff interview.

111. Quoted in Patrick Douglas, "In the Lair of the Panthers," *Seattle Magazine*, V, No. 55 (October, 1968), p. 38.

112. Forman, p. 263.

113. Stokely Carmichael, "Black Power," in *Black Protest*, p. 464.

114. *The Fire Next Time* (New York: Dial Press, 1963), p. 115.

115. Baldwin, p. 108.

116. Student Nonviolent Coordinating Committee (SNCC), "A Position Paper on Race," in *Black Protest*, p. 456.

117. SNCC, p. 454.

118. See, for example, Gunnar Myrdal, *An American Dilemma* (New York: McGraw-Hill, 1962), pp. 927–30.

119. Nathan Glazer and Patrick Moynihan, *Beyond the Melting Pot* (Cambridge, Mass.: M.I.T. Press, 1963), p. 53.

120. Charles Keil, *Urban Blues* (Chicago: University of Chicago Press, 1966), p. 5.

121. Eric Hoffer, "The Negro Is Prejudiced Against Himself," *New York Times Magazine*, November 29, 1964, p. 27.

122. For a critique of the idea of cultural deprivation, see Kenneth B. Clark, *Dark Ghetto* (New York: Harper, Torchbook, 1965), Chapter VI, pp. 111–53.

123. See the discussion of the meaning of Negro family organization in Frank Reissman, "In Defense of the Negro Family," cited in Rainwater and Yancey, pp. 474–78.

124. SNCC, p. 453.

125. According to one black intellectual, 'If Negroes were actually thinking and functioning on a mature political level, then the exclusion of whites—organizationally and politically—should be based not on hatred but on strategy." Cruse, p. 365.

126. See generally James Q. Wilson, *Negro Politics* (New York: Free Press, 1960).

127. Carmichael and Hamilton, p. 10.

128. Harold M. Baron, "Black Powerlessness in Chicago," *Transaction*, VI, No. 1, November, 1968, p. 28.

129. Baron, p. 28.

130. Baron, p. 31.

131. Baron, p. 33.

132. Baron, p. 31.

133. For a history of black separatism in the United States see Essien-Udom.

134. For further discussion of this criticism see Cruse, *Crisis;* Christopher Lasch, "The Trouble with Black Power," in *New York Review of Books*, X, 4, February 29, 1968, pp. 4–14; and Jervis Anderson, "Race, Rage and Eldridge Cleaver," *Commentary*, XLVI, No. 6 (December, 1968), pp. 63–69. We do not feel that this report is the appropriate place to discuss factionalism within the black militant movement. It is a complex and ever-changing problem characteristic of all groups advocating drastic social change, white and black, left and right. We have consequently limited our discussion to the general political thrust of contemporary militancy, especially to its relevance for white America.

135. National Advisory Commission on Civil Disorders, *Report*, p. 112.

136. Forman, p. 281.

137. Carmichael and Hamilton, p. 44.

138. Carmichael and Hamilton, p. 43.

139. Malcolm X, *Autobiography*, pp. 376–77; see also Cleaver.

140. Forman, p. 263.

141. National Advisory Commission on Civil Disorders, *Report*, p. 21.

142. The following analysis is based on incidents reported in the *New York Times* during the month of September for the years 1960–68. This month was chosen on the assumption that protest is most likely to occur when students return to school in the fall.

143. See Jonathan Kozol, *Death at an Early Age* (New York:

Bantam, 1967); Herbert Kohl, *36 Children* (New York: New American Library, 1967); and Clark, *op. cit.*

144. Lemberg Center for the Study of Violence, *Riot Data Review,* No. 2 (Waltham, Mass.: Brandeis University, August, 1968), pp. 73–75.

145. Lemberg Center, p. 75.

146. *New York Times,* October 24, 1967, p. 33.

147. *New York Times,* October 12, 1967, p. 39; November 17, 1967, p. 38; and December 15, 1967, p. 53.

148. *Chicago Sun Times,* September 15, 1967.

149. *Chicago Tribune,* September 15, 1967.

150. *Daily Defender,* September 16, 1967, p. 1.

151. *Nation's Schools,* November, 1967, pp. 26–28.

152. *Chicago Daily News,* September 25, 1967, p. 5.

153. *Chicago Daily News,* September 25, 1967, p. 37.

154. *U.S. News and World Report,* May 20, 1968, p. 37.

155. *Washington Post,* September 24, 1968, p. A3; September 25, 1968, p. B1; and September 26, 1968, p. B1.

156. *New York Times,* September 27, 1968, p. 54.

157. *New York Times,* September 27, 1968.

158. *New York Times,* September 28, 1968, p. 22.

159. *Newsweek,* October 28, 1968, p. 4; and *Chicago Sun Times,* October 25, 1968, p. 11.

160. *New York Times,* December 15, 1967, p. 53.

161. The following editorial excerpt is typical of popular conceptions of youth protests: ". . . student dislocation is not intended to win concessions of peace but is designed to keep the schools in convulsion. . . . We doubt if any but a handful of the black student boycotters in Chicago have the faintest conception that they are being used to generate a revolutionary climate. The cradle is being robbed for radicalism." (*Chicago Tribune,* October 17, 1968.)

162. But see the works of Holt, Kozol, and Clark.

163. Rev. John Fry, "The Subculture of Youth," Chapter 27, in *The People vs. the System: A Dialogue in Urban Conflict* (Chicago: Acme Press, 1968), p. 345.

164. *New York Times,* September 28, 1968, p. 29.

165. *U.S. News and World Report,* May 20, 1968, p. 37.

166. See, for example, the various stories in the *New York Times,* September 6, 1962, p. 22.

167. *New York Times,* September 18, 1960, p. 71.

168. See, for example, *New York Times,* September 3, 1960, p. 1.

169. Forman, p. 281.

170. As we point out on pages 146–48, research on community support for riots supports this contention.

171. *San Francisco Chronicle,* September 12, 1968, p. 32.

172. Elijah Muhammed, quoted in Essien-Udom, p. 253.

173. Forman, p. 281.

174. Edgar Z. Friedenberg, *Coming of Age in America* (New York: Random House, 1965), p. 170.
175. *Newsweek,* October 28, 1968, p. 84.
176. Rev. John Fry, p. 345.
177. Herman Blake, testimony before this commission.
178. Rev. John Fry, p. 344.
179. Lemberg, p. 59.
180. *Ibid.*
181. Lemberg, p. 60.
182. For further discussion of this incident see this report, Chapter VII.
183. Lemberg, p. 74.
184. Lemberg, p. 60.
185. *Chicago Daily Defender,* January 21, 1969, p. 8.
186. *New York Times,* September 10, 1968, p. 30, quoting an unidentified Black Panther.
187. Walker Report, pp. 29–30.
188. It must be emphasized that the exact nature of most of the following incidents is not clear, due to the lack of any information other than short news reports which are difficult to evaluate. They should be understood as *tentative* indications.
189. *New York Times,* September 13, 1968, p. 1.
190. *New York Times,* September 20, 1968, p. 37.
191. *New York Times,* September 29, 1968, p. 37.
192. *Chicago Tribune,* September 30, 1968.
193. *St. Louis Post Dispatch,* September 12, 1968.
194. *Washington Post,* September 6, 1968, p. A3.
195. *New York Times,* January 8, 1969, p. 36.
196. Ray Momboisse, *Riot and Civil Emergency Guide for City and County Officials* (Sacramento, Calif.: MSM Enterprises, 1968), p. 11.
197. Edwin Lemert, "Juvenile Justice—Quest and Reality," *Trans-action,* IV, 1967, p. 32.
198. *Chicago Tribune,* November 8, 1968, p. 4.
199. Robert A. Levin, "Gang-busting in Chicago," *New Republic,* June 1, 1968, pp. 16–18; and *Riots, Civil and Criminal Disorders,* Hearings before the Permanent Subcommittee on Investigations of the Committee on Government Operations, United States Senate (Washington, D.C.: U.S. Government Printing Office, June 28 and July 1 and 2, 1968).
200. Gerald Marwell, "Adolescent Powerlessness and Delinquent Behavior," *Social Problems,* XIV, No. 1 (Summer, 1966), pp. 35–47.
201. National Advisory Commission on Civil Disorders, *Report,* p. 2.

Chapter V

1. National Advisory Commission on Civil Disorders, Otto Kerner, Chairman, *Report* (New York: Bantam Books, 1968).
2. Louis Harris, "Whites, Negroes split on causes of rioting," *The Philadelphia Inquirer,* April 16, 1968.
3. Bruno Bettelheim and Morris Janowitz, *Social Change and Prejudice* (New York: Free Press, 1964); Paul B. Sheatsley, "White Attitudes Toward the Negro," *Daedalus,* XCIV, No. 1, Winter, 1966, pp. 217–38.
4. Robert Merton, "Fact and Factitiousness in Ethnic Opinionaires," *American Sociological Review,* V, No. 1, 1940, pp. 13–24.
5. J. B. Cooper, "Emotion in Prejudice," *Science,* August 7, 1959, pp. 314–18; Gary W. Porier and Albert J. Lott, "Galvanic Skin Responses and Prejudice," *Journal of Personality and Social Psychology,* V, No. 3, 1967, pp. 253–59.
6. Melvin DeFleur and Frank R. Westie, "Verbal Attitudes and Overt Acts: An Experiment on the Salience of Attitudes," *American Sociological Review,* XXIII, No. 6, 1958, pp. 667–73.
7. Thomas F. Pettigrew, "Parallel and Distinctive Changes in Anti-Semitic and Anti-Negro Attitudes," *Jews in the Mind of America,* ed. C. H. Stember (New York: Basic Books, 1966).
8. Richard T. Morris and Vincent Jeffries, *"The White Reaction Study"* (Los Angeles: Report of the Institute of Government and Public Affairs, University of California, June 1, 1967).
9. Hazel Erskine, "The Polls: Demonstrations and Race Riots," *Public Opinion Quarterly,* XXXI, No. 4, Winter, 1967–68, pp. 655–77.
10. Unpublished dissertation (Harvard, 1969) by Michael Ross, "Resistance to Racial Change in the Urban North: 1962–1966."
11. Louis Harris, "After the Riots: A Survey," *Newsweek,* August 21, 1967, pp. 18–19.
12. Melvin M. Tumin, *An Inventory and Appraisal of Research on American Anti-Semitism* (Freedom Books, 1961); Paul B. Sheatsley, "White Attitudes Toward the Negro," *Daedalus,* 1966, Vol. 95, No. 1, pp. 217–38.
13. Sheatsley, pp. 217–38.
14. *Ibid.*
15. Bettelheim and Janowitz, 1964; and Sheatsley, pp. 217–38.
16. Sheatsley, pp. 217–38.
17. Bettelheim and Janowitz, 1964, p. 18.

18. Charles Herbert Stember, *Education and Attitude Change: The Effect of Schooling on Prejudice Against Minority Groups* (New York: Institute of Human Relations Press, 1961).

19. Gordon W. Allport and Michael J. Ross, "Personal Religious Orientation and Prejudice," *Journal of Personality and Social Psychology,* 1967, V, No. 4, 1967, pp. 432–43.

20. Allport and Ross, pp. 432–43; and Gordon W. Allport, *The Nature of Prejudice* (Reading, Mass.: Addison-Wesley Publishing Company, 1954), Chapter 28, "Religion and Prejudice."

21. M. Brewster Smith, Jerome Bruner, and R. W. White, *Opinions and Personality* (New York: Wiley and Sons, 1956).

22. T. W. Adorno, et al., *The Authoritarian Personality* (New York: Harper and Row, 1950). For critical analysis of this approach see generally *Studies in the Scope and Method of the Authoritarian Personality,* eds. R. Christie and M. Jahoda (New York: Free Press, 1954).

23. Gordon W. Allport, *The Nature of Prejudice* (Reading, Mass.: Addison-Wesley Publishing Company, 1954).

24. Allport, 1954; Smith, Bruner, and White, 1956.

25. Leon Festinger, *A Theory of Cognitive Dissonance* (Stanford, Calif.: Stanford University Press, 1957).

26. Frank R. Westie, "The American Dilemma: An Empirical Test," *American Sociological Review,* XXX, No. 4, 1965, pp. 527–38.

27. Milton J. Rokeach, *Beliefs, Attitudes and Values* (San Francisco: Jossey-Bass, Inc., 1968).

28. D. D. Stein, Jane A. Hardyck, and M. B. Smith, "Race and Belief: An Open and Shut Case," *Journal of Personality and Social Psychology,* I, No. 4, 1965, pp. 281–89.

29. Thomas Pettigrew, "Racially Separate or Together?" Presidential Address to the Society for the Psychological Study of Social Issues, September, 1968. *In Press* as a publication of the Anti-Defamation League of B'nai B'rith.

30. William Brink and Louis Harris, *Black and White* (New York: Simon and Schuster, 1966).

31. Samuel A. Stouffer, *Communism, Conformity, and Civil Liberties* (New York: Doubleday, 1955).

32. Angus Campbell and Howard Schuman, "Racial Attitudes in Fifteen American Cities," in *Supplementary Report for the National Advisory Commission on Civil Disorders* (Washington, D.C.: U.S. Government Printing Office, June, 1968), Chapter 3.

33. Bettelheim and Janowitz, 1964, Chapter 1.

34. Richard Hofstadter, "The Pseudo-Conservative Revolt," in *The Radical Right,* ed. Daniel Bell (Garden City, New York: Doubleday, 1963).

35. Erich Fromm, *Escape from Freedom* (New York: Holt, Rinehart and Winston, 1941).
36. Walter Kaufman, "Status, Authoritarianism, and Anti-Semitism," *American Journal of Sociology,* LXII, No. 4, 1957, pp. 379–82.
37. Adorno et al., 1950.
38. Bettelheim and Janowitz, 1964, Chapter 2.
39. Thomas F. Pettigrew, personal communication.
40. Leo J. Strole, "Anomie, Authoritarianism and Prejudice," *American Journal of Sociology,* 1956, LXII, No. 1, pp. 63–67.
41. Richard F. Curtis, et al., "Prejudice and Urban Social Participation," *American Journal of Sociology,* LXXIII, No. 2, 1967, pp. 235–44.
42. Daniel Bell, "The Dispossessed," in *The Radical Right,* ed. Daniel Bell, 1963.
43. Hadley Cantril, *The Pattern of Human Concerns* (New Brunswick, New Jersey: Rutgers University Press, 1965).
44. Campbell and Schuman, 1968, Chapter 1.
45. Philip H. Ennis, *Criminal Victimization in the United States: A Report of a National Survey* (Washington, 1967), p. 54.
46. Ennis, p. 57.
47. Ennis, p. 56.
48. Thomas F. Pettigrew, "Actual Gains and Psychological Losses: The Negro American Protest," *Journal of Negro Education,* XXXII, No. 4, 1963 Yearbook, pp. 493–506. Also appears as Chapter 8 in Thomas F. Pettigrew, *A Profile of the Negro American* (Princeton, New Jersey: D. Van Nostrand Co., 1964).
49. U.S. Department of Labor, *Manpower Report of the President* (Washington, 1967), p. 73—hereafter cited as *Manpower Report.*
50. *Manpower Report,* p. 90.
51. *Manpower Report,* pp. 77–78.
52. Harold M. Baron, "Black Powerlessness in Chicago," *Trans-action,* VI, No. 1, November 1968, pp. 27–33.
53. Campbell and Schuman, 1968.
54. Harris, *Newsweek,* August, 1967.
55. Campbell and Schuman, 1968.
56. Harris, *Newsweek,* August, 1967.
57. Campbell and Schuman, 1968.

Chapter VI

1. Unless otherwise indicated, data for this section are derived from an unpublished paper submitted to this task force by David M. Chalmers.

2. Jacobus ten Broek, Edward N. Barnhart and Floyd W. Matson, *Prejudice, War, and the Constitution* (Berkeley and Los Angeles: University of California Press, 1954), pp. 13–14.
3. ten Broek, et al., p. 11.
4. ten Broek, et al., p. 16.
5. C. Vann Woodward, *The Strange Career of Jim Crow* (New York: Galaxy, Oxford University Press, 1966), p. 23.
6. David M. Chalmers, *Hooded Americanism* (Chicago: Quadrangle Paperbacks, 1968), p. 20.
7. Quoted in Chalmers, pp. 20–21.
8. Chalmers, p. 18.
9. United States Civil Rights Commission Report, *Justice* (Washington, D.C.: U.S. Government Printing Office, 1961), pp. 266–68.
10. Chalmers, p. 3.
11. Quoted in Chalmers, p. 27.
12. John Higham, *Strangers in the Land* (New York: Atheneum, 1963), p. 104.
13. Higham, p. 212.
14. Patrick Renshaw, *The Wobblies* (Garden City, New York: Doubleday, Anchor, 1967), pp. 163-67.
15. Arthur I. Waskow, *From Race Riot to Sit-in* (Garden City, New York: Doubleday, 1966), Chapter 3.
16. Higham, p. 264.
17. U. B. Phillips, quoted in Woodward, p. 8.
18. Allison Davis, "Caste, Economy, and Violence," *American Journal of Sociology*, LI, No. 1 (1945), pp. 7–15.
19. James W. Vander Zanden, *Race Relations in Transition* (New York: Random House, 1965), pp. 6–7.
20. *Baltimore Sun*, September 18, 1968.
21. California Department of Justice, *Paramilitary Organizations in California* (California: Report to State Legislature, 1965).
22. Quoted in Chalmers, p. 372.
23. *Los Angeles Times*, quoting Bowers, July 29, 1968.
24. *Los Angeles Times*, quoting Bowers, July 29, 1968.
25. Chalmers, p. 373.
26. See Chalmers, Chapter 4.
27. *Los Angeles Times*, July 29, 1968.
28. Vander Zanden, p. 43.
29. Vander Zanden, p. 26.
30. Quoted in Peter Young, "Appendix to Consultant's Report," Task Force I, this commission, p. 6.
31. Quoted in Young, p. 14.
32. Quoted in Young, p. 20.
33. Quoted in Young, p. 21.
34. Quoted in Young, p. 32.
35. Quoted in Young, p. 26.
36. Unpublished paper by Robert Wood delivered at the Na-

tional Consultation on Ethnic America, Fordham University, June, 1968.

37. Reported in the *Philadelphia Inquirer,* September 20, 1967.

38. Reported in the *Washington Post,* April 22, 1968.

39. Richard T. Morris and Vincent Jeffries, *The White Reaction Study* (Los Angeles: Institute of Government and Public Affairs, University of California, 1967), p. 7.

40. Morris and Jeffries, pp. 16–26.

41. Morris and Jeffries, p. 7.

42. Arnold Katz, *Firearms, Violence, and Civil Disorders* (Palo Alto: Stanford Research Institute, 1968), p. 45.

43. Angus Campbell and Howard Schuman, "Racial Attitudes in Fifteen American Cities," in *Supplemental Studies for the National Advisory Commission On Civil Disorders* (Washington, D.C.: U.S. Government Printing Office, 1968), pp. 58–59.

44. Unpublished paper by Robert Shellow, et al., "The Harvest of American Racism: The Political Meaning of Violence in the Summer of 1967," November, 1967, pp. 90–92.

45. Waskow, Chapters 3 and 4; see also unpublished dissertation (University of Pennsylvania, 1959), by Allen Grimshaw, "A Study in Social Violence."

46. *Chicago Sun Times,* August 24, 1968.

47. *New York Times,* September 26, 1968.

48. Paul Goldberger, "Tony Imperiale Stands Vigilant for Law and Order," *New York Times Magazine,* September 29, 1968.

49. Higham, p. 66.

50. Quoted in Goldberger.

51. Quoted in Goldberger.

52. Quoted in Young, p. 36.

53. Quoted in Young, p. 41.

54. Quoted in Young, p. 45.

55. J. Harry Jones, Jr., *The Minutemen* (Garden City, New York: Doubleday, 1968), p. 410.

56. See, generally, an unpublished paper by Richard P. Albares (University of Chicago: Center For Social Organization Studies, 1968), "Nativist Paramilitarism in the United States: The Minutemen Organization."

57. Quoted in Albares, p. 8.

58. Albares, pp. 25–26.

59. Jones, Chapter 22.

60. Jones, p. 298.

61. Albares, p. 50.

62. Albares, p. 47.

63. Albares, pp. 14–18.

64. Jones, pp. 399–400.

65. Jones, pp. 295–298.

66. Albares, p. 26.

67. Cf. Albares, p. 26.
68. See generally *The Radical Right,* ed. Daniel Bell (Garden City, New York: Doubleday, Anchor, 1964), Chapter 1.
69. Alan F. Westin, "The John Birch Society," in Bell, p. 239; see also, generally, Benjamin R. Epstein and Arnold Forster, *The Radical Right* (New York: Vintage Books, 1967).
70. Robert B. DePugh, "Blueprint for Victory," 1966, p. 20.
71. Quoted in Albares, p. 11.
72. Quoted in Albares, p. 13.
73. Unpublished dissertation (Columbia, 1957) by Martin Trow, "Rightwing Radicalism and Political Intolerance," pp. 30–31.
74. See John Kenneth Galbraith, *The New Industrial State* (Boston: Signet, 1967).
75. DePugh, p. 32.
76. Quoted in Jones, p. 407.
77. Albares, pp. 62–67.
78. Richard Hofstadter, *The Paranoid Style in American Politics* (New York: Vintage, 1967), pp. 39–40.

Chapter VII

1. James Baldwin, *Nobody Knows My Name* (New York: Dell, 1962), pp. 65–67.
2. *Report of the National Advisory Commission on Civil Disorders* (New York: Bantam Books, 1968). See especially "The Background of Disorder," pp. 135–50 and the charts on pp. 149–50.
3. See, e.g., Robert M. Fogelson, "From Resentment to Confrontation: The Police, the Negroes, and the Outbreak of the Nineteen-Sixties Riots," *Political Science Quarterly,* LXXXIII, No. 2 (June, 1968), pp. 217–47.
4. Among these are: William A. Westley, *The Police: A Sociological Study of Law, Custom and Morality* (unpublished Ph.D. dissertation, Department of Sociology, University of Chicago, 1951); Jerome H. Skolnick, *Justice Without Trial* (New York: Wiley, 1966); Arthur Niederhoffer, *Behind the Shield: The Police in Urban Society* (Garden City, New York: Doubleday, 1967); Burton Levy, "Cops in the Ghetto: A Problem of the Police System," *American Behavioral Scientist* (March-April, 1968), pp. 31–34.
5. Miami Study Team on Civil Disturbances, *Miami Report,* submitted to this commission, January 15, 1969.
6. Unpublished report prepared by the Mayor's Commission on Conditions in Harlem (New York, 1935), *The Negro in Harlem.*
7. Westley, p. 168.

8. "Patterns of Behavior in Police and Citizen Transactions."

9. This and subsequent interview information were derived from interviews carried out by members of this task force, unless otherwise indicated.

10. Robert Conot, *Rivers of Blood, Years of Darkness* (New York: Bantam, 1967).

11. "Book 5" (Washington: U.S. Government Printing Office, 1961), p. 28.

12. See, e.g., Ed Cray, *The Big Blue Line: Police Power vs. Human Rights* (New York: Coward-McCann, 1967); Jerome H. Skolnick, "The Police and the Urban Ghetto," *Research Contributions of the American Bar Foundation,* 1968, No. 3 (Chicago: American Bar Foundation, 1968); Anthony Amsterdam, Testimony to the National Commission on Causes and Prevention of Violence, *Transcript of Proceedings,* especially pp. 2476, 2485, 2491; Paul Chevigny, *Police Power* (New York: Pantheon, 1969); Report of the National Advisory Commission on Civil Disorders: "Task Force Report: The Police," *The President's Commission on Law Enforcement and Administration of Justice* (Washington: U.S. Government Printing Office, 1967), pp. 148, 164, 181–83.

13. According to the *San Francisco Chronicle* of November 5, 1968, p. 4, and the *Detroit Free Press,* November 14, 1968, nine police were suspended for beating black youths at a dance.

14. An off-duty policeman was indicted for shooting a black truck driver following a minor traffic accident, *San Francisco Sunday Chronicle and Examiner, This World,* October 13, 1968, pp. 5–6. He was later acquitted.

15. As reported in the *New York Times,* September 5, 1968, p. 1, 150 off-duty policemen attacked a group of Negroes—some were members of the Black Panthers—in a hallway of the Brooklyn Criminal Courts Building.

16. On-duty policemen were dismissed after firing twelve shots into a Black Panther headquarters, *San Francisco Chronicle,* September 11, 1968, p. 1.

17. In Newark, National Guardsmen and state troopers "were directing mass fire at the Hayes Housing Project in response to what they believed were snipers" (*Report of the National Advisory Commission,* pp. 67–68), although the only shots fired were by Guardsmen. The same pages describe the shooting up of stores with the sign "Soul Brother" in their windows. In Detroit, "Without any clear authorization or direction someone opened fire upon the suspected building. A tank rolled up and sprayed the building with .50 caliber tracer bullets." (*Report of the National Advisory Commission,* p. 97.)

18. In Paterson, New Jersey, according to the *New York Times* (October 30, 1968, p. 18), a grand jury placed blame on

Paterson police for vandalism, brutality, and intimidation in quelling a week of racial disorder. Amsterdam refers to such police tactics as "terrorization as a means of crowd control" in his testimony, p. 2491.

19. Fact-Finding Commission Appointed to Investigate the Disturbances at Columbia University in April and May, 1968, The Cox Commission, *Crisis at Columbia* (New York: Vintage, 1968). See also Chapter III of this report and Daniel Bell, "Columbia and the New Left," *The Public Interest* (Fall, 1968).

20. April 27 Investigating Committee, Dr. Edward J. Sparling, Chairman, *Dissent and Disorder: A Report of the Citizens of Chicago on the April 27 Peace Parade,* August 1, 1968.

21. *Rights in Conflict* (Chicago: November 18, 1968), p. vii; this report is now available in trade editions; for example, New York: Bantam Books, 1968.

22. *Ibid.*

23. *New York Times,* March 23–25, 1968.

24. *New York Times,* April 28, 29, 1968.

25. Los Angeles: Sawyer Press, 1967.

26. *Ibid.,* "Introduction."

27. *Dissent and Disorder,* pp. 30–31.

28. Mayor Richard J. Daley, "Strategy of Confrontation," published as a Special Section in the *Chicago Daily News,* September 9, 1968.

29. *New York Times,* October 28, 1968, p. 3.

30. "A Policeman Looks at Crime," *U.S. News and World Report,* August 1, 1966, p. 52.

31. *Saturday Evening Post,* November 16, 1968, p. 28.

32. *Ibid.*

33. See, e.g., Michael Banton, *The Policeman in the Community* (London: Tavistock Publications, 1964), p. 7, and Arthur L. Stinchcombe, "Institutions of Privacy in the Determination of Police Administrative Practices," *American Journal of Sociology,* LXIX (September, 1963), pp. 150–60, both cited and discussed in Skolnick, *Justice Without Trial,* p. 33.

34. James Q. Wilson, *Varieties of Police Behavior* (Cambridge, Mass.: Harvard University Press, 1968), p. 49. The original is in italics.

35. *Behind the Shield,* pp. 103–52.

36. John H. McNamara, "Uncertainties in Police Work: The Relevance of Police Recruiters' Backgrounds and Training," in *The Police: Six Sociological Essays,* ed. David J. Bordua (New York: John Wiley, 1967), pp. 163–252.

37. According to Richard Wade, a University of Chicago professor of urban history, "Fifty years ago, policemen had an income relatively higher than other trades and there were more applicants than there were jobs"; quoted in A. James

Reichley, "The Way to Cool the Police Rebellion," *Fortune* (December, 1968), p. 113.

38. Interviews in San Francisco have shown that a new recruit faces twelve years of night work before he is "promoted" to daylight work. This undoubtedly is one explanation.

39. *Behind the Shield* . . .

40. Evidence indicates that concurrent with the relative decline in financial rewards for police, the quantity and quality of equipment in some departments has also declined.

41. *Behind the Shield* . . ., p. 16.

42. Reichley, p. 113.

43. Police salaries average only two-thirds that of union plumbers, *Time,* October 4, 1968, p. 27.

44. *Time,* October 4, 1968, pp. 26–27; Sandy Smith, "The Mob: You Can't Expect Police on the Take to Take Orders," *Life,* December 6, 1968, pp. 40–43.

45. Today, according to Reichley, fewer than 10 percent of policemen are college graduates when recruited to the force; most have not more than a high school diploma. And *Time* reported that Detroit recruits are from the bottom 25 percent of high school graduating classes, October 4, 1968, p. 26.

46. *Washington Post,* December 15, 1968, p. B3.

47. Interview with Police Chief William Beall.

48. Quotes from *San Francisco Examiner,* November 13, 1968, pp. 1, 16.

49. In 1960 there were 1.9 police employees per 1,000 population; in 1966, this ratio had increased to 2.0 employees per 1,000. At the same time the number of serious criminal offenses increased 48.4 percent in just the six-year period 1960–66. Thus, while the number of indexed crimes jumped almost 50 percent, the number of employees was augmented by no more than 5 percent. J. Edgar Hoover, Director, Federal Bureau of Investigation. *Uniform Crime Reports for the United States, 1960, 1966* (Washington: U.S. Department of Justice, U.S. Government Printing Office).

50. Charles Saunders, Jr., of the Brookings Institution reports that some departments won't allow new officers to issue tickets—presumably because they have not undergone sufficient training—but require them to carry guns, Reichley, p. 150.

51. *New York Times,* August 30, 1968, p. 10.

52. *Report of the National Advisory Commission,* p. 485.

53. G. Wills, *The Second Civil War* (New York: New American Library, 1968), p. 47.

54. See *Report of the National Advisory Commission,* p. 100.

55. Among numerous other publications *Law and Order* and *The Police Chief* magazines for the past eighteeen months were reviewed. We read them both for an understanding of

the police perspective of their world and for their theories of appropriate response to social problems. Interviews and other reports augmented this study.

56. David Boesel, Richard Berk, W. Eugene Groves, Bettye Eidson, Peter H. Rossi, "White Institutions and Black Rage," *Trans-action* (March, 1969), p. 31.

57. See, e.g., J. Edgar Hoover, quoted in John Edward Coogan, "Religion, a Preventive of Delinquency," *Federal Probation,* XVIII (December, 1954), p. 29.

58. Travis Hirschi and Rodney Stark, "Hellfire and Delinquency," publication A-96, Survey Research Center, University of California at Berkeley.

59. See, e.g., R. R. Sears, et al., "Some Child-rearing Antecedents of Aggression and Dependency in Young Children," *Genetic Psychology Monograph* (1953), pp. 135–234; E. Hollenberg and M. Sperry, "Some Antecedents of Aggression and Effects of Frustration in Doll Play," *Personality* (1951), pp. 32–43; W. C. Becker, et al., "Relations of Factors Derived from Parent Interview Ratings to Behavior Problems of Five Year Olds," *Child Development,* XXXIII (1962), pp. 509–35; and M. L. Hoffman, "Power Assertion by the Parent and Its Impact on the Child," *Child Development,* XXXI (1960), pp. 129–43.

60. *Washington Post,* December 15, 1969, p. B3.

61. Cox Commission, p. 164.

62. *Proceedings,* p. 56.

63. *The Police Chief,* April, 1965, p. 10.

64. The Byrne Commission Report submitted to the Special Committee of the Regents of the University of California on May 7, 1965; most easily available in *Los Angeles Times,* May 12, 1965, Part IV, pp. 1–6. Quoted section, p. 5.

65. Cox Commission, p. 189.

66. *The Police Chief,* April, 1965, p. 36.

67. *Ibid.,* pp. 42–44.

68. Donald Yabush, *Chicago Tribune,* December 3, 1968, p. 1.

69. Chicago Study Team, pp. vii–viii, emphasis added.

70. The variety of intelligence received by law enforcement officials is indicated by this listing of Yippie threats published in the mass media: "There were reports of proposals to dynamite natural gas lines; to dump hallucinating drugs into the city's water system; to print forged credentials so that demonstrators could slip into the convention hall; to stage a mass stall-in of old jalopies on the expressways and thereby disrupt traffic; to take over gas stations, flood sewers with gasoline, then burn the city; to fornicate in the parks and on Lake Michigan's beaches; to release greased pigs throughout Chicago, at the Federal Building and at the Amphitheatre; to slash tires along the city's freeways and tie up traffic in all directions; to scatter razor sharp three-inch

nails along the city's highways; to place underground agents in hotels, restaurants, and kitchens where food was prepared for delegates, and drug food and drink; to paint cars like independent taxicabs and forcibly take delegates to Wisconsin or some other place far from the convention; to engage Yippie girls as 'hookers' to attract delegates and dose their drinks with LSD; to bombard the Amphitheatre with mortars from several miles away; to jam communication lines from mobile units; to disrupt the operations of airport control towers, hotel elevators and railway switching yards; to gather 230 'hyper-potent' hippie males into a special battalion to seduce the wives, daughters and girlfriends of convention delegates; to assemble 100,000 people to burn draft cards with the fires spelling out: 'Beat Army'; to turn on fire hydrants, set off false fire and police alarms, and string wire between trees in Grant Park and Lincoln Park to trip up three-wheeled vehicles of the Chicago police; to dress Yippies like Viet Cong and walk the streets shaking hands or passing out rice; to infiltrate the right wing with short haired Yippies and at the right moment exclaim: 'You know, these Yippies have something to say!'; to have ten thousand nude bodies floating on Lake Michigan—the list could go on." Chicago Study Team, p. 49.

71. Wilson, *Varieties of Police Behavior,* pp. 237–38.
72. Wilson p. 238.
73. Wilson, p. 230.
74. See Wilson generally.
75. See, e.g., Wayne R. LaFave, *Arrest: The Decision to Take a Suspect into Custody* (Chicago: American Bar Foundation, 1965); Skolnick, *Justice Without Trial;* and Wilson, *Varieties of Police Behavior.*
76. A cornerstone of our judicial system is that an accused is presumed innocent until proven guilty. The policeman, however, may feel that this should not be the rule since he would not have arrested the accused unless he was guilty. For a more detailed discussion of these points, see Skolnick, *Justice Without Trial,* Chapter 9, pp. 182–203.
77. Fogelson, p. 226.
78. We have discussed previously the tendency to equate deviance with crime.
79. Interview with John Harrington, President of the Fraternal Order of Police.
80. Certain political activities by police—discussed in detail below—may raise such issues, especially where the activities create sharp antagonism within the policed community and threaten the ability of the civic government to control the police.
81. A "job action" began in response to the city's refusal "to negotiate a new contract" (*New York Times,* October 16,

1968, p. 1). On October 26 the *New York Times* reported that Cassese was in defiance of a court order in his direction to continue the "slowdown" (p. 1). But on October 27, it was reported that he had bowed to the court order (*New York Times,* p. 1).

82. *San Francisco Chronicle,* December 16, 1968, p. 12.
83. *Washington Post,* December 15, 1968, p. B1.
84. For example, in Newark, New Jersey, as reported in *New York Times,* November 30, 1968, p. 1.
85. *Washington Post,* December 15, 1968, p. B1.
86. *Ibid.*
87. *New York Times,* November 18, 1968, p. 1.
88. Chicago Study Team, p. vii.
89. Chicago Study Team, p. 117.
90. *San Francisco Chronicle,* December 11, 1968, p. 41.
91. Chicago Study Team, p. 1.
92. The Chicago Study Team writes that almost three months after the convention no disciplinary action had been taken against most of the police violators (p. xiii).
93. *New York Times,* September 5, 1968, p. 1.
94. *San Francisco Chronicle,* September 11, 1968, p. 1.
95. *San Francisco Chronicle,* November 5, 1968, p. 4, and *Detroit Free Press,* November 14, 1968.
96. *San Francisco Sunday Chronicle and Examiner, This World,* October 13, 1968, pp. 5–6.
97. *Los Angeles Times,* August 16, 1968, p. 4.
98. *New York Times,* August 18, 1968, p. E7.
99. *Los Angeles Times,* August 16, 1968, p. 4.
100. According to a *Washington Post* story, the PBA may have backed down. December 15, 1968, p. B1.
101. *New York Times,* August 16, 1968, p. 38.
102. *New York Times,* September 5, 1968, p. 1.
103. Chicago Study Team, p. xii.
104. Fogelson, pp. 224–25.
105. An example of this phenomenon seems to have been pointed to by the commission's Chicago Study Team: "There has been no public condemnation of these violators of sound police procedures and common decency by either their commanding officers or city officials. Nor (at the time this Report is being completed—almost three months after the convention) has any disciplinary action been taken against most of them. That some policemen lost control of themselves under exceedingly provocative circumstances can perhaps be understood; but not condoned. If no action is taken against them, the effect can only be to discourage the majority of policemen who acted responsibly, and further weaken the bond between police and community" (p. xiii).

Indeed, this might have been predicted from the lack of response to the Sparling Report on the police violence during the Chicago peace march of April 1968.

According to a *Washington Post* study (December 15, 1968, p. B5): "Criticism of the Chicago force has become a symbol of the 'lack of support' that policemen constantly bemoan. Policemen everywhere rallied to the defense of their Chicago colleagues. 'How can people defend the rights [sic] of that filth and attack good police officers?' asks Walter Fahey, a Boston patrolman." And a police chief is reported as observing that Chicago made police feel they had to defend rough and stupid police behavior because they felt criticism of Chicago police was criticism of police everywhere.

106. See John Hersey, *The Algiers Motel Incident* (New York: Bantam, 1968). Reportedly, ten black men and two white girls were severely beaten by police during the Detroit riots; three of the men were found dead, shot at close range, and the police involved failed to report the incident.

107. The following discussion is based on information that is readily available from sources such as the *New York Times* during the period discussed.

108. See, e.g., reports of Boston and Philadelphia in *San Francisco Chronicle,* December 16, 1968, p. 12.

109. An editor's note in a compendium of articles opposing review boards entitled "Police Review Boards," prepared by the National Fraternal Order of Police Committee on Human Rights and Law Enforcement, Cincinnati, Ohio, no date.

110. This discussion draws from the D. J. R. Bruckner article, *Los Angeles Times,* October 2, 1968, pp. 26 ff.

111. See *New York Times,* November 3, 1968, p. 78; our interviews in Oakland, San Francisco, and New York; and Reichley for related information about the Wallace campaign of 1968.

112. *San Francisco Chronicle,* December 16, 1968, p. 12.

113. *Ibid.*

114. *San Francisco Chronicle,* September 28, 1968, p. 9.

115. *Washington Post,* December 15, 1968, p. B1.

116. *Ibid.*

117. One of our staff was present at that reception.

118. *Washington Post,* December 15, 1968, p. B2.

119. *Ibid.*

120. *San Francisco Chronicle,* December 16, 1968, p. 12.

121. *Ibid.*

122. *San Francisco Chronicle,* December 18, 1968, p. 11.

123. John Harrington, National President of the Fraternal Order of Police, has launched a campaign urging Congress to reverse certain Supreme Court decisions on criminal justice, *San Francisco Chronicle,* December 16, 1968, p. 12.

124. *New York Times,* August 16, 1968, p. 38.
125. *New York Times,* September 3, 1968, p. 20; August 16, 1968, p. 38.
126. *New York Times,* August 16, 1968, p. 38.
127. *Ibid.*
128. *Washington Post,* December 15, 1968, p. B1.
129. Henry Wise, the labor lawyer retained to help organize and bargain for the Patrolmen's Association, as quoted in *Washington Post,* December 15, 1968, p. B2.
130. *Washington Post,* December 15, 1968, p. B1.
131. *Washington Post,* December 15, 1968, p. B2.
132. *Washington Post,* December 15, 1968, p. B1.
133. *Washington Post,* December 15, 1968, p. B2.
134. *Ibid.*
135. See 42 U.S.C. 1863.
136. For example, the National Defense Education Program, Chapter 17 of Title 20 of the U.S. Code, and the National Science Foundation, Chapter 16 of Title 42. Grants could also be made to existing institutions to establish special courses, much as the NDEP provides financial assistance to schools for teaching science, mathematics and foreign languages; and on-the-job summer training might also be provided. Such a program should be approached cautiously, however, in light of the currect pressures to deny academic credit to Reserve Officer Training Corps and the comparatively low regard for policemen in the academic community.
137. See, e.g., "Task Force Report: The Police," *The President's Commission on Law Enforcement . . .,* p. 142.
138. *Ibid.*
139. See Herbert L. Packer, *The Limits of the Criminal Sanction* (Palo Alto: Stanford University Press, 1968); The President's Commission on Law Enforcement and Administration of Justice, *The Challenge of Crime in a Free Society* (Washington, D.C.: U.S. Government Printing Office, February, 1967), p. 126; and Skolnick, "Coercion to Virtue," *Research Contribution of the American Bar Foundation,* No. 7 (1968).
140. *Report of the National Advisory Commission,* pp. 311–12.

Chapter VIII

1. National Advisory Commission on Civil Disorders, *Report* (New York: Bantam, 1968), p. 337—hereafter cited as Kerner.
2. W. E. B. Du Bois, *The Philadelphia Negro* (New York: Schocken Books, 1967).
3. St. Clair Drake and Horace Cayton, *Black Metropolis* (New York: Harper, Torchbook, 1962).

4. Governor's Commission on the Los Angeles Riots (1965), *Violence in the City—An End or a Beginning* (Los Angeles: College Book Store, 1965), p. 24.
5. *Kerner,* p. 339.
6. *Ibid.*
7. Chicago Riot Study Committee, *Report* (Chicago, 1968), p. 19.
8. District of Columbia Committee on the Administration of Justice under Emergency Conditions, *Interim Report* (May 25, 1968), p. 5—hereafter cited as *D.C. Report;* and Baltimore Committee on the Administration of Justice under Emergency Conditions, *Report* (May 31, 1968), p. 6—hereafter cited as Baltimore Committee *Report.*
9. *Kerner,* Chapter 13.
10. Chicago Riot Study Committee, *Report,* Chapter XII.
11. *D.C. Report.*
12. Baltimore Committee *Report.*
13. Mayor's Committee, *Administration of Justice under Emergency Conditions* (New York, 1968).
14. *American Criminal Law Quarterly,* VI, 3 (Spring, 1968).
15. "The Administration of Criminal Justice in the Wake of the Detroit Civil Disorder of July, 1967," *Michigan Law Review,* LXIV, 7 (1968), p. 1598—hereafter cited as *Michigan Law Review Riot Study.*
16. *Kerner,* p. 341.
17. Ronald L. Goldfarb, "The Administration of Justice in Washington, D.C., During the Disorder of April, 1968," an unpublished manuscript, p. 6.
18. Goldfarb, pp. 10–11.
19. Anthony Platt and Sharon Dunkle, *The Administration of Justice in Crisis: Chicago, April, 1968* (Center for Studies in Criminal Justice: University of Chicago, 1968).
20. Information from staff interview.
21. Jerome E. Carlin and Jan Howard, "Legal Representation and Class Justice," *UCLA Law Review,* XXII (January, 1965), pp. 381 and 437.
22. *Kerner,* p. 342.
23. *Kerner,* p. 342; Platt and Dunkle, pp. 9–24.
24. *Michigan Law Review Riot Study,* p. 1553.
25. *Michigan Law Review Riot Study,* p. 1600.
26. *Kerner,* p. 357.
27. Platt and Dunkle, pp. 22–23.
28. Platt and Dunkle, pp. 17–19.
29. *Michigan Law Review Riot Study,* p. 1553.
30. Platt and Dunkle, p. 8.
31. Information from staff interview.
32. Goldfarb, p. 28.
33. Ben W. Gilbert, *Ten Blocks from the White House: Anatomy of the Washington Riots 1968* (New York: Frederick

A. Praeger, 1968), Chapter 8; *Michigan Law Review Riot Study,* p. 1604.

34. Gilbert, p. 125; Goldfarb, p. 29.
35. Platt and Dunkle, pp. 19–24.
36. Information from staff interviews.
37. *Kerner,* p. 357.
38. Judge George W. Crockett, Jr., "Recorder's Court and the 1967 Civic Disturbance," *Journal of Urban Law,* XLV (Spring and Summer, 1968), p. 846.
39. Information from staff interview.
40. *Detroit Free Press,* July 28, 1967.
41. *Detroit Free Press,* October 15, 1967.
42. *Detroit Free Press,* July 26, 1967.
43. Crockett, p. 846.
44. *Ibid.*
45. Crockett, p. 841.
46. E. Philip Colista and Michael G. Domonkos, "Bail and Civil Disorder," *Journal of Urban Law,* XLV (Spring and Summer, 1968), pp. 815–39.
47. Colista and Domonkos, p. 818.
48. Information from staff interview.
49. *Newark Evening News,* July 14, 1967.
50. *Kerner,* p. 357.
51. Information provided by Chicago Civil Liberties Union.
52. *Chicago Daily News,* February 8, 1967.
53. *Ibid.*
54. Illinois Special Legal Project, The Roger Baldwin Foundation of the ACLU, "Preliminary Report and Evaluation on the Bail Procedures in Chicago's Looting Cases—Winter, 1967" (Chicago, August, 1967).
55. *Chicago Tribune,* February 1, 1967.
56. Platt and Dunkle, *passim.*
57. Information from staff interview.
58. Information from University of Chicago Law Review Riot Study Project.
59. Baltimore Committee *Report,* p. 48.
60. *Ibid.*
61. Baltimore Committee *Report,* pp. 48-49.
62. Baltimore Committee *Report,* p. 57.
63. *D.C. Report,* p. 83; Goldfarb, p. 34.
64. Goldfarb, p. 35.
65. The President's Commission on Law Enforcement and Administration of Justice, *Task Force Report: The Courts* (Washington, D.C.: U.S. Government Printing Office, 1967), p. 29, hereafter cited as *Task Force.*
66. *Task Force,* p. 32.
67. President's Commission on Crime in the District of Columbia, *Report* (Washington, D.C.: U.S. Government Printing Office, 1966), p. 351.

68. *Task Force,* p. 30.
69. *Stack v. Boyle,* 342 U.S. 1 (1951); *Williamson v. U.S.,* 184 F. 2d 280 (2nd Cir. 1950).
70. Caleb Foote, "Compelling Appearance in Court; Administration of Bail in Philadelphia," *University of Pennsylvania Law Review,* CII (1954), p. 1031; Caleb Foote, "New York Bail System," *University of Pennsylvania Law Review,* CVI (1958), p. 633.
71. Foote, "Compelling Appearance in Court: Administration of Bail in Philadelphia," p. 1031.
72. See, for example, the testimony before this commission of Professor Anthony Amsterdam on October 31, 1968.
73. See, for example, the various bail studies of Caleb Foote, and works of the Vera Foundation in New York.
74. *Task Force,* p. 30.
75. *Michigan Law Review Riot Study,* p. 1556.
76. Francis A. Allen (Chairman), *Poverty and the Administration of Federal Criminal Justice* (Washington, D.C.: U.S. Government Printing Office, 1963), pp. 10–11.
77. Jerome E. Carlin, *Lawyers' Ethics* (New York: Russell Sage Foundation, 1966).
78. Arthur Lewis Wood, *Criminal Lawyers* (New Haven, Connecticut: College and University Press, 1967); Jack Ladinsky, "Careers of Lawyers, Law Practice and Legal Institutions," in Rita James Simon, ed., *The Sociology of Law* (San Francisco: Chandler Publishing Company, 1968), pp. 275–89.
79. Ladinsky, p. 279.
80. Wood, p. 149.
81. *Task Force,* p. 4.
82. Jerome H. Skolnick, "Social Control in the Adversary System," *Journal of Conflict Resolution,* XI (1967), pp. 52–70. For studies of the impact of the *Gault* decision on juvenile court which point to similar conclusions, see Anthony Platt and Ruth Friedman, "The Limits of Advocacy: Occupational Hazards in Juvenile Court," *University of Pennsylvania Law Review,* CXVI (May, 1968), pp. 1156–84; Anthony Platt, Howard Schechter, and Phyllis Tiffany, "In Defense of Youth: A Case Study of the Public Defender in Juvenile Court," *Indiana Law Journal,* XLIII (Spring, 1968), pp. 619–40.
83. *Task Force,* pp. 11–12. See also the recent criticisms by Chief Judge David L. Bazelon, of the United States Court of Appeals (D.C. Circuit), reported in the *Washington Post,* February 14, 1969.
84. David Sudnow, "Normal Crimes: Sociological Features of the Penal Code in a Public Defender's Office," *Social Problems,* XII (1965), pp. 255–76.
85. *Task Force,* p. 10.

86. *Detroit Free Press,* July 27, 1967.
87. Crockett, p. 846.
88. *Newark Evening News,* July 16, 1967.
89. *Newark Evening News,* August 2, 1967.
90. Information from staff interview.
91. Federal Bureau of Investigation, *Prevention and Control of Mobs and Riots* (Washington, D.C.: U.S. Government Printing Office, 1968), Chapter 7.
92. See pages 300–301.
93. Martin Shapiro, "Political Jurisprudence," *Kentucky Law Journal,* LII (1963), pp. 294-343; Richard Quinney, "Crime in Political Perspective," *The American Behavioral Scientist,* 8 (1964), pp. 19–22.
94. Otto Kirchheimer, *Political Justice* (Princeton: Princeton University Press, 1961).
95. *Proceedings,* pp. 1745–46.
96. This view, of course, is not without factual basis. The Chicago Commission on Race Relations which studied the 1919 riot concluded that black citizens received harsher judicial treatment than white citizens under both routine and emergency conditions: "It . . . appears, from the records and from the testimony of judges in the juvenile, municipal, circuit, superior, and criminal courts, of police officials, the state's attorney, and various experts on crime, probations, and parole, that Negroes are more commonly arrested, subjected to police identification, and convicted than white offenders; that on similar evidence they are generally held and convicted of more serious charges, and that they are given longer sentences." Chicago Commission on Race Relations, *The Negro in Chicago: A Study of Race Relations and a Riot* (Chicago: University of Chicago Press, 1922), pp. 622–23.
97. W. E. B. DuBois, *The Souls of Black Folk,* 1903, p. 176.
98. Information from staff interview.
99. *Kerner,* p. 333.
100. Harold H. Greene, "A Judge's View of the Riots," *D.C. Bar Journal,* XXXV (August, 1968), p. 28.
101. Frederic S. LeClercq, "The San Francisco Civil Rights Cases," unpublished paper, Center for the Study of Law and Society, University of California, Berkeley, 1964, pp. 14–15.
102. Edmund Cahn distinguishes between the "official" and "consumer" perspectives on law. "Law in the Consumer Perspective," *University of Pennsylvania Law Review,* CXII (November, 1963), pp. 1–21.
103. Quoted in Jerome H. Skolnick, "The Berkeley Rebels and the Courts," unpublished paper, Center for the Study of Law and Society, University of California, 1965.
104. Special Committee of the Regents of the University, *Report,* May 7, 1965.

105. The April 27 Investigating Commission, "Dissent and Disorder," Chicago, August 1, 1968, p. 108.
106. Irving Louis Horowitz and Martin Liebowitz, "Social Deviance and Political Marginality: Toward a Redefinition of the Relation between Sociology and Politics," *Social Problems*, XV (1968) pp. 280–96.
107. *Kerner*, p. 357.
108. See, for example, Baltimore Committee *Report*, Chapter 3; *D.C. Report*, p. 86; and *American Criminal Law Quarterly* (Spring, 1968).
109. Baltimore Committee *Report*, pp. 38–39.

Chapter IX

1. Chicago Commission on Race Relations, *The Negro in Chicago: A Study of Race Relations and a Race Riot* (Chicago: University of Chicago Press, 1922)—hereafter cited as *The Negro in Chicago*.
2. From an unpublished paper by William Kornhauser quoted in Henry Bienen, *Violence and Social Change* (Chicago: University of Chicago Press, The Adlai Stevenson Institute of International Affairs, 1968), p. 106.
3. Gustave Le Bon, *The Crowd* (London: Ernest Benn, 1952), p. 32. Also available in Viking Compass Book (New York, 1960), p. 32.
4. Le Bon, Chapter 2.
5. Le Bon, Chapter 5.
6. Leon Bramson, *The Political Context of Sociology* (Princeton, New Jersey: Princeton University Press, 1961).
7. See Kurt Lang and Gladys Engel Lang, "Collective Behavior," in *International Encyclopedia of the Social Sciences*, 1968, pp. 556–64.
8. See, e.g., Roger Brown, *Social Psychology* (New York: Free Press, 1965); Herbert Blumer, "Collective Behavior," in *Review of Sociology: Analysis of a Decade*, ed. J. B. Gittler (New York: John Wiley, 1957), pp. 127–58; Neil J. Smelser, *Theory of Collective Behavior* (New York: The Free Press, 1962); and R. H. Turner and L. M. Killian, *Collective Behavior* (Englewood Cliffs, N.J.: Prentice-Hall, 1957).
9. Roger Brown, p. 709.
10. Smelser, p. 74.
11. Smelser, p. 1.
12. Smelser, esp. p. 72.
13. *Ibid.*
14. *Ibid.*
15. The work of Blumer, especially, emphasizes the creative potential of collective behavior: see Blumer, *op. cit.* Smelser's work specifically notes the "reconstitutive" character of col-

lective behavior, but in the same breath judges it as "uninstitutionalized" and based on extravagant beliefs; see Neil J. Smelser, *Essays in Sociological Explanation* (Englewood Cliffs, N.J.: Prentice-Hall, 1968), pp. 96–97.

16. But see Smelser's more recent work in which an attempt is made to get at the "deeper psychological meanings" of collective episodes, especially his statement that "the striking feature of the protest movement is what Freud observed: it permits the expression of impulses that are normally repressed." Smelser, *Essays,* p. 121.

17. Turner and Killian, pp. 20–21.

18. Smelser, *Theory of Collective Behavior,* p. 246.

19. Smelser, *Theory of Collective Behavior,* pp. 261, *et passim.*

20. Morris Janowitz, *Social Control of Escalated Riots* (Chicago: University of Chicago Center for Policy Study, 1968), p. 7.

21. *Ibid.*

22. Janowitz, p. 14.

23. Janowitz, p. 13.

24. Federal Bureau of Investigation, *Prevention and Control of Mobs and Riots* (Department of Justice, April 3, 1967), p. 25.

25. National Advisory Commission on Civil Disorders, *Report* (New York: Bantam, 1968), Chapter 2.

26. Carl J. Couch, "Collective Behavior: An Examination of Some Stereotypes," *Social Problems,* XV, No. 3 (1968), pp. 310–22.

27. Throughout this chapter, we have applied the perspective of labeling theory—usually associated with the field of deviant behavior—to the theory of collective behavior. See, for example, the work of Howard Becker and Edwin Lemert.

28. Jules J. Wanderer, "1967 Riots: A Test of the Congruity of Events," *Social Problems* XVI, No. 2 (1968), pp. 193–98.

29. Eric Hobsbawm, *Primitive Rebels* (New York: Norton, 1959); George Rudé, *The Crowd in History, 1730–1848* (New York: Wiley, 1964).

30. Hans W. Mattick, "Form and Content of Recent Riots," *Midway,* IX, No. 1 (Summer, 1968), pp. 18–19.

31. *The Negro in Chicago,* p. 342.

32. Unpublished report prepared by the Mayor's Commission on Conditions in Harlem (New York, 1935), *The Negro in Harlem,* pp. 7 and 99.

33. Governor's Commission on the Los Angeles Riots, *Violence in the City—An End or a Beginning?* (Los Angeles: College Book Store, 1965), pp. 1, 4–5—hereafter cited as *Violence in the City.*

34. See e.g., Chicago Riot Study Committee, *Report* (Chicago, 1968), p. 3; Mayor's Special Task Force, *Progress Report* (Pittsburgh, 1968), p. 4.

35. Chicago Riot Study Committee, *Report,* p. 112.
36. E. L. Quarantelli and Russell R. Dynes, "Patterns of Looting and Property Norms: Conflict and Consensus in Community Emergencies," 1968, paper submitted to this commission.
37. FBI, *Prevention and Control of Mobs and Riots,* p. 86.
38. *The Negro in Chicago,* p. xiii.
39. *Violence in the City,* p. 9.'
40. Chicago Riot Study Committee, *Report,* p. 3.
41. Mayor's Special Task Force, Pittsburgh, p. 5.
42. National Advisory Commission on Civil Disorders, *Report,* p. 2.
43. *Supra,* note 27.
44. Hobsbawm, p. 114.
45. Lewis A. Coser, *Continuities in the Study of Social Conflict* (New York: Free Press, 1967), p. 83.
46. Eric Hobsbawm, *Labouring Men: Studies in the History of Labor* (New York: Basic Books, 1964), p. 16.
47. Gaston Rimilinger, "The Legitimation of Protest: A Comparative Study in Labor History," *Comparative Studies in Society and History,* II (April, 1960), p. 343.
48. *The Negro in Harlem,* p. 109.
49. National Advisory Commission on Civil Disorders, p. 18.
50. G. Wills, *The Second Civil War* (New York: New American Library, 1968), p. 47.
51. Smelser, *Theory of Collective Behavior,* p. 73.
52. Janowitz, p. 20.
53. *Ibid.*
54. Bienen, *Violence and Social Change,* Chapter 3.

Selected Bibliography

Chapter I. Protest and Politics

There is no comprehensive study of the history of political violence, and the social-scientific literature on the social meaning of violence is undeveloped. The works which we criticize in the chapter are cited in the notes at the appropriate place. See Richard Rubenstein's forthcoming book *Rebels in Eden: Mass Political Violence in the United States.*

Chapter II. Anti-War Protest

Documents

Clergy and Laymen Concerned about the War. *In the Name of America.* New York: Dutton, 1968.

Fulbright, J. William. *The Vietnam Hearings.* New York: Vintage, 1966. Introduced by Senator Fulbright, the book includes the testimony before the Senate Foreign Relations Committee by Dean Rusk, James M. Gavin, George F. Kennan, and Maxwell D. Taylor.

Gettleman, Marvin E., ed., *Vietnam: History, Documents, and Opinions on a Major World Crisis.* New York: Fawcett, 1965.

Raskin, Marcus G., and Bernard B. Fall. *The Viet-Nam Reader: Articles and Documents on American Foreign Policy and the Viet-Nam Crisis.* New York: Vintage, 1965.

The Draft

American Friends Service Committee, Peace Education Division. *The Draft?* New York: Hill and Wang, 1968.

Carper, Jean. *Bitter Greetings; The Scandal of the Military Draft.* New York: Grossman, 1967.

Tax, Sol, ed. *The Draft, A Handbook of Facts and Alternatives.* Chicago: University of Chicago Press, 1967.

Historical Analysis

Ashmore, Harry S., and William C. Baggs. *Mission to Hanoi: A Chronicle of Double-Dealing in High Places, A Special Report from the Center for the Study of Democratic Institutions.* New York: Berkley Publishing, 1968. Includes a valuable chronology.

Fall, Bernard B. *Street Without Joy: From the Indochina War to the War in Viet-Nam.* Harrisburg, Pa.: The Stackpole Company, 1961. A military history of the war from 1946 to 1954.

————. *The Two Viet-Nams: A Political and Military Analysis.* New York: Praeger, 1964. Rev. ed. Developments from the end of World War II through early 1964.

————. *Viet-Nam Witness, 1953–66.* New York: Praeger, 1966. Collection of articles.

Gavin, James. *Crisis Now.* New York: Vintage, 1968. Exposition of the relationship between foreign and domestic issues.

Goodwin, Richard N. *Triumph or Tragedy: Reflections on Vietnam.* New York: Vintage, 1966. By the former assistant to Presidents Kennedy and Johnson, first appearing as an article in *The New Yorker.*

Halberstam, David. *The Making of a Quagmire.* New York: Random House, 1965. Pulitzer prizewinning account based on observations between 1961 and 1964.

Hanh, Thich Nhat, *Vietnam: Lotus in a Sea of Fire.* New York: Hill and Wang, 1967. Analysis by a prominent Vietnamese Buddhist.

Harvey, Frank. *Air War: Vietnam.* New York: Bantam, 1967.

Kahin, George McTurnan, and John W. Lewis. *The United States in Vietnam.* New York: Delta, 1967. Detailed historical, political, and military analysis.

Lacouture, Jean. *Vietnam: Between Two Truces.* New York: Random House, 1966. By the correspondent of *Le Monde.*

Lynd, Staughton, and Thomas Hayden. *The Other Side.* New York: New American Library, 1967. Sympathetic view of North Vietnam by two American radicals.

McCarthy, Mary. *Vietnam.* New York: Harcourt, 1967. Vivid narrative by an eminent novelist.

Mecklin, John. *Mission in Torment.* Garden City, New York: Doubleday, 1965. By a former high officer of the U.S. Information Agency in Saigon.

Menashe, Louis, and Ronald Radosh, eds. *Teach-Ins: U.S.A.: Reports, Opinions, Documents.* New York: Praeger, 1967.

Pike, Douglas. *Viet-Cong.* Cambridge, Mass.: M.I.T. Press, 1966. The most scholarly study of enemy organization.

Ray; Michele. *The Two Shores of Hell.* New York: McKay, 1968.

Salisbury, Harrison. *Behind the Lines: Hanoi, December 23–January 7.* New York: Harper and Row, 1967.

Schell, Jonathan. *The Village of Ben Suc.* New York: Vintage, 1967. An account of American treatment of the South Vietnamese countryside.

————. *The Military Half.* New York: Vintage, 1968. First-hand reportage of military operations in two South Vietnamese provinces.

Schlesinger, Arthur M., Jr. *A Thousand Days.* Boston: Houghton Mifflin, 1965. President Kennedy's approach to Vietnam.

Schurmann, Franz, Peter Dale Scott, and Reginald Zelnik. *The Politics of Escalation in Vietnam.* New York: Fawcett, 1966. Analyzes the political basis of American military decisions.

Senate Republican Policy Committee. "The War in Vietnam." May 1, 1967.

Sontag, Susan, *Trip to Hanoi.* New York: Farrar, Straus & Giroux (Noonday ed.), 1968.

International Law

Falk, Richard A. *The Vietnam War and International Law.* Princeton, N.J.: Princeton University Press, 1968. Contains also pertinent documents.

Lawyers Committee on American Policy Toward Viet-Nam, Consultative Council. *Vietnam and International Law: An Analysis of the Legality of the United States Military Involvement.* Flanders, New Jersey: O'Hare, 1967.

Chapter III. Student Protest

General Bibliographies

Altbach, Philip. *A Select Bibliography on Students, Politics and Higher Education.* Cambridge, Mass.: Harvard University Center for International Affairs, 1967.

————. *Student Politics and Higher Education in the U.S., a Select Bibliography.* Cambridge, Mass.: Harvard University Center for International Affairs, 1968.

International Student Politics

Lipset, Seymour Martin, ed. *Student Politics.* New York: Basic Books, 1967.

"Students and Politics," *Daedalus* (Winter, 1968).

Empirical Data

Kenniston, Kenneth. *Young Radicals.* New York: Harcourt, Brace, 1968.

Peterson, Richard. *The Scope of Organized Student Protest in the U.S., 1967–68.* Princeton, N.J.: Educational Testing Service, 1968.

Sampson, Edward, ed. "Stirring out of Apathy," *Journal of Social Issues* (July, 1967).

"Special Issue: The Universities," *The Public Interest* (Fall, 1968).

Columbia and After

"American Youth: Its Outlook is Changing the World: A Special Issue," *Fortune* (January, 1969).

Fact-Finding Commission Appointed to Investigate the Disturbances at Columbia University in April and May, 1968, The Cox Commission. *Crisis at Columbia.* New York: Vintage, 1968.

"Special Issue on the American University and Student Protest," *American Behavioral Scientist,* XI (May-June, 1968).

The New Left

Kennan, George. *Democracy and the Student Left.* New York: Bantam, 1968.

Newfield, J. *A Prophetic Minority.* New York: New American Library, 1966.

Chapter IV. Black Militancy

There is an abundant and increasing literature on black protest in America. The following works should be considered basic:

Carmichael, Stokely, and Charles V. Hamilton. *Black Power; The Politics of Liberation in America.* New York: Vintage, 1967. A concise discussion of the need for black political and cultural autonomy.

Clark, Kenneth B. *Dark Ghetto; Dilemmas of Social Power.* New York: Harper, Torchbooks, 1965. An analysis, by a black social scientist, of the social, political, and economic structure of the urban ghetto.

Cleaver, Eldridge. *Soul on Ice.* New York: McGraw-Hill, Ramparts Book, 1968. A collection of writings by the Minister of Information of the Black Panther Party.

Dollard, John. *Caste and Class in a Southern Town.* Garden City,

New York: Doubleday, Anchor, 1949. A classic study, still useful, of race and racism in the South in the 1930's.

Essien-Udon, E. U. *Black Nationalism.* New York: Dell, 1962. A study of Black Nationalist movements in American history, with special reference to the Nation of Islam.

Fanon, Frantz. *The Wretched of the Earth.* New York: Grove Press, 1963. An extremely influential treatment of the politics and psychology of colonialism and anti-colonialism.

Grant, Joanne, ed. *Black Protest.* Greenwich, Conn.: Fawcett Premier Books, 1968. An anthology of documents and writings on black protest from the seventeenth century to the 1960's.

Malcolm X. *The Autobiography of Malcolm X.* New York: Grove Press, 1966. An indispensable account of the thought and development of Malcolm X, whose influence on contemporary black militancy has been enormous.

National Advisory Commission on Civil Disorders. *Report.* Washington, D.C.: U.S. Government Printing Office, 1968. The Kerner Report. Indispensable for an understanding of the 1967 riots and official reaction.

Waskow, Arthur I. *From Race Riot to Sit-in.* Garden City, New York: Doubleday, Anchor, 1966. Historical analysis of the 1919 race riots and the nonviolent civil rights movement.

Chapter V. The Racial Attitudes of White Americans

General Introduction

Encyclopedia of the Social Sciences. New York: Macmillan and Free Press, 1968. For brief, informative entries on such topics as "Prejudice: The Concept" by Otto Klineberg, "Race Relations: Social-Psychological Aspects" by Thomas F. Pettigrew, and "Prejudice: Social Discrimination" by J. Milton Yinger.

Simpson, George, and J. Milton Yinger. *Racial and Cultural Minorities,* 3rd ed. New York: Harper and Row, 1965. Comprehensive and up-to-date general introduction to prejudice and discrimination.

Personality and Prejudice

Adorno, T. W., et al. *The Authoritarian Personality.* New York: Harper and Row, 1950. Most influential work examining prejudice from a psychoanalytic perspective.

Allport, Gordon W. *The Nature of Prejudice.* Reading, Mass.: Addison-Wesley, 1954. Though published fifteen years ago, it remains the definitive social-psychological account of this topic.

Brown, Roger. *Social Psychology.* New York: Free Press, 1965. Especially Chapter 10. Summary of Adorno as well as methodological and conceptual criticisms inspired by *The Authoritarian Personality.*

Pettigrew, Thomas F. "Personality and Sociocultural Factors in Intergroup Attitudes: A Cross-national Comparison," *Conflict Resolution,* II, No. 1 (1958), pp. 29–42. Illustrates an application of the Smith et al. (see below) functional approach to racial prejudice.

Rokeach, Milton. *Beliefs, Attitudes and Values.* San Francisco: Jossey-Bass, Inc., 1968. Research testing theory of perceived belief dissimilarity as a determinant of the selection of a target for prejudice.

——. *The Open and Closed Mind.* New York: Basic Books, 1960. Analysis of the relationship between prejudice and rigid, dogmatic thinking.

Smith, M. Brewster, Jerome Bruner, and R. W. White. *Opinions and Personality.* New York: Wiley, 1956. Discussion of the psychological functions of social attitudes broader than the psychoanalytically oriented Adorno.

Prejudice and the Social Context

Bell, Daniel, ed. *The Radical Right.* New York: Doubleday, 1963. Contains a number of essays which trace the sources of rootlessness and status anxiety in American society which may foster a predisposition to participate in racist social movements.

Bettelheim, Bruno, and Morris Janowitz. *Social Change and Prejudice.* New York: Free Press, 1964. An account of the psychological effects of social change upon racial and religious intolerance. Chapter 2 reviews studies of the effects of social mobility upon prejudice.

Blalock, Hubert M. *Toward a Theory of Minority Group Relations.* New York: Wiley, 1967. A methodologically sophisticated discussion of personality and prejudice, but primarily an attempt to systematize "macro" or social system level theoretical propositions about racial discrimination and intergroup conflict.

Williams, Robin. *Strangers Next Door.* Englewood Cliffs, New Jersey: Prentice-Hall, 1964. Description of a series of empirical studies which examine the effects of both personality and sociocultural factors upon prejudice.

Public Opinion Surveys of Racial Attitudes

Brink, William, and Louis Harris. *Black and White.* New York: Simon and Schuster, 1966. See especially Chapter 5, "White

Attitudes: Political Cross Fire," and Chapter 6, "White Attitudes: The Age-Old Dilemma."

———. *The Negro Revolution in America*. New York: Simon and Schuster, 1964. Especially Chapter 9, "What Whites Think of Negroes."

Pettigrew, Thomas F. "Parallel and Distinctive Changes in Anti-Semitic and Anti-Negro Attitudes," in C. H. Stember, ed., *Jews in the Mind of America*. New York: Basic Books, 1966. A discussion of changing white racial attitudes which convincingly debunks many of the myths concerning the "white backlash."

Sheatsley, Paul B. "White Attitudes Toward the Negro," *Daedalus*, XCV, No. 1 (1966), pp. 217–38. Very useful summary of trends in white racial attitudes over the past twenty-five years.

Finally, newspaper columns by George Gallup and Lou Harris and occasional articles in weekly magazines—*Newsweek* especially—provide sensitive barometers of changing racial beliefs and feelings. More detailed information is published as the *Gallup Monthly Political Index*.

Chapter VI. White Militancy

There is a relatively small amount of literature on the militant white. This is especially true in the case of the organization and structure of contemporary white militant groups. The following works are helpful:

Albares, Richard P. *Nativist Paramilitarism in the United States: The Minutemen Organization*. University of Chicago: Center for Social Organization Studies, 1968. The most thorough analysis of the Minutemen.

Bell, Daniel, ed. *The Radical Right*. Garden City, New York: Doubleday, Anchor, 1963, 1964. An influential collection of essays on right-wing politics in the United States, guided by the questionable assumption of the pathological character of "extremist" politics.

Chalmers, David M. *Hooded Americanism*. Chicago: Quadrangle Paperbacks, 1968. A thorough history of the various Ku Klux Klans, from Reconstruction to the present.

Higham, John. *Strangers in the Land: Patterns of American Nativism*. New York: Atheneum, 1963. An indispensable study of nativist thought and action in the United States.

Hofstadter, Richard. *The Paranoid Style in American Politics*. New York: Vintage, 1965, 1967. Historical analysis of extreme political ideologies in the United States. Similar in conception to the Bell collection.

Vander Zanden, James W. *Race Relations in Transition*. New

York: Random House, 1965. Contains materials on the modern Klan and White Citizens' Councils.

Chapter VII. The Police in Protest

The following are part of a growing collection of information on the police, their actions and interactions:

April 27 Investigating Commission, Dr. Edward J. Sparling, Chairman. *Dissent and Disorder: A Report to the Citizens of Chicago on the April 27 Peace Parade*. Chicago, August 1, 1968. The report of a blue-ribbon committee investigation of police violence against a peace march in Chicago during April, 1968.

Black, Donald Jonathan. *Police Encounters and Social Organization: An Observation Study*. Unpublished Ph.D. dissertation, Department of Sociology, University of Michigan, 1968. The results of systematic field observation of police-public contacts.

Bordua, David J. *The Police*. New York: Wiley, 1967. A collection of important essays on the contemporary police, it includes a superb bibliography.

Chevigny, Paul. *Police Power: Police Abuses in New York City*. New York: Pantheon, 1969. A lawyer's report on the almost impossibility of fighting police malpractices through the courts.

Cray, Ed. *The Big Blue Line: Police Power vs. Human Rights*. New York: Coward-McCann, 1967. A compendium of recent police malpractices.

Jacobs, Paul. *Prelude to Riot; A View of Urban America from the Bottom*. New York: Vintage, 1968. A study of the conditions of poverty and bureaucracy which lie behind the grievances of rioters.

Levy, Burton. "Cops in the Ghetto: A Problem of the Police System," *American Behavioral Scientist* (March-April, 1968), pp. 31–34. An unhopeful reappraisal of police community relations efforts.

National Advisory Commission on Civil Disorders. *Report*. New York: Bantam, 1968. The Kerner Commission's report and interpretation of 1967 riots.

National Commission on the Causes and Prevention of Violence, Chicago Study Team. *Rights in Conflict*. Chicago, November 18, 1968. Also available in trade editions; for example, New York: Bantam, 1968. Daniel Walker's celebrated report on the events surrounding the Democratic National Convention in Chicago, August, 1968.

Niederhoffer, Arthur. *Behind the Shield: The Police in Urban Soci-*

ety. Garden City, New York: Doubleday, 1967. A study of police training and recruitment in New York City.

President's Commission on Law Enforcement and Administration of Justice. *Task Force Report: The Police.* Washington, D.C.: U.S. Government Printing Office, 1967. On the organization, personnel, resources, and relations with the community.

Reiss, Albert J., Jr. "How Common Is Police Brutality?" *Transaction* (July-August, 1968), pp. 10–19. Based on the same data as Black's study, this article shows how frequently police use excessive force.

Skolnick, Jerome H. *Justice without Trial.* New York: Wiley, 1966. A study of police use of discretionary powers.

Westley, William A. *The Police: A Sociological Study of Law, Custom and Morality.* Unpublished Ph.D. dissertation, Department of Sociology, University of Chicago, 1951. A study of a Midwestern police department focused on how the police subculture sustains illegal police practices.

Wilson, James Q. *Varieties of Police Behavior.* Cambridge, Mass.: Harvard University Press, 1968. A case study of police in eight communities; their styles of policing.

Chapter VIII. Judicial Response in Crisis

Until the Kerner Report (1968), there was little scholarly interest in the activities of the judicial system in times of civil disorder. Furthermore, there are few empirical studies of the routine operations of the criminal courts. The following are examples of the current work:

April 27 Investigating Commission. *Dissent and Disorder.* Chicago, August 1, 1968. Independent, critical study of the suppression of dissent in Chicago.

Baltimore Committee on the Administration of Justice under Emergency Conditions. *Report.* Baltimore, May 31, 1968. Report by an official committee on response of judicial system to the riot in Baltimore, 1968.

Bledsoe, William. "The Administration of Criminal Justice in the Wake of the Detroit Civil Disorder of July, 1967," *Michigan Law Review* (1968). Cited from prepublication galley proofs. Comprehensive study of response of judicial system to the Detroit riot, 1967.

Carlin, Jerome E., and Jan Howard. "Legal Representation and Class Justice," *UCLA Law Review,* XXII (January, 1965). Study of accessibility to and use of legal system by the poor.

Chicago Riot Study Committee. *Report.* Chicago, 1968. Includes superficial analysis of response of judicial system to the riot in Chicago, 1968.

District of Columbia Committee on the Administration of Justice under Emergency Conditions. *Interim Report.* District of Columbia, May 25, 1968. Official committee report on response of judicial system to the riot in Washington, D.C., April, 1968.

Gilbert, Ben W. *Ten Blocks from the White House: Anatomy of the Washington Riots 1968.* New York: Frederick A. Praeger, 1968. Independent, critical study by a lawyer of judicial system response to the Washington, D.C., riot.

Kirchheimer, Otto. *Political Justice.* Princeton: Princeton University Press, 1961. Influential study of the uses of the judicial system for political ends.

National Advisory Commission on Civil Disorders. *Report.* New York: Bantam 1968. Especially Chapter 13. Pioneering critique of the response of the judicial system to the 1967 riots. Includes statement of principles for future reference.

Platt, Anthony, and Sharan Dunkle. *The Administration of Justice in Crisis: Chicago, April, 1968.* Chicago: Center for Studies in Criminal Justice, University of Chicago, 1968. Independent, critical study by University of Chicago researchers on response of judicial system to the April riot in Chicago, 1968.

President's Commission on Law Enforcement and Administration of Justice. *Task Force Report: The Courts.* Washington: U.S. Government Printing Office, 1967. Official survey of criminal courts in the United States.

Skolnick, Jerome H. "Social Control in the Adversary System," *Journal of Conflict Resolution,* XI (1967), pp. 52–70. Empirical study of routine operations of criminal lawyers and public defenders.

Sudnow, David. "Normal Crimes: Sociological Features of the Penal Code in a Public Defender's Office," *Social Problems,* XII (1965), pp. 255–76. Empirical study of routine operations of the Public Defender's Office.

Wood, Arthur Lewis. *Criminal Lawyer.* New Haven, Conn.: College and University Press, 1967. Formal survey of background, interests, and competence of criminal lawyers.

Chapter IX. Social Response to Collective Behavior

Blumer, Herbert. "Collective Behavior," in J. B. Gittler, ed., *Review of Sociology: Analysis of a Decade.* New York: Wiley, 1957. Classic review of the social-scientific literature on collecting behavior, and a presentation of Blumer's own approach, stressing the creative character of collective behavior.

Bramson, Leon. *The Political Context of Sociology.* Princeton, New Jersey: Princeton University Press, 1961. Historical study of theories of mass society and collective behavior, emphasizing differences between European and American conceptions.

Chicago Commission on Race Relations. *The Negro in Chicago.* Chicago: University of Chicago Press, 1922. The first major "riot commission" report, strongly influenced by early collective behavior theories.

Governor's Commission on the Los Angeles Riots. *Violence in the City: an End or a Beginning?* Los Angeles: College Book Store, 1965. The McCone Report on the Watts riot of 1965, best seen as a case study in official misunderstanding.

Janowitz, Morris. *Social Control of Escalated Riots.* Chicago: University of Chicago Center for Policy Studies, 1968. An example of the application of conventional collective behavior theory to the problem of riot control, and a case study of the pitfalls in this approach.

National Advisory Commission on Civil Disorders. *Report.* New York: Bantam Books, 1968. The Kerner Report, an example of the strengths and limitations of conventional approaches to civil disorders.

Smelser, Neil J. *Theory of Collective Behavior.* New York: Free Press, 1962. The most prominent recent attempt to provide a sociological framework for the study of all forms of collective behavior. An example of the several problems inherent in the conventional social-scientific approach to collective disorder.

Index

AAAS, 53
Abnormality, riots and, 340–42
Abolitionists, 12–13, 128
Abram, Morris B., 120
Academic institutions, *See also* student protest; Universities.
  war effort and, 102–3
Administration, university, 117–18
AFL-CIO, Vietnam and, 58
Africa
  culture of, 139–41
  power and politics in, 141, 142, 143
Afro-American Associations, 109
Age differences in prejudice, 189, 198
"Agitational" theory, 262 ff.
Alabama, Ku Klux Klan in, 222
Albany, Georgia, 134, 268
Aliens, 13
  vigilantism and, 213
  in wartime, 154
Allen, Ethan, 18
Allport, Gordon, 191
American Civil Liberties Union, 247, 297, 300
  bail and, 305
American Criminal Law Quarterly, 295
American Friends Service Committee, 35
American Institute of Public Opinion, xviii
Anti-colonialism, 137 ff.
Anti-ranking protests, 96
Anti-war protest, 27 ff.
  administration arguments and, 38 ff.
  black Americans in, 61 ff., 136–37

clergy and, 61
course of war and, 45–47
dialogue and, 65–66
disorganization of, 30 ff.
domestic scene and, 57
"doves" and "hawks," 43–44, 48
draft and, 47–49
future of, 76–78
growth of, reasons for, 35 ff.
media and, 42 ff.
opinion leaders and, 42 ff.
police and, 245
Presidential campaign of 1964 and, 37–38
size of movement, 32
South Vietnam regime and, 54–56
students in, 59–61, 72, 102
tactics of, 65 ff.
time factor and, 35–37
varieties of protesters, 68 ff.
violence in, 66–68
war crimes issue, 49 ff.
Appalachian farmers, 11
Apple, R. W., 47
Arguedas, Antonio, 56
Arnett, Peter, 52
Asian-American students, 111
Assimilationism in colonialism, 140
Atlantic City convention, 92
Authoritarianism, prejudice and, 192

Backlash
  of confrontation, 108
  white, 184 ff., 208–9
Bacon, Warren, 247
Bail, 300 ff., 310

Baldwin, James, 155, 241, 250
Baltimore judicial system, 296, 307–8
Barca, Charles, 255
Baugh, Jack, 282
Beall, William, 255
Becker, Howard, xviii
Behavioral theories of riots, 329 ff.
Belief differences, racism and, 195–97
Bell, Daniel, 105, 123
Berkeley, xvii, 101–2, 113
  anti-war movement, 70–71
  communists and, 263–64
  draft protests, 96, 98
  Free Speech Movement, 93, 263–64, 265, 266, 322
  police, 255
  Presidential campaign of 1964 and, 92–93
  rebellion of 1964, 79
  SLATE and, 88
  Vietnam Day Committee, 94–95
Berrigan, Daniel and Philip, 61
Bettelheim, Bruno, 189, 190, 199
Birch Society, 236
Birth of a Nation, 216
Black, Donald J., 243
Black Codes, 215
Black Metropolis, 294
Black militancy, 125 ff.
  African history and, 156
  anti-colonialism and, 137–39
  anti-war movement and, 61 ff., 136–37
  assimilation and, 140
  Berkeley and, 88
  civil rights and decline of faith, 129 ff.
  community control and, 158 ff.
  culture and, 139–41, 154 ff.
  direction of, 149 ff.
  factionalism, 377
  federal intervention and, 133–34
  historical violence of, 15
  judicial system and, 393
  liberals and, 134–35
  middle class and, 110
  Mississippi Freedom Democratic Party and, 92, 135, 136
  peaceful progress myth and, 9
  police and, 152–53, 203, 241 ff., 275–76
  policy-making positions and, 159, 160, 205
  politics and, 143–45, 158 ff.
  power and, 141–43
  "riffraff" theory, 146–48
  riots, impact of, 145 ff.
  roots of, 128 ff.
  satisfaction with life and, 202 ff.
  self-defense and, 150 ff.
  socioeconomic status and, 204
  student movement and, 88, 104, 109–11, 124, 132, 163 ff.
  violence and, 127, 144, 145 ff.
  white attitudes and, 179 ff. *See also* Racism.
  youth in, 162 ff.
Black Panther Party, 149, 152–53, 162, 275, 276, 277
"Black Power," 160–61
Black Student Unions, 109
Blackstone Rangers, 168, 171
Blake, Herman, 171, 348
Bledsoe, William, 295
"Blue flu," 273
Blumer, Herbert, xviii
Boston Five, 74
Boston police, 243, 283
Bowers, Sam, 221
Boyle, John, 305
Brandeis University, 120
Breakthrough, 229
Brewster, Kingman, 347
Brink, William, 197
Broek, Ten, 214
Brooklyn
  Criminal Court attack, 152, 275, 277
  police training, 256
Brown, H. Rap, 9
Brown, Robert McAfee, 61
Brown, Sam, 347
Brown v. Board of Education, 130
Brown University, 98
Bruckner, D. J. R., 281
Burchett, Wilfred, 33
Bureau of Labor Statistics, 203, 253

Campbell, Angus, 198, 202, 206, 208
Cantril, Hadley, 202
Capitalism, paramilitarism and, 236
Carey, Charles, xviii
Carmichael, Stokely, 137

Cassese, John, 272, 276–77
Catonsville Nine, 72
Cedar Falls, Operation, 52
Center for the Study of Law and Society, xvii
Central Intelligence Agency, 56
  academic institutions and, 103
Centralization, political, 18
Chalmers, David, xvii
Chemical warfare, 53, 357
Chessman, Caryl, 88
Chicago, 294
  anti-war protest, 66, 245, 247
  bail policy, 304 ff.
  Democratic convention in, 6, 31, 66, 246–48, 274–75
    black participation, 173
    radicals and, 267
  high school protests, 164–65, 167, 168
  job training, 175
  judicial system, 296, 298, 299–300, 314, 322
  police, 243, 246–48, 265, 274–75, 278
  policy-making positions in, 159, 160, 205
  riot of 1968, 146
  white militancy in, 228
  Yippie threats, 385
Chicago, University of, 93, 96, 123
Chicago Study Team, 6, 66, 67, 146, 246, 265, 267, 274, 278
Chicago Tribune, 265
Child-rearing, permissiveness in, 261
Children's Crusade, 65
Chinese, vigilantism and, 213–14
Chomsky, Noam, 60
Christian Science Monitor, 47
Churns, Michael, 282
Cincinnati, 166
CIO, 15
Cioffi, Lou, 46
Citizens' Councils, 223
Civil rights movement. See also Black militancy.
  decline of faith in, 129 ff.
  federal intervention, 133–34
  middle class and, 110
  nonviolence, 77, 101, 131–32, 150
  in North, 130, 135, 151 ff.
  in South, 101, 128 ff.
  youth in, 162–63

Civil Rights Commission, 244
Civilian review boards, 278 ff.
Cleaver, Eldridge, 162
Clergy, anti-war protest and, 61
Cleveland, Grover, 14
Cleveland, Ohio, 172, 173
  police, 244, 276
Clifford, Clark, 55
Coal industry, violence and, 14
Cobbs, Price, i, ii, xiv, 348
Coffin, William Sloane, 61, 73
Cognitive dissonance, 194
Cohen, Nathan, 148
Cold War
  anti-colonialism and, 142
  Korea and, 36
  Vietnam and, 56
  white paramilitarism and, 232–33
Cole, Robert, xviii
Coleman, Kermit, xvii
Collective behavior, 329 ff.
  abnormality and, 340–42
  crowds and, 330–31
  political aspects, 345–46
  riots, 331 ff.
    control, 342 ff.
    official conceptions of, 339 ff.
  theories of, 330 ff.
Colleges. See also Student protest; Universities.
  in crisis, 111 ff.
Colonialism
  in America, 11–12
  black militancy and, 137 ff.
  welfare, 157
Columbia University, 118
  "agitators," 262, 264
  anti-war movement, 61
  community and, 124
  Cox Commission and, 80
  police at, 105, 123
  SDS at, 98, 100, 105, 123
Columbians, 220
Commission on Law Enforcement and Administration of Justice, 309, 310
Committee for Draft Resistance, 34
Committee for Nonviolent Action, 35
Committee for a Sane Nuclear Policy, 35
Communists, 35
  agitation by, 263–65
  Hoover, J. Edgar, on, 263

paramilitarism and, 232–33
Vietnam and, 39–40, 353
Community Action Patrol, 152
Community control, black militancy and, 158 ff.
Congress, racism and, 208–9
Conot, Robert, 244
Conspiracy in student protest, 266, 267
Contagion, social, 334
Control, social, 342 ff.
  in student protest, 120 ff.
Con Thien, 46
CORE, 63, 131–32
Counter-Insurgency Council, 235
Counsel, legal, 297 ff., 310 ff.
Courts. *See also* Judicial systems.
  police and, 285
Cox Commission, 80, 245, 262, 263
Craig, David, 348
Crawford, Thomas, xvii
Cray, Ed, xvii
Credibility gap, 102
Crews, Frederick, xvii
Crime
  definition of, 292
  judicial system and, 323
Crockett, George W., Jr., 301, 302
Crowd control, 7
  theories of, 330–31
Cuban interventions, 28
Culture, black militancy and, 139–41, 154 ff.
Currie, Elliott, xvii
Czechoslovakia, 82, 337

Dak To, 46
Deadly force, decision to use, 6–7
Defense, Department of
  defoliation and, 53
  universities and, 103
Deferments, draft, 103–4
Dellinger, David, 77
Democratic Party
  Atlantic City convention, 92
  black militants and, 135
  Chicago convention, 6, 31, 66, 173, 246–48, 267, 274–75, 385
Demonstration, peaceful, right of, 23
DePugh, Robert, 235, 237, 238
Detroit, 294
  gun registry, 227
  judicial system, 295, 296, 298, 299, 311, 314

bail policy, 301–3
police, 257–58, 273
riot of 1967, 148, 257–58
white militancy, 228, 229
Detroit Free Press, 302
Diem, Ngo Dinh, 36, 38, 102, 352, 353
Dominican Republic, 28, 351
Douglass, Frederick, 128
Dounis, George, 49
"Doves," 43–44
Dow Chemical Company, 98–99
Draft protest, 47–49
  black Americans and, 61 ff.
  deferment and, 95, 103–4
  judicial system and, 322, 356
  in Oakland, 62–63
  students in, 47–49, 96, 98, 103–4
Drake, St. Clare, 294
DuBois, W. E. B., 138, 294, 319
Dulles, John Foster, 355, 356–57

East St. Louis, 166
Economy
  education and, 113
  inertia of, 16
Education
  economy and, 113
  racism and, 190, 198
Educational Testing Service, 89, 115
Erlanger, Howard, xviii
Ethnocentric preferences, 195–97
Etzioni, Amitai, xvii

Faculty, university, 117–18
Fanon, Frantz, 138, 144, 145
Farmers, Appalachian, 11
Federal Bureau of Investigation, 255
  Ku Klux Klan and, 223
  riots and, 146
Ferber, Michael, 73
Fifth Avenue Peace Parade Committee, 34
Fight Back, 229
Fi-Po, 284
Flacks, Richard, xvii
Flint, Michigan, 166
Ford, Gerald, 55
Fogelson, Robert M., 147, 148
Forman, James, 110, 155, 161, 169
Forrest, Nathan B., 215

Fort Hood Three, 75
Fortas, Abe, 285
Fortune, 80
Fox, Sylvan, 277
France, student movement in, 85
Fraternal Order of Police, 271, 272, 276
Free Speech Movement, 93, 263–64, 265, 266, 322
Freedom Democratic Party, 92, 135, 136
Freedom Riders, 132
Frick, Henry Clay, 14
Friedenberg, Edgar, 170
Friends Service Committee, 35
Frustration, 334, 337
Fry, John, 171
Fulbright, J. W., 41, 57
Furey, John F., 284

Gallup polls
  racism and, 185, 187
  Vietnam War and, 44, 48
Garveyism, 129, 138, 140
Geertz, Clifford, 8
Gellhorn, Martha, 50
Geneva Accords of 1954, 38
Germany, student protest in, 85–86
Ghettos
  police and, 241 ff.
  political autonomy of, 158 ff.
  self-defense in, 151 ff.
GI teach-ins, 77
Ginsburg, David, 348
Girardin, Ray, 273
Goldfarb, Ronald, 299
Goldwater, Barry, 92
  police support for, 282
Goodman, Mitchell, 73
Grand Central demonstration, 247
Great Committee of 1856, 213
Griffith, D. W., 216
Grimshaw, Allen, xviii
Group for Research on Social Policy, 260
Guerrilla theater, 77
Gusfield, Joseph, xvii

Hague Convention, 357
Hanh, Thich Nhat, 39
Hannon, Robert, 282
Hanoi, 50

Happiness, prejudice and, 202 ff.
Harlem
  police and, 174
  riots
    1935: 147, 243, 343
    1964: 136
Harrington, John, 268, 348
Harrington, Michael, 91
Harris polls
  labor strikes, 23
  racism, 187, 197, 205–7
  self-defense, 226
Hartz, Louis, 9
Harvey, Frank, 52
Hattiesburg, Mississippi, 221
"Hawks," 43–44, 48
Hayden, Tom, 31, 319, 347
Headley, Chief, 242
Herbicides, 53
Herblock, 47
Hershey, Lewis, 95, 322
Herskovits, Melville, 139
Heyman, Ira M., xvi
High school protests, 163 ff.
Hill, Robert B., 147, 148
Historical background of violence, 8 ff.
Hobsbawn, Eric, 341
Hofstadter, Richard, 199, 238
Hollingworth, Clare, 46
Hoover, J. Edgar, 263, 280
Horowitz, Irving, xvii, 347
House Un-American Activities Committee, San Francisco and, 88
Hutchins, Robert, 77

Immigrant groups, 13, 154, 213
Imperiale, Anthony, 224, 229, 231
Imperialism, 56, 137 ff.
Independence, violence and, 20
Indians, American, 10–11
  vigilantism and, 213
Individuals, integration as, 21
Institutional violence, 5
Institutionalized behavior, 333
Integration of people as individuals, 21
Intellectuals
  anti-war protest and, 59
  student protest and, 84
International Voluntary Services, 43
International War Crimes Tribunal, 33

Iron Triangle campaign, 52
Islam, Nation of, 169–70

Jail facilities, 302 ff.
Janowitz, Morris, 189, 190, 199
Jefferson, Thomas, 15
Jencks, Christopher, 121
Job training in Chicago, 175
John Birch Society, 236
Johnson, Lyndon B.
　campaign of 1964, 37
　deceitfulness of spokesmen, 102
　Dominican Republic and, 28
　SDS support for, 92
　Vietnam and, 354
　　bombing policy, 45
　　legality of intervention, 40
Jones, LeRoi, 138
Judicial system, 293 ff.
　bail in, 300 ff., 310–11
　counsel and, 297 ff., 310 ff.
　disenchantment with, 316 ff.
　draft resistance and, 322
　lack of preparation, 295–97
　law enforcement and, 313 ff.
　neutrality and, 321
　police and, 285, 287–88, 290
　recommendations, 324–26
　routine vs. riot procedures, 308–
　　10
Junction City, Operation, 52

Kadish, Sanford, xviii
Kahin, George McT., 54
Kalven, Harry, Jr., 247
Katzenbach, Nicholas, 41
Kennedy, Robert F., 5, 45, 46, 58
Kennedy, John F., 91
Kerner Report, 3
　black militancy and, 126, 147,
　　162, 170, 175
　collective behavior and, 334,
　　336, 343
　judicial response and, 295, 298,
　　301, 304, 319, 325
　police and, 242, 245, 257
　racism and, 179, 198, 201
　white militancy and, 227
Kerr, Clark, 102, 117
Khe Sanh, 46
King, Martin Luther, Jr., 56, 61,
　131, 149, 150
　aftermath of death, 153, 164,
　　168, 172, 294, 304

draft and, 63
Knox, P. C., 28
Korean War, 29, 36
Kornhauser, William, xviii, 330
Kroninger, Robert, 322
Ku Klux Klan, 150, 214 ff.
　First World War era, 217
　membership, 222–23
　organizations, 220 ff.
Ky, Nguyen Cao, 33, 55

Labor
　historical violence of, 14–15
　strikes, beginnings of, 23
　Vietnam War and, 58
Ladies' Home Journal, 50
Laino, Leon, 285
Law, disenchantment with, 316 ff.
Law Enforcement Group, 277, 282,
　284–85
Lawyers, 297 ff., 310 ff.
"Leaders" in mass protest, 262 ff.
Leary, Howard R., 277
Le Bon, Gustave, 331
leDivelec, Marie-Helene, xvii
Lee, Maurice, 306
Legal system. See also Judicial
　system.
　police role in, 269–70
Lemberg Center, 164
Leonard, Nancy, xviii
Levy, Howard, 43, 75
Lewis, John, 134
Liberals, black militancy and, 134–
　35
Liebowitz, Martin, xvii
Life, 22
Lincoln, Abraham, 28
Lincoln Park, 68
Lindsay, John V., 279, 283, 286
Lipset, S. M., 82, 83
Liuzzo, Mrs. Viola, 220
Lockman, Ronald, 43, 64, 75
London police, 248
London Daily Telegraph, 46
Looter, concept of, 7
Los Angeles
　guns in, 227
　high school protests, 164
　police, 247, 261
　socioeconomic status in, 204
　Riot Study, 148
Los Angeles Times, 14, 281
Lovestone, Jay, 58
Lowell, Robert, 60

Luce, Don, 43
Lynching in South, 216
Lynd, Staughton, 60

MACE, 69
Maddox, 41
Mailer, Norman, 60
Malcolm X, 63, 128, 136, 142, 149, 151
Marks, Sharon Dunkle, xvii
Masotti, Louis, 350
Mass protest
  behavioral theories of, 329 ff.
  institutions and, 4
  police and, 262 ff.
Mattick, Hans W., 336
Matza, David, xviii
Mayer, Henry, 347
Mayer, Jean, 53
Maywood, Illinois, 165–66
McCabe, Charles, 275
McCarthy, Eugene, 65
McComb, Mississippi, 136
McCormack, Sam, xviii
McDermott, John, 77
McNamara, John H., 252
McNamara, Robert S., 54, 64
McNanamon, Joseph F., 276
Meany, George, 58
Media, Vietnam War and, 42 ff.
Mensh, Maurice, 254
Messinger, Sheldon, xvii
Mexican-Americans
  students, 111
  vigilantism and, 213
Mexico, annexation of, 28
Miami police, 242
Michigan State University, 102
Midwest, Minutemen in, 233, 235
Middle class
  civil rights and, 110
  confrontation tactics and, 108
  white militancy and, 227
Military agencies, academic co-operation with, 102–3, 121
Mills, C. Wright, 89
Milwaukee Fourteen, 72
Mining industry, violence in, 14–15
Minorities
  higher education and, 114
  power and, 142
Minutemen, 232 ff.
Misner, Gordon, 347
Mississippi, 151

Freedom Democratic Party, 92, 135, 136
Ku Klux Klan in, 220 ff.
Mobility, social, prejudice and, 199–200
Mohr, Charles, 39, 51
Molly Maguires, 14
Monroe, North Carolina, 151
Morrison, Norman, 70
Moynihan Report, 135
Muhammed, Elijah, 131
Multiversity, 93, 117

Napalm, 50
Natchez, Mississippi, 221
National Advisory Commission on Civil Disorders. *See* Kerner Report.
National Association for the Advancement of Colored People, 130–31
  high school protests and, 165
  in Mississippi, 221
  self-defense and, 151
National Guard troops, 172, 173
  in Detroit, 257
  in Newark, 382
National Liberation Front
  communism and, 39–40
  tactics of. 52
National Mobilization Committee to End the War in Vietnam, 33, 34, 68
National Opinion Research Center, xviii, 181, 186, 188
National States Rights Party, 220, 238
National Student Association, 79
Negroes. *See also* Black militancy.
  peaceful progress myth and, 9
Nelson, Gaylord, 41
Neshoba County, 151, 221, 223
Neutrality of justice, 321
New left activist tactics, 107–8
New Politics convention, 64
New York. *See also* Columbia University.
  high school protests, 168
  Minutemen in, 234, 235
  police, 247, 251
    attacks on, 174
    authority and, 276–77
    civilian review board and, 279–80
    politics and, 272, 282, 283, 284

salary of, 252–53
strikes, 273
training, 256–57
violence, 247, 275
New York City College, 93
New York Times, 3, 39, 47, 50, 51, 54, 248, 257, 277
Newark, 294
judicial system, 314
bail, 303–4
National Guard in, 382
white militancy in, 227, 229–31
Newark Evening News, 304
Newsweek, 187
Newton, Huey P., 152, 276
Nhu, Madame, 36
Niederhoffer, Arthur, 252
Nitze, Paul, 51
Nkrumah, Kwame, 138
Nonconformity
police and, 261–62
riots and, 332
Nonviolence, 77
civil rights movement and, 101, 131–32, 150
North
abolitionists, 12–13
civil rights movement, 130, 135, 151 ff.
prejudice in, 193
riots in, 145 ff.
white militancy in, 224 ff.
North Carolina, 151, 223
North Ward Citizens Committee, 229–31

Oakland, California, 62–63, 69
Black Panther Party and, 152, 153, 276
police, 253–54, 360
Official violence, 6–7, 18, 154
in South, 220
Order, definition of, 5
Orientals in California, 214

Pacification in Vietnam, 55
Pacifists, 68
Pan-Africanism, 140
Panic, 332
Paramilitarism, white, 231 ff.
Parks, Mrs. Rosa, 130–31
Paterson police, 382
Patriotic Party, 237

Patrolmen's Benevolent Asociation, 272, 276, 279–80, 283
Peace movement. *See* Anti-war protest.
Peaceful demonstration, rights of, 23
Peaceful progress, myth of, 9
Penn, Lemuel, 220
Permissiveness, 261
Perry, Richard E., 50
Perry, Thomas O., 53
Personality, prejudice and, 192 ff.
Peterson, Richard, 89
Pettigrew, Thomas, 184, 193, 203
Philadelphia
bail policy, 310
police, 284
Philadelphia Negro, 294
Philippine nationalism, 28
Pittsburg, California, 166
Platt, Anthony, xvii
Police, 108, 241 ff.
activism
for material benefits, 272–74
for social policy, 274 ff.
"agitators" and, 262
anti-war protesters and, 245 ff.
black views of, 152–53, 203, 241 ff., 275–76
federal government and, 290
judicial analogy, 287–88
manpower problems, 252 ff.
mass protest and, 262 ff.
military analogy, 286–87
nonconformity and, 261–62
permissive child-rearing and, 261
political involvement, 268 ff., 281 ff.
predicament of, 249 ff.
resources of, 252 ff.
retirement of, 254–55
review boards and, 278 ff.
revolt against higher authority, 276–78
role of, 269–70
"rotten apple" theory and, 259 ff.
salaries, 252–53
solidarity of, 278 ff.
sporadic violence against, 174
strikes, 273
student protests and, 105, 123, 245 ff., 262 ff.
training, 255 ff.
views of protesters, 258–59
violence of, 246 ff., 274–76
white views of, 203

Police Chief, The, 263, 264
Police Officers Association, 283
Politics
    black militancy and, 143–45,
      158 ff.
    centralization of, 18
    inertia in, 16
    police involvement, 268 ff.,
      281 ff.
    riots and, 345–46
    violence in American history,
      8 ff.
    white paramilitarism and, 237–
      38
Polls
    on labor strikes, 23
    on racism, 183 ff., 197, 205–7
    on self-defense, 226
    on Vietnam, 44, 48
Poor People's March, 206
Port Chicago, California, 34
Port Huron SDS convention, 90
Poverty, student protest and, 101,
    104
Power
    black militancy and, 141–43
    structure of university, 121–22
Prejudice. *See also* Racism.
    decline in, 181
Presidential campaign of 1964,
    92–93, 282
Press, Vietnam War and, 43
Price, Cecil, 221
Progress, peaceful, myth of, 9
Progressive Labor Party, 33
Protest
    contemporary, 21 ff.
    definition problems, 3 ff.
    force to control, 6–7
    historical background, 8 ff.
Proviso East High, 165–66

Racism, 133, 179 ff.
    age differences and, 189, 198
    backlash and, 184 ff., 208–9
    belief differences and, 195–97
    Congress and, 208–9
    decline in, 182
    education and, 190, 198
    personality and, 192 ff.
    politics and, 160
    protests and, 104–5, 205–6
    religion and, 190–91
    riots and, 206–7

    satisfaction with life and, 202 ff.
    social change and, 197 ff.
    socioeconomic status and, 189–
      90, 199–200, 204
    students and, 104–5
    subgroup differences in, 188 ff.
    surveys of, 183 ff.
    urbanization and, 189, 198
    widening gap in, 201 ff.
Radicals
    police and, 265, 267
    student movement and, 84, 89,
      107–8
Railroad strikes, 14
Randolph, A. Philip, 131
Raskin, Marcus, 60, 73
Redbook, 50
Redmon, Washington, 235
Reisman, David, 121
Reiss, Albert J., Jr., 243
Religion, racism and, 190–91
Republican Blue Book, 33, 44
Research, economy and, 113
RESIST, 34
Resistance, The, 34
Resistance tactics, student, 105 ff.
Reston, James, 22
Review boards, civilian, for police,
    278 ff.
Rhee, Syngman, 36
"Riffraff" theory, 145 ff.
"Right-wing" militancy, 236
Rights in Conflict, 67
Riots
    behavioral theories of, 330 ff.
    control of, 258, 334, 342 ff.
    feedback to, 301
    impact of, 145 ff.
    inappropriateness of, 336
    liberals and, 135–36
    opinions on causes of, 207
    participants in, 146 ff., 339
    racism and, 206–7
    vigilantism and, 217
    white reactions to, 185
Rizzo, Frank L., 284, 286
Rokeach, Milton, 195, 197
Roper Research Associates, xviii
Ross, Michael, 187, 191
ROTC, black youth and, 170
"Rotten apple" theory, 259 ff.
Rubenstein, Richard, xvii
Rudd, Mark, 100
Rusk, Dean, 39, 56, 67
Russell, Bertrand, 33

Rustin, Bayard, 136

Saigon, 39, 46, 54
St. Louis, 174, 251, 280
Salisbury, Harrison, 33, 50, 51
San Francisco, 67
    HUAC demonstration, 88
    judicial system, 321
    police, 254–55, 282
    vigilantism, 213
San Francisco Chronicle, 254, 282
San Francisco State College, 111
Sane Nuclear Policy, 35
Saturday Evening Post, 251
Schell, Jonathan, 52
Schuman, Howard, 198, 202, 206, 208
Schurmann, Franz, 60
SDS. See Students for a Democratic Society.
Selective Service, 49
    deferments, 103–4
    Qualification Test, 95
Self-Anchoring Striving Scale, 202
Self-defense, black militancy and, 150 ff.
Selznick, Philip, xvii
Senate Preparedness Committee, 56
Senate Republican Policy Committee, 44
Shelly v. Kraemer, 130
Shelton, Robert, 218, 220
Shoup, David M., 76
Skolnick, Alexander Nathan, xviii
Skolnick, Arlene, xviii
Skolnick, Jerome H., ii
Slavery, 128
Smelser, Neil, xviii, 332
Smith, Bruce L. R., xvi
SNCC. See Student Nonviolent Coordinating Committee.
Social responses, 329 ff.
    anti-war movement and, 58 ff.
    control, 120 ff., 334
    police activism and, 274 ff.
    prejudice and, 197 ff.
Social Service Academy, 291
Socioeconomic status
    paramilitarism and, 236
    racism and, 189–90, 199–200, 204
Sons of Liberty, 12
South

    Black Codes of, 215
    civil rights movement in, 101, 128
    historical violence in, 12–13, 19
    KKK in, 214 ff., 220 ff.
    lynching in, 216
    prejudice in, 193
    self-defense of blacks in, 150–51
    slavery in, 128
    SNCC and, 110
    white violence in, 12–13, 133, 218 ff.
South Vietnam, 54 ff. See also Anti-war protest; Vietnam War.
Southern Christian Leadership Conference, 63, 169
Sparling Commission, 245, 247
Speiglman, Richard, xviii
Spellman, Cardinal, 61
Spock, Benjamin, 73
Stark, Rodney, xvii
Starr, Roger, 124
State Department White Papers, 36, 38
Stevenson, Adlai, 90
Stokes, Carl B., 244, 276
Stop the Draft Week, 62–63, 69
Stouffer, Samuel, 197
Strain, social, 333–34, 337
Strikes, labor, beginnings of, 23
Student Mobilization Committee, 34
Student protest, 79 ff.
    anti-war, 59–61, 72
    black, 88, 104, 109–11, 124, 132, 163 ff.
    confrontation tactics, 105 ff.
    contemporary, 87 ff.
    control measures, 120 ff.
    crisis of colleges and, 111 ff.
    decision - making participation and, 122
    draft, 103–4
    faculty and administration and, 117–18
    fragmentation of university interests and, 115
    in France, 85
    high school, 163 ff.
    idealism and, 82
    international perspective, 81 ff.
    "normal channels" and, 91
    optimism in, 91–92
    phases of movement, 99–100

police and, 105, 123, 245 ff.,
262 ff.
power and influence in, 97, 119
radicalism, 84, 89, 107–8
reasons underlying, 107–8
response to, 120 ff.
role of higher education and,
112 ff.
syndicalism, 97
Third World, 109–11, 124, 149
trustees and, 115–17
in West Germany, 85–86
Student Nonviolent Coordinating
Committee, 131–32, 134
draft and, 63
formation of, 88
middle class and, 110
Mississippi Freedom Democratic
Party and, 92
Vietnam and, 136–37
white exclusion from, 157
Students for a Democratic Society,
33
aims of, 89–90
anti-Dow demonstrations, 98–99
class consciousness of, 97
at Columbia, 98, 100, 105, 123
draft and, 96, 98
Johnson (L. B.) and, 92
membership, 89, 364
1963 optimism of, 91
phases of movement, 99–100
Port Huron convention, 90
Students for Freedom, 164
Supreme Court decisions
civil rights, 130
defense counsel, 312
draft resistance, 356
Surveys of racism, 183 ff.
Syndicalism, student, 97

Tarbi, Frank, 73
Teach-ins (1965), 59, 94–95
Television, Vietnam War and, 42
Tension, social, 333–34, 337
Tet Offensive, 47
Third World Liberation Front,
109–11, 124, 149
Thoreau, Henry, 28
Tocsin, 264
Tonkin Gulf Resolution, 41
Trenton, New Jersey, 167
True, Arnold, 76
Trustees, university, 115–17

Truth Teams, 59
Tucker, Sterling, 145, 348
Turner Joy, 41
Tuscaloosa, Alabama, 220
Tuskegee Institute, 132, 216
Twain, Mark, 28

United Klans of America, 220
United Nations, anti-colonialism
and, 142–43
Universities. See also Student protest.
changing roles of, 112 ff.
as community, 112
in crisis, 111 ff.
dialogue in, 91
military agencies and, 102–3,
121
faculty and administration, 117–
18
fragmentation of interests, 115
power structure, 121–22
response to protest, 120 ff.
trustees, 115–17
University of California, Berkeley.
See Berkeley.
University of Michigan Survey Research Center, xviii
Urban League, 134, 145
Urbanization
racism and, 189, 198
white militancy and, 224 ff.
Ursin, Edmund C., xvii
U. S. News and World Report, 47

Vasquez de Ayllon, Lucas, 128
Vietnam Commencements, 72
Vietnam Day Committee, 94
Vietnam Summer, 69
Vietnam War. See also Anti-war
protest.
black militancy and, 136–37
chemical warfare, 53
Communism and, 39–40
course of, 45–47
defoliation, 53
desertions, 46
draft, 47–49. See also Draft protest
elections and, 352–53
Korean War vs., 29, 36
legality of intervention, 40
regimes, 54 ff.

student movement and, 102
Vigilantism, 211 ff.
Violence. *See also* Riots.
  anti-war protest and, 65 ff.
  black militancy and, 127, 144,
    145 ff.
  definition of, 4–6
  institutional, 5
  nonviolence vs., 77
  official, 6–7, 18, 154, 220
  police, 245 ff., 274–76
  political, in history, 8 ff.
  sporadic acts of, 174
  usefulness of, 341
  white, 210 ff. *See also* Whites,
    militancy of.

Wagner Act, 15
Walker, David, 128
Wall Street Journal, 45
Wallace, George, 58
War crimes issue, 49 ff.
War on Poverty, 101, 104
Warren, Michigan, 229
Washington, D. C., 294
  crime in, 309–10
  high school protests, 166
  judicial system, 296, 299
    bail policy, 308
  peace marches, 88, 134
  police, 243, 254
  Poor People's March on, 206
Washington Post, 3
Washington Report, 264
WASPs, 13–14, 211
Watts riot, 147, 152, 294, 339–40
Welfare colonialism, 157
West Frankfort, Illinois, 217

West German students, 85–86
Westley, William A., 243
White, Kevin, 283, 286
White Knights of the Ku Klux
  Klan, 220 ff.
White Papers, State Department,
  36, 38
Whites, 13–14, 211
  backlash, 184 ff., 208–9
  colonialism and, 137 ff.
  culture and, 156–58
  dominance in politics, 143
  militancy of, 210 ff.
    in North, 224 ff.
    paramilitarism, 231 ff.
    in South, 12–13, 133, 218 ff.
    vigilantism, 211 ff.
  racial attitudes of, 179 ff. *See
    also* Racism.
  satisfaction with life, 202 ff.
  student, 85
Wilmington, Delaware, 173
Wilson, James Q., 251, 268
Wilson, O. W., 250
Witnesses at Task Force hearings,
  347–48
Women, militance of, 15
Wood, Robert, 225
Working class. *See also* Labor.
  militancy of white, 224 ff.
Wui Nhon, 50

Yippie threats in Chicago, 385
Young, Whitney, 134
Younge, Sammy, Jr., 132

Zinn, Howard, 60, 134

About The Authors

JEROME H. SKOLNICK is presently in residence at the Center for the Study of Law and Society, University of California, Berkeley, and has just accepted an appointment as Professor of Sociology, University of California, San Diego. He is on leave from the University of Chicago, where he is Associate Professor of Sociology. He is also Senior Social Scientist, American Bar Foundation, and Research Associate, Center for Studies in Criminal Justice, University of Chicago Law School.

He has taught at the University of California, Berkeley, the Yale Law School, and the New York University Law School. During 1965–66 he was Carnegie Fellow in Social Science at Harvard Law School.

Born in 1931, he attended public schools in New York City, graduated in 1952 from the City College of New York, and was granted a Ph.D. in Sociology by Yale University in 1957.

He is the author of *Justice Without Trial: Law Enforcement in a Democratic Society* (1968), and his many articles include an analysis of trends in American sociology of law, an analysis of police-community relations written for the National Advisory Commission on Civil Disorders, and a report on law and morals prepared for the President's Commission on Law Enforcement and Administration of Justice.

WILLIAM H. GRIER and PRICE M. COBBS are Assistant Professors of Psychiatry at the University of California Medical Center, San Francisco, and are psychiatrists in private practice. Their book *Black Rage* was published in 1968.